Learning, Problem Solving, and Mindtools

Learning, Problem Solving, and Mindtools is inspired by the substantial body of learning research by David H. Jonassen in the areas of mindtools and problem solving. The focus of the volume is on educational technology, especially with regard to how new technologies have facilitated and supported problem solving and critical thinking. Each chapter focuses on a particular aspect of learning with technology and elaborates the implications for the design and implementation of learning environments and activities aimed at improving the conceptualization of problems, reasoning and higher-order thinking, and solving challenging problems.

This collection of scholarly essays provides a highly engaging treatment of using tools and technologies to improve problem solving; multiple perspectives on integrating educational technology to support learning in complex and challenging problem-solving domains; guidance for the design of instruction to support problem solving; a systemic account of the relationships between mental models, instructional models, and assessment models; and a look into the future of educational technology research and practice.

J. Michael Spector is Professor and Chair of the Department of Learning Technologies at the University of North Texas, USA.

Barbara B. Lockee is Professor of Education and Associate Director of the School of Education at Virginia Polytechnic and State University, USA.

Sharon E. Smaldino is the L.D. and Ruth Morgridge Endowed Chair for Teacher Education at Northern Illinois University, USA.

Mary C. Herring is the Associate Dean of the College of Education at the University of Northern Iowa, USA.

All four co-editors of this volume are Past Presidents of the Association of Educational Communications and Technology (AECT; see http://www.aect.org), which has supported and facilitated this effort.

Learning, Problem Solving, and Mindtools

Essays in Honor of
David H. Jonassen

**Edited by
J. Michael Spector,
Barbara B. Lockee,
Sharon E. Smaldino,
and Mary C. Herring**

Routledge
Taylor & Francis Group

NEW YORK AND LONDON

First published 2013
by Routledge
711 Third Avenue, New York, NY 10017

Simultaneously published in the UK
by Routledge
2 Park Square, Milton Park, Abingdon, Oxon OX14 4RN

*Routledge is an imprint of the Taylor & Francis Group,
an informa business*

Library of Congress Cataloging in Publication Data
Learning, problem solving, and mindtools: essays in honor of
David H. Jonassen / edited by J. Michael Spector, Barbara B. Lockee,
Sharon E. Smaldino, and Mary C. Herring.
p. cm.
Includes bibliographical references and index.
1. Problem solving—Study and teaching. I. Jonassen, David H.,
1947- II. Spector, J. Michael, editor of compilation. III. Lockee,
Barbara B., editor of compilation. IV. Smaldino, Sharon E., editor of
compilation. V. Herring, Mary C., editor of compilation. VI. Spector,
J. Michael. Introducing mindtools and problem solving.
LB1590.3.L44 2013
370.15'24—dc23   2012034711

ISBN: 978-0-415-52435-3 (hbk)
ISBN: 978-0-203-11106-2 (ebk)

Typeset in Sabon
by Cenveo Publisher Services

Printed and bound in the United States of America by Publishers Graphics,
LLC on sustainably sourced paper.

This volume is inspired by the works of David H. Jonassen. As a consequence, we dedicate this volume to those whom have been directly influenced by David – namely, his students and colleagues, several of whom have contributed chapters.

J. Michael Spector, Barbara B. Lockee,
Sharon E. Smaldino, and Mary C. Herring
Summer 2012

In Memoriam

David H. Jonassen passed away December 2nd 2012 prior to the publication of this book. During the last two years of his life, while struggling with cancer, Dave not only contributed to this volume by recommending authors and writing the final chapter, but he was also named a Fellow to the American Educational Research Association based on a lifetime of substantial contributions, and he earned the 2012 Outstanding Reviewer Award for the Development Section of *Educational Technology Review & Development* based on both quality and quantity of reviews while serving on the *ETR&D* Research Section's Editorial Board. The Monday before he passed away, he participated in a dissertation defense. For these and so many other remarkable achievements, Dave was named the first recipient of the David H. Jonassen AECT Excellence in Research Award. His family, friends, and colleagues will remember his many contributions over the years as well as the superb quality of his intellect and character.

Contents

Acknowledgments

We wish to thank the authors and reviewers who have made this book possible. While the idea for the volume arose about six years ago, we only began in earnest to develop this volume in the summer of 2011. We had the support of Lane Akers, senior editor at Routledge, and the ongoing support and encouragement from the Routledge editor for this volume, Alex Masulis. We talked with many persons while formulating the volume and asked for advice on particular aspects of the contents, and we are most grateful for the great counsel provided by so many interested persons.

J. Michael Spector, Barbara B. Lockee,
Sharon E. Smaldino, and Mary C. Herring
Summer 2012

Preface

This collection of scholarly essays is inspired by the substantial body of learning research by David H. Jonassen in the areas of mindtools and problem solving; see, for example, Jonassen's *Modeling with technology: Mindtools for conceptual change* (2006) and *Learning to solve problems: A handbook for designing problem-solving learning environments* (2011). Jonassen's work has inspired educational development, instructional design, and learning research in many areas and in many different contexts. Educational research and development in the following areas, among others, have been significantly influenced by Jonassen's research: case-based learning, constructivist designs and paradigms, hypermedia, individual differences, problem solving, simulation-based learning, task analysis, virtual reality and so much more.

The co-editors contributed equally to this effort and are all past presidents of the Association for Educational Communications and Technology (AECT) in which Jonassen has been active for many years. We initiate the volume with a unifying rationale and description of the contents. This is followed by contributions from some 20 researchers who write about an aspect of Jonassen's published work and elaborate the subsequent educational research and development that has evolved. The volume concludes with a forward-looking reflective piece by Jonassen entitled "First Principles of Learning" that considers where educational technology should be headed.

The focus of the volume is on educational technology, especially with regard to how new technologies have facilitated and supported problem solving and critical thinking. Each chapter focuses on a particular aspect of learning with technology and elaborates the implications for the design and implementation of learning environments and activities aimed at improving the conceptualization of problems, reasoning and higher-order thinking, and solving challenging problems.

We know that Jonassen's substantial body of scholarly work has influenced research and practice pertaining to educational technology, broadly conceived. We hope that these essays will extend that influence and add to the already impressive impact on researchers, designers, teachers and others.

References

Jonassen, D. H. (2006). *Modeling with technology: Mindtools for conceptual change.* Columbus, OH: Merrill/Prentice-Hall.
Jonassen, D. H. (2011). *Learning to solve problems: A handbook for designing problem-solving learning environments.* New York: Routledge.

*J. Michael Spector, Barbara B. Lockee,
Sharon E. Smaldino, and Mary C. Herring
Summer 2012*

1 Mindtools and Problem Solving

An Introduction

J. Michael Spector, Barbara B. Lockee,
Sharon E. Smaldino, and Mary C. Herring

Learning, Complexity and Problem Solving

When one thinks about the nature of working and living in the twenty-first century, what comes to mind? Of course the answers will vary from person to person, region to region, and situation to situation. For many, the answers are likely to be related, however indirectly, to the problems one encounters or expects to encounter. Typical/generic problems include selecting a career, deciding to get married and have children, purchasing a home or car, planning an event, ending a relationship, resolving a dispute, being productive at work, and so on. Many have argued that such problems have become more challenging and complex in the twenty-first century due to new technologies, globalization, and rapidly changing circumstances surrounding many of the problems we are likely to confront. Not surprisingly, one of the central objectives of education and many instructional programs is to improve problem-solving skills and abilities (Borgman, 2008; Bransford, Brown & Cocking, 2000; Jonassen, 2004, 2006, 2007, 2011; NRC, 2011).

Once one decides that addressing problem solving in an instructional sequence or educational program is critically important, this question arises: what is it that makes some problems especially challenging for different learners? What are the sources of complexity in various problem-solving situations? Some complexity is inherent in a problem itself. For example, understanding all the complexities involved in purchasing a house compared with those needed to balance a checking account. Problems tend to become more complex when the system or situation involves non-linear relationships among some of the system components, when there is internal feedback and when there are delayed effects. For example, in a manufacturing environment when production is faced with a large backlog of orders, one tactic is to pay people to work overtime to meet that backlog. However, if the overtime persists, the result may be that after a short period of improved productivity and backlog reduction, people begin to make mistakes with the result that orders are misplaced and work has to be re-accomplished. In short, what appeared for a short period of time to be a linear improvement in backlog reduction may turn into a non-linear situation resulting in worsening backlog.

Another source of complexity concerns the people involved in a problem situation. A person with limited knowledge of land prices, home inspection, the cost of remodeling, school districts, and city codes would find it very challenging, while a realtor might regard these issues as quite simple. A person's background and prior experience is clearly relevant to the perceived complexity of a problem situation. Likewise, a person who is distracted by other matters (e.g., a family crisis, an illness, etc.) may not be able to concentrate on the problem at hand which might have otherwise been easily managed.

In addition, there are general limitations to human reasoning, such as the limits on working memory (Miller, 1956). There is also strong evidence that many people do not reason well when non-linear relationships and delayed effects are involved (Dörner, 1996). Couple these facts about the limitations and constraints of human reasoning with the increasing complexity of problems that we are likely to confront, and one can sense that the educational challenges of the twenty-first century are far from trivial.

What can be done to extend reasoning abilities and better cope with the complex problems we are likely to encounter? Given the history and success of the human experience with tools, the notion of tools to extend our problem-solving abilities is a natural course of action. Agriculture tools allowed early civilizations to thrive in one location and abandon nomadic traditions. Manufacturing tools enabled modern civilizations to create healthier and more productive living arrangements. Of course tools have also been used destructively. A tool in and of itself is perhaps value neutral. For now, we want to focus on how tools might extend our problem-solving abilities, which brings us to the domain of cognitive tools, also known as mindtools (Jonassen, 2000; Jonassen, Carr, & Yueh, 1998).

Before discussing powerful mindtools that support and extend our problem solving and critical reasoning abilities, first take a quick look at a simple mind tool so as to develop a common point of reference. Table 1.1 depicts a simple cost estimation for a vacation. This table was created in Word using a formula to automatically calculate the total.

Imagine that one of the two persons involved in this vacation plan brings this simple table to the other person. A discussion begins. Soon other locations are being considered along with a different length of stay and alternative lodging arrangements. The initial table would then need to be recreated for each scenario to compare outcomes. Suppose the couple has a fixed

Table 1.1 Simple mindtool example

Description	Estimated cost
Travel to and from location	$2,000
Lodging at destination	$1,500
Meals and entertainment	$875
Total	$4,375

maximum budget of $5,000 for the vacation and they want to stay within that limit. In such a case, a spreadsheet would be more helpful in exploring alternatives. A spreadsheet will allow multiple types of formulas to be used along with a variety of constants that can easily be changed to support multiple "*what if?*" analyses. For example, one cell in the spreadsheet might be used for the number of days involved. This cell can then be referred to when calculating the cost of lodging. Moreover, the couple can then manipulate that single cell to see what would happen if they extend the vacation from four to five days, for example. Such a spreadsheet then becomes a valuable extension of the couple's reasoning repertoire and might enable them to reach a desirable solution more quickly than might otherwise be possible without such a tool. It allows them to externalize their internal mental models using the spreadsheet as a mindtool (Jonassen, 2006).

Use of the computer as a mindtool to construct better mental models is now quite familiar to many people thanks to David Jonassen's work. Using mindtools to construct technology-mediated model of phenomena can be considered among the most conceptually engaging task that students can undertake (Jonassen, Howland, Marra, & Chrismond, 2008). The next step is to extend this notion of mindtools to more challenging problems and problem domains. As this is done, it is worth noting that many environments such as home, school, and work, have developed and deployed such tools to support various problem-solving tasks. Given that fact, the integration of mindtools into an instructional sequence and throughout an educational system becomes more than merely a good thing to do – it becomes part of responsible education and training in the twenty-first century.

Part 1 of this volume presents three additional contributions that provide a multi-dimensional context for mindtools. In Chapter 2, Seel, Ifenthaler, and Pirnay-Dummer addresses the dimensions of learning, complexity and problem solving from a psychological perspective involving the successive and cumulative development of useful and productive mental models. In Chapter 3, Wilson addresses the dimensions of learning, complexity and problem solving from an instructional design perspective, emphasizing the critical importance of meaningful practice in developing knowledge and understanding. In Chapter 4, Reeves provides a synthesis of these dimensions and perspectives as applied to the challenging and complex domain of healthcare.

Representation and Visualization Affordances

Technological innovations for teaching and learning have brought significant advancements in pedagogical approaches, especially since the advent of personal computing technologies. The methods available for the representation of information have evolved to provide a broader array of options in the way that information can be represented and, consequently, engaged with by the learner. The construct that Levie and Dickie (1973) described as media attributes, or features of the instructional delivery system, has been more recently explored as *affordances* of learning environments (Gibson, 1977; Gaver, 1991; Norman, 1988; Kirschner & Wopereis, in press). Jonassen's examination of the computer as a mindtool reflects the ability of such technological systems to support learning, in part due to the inherent features of these systems to facilitate different strategies for visual representations of information. On the part of the designer, computers can represent the learning context, supporting the use of problem-based approaches that situate the learner in real-world, meaningful challenges. On the part of the learner, the visual dimension of such systems can reflect interactions with and resulting representations of learning with mindtools.

While the notion of computers as mindtools was not among Jonassen's initial works related to the use of technology for learning, his early work did explore strategies for the creation of effective learning environments by leveraging the visual features, or affordances, of media to support learning. For example, in his book, *The Technology of Text: Principles for Structuring, Designing, and Displaying Text* (1982), Jonassen presented message design guidance for the use of various types of text (printed, electronic, teletext), as well as design principles for supplemental visual information such as diagrams, charts, and so on. The principles featured in this book have continuing relevance to current message design needs, particularly with the proliferation of distance learning, so much of which is delivered primarily through text-based information. Researchers and practitioners alike still examine and employ aspects of this important work – see Chapter 8 by Wijekumar and Meyer.

The affordances of technologies to represent visual understanding continue to develop, as innovations have brought forth new ways to support instructional design and learner engagement. In Chapter 5, Warren and Wakefield examine how educational games provide constructivist learning environments that align with Jonassen's notion of mindtools that support critical thinking and, therefore, cognition. Kirschner and Wopereis contend in Chapter 6 that Web 2.0 tools not only facilitate collaborative, constructivist learning activities for students, but they can also provide the infrastructure for networked *communities of practice*, a newly conceived mindtool for teacher professional development.

In Chapter 7, Laffey, Schmidt, and Galyen advocate the use of three-dimensional virtual environments (3D VE) as *experience tools* that would support authentic learning experiences that are at the same time social, embodied, meaningful and playful. Also related to the social affordances of technological learning environments, As technologies for learning continue to evolve, so will mechanisms to design and assess visual representations of knowledge. In Chapter 9, Tan discusses potential ways to advance the foundational research to which Jonassen (2000, 2004, 2006) contributed so significantly in this area, asking us to examine our own beliefs and ideologies related to the design of technology-supported, problem-based learning environments.

In sum, Part 2 of this volume provides a reminder of how very important support for representation and visualization are in the process of coming to know and understand. Jonassen's many publications have helped us learn this valuable lesson.

Problem Solving and Critical Thinking

In his many published works, David Jonassen has contributed much to the context of problem solving and the critical thinking relevant to the process of solving problems. In Part 3, the five authors have focused on issues associated with these elements.

In Chapter 10, Michael Hannafin explores the connection between theory and design in addressing learning needs. His focus on the implications of differences in theory and epistemology demonstrates their impact on learning and design of instruction. In Chapter 11, Woei Hung advocates for the integration of problem-based learning (PBL) as an instructional strategy to challenge students to address real-world issues. The suggestion is that PBL provides students of any age the opportunity to explore a learning problem and develop approaches to resolution of that circumstance. In Chapter 12, Lee and Murcia offer a view of problem solving and elements of conceptual change. They propose that when students engage in problem solving they become aware of the inconsistencies in their own thinking and subsequently gain a better understanding of their own way of thinking and learning needs. In Chapter 13, Land, Smith, and Zimmerman offer the use of computer tools to be adapted or created to extend thinking and problem solving. Using Jonassen's (2000) model of mindtools, they apply that model to three examples where mobile technologies can serve as the vehicles to support student thinking and creative learning in all settings. In Chapter 14, Brian Belland focuses on Jonassen's work pertaining to ill-structured problems and how students need to apply argumentation in their thinking process as they try to resolve those problems (Jonassen & Kim, 2010). Without simple solutions, students need to develop their skills in preparing arguments to support resolutions.

In each chapter of this section of the book, the interrelated themes of problem solving and critical thinking are central to the ideas presented. Whether advocating for the connections to theory or the use of particular technology tools, the notion that as designers and instructors we are responsible for providing the opportunity to explore problems, no matter how complex or ill-structured, and to facilitate the learning process for students.

Integrating Mindtools into Teaching and Learning

There is much discussion these days about the need to change the way we go about educating students for the twenty-first century. Within these discussions is often included the concept that technology is another tool in the toolkit. David Jonassen has reminded us for years that they are not just tools, but instead that technology can be used as a mindtool to address ill-structured problems. Mindtools are not machines and systems; instead they represent a concept. It is a concept that embraces the use of constructive, higher-order critical thinking that is modeled and supported by the use of a computer application (Jonassen et al. 2008).

The Partnership for 21st Century Skills (P-21) is a primary mover in the area of educating for the twenty-first century needs. P-21 (see http://www. p21.org/) argues that students must not only learn content but also develop essential skills for success such as critical thinking, problem solving, collaboration and communication (Partnership, 2009). The use of the mindtools concept aligns well with the P-21 concepts with its focus on "active, constructive, intentional, authentic, and collaborative" mindful thinking (Jonassen et al., 2008, p. 96).

Jonassen, in his contribution to this volume, reminds us that learning is problem-focused necessarily engages the deeper processing of information and results in more meaningful kinds of knowledge. Knowledge can be categorized in multiple forms. A main aspect of all educational models or curricula used to categorize knowledge is a focus on intended learning outcomes. These outcomes are key to the design of any instructional system. Jonassen and Tessmer (1996/1997) and Tristen (see Chapter 15) have categorized various types of learning outcomes into taxonomies that can be used to design or evaluate instructional systems and to generate research questions about them. These authors expanded upon previous taxonomies noting that as learning theories, systems, and settings changed so too would the types of learning systems.

Taxonomies provide a way of classifying and identifying the levels of complexity of a thinking process typically associated with a type of knowledge and a set of evidences. Use of taxonomical categories help to verify that learning of the type and quality established by the curriculum or educational program has occurred, an important piece in our present age of educational accountability for not only learning but also the use of resources such as technology. Taxonomies assist in identifying and creating the type of intended learning. Expanded opportunities for learning have extended the use of mindtools in a variety of educational settings. An example of primary areas of expansion in the twenty-first century is distance learning.

Jonassen conceptualized mindtools in the 1990s. At this time, online learning held minimal importance for educators. Times have changed! During the fall 2010 term, over 6.1 million American college students were taking at least one online course; an increase of 560,000 students over the number reported the previous year (Allen & Seaman, 2011). Meanwhile, K-12 online learning is growing at an annual rate of 30 percent in the USA and similar growth is occurring in other countries. State-led virtual schools are found in 34 of the 50 states in the USA, and 70 percent of American school districts offer at least one online course to students (iNACOL, 2012). Do mindtools concepts still work in these new learning settings? Yes!

Mindtools can help to overcome some of the challenges of enabling meaningful learning online. Mindtools port easily to the online setting as long as they are part of instructional activities that are supportive and meaningful. Mindtools are still relevant because they are not discipline specific and they are financially and cognitively accessible. When an online educator incorporates mindtool activities it means that the learners represent what they know by working *with* the technology (e.g. pose a real-world problem that students must solve using online data) rather than learning *from* the technology in forms such as tutorials or drill and practice applications, as Rose Marra argues in Chapter 16.

Jonassen et al. (2008) remind us that to have meaningful learning we must create activities that are active, constructivist, cooperative, authentic, and intentional (see also Gagné & Merrillm, 1990). These are not just terms, but a frame for instructional designers to use when designing and implementing instruction in any setting. He argues that the most powerful modes of thinking that lead to the most meaningful learning are problem solving, analogizing, modeling, reasoning causally, and arguing. No matter the mode, all learning environments should support productive thinking by students, which is Jonassen's closing remark in his contribution to this volume.

Concluding Remarks

In one sense, Jonassen falls within the mainstream of instructional design researchers. In his contribution to this volume, Jonassen makes a strong case that problem-centered learning is vitally important in developing productive and useful thinking and reasoning skills. Many others agree. Merrill's (2002) instructional design model has problems at the center. van Merriënboer's (1997) Four-Component/Instructional Design (4C/ID) model also puts problem solving on center stage, distinguishing two quite different kinds of problems – those involving recurrent tasks and those involving non-recurrent tasks, each of which requires somewhat different kinds of instructional support.

The notion that the type of thing to be learned can be traced back to Gagné (1965) and perhaps to instructional design researchers prior to Gagné. Jonassen's focus on types of problems culminated in a handbook for designing meaningful problem-solving environments to support learning (2011). That is what instructional designers do – they devise methods to support learning.

While Jonassen's many contributions now seem well within the mainstream of instructional design and educational research, when first introduced they were clearly at the leading edge of where learning and instruction was headed. As a result of his untiring efforts, it is now expected that learning environments will include scaffolding for analogical reasoning, interactions with models, opportunities to develop causal reasoning, support for argumentation and many other affordances in support of improving human problem solving. As Jonassen so appropriately concludes in Chapter 17, instruction and learning environments should support productive thinking and problem solving. By stirring up the muddy waters of previous research and development in the area of instructional systems and learning environments, Jonassen has created a clear focus on the first principle of learning – support productive thinking.

As you move through the chapters in this *festschrift* for David Jonassen, you will find the embodiment of his lifelong commitment to meaningful learning and see the impact of his work around the world. Thank you, David, for inspiring so many to do so much.

References

Allen, I. E., & Seaman, J. (2011). *Going the distance: Online education in the United States*. Babson Park, MA: Babson Survey Research Group. Retrieved from http://www.onlinelearningsurvey.com/reports/goingthedistance.pdf

Borgman, C. L. (Ed.), (2008). *Fostering learning in the networked world: The cyberlearning opportunity and challenge*. Report of the NSF Task Force on Cyberlearning, National Science Foundation, Washington, DC.

Bransford, J. D., Brown, A. L., & Cocking, R. R. (Eds.), (2000). *How people learn: Brain, mind, experience and school*. Washington, DC: National Academy Press.

Gagné, R. M. (1965). *The conditions of learning and theory of instruction* (1st ed.). New York: Holt, Rinehart & Winston.

Gagné, R. M., & Merrill, M. D. (1990). Integrative goals for instructional design. *Educational Technology Research and Development, 38*(1), 23–30.

Gaver, W. W. (1991). Technology affordances. In S. P. Robertson, G. M. Olson, & J. S. Olson (Eds.), *Proceedings of the ACM CHI 91 Human Factors in Computing Systems Conference*, April 28–June 5, 1991 (pp. 79–84). New Orleans, LA: ACM.

Gibson, J. J. (1977). The theory of affordances. In R. Shaw & J. Bransford (Eds.), *Perceiving, acting and knowing* (pp. 67–82). Hillsdale, NJ: Erlbaum.

iNACOL (International Association for K-12 Online Learning) (2012). *iNACOL National Standards for Quality Online Courses*. Retrieved from http://www.inacol.org/research/nationalstandards/.

Jonassen, D. H. (1982). *The technology of text: Principles for structuring, designing, and displaying text*. Englewood Cliffs, NJ: Educational Technology Publications.

Jonassen, D. H. (2000). *Computers as mindtools for schools: Engaging critical thinking* (2nd ed.). Columbus, OH: Prentice-Hall.

Jonassen, D. H. (2004). *Learning to solve problems: An instructional design guide*. San Francisco, CA: Jossey-Bass.

Jonassen, D. H. (2006). *Modeling with technology: Mindtools for conceptual change*. Columbus, OH: Merrill/Prentice-Hall.

Jonassen, D. H. (2007). *Learning to solve complex, scientific problems*. Mahway, NJ: Erlbaum.

Jonassen, D. H. (2011). *Learning to solve problems: A handbook for designing problem-solving learning environments*. New York: Routledge.

Jonassen, D. H., & Kim, B. (2010). Arguing to learn and learning to argue: Design justifications and guidelines. *Educational Technology Research & Development, 58*(4), 439–457.

Jonassen, D. H., & Tessmer, M. (1996/1997). An outcomes-based taxonomy for the design, evaluation, and research of instructional systems. *Training Research Journal, 2*, 11–14.

Jonassen, D. H., Carr, C., & Yueh, H-P. (1998). Computers as mindtools for engaging learners in critical thinking. *TechTrends, 43*(2), 24–32.

Jonassen, D. H., Howland, J., Marra, R. M., & Chrismond, D. (2008). *Meaningful learning with technology*. Upper Saddle River, NJ: Pearson, Merrill, Prentice Hall.

Levie, W. H., & Dickie, K. E. (1973). The analysis and application of media. In R. M. W. Travers (Ed.), *The second handbook of research on teaching* (pp. 858–882). Chicago: Rand-McNally.

Merrill, M. D. (2002). First principles of instruction. *Educational Technology: Research and Development, 50*(3), 43–59.

Norman, D. A. (1988). *The design of everyday things.* New York: Doubleday.

Partnership (2009). The MILE guide: Milestones for improving learning and education. Retrieved from http://p21.org/storage/documents/MILE_Guide_091101.pdf.

van Merriënboer, J. J. G. (1997). *Training complex cognitive skills: A four-component instructional design model for technical training.* Englewood Cliffs, NJ: Educational Technology Publications.

2 Mental Models and Their Role in Learning by Insight and Creative Problem Solving

Norbert M. Seel, Dirk Ifenthaler, and Pablo Pirnay-Dummer

Introduction

In the literature on great inventions we can find some illustrative examples referring to *insight and restructuring* in creative problem solving. So, for example, the famous chemist Kekulé reports that he found the ring structure of Benzol after a long and tedious period of cogitation when he dreamed about a snake biting its tail. The mathematician Poincaré (1908) reports that his idea of a new class of mathematical functions appeared suddenly and unexpectedly while he was boarding his vehicle during a journey. Amazingly, the purpose of his journey was to take a break from his unsuccessful and frustrating work on this problem. Similar anecdotes have been reported with regard to other scientific inventions, such as the decoding of genetic information. When Watson (1968) was asked how he deciphered the double helix structure he answered that he discovered this structure while playing with model devices that represented the already known basic sequences of deoxyribonucleic acid (DNA). While playing with the devices he arrived at the spontaneous insight that these devices had to be arranged as a spiral stairs.

Already across the first half of the twentieth century, some researchers attempted to develop theoretical models of insightful problem solving on the basis of such subjective reports. Among these attempts, the model of problem solving developed by Wallas (1926) became popular. The initial phase of this model is the *preparation phase*, which is concerned with the formulation and specification of the problem and a search for solutions that, however, fail within the realm of the original problem specification. Thus, at the end of this initial phase the feeling arises that the problem is not solvable. Therefore, another phase follows where the active search for a solution is interrupted and the problem solver puts the problem aside. This phase is called the *incubation phase*. Suddenly, the problem solver achieves insight into the problem. This phase is called the *illumination phase* and is characterized by the fact that the problem's solution appears unexpectedly in the consciousness of the problem solver. Finally, the *verification phase* involves working out the implications of the new insight. Clearly, the heart of this model is the incubation phase followed by a spontaneous illumination, the so-called insight. Wegner (2002) described this phenomenon with the following words:

> The happiest inconsistency between intention and action occurs when a great idea pops into mind. The action in this case is the occurrence of the idea, and our tendency to say "Eureka!" or "Aha!" is our usual acknowledgement that this particular insight was not something we were planning in advance. Although most of us are quite willing to take credit for our good ideas, it is still true that we do not experience them as voluntary.
>
> (Wegner, 2002, p. 81f)

This statement illustrates the paradox of insight. While consciously managed, and when volitional and strenuous attempts of problem solving fail, a sudden and unconsciously generated and inadvertent idea unforeseeably provides the solution.

For a long time, Gestalt psychologists, such as Wertheimer, Köhler, Duncker, and Maier, explained the phenomenon of creative problem solving as a matter of spontaneous and unconscious insight. Based on the results of his ingenious experiments on the *two-string* or pendulum problem, which have been described extensively in the psychological literature (e.g. Eysenck, 2004; Saugstad, 1957), Maier concluded:

> Before the solution is found there is disharmony. The reasoner cannot quite see the relation of certain things in the room to the solution of the problem. The next experience is that of having an idea. The "transformation" or "organization" stage is not experienced in reasoning any more than in reversible perspective. *The new organization is suddenly there.* It is the dominant experience and covers any factor which just preceded it.
>
> (Maier, 1931, p. 191)

The assumption of illumination as a sudden insight into a problem was the mantra of Gestalt psychology and cognitive psychology until the emergence of mental model theory in the 1980s, according to which the solution of a problem is found by means of a mental model (Seel, 1991). Unlike the earlier explanations of Gestalt psychologists, mental model theory considers insight and restructuring as a matter of *conscious* changes of the problem representation by means of a working model, which allows the problem solver to perform actions entirely internally to judge their consequences, interpret them, and draw conclusions based on them (Rumelhart, Smolensky, McClelland, & Hinton, 1986). According to mental model theory, a problem is represented at the beginning in such a way that an immediate solution is not possible. All initial attempts to solve the problem fail, and the problem solver reaches a dead end (i.e. the incubation phase). To leave the dead end, the problem solver must change the problem representation iteratively until a plausible solution becomes possible. This is based on the learning-dependent progression of a mental model, which involves processes of restructuring and reorganizing world knowledge, resulting in changes to the problem representation and finally in the solution.

In this chapter, we describe how mental models operate to afford insight into a problem and its solution. First, we describe briefly the theory of mental models and its implications for creative problem solving. Then we focus on the effects of the learners' semantic sensitivity on the construction and revision of mental models. After reporting some results of empirical research, we discuss the instructional implications.

The Theory of Mental Models

In the 1980s, the theory of mental models emerged and introduced a constructivist approach to modeling into cognitive science and related fields of interest (Johnson-Laird, 1983) that complemented the prevalent pragmatic approaches to model building of the time. The theory of mental models is based on the assumption that cognition takes place in the use of mental representations in which individuals organize symbols or representations of experience or thought in such a way that they effect a systematic representation of this experience or thought, as a means of understanding it – or explaining it to others (Seel, 1991).

In a historical review, Johnson-Laird (2004) traced the theory of mental models back to Peirce (1883) as well as to Wittgenstein (1922) and the Gestalt psychologists. In accordance with Peirce's semiotics, cognitive psychology differentiates at the very least between (picture-like) images and (language-like) propositions as forms of mental representation. Johnson-Laird (1983) added mental models as a particular form of representation that mediates between images and propositions (Markman, 1998). In addition, Johnson-Laird (1983, 2004) referred to the work of Craik (1943), who argued that an individual who intends to give a rational explanation for something must develop practicable methods in order to generate adequate explanations from the available knowledge of the world and a limited information processing capacity. Thus, in order to create subjective plausibility the individual constructs an internal model that both integrates the relevant semantic knowledge and meets the perceived requirements of the situation. Accordingly, this model works when it fits the subject's knowledge as well as the explanatory need with regard to the concrete situation. More generally, Craik points out:

> If the organism carries a "small-scale model" of external reality and of its own possible actions within its head, it is able to try out various alternatives, conclude which is the best of them, react to future situations before they arise, utilize the knowledge of past events in dealing with the present and the future, and in every way to react in a much fuller, safer, and competent manner to the emergencies which face it.
>
> (Craik, 1943, p. 61)

Since the concept of mental models was introduced into cognitive science it has been criticized by proponents of schema theories, who consider mental models as mere instantiations of local schemas (e.g. Brewer, 1987; Rips, 1987). In contrast, the schema concept is not widely accepted in the field of cognitive science. For example, Anderson (1983) and Johnson-Laird (1983) did not operate with the schema concept, and other researchers, such as Brown (1979) and Prinz (1983), have rejected schemas as an unnecessary and insufficiently defined construct of cognitive psychology. This is not the place to expound on the arguments of this controversial debate about schemas and mental models. Today, most cognitive scientists agree on the point that schemas and mental models serve different cognitive functions. Schemas represent generic and abstract knowledge acquired on the basis of manifold individual experiences with objects, persons, situations, and behaviors (Mandler, 1984). As soon as a schema is fully developed it can be applied immediately to assimilate information about new experiences. But how do people operate cognitively in the case of novel problems for which no schema can be retrieved from memory? The answer for those who advocate mental model theory is that people construct a mental model of the situation or problem to be solved. In accordance with this argumentation, the next section of this article will describe a theoretical model that integrates schemas and mental models into a comprehensive architecture of cognition with the aim of explaining their unique functions in cognition.

According to Rumelhart et al. (1986), people have three essential abilities for processing information and acting successfully in various environments. First of all, people are very good at *pattern matching*. They are obviously able to quickly settle on an interpretation of an input pattern. This ability is central to perceiving, remembering, and comprehending. It is probably *the* essential component of most cognitive behavior – and it is based on the activation and instantiation of schemas. Second, people are very good at *modeling* their worlds due to their ability to anticipate new states of affairs resulting from actions in the world or from an event they might observe. Both pattern matching and modeling are grounded on building up expectations by *internalizing* experiences and are crucial for making inferences (Seel, 1991). Third, people are good at *manipulating* their environments. This can be considered as a version of man-the-tool-user, which is perhaps the crucial skill for building a culture. Especially important here is the ability to manipulate the environment and to create artifacts as *external representations* which can be manipulated in simple ways to get answers to very difficult and abstract problems. Jonassen has referred to external representations as "mind tools" closely related with the use of computers (Jonassen, Carr, & Hsiu-Ping, 1998). As people gain experience with the world created by their actions they internalize their experiences with external representations to develop mental models.

In order to explain the aforementioned basic capabilities, Rumelhart et al. (1986) divide the cognitive system into two modules or sets of units. One module – called an *interpretation network* – is concerned with producing appropriate responses to any input from the external world, while the other module is concerned with constructing a *model of the world* and producing an interpretation of *what would happen if we did that* with a particular external representation. The modeling part of the cognitive architecture is concerned with generating expectations about possible changes to the world as a result of imagining an external representation and operating on it. The interpretation network receives input from the world and reaches a relaxed mental state by producing relevant cognitive responses, whereas the model of the world predicts how the input would change in accordance with these responses. From a psychological point of view, it can be argued that the interpretation network operates with *schemas,* which help the learner to assimilate new information into cognitive structures and constitute the fundamental basis for the *construction of mental models* of the world as well. In cognitive psychology, as well as in parallel distributed processing (PDP) models, schemas are characterized as slot-filler structures used to organize concepts, relations between them, and operations with them semantically. However, PDP models do not consider schemas as stored structures of the semantic memory that can be activated when necessary but rather as representations of complex constraint satisfaction networks that trigger the interpretation of input information. Schemas emerge at the moment they are needed to interpret new information. Each schema results from the interaction between a large number of simpler units, which all work together to come to an interpretation of input information. Schemas are implicit in people's knowledge and are triggered by the events that they have to interpret. This conception clearly contradicts the conventional belief of educational psychologists that schemas are stored in memory. From the point of view of the PDP approach, *nothing stored actually corresponds directly to a schema*; rather, "what is stored is a set of connection strengths which, when activated, have implicitly in them the ability to generate states that correspond to instantiated schemata" (Rumelhart et al., 1986, p. 21). Schemas are active processes but not products. They can be understood as recognition devices aiming at the evaluation of their goodness-of-fit to the data being processed.

Basically, Rumelhart et al. (1986) see the emergence of models of the world or *mental models* in the same way. A mental model also consists of a network, which, however, does not take its input from the external world but rather from the interpretation network with the aim of specifying the actions that can be carried out in pure imagination. Its product consists of an interpretation of what can happen when actions are performed. Accordingly, the function of the mental model is to simulate actions in the mind, to assess their consequences, to interpret them, and to use these interpretations for making inferences. While the interpretation network takes its inputs from the world, the model-based network takes its inputs from actions of the interpretation network and predicts what changes they will bring about. Therefore, the model-based network can also be considered as an "action network" and constitutes the space for mental simulations.

According to Seel (1991), this cognitive architecture proposed by Rumelhart et al. (1986) corresponds to Piaget's (e.g. 1976) fundamental idea that cognition is regulated by the interaction between assimilation and accommodation, which aims at adjusting the mind to meet the necessities of the external world. Assimilation can be considered as the fundamental basis of the interpretation network and is dependent on the activation of schemas, which allow new information to be integrated into existing cognitive structures. In cognitive psychology, schemas are understood as slot-filler structures that serve central cognitive functions, such as integrating information into cognitive structures, regulating attention, making inferences in the process of acquiring knowledge, and reconstructing it from memory. As soon as learners have consolidated schemas to a sufficient extent through learning and development, they provide them with the cognitive framework for matching information from stimuli with content from knowledge memory, thus allowing them to select the information that is consistent with a schema. Anderson (1984) captures the essence of these functions of schemas when he remarks: "Without a schema to which an event can be assimilated, learning is slow and uncertain" (p. 5). Schemas represent the *generic* knowledge a person has acquired in the course of numerous individual experiences with objects, people, situations, and actions. As soon as a schema can be activated, it is automatically used and regulates the assimilation of new information in a top-down procedure. This allows information to be processed very quickly, a function which is vital for humans as it enables them to adapt to their environment more quickly.

Assimilation is a basic form of cognitive processing, but certainly not the only one. Another basic form consists in accommodation aiming at restructuring knowledge. Accommodation aims, first of all, at a modification of a schema by means of accretion, tuning, or the reorganization of its structures and content (Norman & Rumelhart, 1978). This kind of accommodation presupposes an adjustment of existing schemas to new but familiar input information. In accordance with this view, Chi (2008) distinguished between three types of conceptual change. First, if there is no prior knowledge of the concept to be learned, learning consists of adding new knowledge. Second, if the available knowledge is incomplete learning consists of gap filling. In both of these situations, learning consists of enriching existing knowledge structures, whereas in a third situation existing preconceptions may be incorrect and contradict the concepts to be learned. In this case, a conceptual change is necessary. What these kinds of learning have in common is that schematically organized knowledge exists and can be adjusted to fit new information. However, speaking about mental model transformation is somewhat misleading because schemas are modified in accordance with the distinction made by Norman and Rumelhart (1978).

If an adjustment of a schema is not possible – that is, if the accretion, tuning, and/or reorganization of a schema fail, or if no schema can be activated at all – the learner either can abandon the cognitive processing or else invest some mental effort to develop a mental model. Accordingly, mental

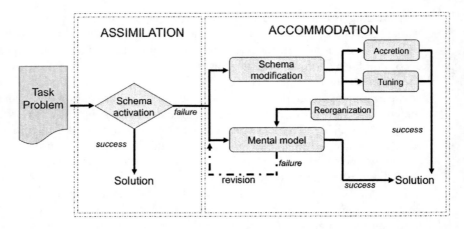

Figure 2.1 Cognitive functions of assimilation and accommodation (Ifenthaler & Seel, 2011, p. 539).

models must be seen as products of accommodation (as discussed in Piaget's epistemology) that aim at adjustments of cognitive structures to the environment whenever the subject is not able to activate and modify an appropriate schema (Seel, 1991, 2006). In contrast to schemas, mental models operate from the "bottom up" under the continuous control of consciousness. As long as the information being processed can be assimilated promptly into cognitive structures and as long as schemas can be modified by means of accretion, tuning, and reorganization, there is no need to construct a mental model. This theoretical conception can be illustrated as in Figure 2.1.

Mental models constitute the fundamental basis for developing models of the world and may serve as *models for reasoning* as well as *models for understanding* (Mayer, 1989). In both cases, mental models are constructed to meet the specific requirements of situations and problems the subject is faced with for which the activation and/or modification of a schema fails. In contrast to schemas as slot-filler structures, mental models contain sets of assumptions that must be justified by observations or by mapping them to world knowledge. This justification of assumptions is closely connected with a *reduction to absurdity* (Seel, 1991), that is, a process of testing continuously whether a model can be replaced with a better model. As long as this is not possible, the model is considered suitable.

Models for understanding, which are necessary for problem solving, have their starting point in the tentative integration of relevant simple structures or even single bits of domain-specific knowledge step by step into the coherent design of a working model to meet the requirements of the problem to be solved. Johnson-Laird (1983) considers this process of a stepwise enrichment of a model with more and more information units as a process of elaboration. Models for understanding *represent the structure of world knowledge* because they are generated to structure it and not to reproduce or copy a given external structure. Nevertheless, models for understanding can be externalized by means of particular symbol systems (e.g. mindtools) and generate subjective plausibility with regard to complex phenomena to be understood and explained. It is noteworthy that models for understanding are cognitive artifacts which correspond only more or less to the external world, since people can also construct pure thought models which bear no direct correspondence to the external world but rather only to world knowledge. This corresponds to the idea of *coherence epistemology* (Seel, 1991) as described in detail by Al-Diban (2002, 2012). In general, models for understanding share the following characteristics: (a) They are incomplete and constantly evolving; (b) they are usually not an accurate representation of a phenomenon but typically may contain errors and contradictions; (c) they are parsimonious and provide simplified explanations of complex phenomena; and (d) they often contain measures of uncertainty about their validity that allow them to be used even if incorrect (see Pirnay-Dummer, Ifenthaler, & Seel, 2012).

The functions of a model are defined on the basis of the intentions of the model-constructing person. Therefore, the term 'model' is principally used in accordance with functional intentionality. In general, external representations of models may serve as means of *simplifying* an investigation to particular and relevant phenomena in a domain. In addition, externalizations of models may serve to help its user to *envision* the phenomenon to be understood or explained by making the invisible visible. Beyond these basic functions of models in general, mental models in particular are often constructed as analogies in order to identify relationships within an unknown domain to be explained (e.g. quantum mechanisms) with the help of the relationships within a known domain (e.g. Rutherford's atomic model). Such models are essentially heuristic and suggest structural similarities between or among different domains. Usually, they are called *analogy models*. However, probably the most important function of mental models is their capacity to aid in the simulation of a cognitive system's processes, as already emphasized by Craik (1943) and others (e.g. Forbus and Gentner, 1997; Greeno, 1989; Seel, 1991). Actually, by means of a mental model an individual is able to simulate real actions in the pure imagination. A mental simulation enables the imagination to envision events that would take place in the world if particular actions were to be performed (Markman, 1998). Within the realm of problem solving, the mental model simulates specific transformations of a problem representation as a kind of *thought experiment* to produce qualitative inferences with respect to the problem to be solved. Thus, we can conclude this section of our paper with Johnson-Laird's (1983) precept that:

> [m]ental models play a central and unifying role in representing objects, states of affairs, sequences of events, the way the world is. ... They enable individuals to make inferences and predictions, to understand phenomena, to decide what action to take and to control its execution, and, above all, to experience events by proxy.
>
> (Laird's, 1983, p. 397)

As a consequence, mental models are indispensible with regard to problem solving in general and to creative invention in particular.

Mental Models for Creative Problem Solving

In the literature of the 1960s, creativity and creative problem solving were considered as closely related to the formation of *new schemas of thinking* (e.g. Guilford, 1967). However, Bransford (1984) has pointed out that schema activation and the formation of a new schema are two different problems. Although it may be possible to activate existing schemas with a given topic, this does not necessarily imply that a learner can use this activated knowledge to develop new knowledge in order to solve a given problem. Moreover, the development of new schemas is a long process and presupposes manifold and repeated experiences with many similar objects and events. In cognitive psychology, a schema is conceptualized as a unit of mental representation in which the conceptual structures, relations, and processes of a particular semantic phenomenon of the world are organized as slot-filler structures that run automatically when triggered by input information that fits with the default values of a schema. In consequence, schemas are not appropriate devices for problem solving at all (Brown, 1979), because a problem is defined by three components: (1) a given initial state s_i; (2) a desired final state s_j; and (3) a barrier which hinders the solution of the problem. By definition, a problem always occurs if a person does not know how to proceed from a given state to a desired goal state.

Certainly, most learning tasks in the classroom as well as well-structured problems, such as the Towers of Hanoi task or Duncker's famous x-ray task (Duncker, 1945), can be solved by means of restructuring available schemas, but ill-structured problems and problems which require insight and creativity cannot. As Jonassen and Hung (2012) have pointed out, ill-structured problems regularly possess aspects that are unknown. Additionally, such problems might have multiple solutions, varied solution methods, or even no solutions at all. Ill-structured problems often require learners to make judgments and express personal opinions or beliefs about the problem and basically presuppose the construction of mental models. This especially holds true with regard to problems that require insight and creative solutions.

Creative Problem Solving

Creative problem solving presupposes that people actively construct meaningful representations, such as coherent mental models, which represent subjective experiences, ideas, thoughts, and feelings. Explanatory mental models needed for creative problem solving are usually designed without a specific end in mind. In accordance with the principle of reduction to absurdity (Seel, 1991), the problem solver explores possible models by developing hypotheses and then varying significant parameters to investigate how well his or her conjectures align with the models. This is how mental models guide the necessary understanding of the problem space as well as the necessary operations within it. Creative problem solving requires iterative steps of hypothesis testing as well as an increased time for constructing appropriate mental models (Funke, 1992). This constitutes a problem in itself because mental models are regularly incomplete and constantly evolving. They are usually not an accurate representation of a phenomenon but rather typically contain errors and contradictions.

However, mental models are parsimonious and provide simplified explanations of complex phenomena; they often contain measures of uncertainty about their validity that allow them to be used even if they are incorrect. Mental models, like heuristics in general, often become apparent when the problem solver encounters a kind of resistance to explain something. For example, an expert who solves a particular class of problems automatically by triggering schemas may have to struggle to find a solution for a novel problem and may be forced to develop a mental model. Accordingly, creative invention necessitates the construction and gradual improvement of a mental model.

It is generally assumed that creative problem solvers, such as inventors, use mental models as sets of heuristics to develop their ideas and inventions. Accordingly, a mental model can also be defined as the ideas and concepts an inventor has about an invention. Mental models are dynamic prototypes an inventor can run in the mind's eye. Their decisive advantage is that they allow an inventor to radically reconstruct previous knowledge about various domains to help solve a complex problem. In other words: Mental models for invention often are based on analogies between different domains. This can be illustrated with the example of the invention of the telephone. Its inventor, Alexander Bell, had an expertise in human anatomy that he used to develop a mental model of the telephone (Gorman & Carlson, 1990). Another example is provided by Thomas Edison, who made a career out of taking parts from one invention and fitting them together with a different invention to produce a third. Edison's use of mental models also demonstrates one of the problems of using such techniques. When Edison was trying to develop the kinetoscope, having the same mental model for motion pictures as he did for the phonograph hampered him. He saw the kinetoscope as a single-use device, and in the end, his mental model of a phonograph with pictures had to be discarded (Carlson & Gorman, 1990). This is an example of the observation that a mental model can also make one blind to facts and ideas that challenge or defy deeply held beliefs.

Mental Models for Inventions

Creativity is often put on a level with spontaneity, but creative invention is usually not the result of spontaneous ideas but rather the endpoint of a long-term cognitive contention with a complex problem. First: *invention is hard work* and second: *necessity is the mother of invention*. Third: mental models provide the frame for an invention by constraining proto-inventions to an applicable product, which is generally considered as both sufficiently new and useful. The use of the prefix 'proto-' indicates a precondition or an early stage of development of a solution to a problem. According to mental model theory, inventors develop tentative mental models of the problem in order to generate proto-inventions by design heuristics. In mental model theory, this is called a reduction to absurdity, which denotes a continuous process of a testing and revising a mental model and the resulting proto-invention. A small number of design heuristics can generate an abundance of proto-inventions, but a really successful invention will be rare.

The probability of constructing an effective mental model for creative invention can be substantially increased through the development of *analogy models*, which are built on what is known and on what can be successfully transferred to a new problem. The person creating a model for a proto-invention constructs an initial solution model by selecting only a few attributes from a known base domain and then mapping them to the target domain. This can be illustrated by an example provided by Holyoak and Thagard (1995):

> Our knowledge of water provides us with a kind of internal model of how it moves. Similarly, our knowledge of sound provides us with a kind of model of how sound is transmitted through the air. Each of these mental models links an internal representation to external reality. But when we consider the analogy between water waves and sound propagation, we are trying to build an isomorphism between two internal models. Implicitly, we are acting as if our model of water waves can be used to modify and improve our model of sound.
>
> (Thagard, 1995, p. 33)

If this process of building an isomorphism between two mental models leads immediately to an acceptable conclusion by analogy, the procedure will be finished. But in the case of creative inventions this situation should arise relatively infrequently since usually it is not easy to construct a mental model to explain an unknown phenomenon on the basis of previous experiences with similar phenomena within another domain.

Naturally, there is a substantial lack of empirical research on the role of mental models for great inventions because they cannot be forced by experimental treatments. However, one can find some good case descriptions of great inventions in the literature that demonstrate how one can use mental models for creative inventions by performing analogical reasoning and thought simulations and then ruling out unpromising designs and following up on promising ones. A nice example for this thought simulation by means of a mental model that can be found in the literature is Oatley's (2011) essay about Shakespeare's invention of the theater. Other good examples of the role of mental models for inventions refer to Thomas Edison (1847–1931), with a particular emphasis on the cognitive processes involved in his creative inventions (Carlson & Gorman, 1990; Gorman & Carlson, 1990).

Referring to the invention of the light bulb, one can state that Edison began his efforts to solve the problem by creating a regulating system that kept a platinum filament between the incandescent and melting temperatures. This phase of operating exclusively in the design space of regulated platinum-filament bulbs lasted some months and resulted in Edison's first design of a light bulb in 1878.

In the following phase (January 1879 to October 1879), Edison adopted a strategy of functional decomposition of the complex problem when he discovered that gases boil out of a platinum filament raised to incandescence and damage the wire. He now explored changes in different filaments due to high temperatures generated by a blowtorch. During the next months (to December 1879) Edison developed the first practical high-resistance carbon bulbs. Edison's invention of the light bulb took nearly one year and was associated with cognitive processes that are characteristic to the construction and revision of a mental model. First, he referred to his broad knowledge of mechanisms to develop self-regulating bulbs, but these efforts to find an analogy model were not successful until Edison came up with a functional decomposition of the complex problem and employed a kind of "beam search" at various phases.

Beam search is a heuristic search which optimizes a best-first search to reduce memory requirements as well as to order partial solutions to a problem in accordance with a heuristic which aims at predicting how close a particular solution is to a successful overall solution. In terms of mental model theory, beam search corresponds largely to a reduction to absurdity of model candidates. Beam search uses a breadth-first search strategy to generate all possible consequences of a current model and to sort them in increasing order of heuristic cost.

The effectiveness of mental models and related heuristics (such as beam search) can also be demonstrated by referring to other great inventors, such as Nikola Tesla (1856–1943), who electrified the world. In his autography (Johnston, 1981), Tesla reports that he relied heavily on his capabilities of visualization and mental simulation in making his inventions. More specifically, Tesla (1919) informs us about his creative inventions by using a kind of mental model:

> My method is different. I do not rush into actual work. When I get an idea I start at once building it up in my imagination. I change the construction, make improvements and operate the device in my mind. It is absolutely immaterial to me whether I run my turbine in thought or test it in my shop. I even note if it is out of balance. There is no difference whatever, the results are the same. In this way I am able to rapidly develop and perfect a conception without touching anything. When I have gone so far as to embody in the invention every possible improvement I can think of and see no fault anywhere, I put into concrete form this final product of my brain. Invariably my device works as I conceived that it should, and the experiment comes out exactly as I planned it.

In twenty years there has not been a single exception. ... The incessant mental exertion developed my powers of observation and enabled me to discover a truth of great importance. (online translation)

However, creative problem solving by insight and restructuring is not limited to inventors and ingenious people but is a common feature of humans and other animals in general, as the seminal research of Köhler (1921) on problem solving of chimpanzees demonstrates. Furthermore, there is sufficient research on the effectiveness of instructional aids on problem solving.

Creative Problem Solving Under the Condition of Instruction

The idea of assisting students in problem solving by means of particular hints has a long tradition in research on learning by insight and creative problem solving. For example, Maier (1930, 1931) investigated the effects of hints in his experiments on the pendulum and two-string problem. In his pendulum experiment, Maier focused on the effect of prior knowledge on problem solving. The control group had to solve the pendulum problem without any help, whereas the subjects of another group were provided with the three necessary steps for solving the given problem. According to behaviorism, this should increase the probability of finding the solution to the problem. In a third condition, the subjects were additionally provided with a specific hint to direct their thinking to the correct solution and organize their thinking more effectively. The overall results of this experiment show that the pendulum problem was very difficult to solve. None of the 15 subjects of the control group were able to solve the problem, and only one subject could solve the problem when provided with hints, whereas eight of 22 subjects could solve the problem when they were provided with the direction. In view of this result, Maier concluded that the solution to the problem did not result only from a combination of single cues but rather that the direction can be considered as the decisive factor in problem solving. Direction is defined as the way of approaching a problem or the difficulty expected in a problem. Prior experiences only facilitate the overcoming of the problem's difficulty.

In accordance with these results, Maier (1931) investigated the effects of hidden hints on solving the two-string problem. The experimenter ambled across the room and touched the sail in the middle of the room, which began to swing slightly. The subjects didn't know that this was a hint for the problem solution. If the problem could not be solved after this hint, another (result-oriented) hint was given. If this hint was not helpful either, the first hint was repeated. Twenty-four of a total of 61 subjects succeeded in solving the problem independently, 23 could solve the problem as a result of the hints they had been given, and 14 subjects could not solve the problem at all. Maier was especially interested in the subjects who could solve the two-string problem with the help of the hints. Interestingly, many of the subjects solved the problem in less than one minute after observing the first hint. Amazingly, none of these subjects stated that they had noticed the hint. This result is really striking because the hint was effective unless it was noticed consciously. The same observation resulted in an experiment by Dreistadt (1969) in which adults had to solve two well-defined problems. In the first problem, the subjects had to separate the area of a farm into four parts of equal size and shape, and in the other problem they had to plant 20 trees in five straight rows of four trees each. For the experimental condition, Dreistadt provided pictures of various objects in the experimental room that supplied analogs to the given problems and indicated an idea for a solution. The first experiment, for example, provided the subjects with a map of the USA on which Texas and several flight paths were highlighted, a diagram with curves, and a clock on a dresser half covered by a radio. The results of Dreistadt's experiments not only support the former studies of Maier but also show a substantial *context sensitivity* of the learners if they were given enough time to solve the problems. This context sensitivity of learners was also demonstrated in some experimental studies on mental models (e.g. Anzai & Yokoyama, 1984; Seel & Dinter, 1995). From our point of view, context sensitivity is an important ingredient of instructional support for problem solving.

Effects of Semantic Sensitivity

The concept of context sensitivity refers to people's ability to recognize key stimuli in their environment and to use them to make a given task or situation subjectively plausible. This corresponds to a constructivist perspective, which considers human learning as an active process of knowledge construction that is dependent to a large extent on the learner's ability to strategically manage and organize all available information resources. Besides the information already stored in memory, information presented by the external environment, the duration of that availability, and the way the information is structured are especially relevant for cognitive learning and problem solving (Kozma, 1991).

In contrast with schema-based argumentations, researchers in the field of mental models argue that context sensitivity occurs consciously and intentionally. Among others, Anzai and Yokoyama (1984) assume that learners encode information on a problem in a mental model as soon as they begin working on it to gain a basic understanding of the situation and its demands. This initial experiential model can be false or insufficient for accurately representing the subject domain in question and the learner is generally aware of this. However, it is semantically sensitive toward key stimuli in the learning environment and can thus be transformed into a new model through accurate processing and interpretation of these key stimuli. The results of the experimental study of Anzai and Yokoyama (1984) as well as those of other studies (e.g., Ifenthaler & Seel, 2005, 2011; Seel & Dinter, 1995) indicate the following characteristics of context sensitivity in the learning-dependent progression of mental models:

- If the learner's initial mental model is strongly dependent on previous knowledge from experience rather than on acknowledged principles (e.g. of physics) and if specific key stimuli from the learning environment capture the learner's attention, the initial experiential model is sensitive toward these key stimuli and can be changed into a more correct model.
- Context sensitivity requires for the key stimuli to be related to the knowledge on which the initial model is based. Key stimuli which capture the learner's attention but are not related to the knowledge on which the "experiential model" is based are ineffective for changing this mental model.
- Which key stimuli in the environment are taken into account for the further development of a model depends primarily on the learner's domain-specific knowledge. The mental model created at the beginning of a problem-solving process is only sensitive toward key stimuli in the environment if the learners are able to recognize the principles which their knowledge indicates to be relevant for mastering the given situation.

Guided Discovery Learning and Mental Models

Since its introduction into the literature in the 1980s, the concept of mental models has played an increasing role in math and science education literature. Franco et al. (1999), for instance, discuss the relationships between external representations, mental models and ideational realizations by referring to scientists' and inventors' mental models as working devices for creative inventions. Innovation and creative inventions are inherently very complex phenomena and subject to manifold cognitive and social requirements. As the evidence grows for the close link between invention and mental models (and its basic functions) there is no doubting the need for theoretical and practical advances in the understanding of how mental models work at creative problem solving.

Since the seminal work of Piaget (e.g. 1975) it has been well known that even young children possess more or less stable preconceptions, these are not isolated units, but rather parts of conceptual structures that provide a sensible and coherent understanding of the physical world. With regard to mental models, some studies reported, for example, that children have naive mental models of the day/night cycle and of the earth and believe, for example, that the earth is flat or hollow (Vosniadou & Brewer, 1992, 1994). However, more recent research (Panagiotaki, Nobres, & Potton, 2009) clearly shows that (six- and seven-year-old) children show substantially more indications of having scientific understanding and less of having naive mental models of the earth, suggesting that the misconceptions reported in former studies are largely methodological artifacts. Nevertheless, even given the case that learners' preconceptions are vague and incomplete, they strongly affect the construction of mental models needed for problem solving. Preconceptions are not easy to modify or to change if an individual is convinced of their plausibility – but it is possible in principle, as the studies on context sensitivity show.

This leads to the question of how carefully designed instruction can affect problem solving by means of mental models. Although it is possible in principle to initiate and facilitate free explorations and learning by invention within the realm of free learning environments (Farnham-Diggory, 1972), instruction is usually realized in well-prepared learning environments which constrain learning processes to different extents. It is certainly true that discovery learning and creative problem solving are very popular in the educational literature, but it is also true that it is a rare event in practice. Accordingly, it is easy to find an abundance of studies in which the problem of problem solving is solved by means of worked examples. That's of course easier than designing learning environments which provide opportunities for reflective thinking and creative problem solving. In contrast to the many studies in which learners are provided with ready-made conceptual models and with worked examples aiming at bypassing mental efforts in constructing mental models, there are only few studies which focus on exploratory and discovery learning and problem solving (Dugdale, 1994; Hammer, 1997). In one of them, Seel and Dinter (1995) compared two strategies of guided discovery, a result-oriented strategy aiming at the comprehension of regularities in numerous situations with a similar structure and a process-oriented strategy aiming at a deep understanding of problems (see Table 2.1).

Table 2.1 Comparison of the characteristics of different guided-discovery teaching strategies

Problem-oriented aids	*Result-oriented aids*
Instructions with the aim to influence the organization of the students' learning and thinking process.	
Problem-centered organization of the learning process	*Object-centered organization of the learning process*
Instructions with the aim to direct the learning and the thinking process (situated aids)	
Aids for structuring	*Aids for solution finding*
• Help to make the problem more precise • Help to develop hypotheses • Help to test these hypotheses • Help to summarize the acquired knowledge	• Providing tasks and instructions to deal with these tasks – but without reference to the problem in question • Help to identify relevant components • Help to generalize the relevant relations • Help to stabilize what is to be learned

The participants of this study were 131 students (grades 5 and 9) from several secondary schools with different prior school experience concerning the subject matter of Newtonian physics. Two programs of instruction aimed at discovery learning. Accordingly, the instruction was designed to engage the learners in inquiry processes to gather facts from given data sources and detect similarities and differences between the tasks. The effectiveness of the instruction was measured by a pretest–posttest comparison of domain-specific knowledge as well as two complex tasks demanding a transfer of the acquired knowledge. The overall results of this study show that the subjects of both instructional treatments encountered severe difficulties solving the problems as well as transferring newly acquired knowledge to similar new problems. Despite this, the strategy of process-oriented aids for restructuring the problems and arriving at solutions was revealed to be significantly better than the product-oriented aids for finding solutions. This result corresponds to Maier's finding concerning the effectiveness of direction.

This general result, indicating that students have big problems with exploratory problem solving and learning by inquiry, was also reported in a series of experiments on inductive reasoning carried out by Ifenthaler and Seel (e.g. Ifenthaler, Masduki, & Seel, 2011; Ifenthaler & Seel, 2011). Ifenthaler et al. (2011) conducted an experimental study to track the development of cognitive structures over time. In this study, it is demonstrated how various indicators derived from graph theory can be used for a precise description and analyses of progressing cognitive structures. The in-depth analysis of 125 cognitive structures at five measurement points revealed several patterns that provided a better understanding of their construction and development during learning processes. The results of a HLM analysis revealed significant growth in the *organizational measures* between measurement points one and five. The overall size of the cognitive structure increased many times over. Accordingly, this is an indicator for an accommodation process (see Piaget, 1976; Seel, 1991), this is to say, the individuals continuously added new concepts and links between concepts to their cognitive structure while learning. As a consequence, the complexity of the externalized cognitive structure also increased. Therefore, Ifenthaler et al. (2011) concluded that while learning and understanding more and more of a given subject matter, individuals are able to more tightly integrate single concepts and links. Additionally, the HLM analysis revealed a significant growth in the *semantic measure*. The individuals use more and more semantically correct concepts during the learning process. As individuals become more familiar with the terminology of the subject domain (in our study research methods), they use these concepts more frequently. This learning process enables individuals to communicate their cognitive structure more precisely and more like experts. In summary, a precise and stepwise diagnosis of cognitive structure helps us to better understand the differences within and between individuals as they develop over time. This will enable us to identify the most appropriate instructional materials and instructor feedback to be provided at suitable times during the learning process.

Based on previous findings, Ifenthaler and Seel (2011) conducted a longitudinal experiment with ten measurement points. The overall research interest was to identify specific transition points within a learning progression at which the shift of a cognitive structure from mental model (fluctuation in probability of change) to schema (decrease in probability of change) occurs. It is argued that there is strong evidence that the research on mental models and schemas has to move beyond the traditional two-wave design to capture these changes more precisely (Ifenthaler, 2008, 2010). In order to model and analyze the likelihood that one given state of a cognitive structure (mental model or schemas) will be followed by another, Ifenthaler and Seel (2011) computed transition probabilities from one measurement point to another. Overall, the transition probabilities and state diagrams for participants revealed a possible schematization during the ten measurement points, because it was very likely that once they had applied a correct strategy for solving an inductive reasoning task they would not revert to an incorrect strategy. Additionally, experimental variations revealed that it is more effective to construct flexible mental models like those required by the variation of tasks than to apply available schemas within new and unknown contexts (Ifenthaler, 2011).

Conclusion

The review and discussion of mental models and creative invention reveal not only numerous advances, but also substantial research questions that require more complex and comprehensive approaches than the previous case studies to be found in the literature (Calabrese-Barton, 1998). The nature of mental models is now a well-developed issue in cognitive and instructional psychology, and some researchers have borrowed psychological theories to carry out basic research in instructional design. Although we consider this route to be fruitful, we argue for the need of theoretical work on mental models within the field of science education.

Mental models play a key part in all reasoning processes. They are the only mental entities flexible enough to react to unpredictable (or at least unpredicted) change in the world and to adapt thought, decisions and action to the workings of the world. Thus, they are the basis and the guide to human response to the world. Moreover, they make decisions fast enough due to their heuristics and allow humans to respond and change their cognition in real time. Real time decisions are necessary in most of the conceivable decision-making processes, for example, when running from the lion or when reacting to a very creative chat-up line. Therefore, their role in learning is also crucial. Learning is change – of behavior, of thought. And most of the time even manual learning goes at least along with the change of thought. For facilitated and induced learning, there is always a challenge to the model-building process within the learner. This challenge is provided on the basis of expert ideas that are transformed (designed) into learning environments or learning experiences. The experiences have to be constructed so that they address the learners' current schemas and carry the experts' ideas at the same time. This is in itself a reciprocal process between the mental constructs of the learners and the manifestation of the expert ideas within the designed learning environment. A proper balance between the two different constructs of understanding will affect the learners' model-building process on the basis of the experts' model-building process, which resembles the design-decisions for the learning experiences.

On the other hand, the models of understanding are in almost no other context so different – while still being on the same subject – as in learning situations. Moreover, the supposed differences are the key reason for teaching and instruction: Somebody who knows or is skilled differs from someone who lacks knowledge and experience. The model that guides the learning experience or learning environment is called the LE Model (model that guides and constitutes the *learning* environment). The learners' understanding that is subject to change is called the L Model (*model* within the *learner*). With the differences comes a set of design principles to help the process of model-based learning and instruction as introduced by Pirnay-Dummer et al. (2012):

• Analytical Access
• Analytical Access – proper sources for the LE model
• Epistemic Access – the matching of the L model and LE model and the processes of curiosity
• Cognitive Conflict and Puzzlement – to induce a change in beliefs
• Diversity of Surfaces – to induce generalization and transfer
• De-Contextualization – to stabilize (and limit) generalization and transfer
• Multiplicity of Goals and Performance Evaluation – to allow development and tracking of understanding
• Diagnostic Access to Learning (i.e. to change) – to monitor the process of learning.

The analytical access to the LE model is the starting point. It connects the goals to the actual states by describing either a gap or a potential, starting always with the learner and his or her prior knowledge and skills. Then, a complete construct of what is to be learned is described, as well as how it is to be learned and what the learner may take from the learning experience. Usually experts are consulted to create this model.

Epistemic Access

The learners' actual knowledge and skills are part of the personal schemas which constitute their belief network. The learners' schemas hold all the facts and things that they picture to themselves as being either true or at least valid for their actions. The fact that the learners have certain beliefs in relation to the subject matter when they enter the learning environment needs to be taken into consideration before one creates it – even more so when the learning environment is to address an inhomogeneous group, that is to say, with learners who differ in their beliefs.

Cognitive Conflict and Puzzlement

After the learner has understood the different model, learning needs to be induced. This principle aims at the change of knowledge and skills within the learner. If the goals carry something really new for the learner, this means that the learner will have to let go of currently existing beliefs about the subject matter. These situations are a key indicator for the use of model-based learning environments. They provide a good chance for knowledge change. In order to be successful in this regard, the learning environment needs to induce puzzlement or cognitive conflict.

Diversity of Surfaces

Aside from feedback, multiple similar learning experiences are needed to consolidate the learning experience (Aebli, 1991). Thus, the learning environment needs to change either the sequence of events, the perspective (e.g. through multiple roles or cover stories), the time on task, or even its immediate goals – goals inherent to the environment (e.g. rescue a maiden or consult with a city planner) – while at the same time not losing sight of the learning goals. Repeating the same path through a learning environment over and over again stabilizes both the misconceptions and the intended knowledge alike and should, therefore, be avoided within model-based learning environments.

De-Contextualization

A learning environment always comes with a context. And as context is particularly important for the learning process and for the learning outcome within the puzzlement and orientation of model-based and model-oriented learning environments (Schnotz & Preuss, 1997; Seel, 2003), it needs to be considered properly. In many cases (e.g. simulations) the learning experience is not a real life experience. Dealing with the LE models is not entirely like dealing with the real world. In fact, even in the design process there are two transfers involved (see Figure 2.2; Wein, Willems, & Quanjel, 2000).

(1) The first is the transfer from the real world to the analytical knowledge that some experts have about the world. The analytical knowledge is therefore with certainty less complex than the world, due to simplifications and incompletion. (2) The second transfer has to do with the expert knowledge that makes it into the learning environment (LE model). The expert necessarily synthesizes this knowledge and offers it in abbreviated form in the LE model, because the learner cannot grasp all there is to know in a single learning experience in the learning environment. Moreover, the analytical model has to be constrained to the LE model (synthesis) to run feasibly, for example, as a simulation (see Figure 2.2).

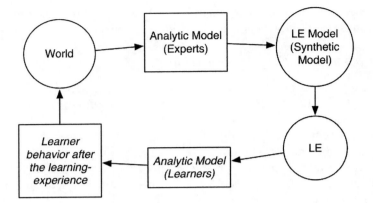

Figure 2.2 Analytic and synthetic models of the domain (Pirnay-Dummer, et al. 2012, p. 74).

Multiplicity of Goals and Performance Evaluation

There are two kinds of performances within learning environments, especially within games and simulations, that may get confused during evaluation. The first is easy to predict: If an expert explores the environment, then he or she will obviously put in a good performance unless the design has an LE model that does not correspond to the analytical model at all – a pure game of luck in other words. Once there is something systematic to the design, then experts will perform well when running the environment on their own. The second kind of performance is very similar on the behavioral level: It is the learners' performance that might improve over time. Given that the learning goals correspond to expertise, or more precisely to the experts' behavior, this design expectation, which lays the foundation for the learning environment, may create the illusion of behavior that is caused by understanding. Thus, only a multiplicity of evaluations allows one to retrace the gain in understanding. Simple or simplified tasks may still be used to introduce expertise to the learners. But the larger the gap between the LE model and the analytical model is, the more care is needed in tracking the understanding of the learners – to make sure that they do not base large parts of their behavior on hidden misconceptions.

Diagnostic Access to Learning

Mental models are constructed ad hoc (on the fly) for a given purpose, usually strongly influenced by the task and context. They are involved in the learning process and are a means of reasoning (i.e. they help the learner understand and reflect on the environment.) By coming to their own conclusions, the learners learn. Because mental models are not stable mental constructions, they cannot be the ends of learning; they are rather the means of learning. They help the learning proceed from the current mental model to the knowledge and skills described in the goals – assuming that the goals are at all reachable for the learner with the given time and other resources. In many cases – and not only in research – it is mandatory to know something about what is going on in the learner during learning. Not only may this understanding help one to track down possible sources and concrete learning experiences that lead to misunderstanding or misconceptions on the way through the learning environment; the insight into the process will also help tremendously with the designing and redesigning of good learning environments.

In a somewhat weaker sense, the principles also hold true for all communication situations where different beliefs (and models thereof) are confronted with each other in any given interaction. In most of these cases, there is rarely time for a design phase or for a transition between an analytical model and a design (LE Model). But still the same problems and needs arise the more models differ from each other. For future research it will be very interesting to investigate the impact of effects of model-negotiation, for example, within diplomatic or cultural settings.

As central as mental models are for learning, their central processes and constraints are still very much open for investigation as to their role *within* the learning processes. While the assumptions have a good empirical backup for smaller and, in particular, deductive reasoning tasks, the investigation of the role of mental models in more complex situations is still a partly uncharted territory. Their iteration with the learning process on the micro-level, especially, is still waiting for a big leap in methodological development (e.g. Pirnay-Dummer & Ifenthaler 2010).

References

Aebli, H. (1991). *Zwölf Grundformen des Lehrens: eine allgemeine Didaktik auf psychologischer Grundlage,* (6th ed.). Stuttgart: Klett-Cotta.

Al-Diban, S. (2002). *Diagnose mentaler Modelle.* Hamburg: Kovac.

Al-Diban, S. (2012). Mental models. In N. M. Seel (Ed.), *The encyclopedia of the sciences of learning* (Vol. 5, pp. 2200–2204). New York: Springer.

Anderson, J.R. (1983). *The architecture of cognition.* Cambridge, MA: Harvard University Press.

Anderson, R.C. (1984). Some reflections on the acquisition of knowledge. *Educational Researcher, 13*(9), 5–10.

Anzai, Y., & Yokoyama, T. (1984). Internal models in physics problem solving. *Cognition and Instruction, 1*(4), 397–450.

Bransford, J. D. (1984). Schema activation versus schema acquisition. In R. C. Anderson, J. Osborn & R. Tierney (Eds.), *Learning to read in American schools: Basal readers and content texts* (pp. 259–272). Hillsdale, NJ: Lawrence Erlbaum.

Brewer, W. F. (1987). Schemas versus mental models in human memory. In P. Morris (Ed.), *Modelling cognition* (pp. 187–197). Chichester: Wiley.

Brown, A. L. (1979). Theories of memory and the problems of development: Activity, growth, and knowledge. In L.S. Cermak & F.I.M. Craik (Eds.), *Levels of processing in human memory* (pp. 225–258). Hillsdale, NJ: Lawrence Erlbaum.

Calabrese-Barton, A. (1998). Examining the social and scientific roles of invention in science education. *Research in Science Education, 28*(1), 133–151.

Carlson, W. B., & Gorman, M. E. (1990). Understanding invention as a cognitive process: The case of Thomas Edison and early motion pictures, 1888–1891. *Social Studies of Science, 20*(3), 387–430.

Chi, M. T. H. (2008). Three types of conceptual change: Belief revision, mental model transformation, and categorical shift. In S. Vosniadou (Ed.), *Handbook of research on conceptual change* (pp. 61–82). Hillsdale, NJ: Erlbaum.

Craik, K. J. W. (1943). *The nature of explanation.* Cambridge, UK: Cambridge University Press.

Dugdale, S. (1994). Using students' mathemetical inventiveness as a foundation for software design: Toward a tempered constructivism. *Educational Technology Research and Development, 42*(1), 57–73.

Duncker, K. (1945). On problem-solving. *Psychological Monographs, 58*(5), Whole No. 270.

Eysenck, M. W. (2004). *Psychology. An international perspective.* New York: Psychology Press Ltd.

Farnham-Diggory, S. (1972). *Cognitive processes in education: A psychological preparation for teaching and curriculum development.* New York: Harper & Row.

Forbus, K.D., & Gentner, D. (1997). Qualitative mental models: Simulations or memories? In *Proceedings of the Eleventh International Workshop on Qualitative Reasoning*, Cortona, Italy.

Franco, C., de Barros, H. L., Colinvaux, D., Krapas, S., Queiroz, G., & Alves, F. (1999). From scientists' and inventors' minds to some scientific and technological products: Relationships between theories, models, mental models and conceptions. *International Journal of Science Education, 21*(3), 277–291.

Funke, J. (1992). Dealing with dynamic systems: Research strategy, diagnostic approach and experimental results. *The German Journal of Psychology, 16*(1), 24–43.

Gorman, M. E., & Carlson, W. B. (1990). Understanding invention as a cognitive process: The case of Alexander Graham Bell, Thomas Edison, and the telephone. *Science, Technology and Human Values, 15*(2), 131–164.

Greeno, J. G. (1989). Situations, mental models and generative knowledge. In D. Klahr & K. Kotovsky (Eds.), *Complex information processing* (pp. 285–318). Hillsdale, NJ: Lawrence Erlbaum.

Guilford, J. P. (1967). *The nature of human intelligence.* New York: McGraw-Hill.

Hammer, D. (1997). Discovery learning and discovery teaching. *Cognition and Instruction, 15*(4), 485–529.

Holyoak, K. J., & Thagard, P. (1995). *Mental leaps: Analogy in creative thought.* Cambridge, MA: MIT Press.

Ifenthaler, D. (2008). Practical solutions for the diagnosis of progressing mental models. In D. Ifenthaler, P. Pirnay-Dummer, & J. M. Spector (Eds.), *Understanding models for learning and instruction. Essays in honor of Norbert M. Seel* (pp. 43–61). New York: Springer.

Ifenthaler, D. (2010). Zur Notwendigkeit einer systematischen Erfassung von Bildungsverläufen. Methodologische Anforderungen einer Veränderungsmessung. *Lehrerbildung auf dem Prüfstand, 3*(Sonderheft), 86–105.

Ifenthaler, D. (2011). Identifying cross-domain distinguishing features of cognitive structures. *Educational Technology Research and Development, 59*(6), 817–840. doi: 10.1007/s11423-011-9207-4

Ifenthaler, D., & Seel, N. M. (2005). The measurement of change: Learning-dependent progression of mental models. *Technology, Instruction, Cognition and Learning, 2*(4), 317–336.

Ifenthaler, D., & Seel, N. M. (2011). A longitudinal perspective on inductive reasoning tasks. Illuminating the probability of change. *Learning and Instruction, 21*(4), 538–549. doi: 10.1016/j.learninstruc.2010.08.004.

Ifenthaler, D., Masduki, I., & Seel, N. M. (2011). The mystery of cognitive structure and how we can detect it. Tracking the development of cognitive structures over time. *Instructional Science, 39*(1), 41–61. doi: 10.1007/s11251-009-9097-6.

Jonassen, D. H., & Hung, W. (2006). Learning to troubleshoot: A new theory-based design architecture. *Educational Psychology Review, 18*, 77–114.

Jonassen, D. H., Carr, C., & Hsiu-Ping, Y. (1998). Computers as Mindtools for engaging learners in critical thinking. *TechTrends, 43*(2), 24–32.

Johnson-Laird, P. N. (1983). *Mental models. Towards a cognitive science of language, inference, and consciousness.* Cambridge, UK: Cambridge University Press.

Johnson-Laird, P. N. (2004). The history of mental models. In K. Manktelow & M.C. Chung (Eds.), *Psychology of reasoning: Theoretical and historical perspectives* (pp. 179–212). New York: Psychology Press.

Johnston, B. (1981). *My inventions: The autobiograhy of Nikola Tesla.* New York: Experimenter Publishing Co.

Köhler, W. (1929). *Gestalt psychology.* New York: Liveright.

Kozma, R. B. (1991). Learning with media. *Review of Educational Research, 61*(2), 179–211.

Maier, N. R. F. (1931). Reasoning in humans. II. The solution of a problem and its appearance in consciousness. *Journal of Comparative Psychology, 12*, 181–194.

Mandler, J. M. (1984). *Stories, scripts, and scenes: Aspects of schema theory.* Hillsdale, NJ: Lawrence Erlbaum Associates.

Markman, A. B. (1998). *Knowledge representation.* Mahwah, NJ: Erlbaum.

Mayer, R. E. (1989). Models for understanding. *Review of Educational Research, 59*(1), 43–64.

Norman, D. A., & Rumelhart, D. E. (Eds.), (1978). *Strukturen des Wissens. Wege der Kognitionsforschung.* Stuttgart: Klett.

Oatley, K. (2011). Fiction and its study as gateways to the mind. *Scientific Study of Literature,* 153–164.

Panagiotaki, G., Nobres, G., & Potton, A. (2009). Mental models and other misconceptions in children's understanding of the earth. *Journal of Experimental Child Psychology, 104*(1), 52–67.

Piaget, J. (1975). *Das Erwachen der Intelligenz beim Kinde.* Stuttgart: Klett.

Piaget, J. (1976). *Die Äquilibration der kognitiven Strukturen.* Stuttgart: Klett.

Peirce, C. S. (1898). *Reasoning and the logic of things: The Cambridge conference lectures of 1898.* Cambridge, MA: Harvard University.

Pirnay-Dummer, P., & Ifenthaler, D. (2010). Automated knowledge visualization and assessment. In D. Ifenthaler, P. Pirnay-Dummer, & N. M. Seel (Eds.), *Computer-based diagnostics and systematic analysis of knowledge* (pp. 77–115). New York: Springer.

Pirnay-Dummer, P., Ifenthaler, D., & Seel, N. M. (2012). Designing model-based learning environments to support mental models for learning. In D. H. Jonassen & S. Land (Eds.), *Theoretical foundations of learning environments* (2nd edn, pp. 66–94). New York: Routledge.

Poincaré, H. (1908). *Science et méthode.* Paris: Flammarion.

Prinz, W. (1983). *Wahrnehmung und Tätigkeitssteuerung.* Heidelberg: Springer.

Rips, L. J. (1987). Mental muddles. In M. Brand & R. M. Harnish (Eds.), *The representation of knowledge and belief* (pp. 259–286). Tuscon, AZ: University of Arizona Press.

Rumelhart, D. E., Smolensky, P., McClelland, J. L., & Hinton, G. E. (1986). Schemata and sequential thought processes in PDP models. In J. L. McClelland & D. E. Rumelhart (Eds.), *Parallel distributed processing. Explorations in the microstructure of cognition. Volume 2: Psychological and biological models* (pp. 7–57). Cambridge, MA: MIT Press.

Saugstad, P. (1957). An analysis of Maier's pendulum problem. *Journal of Experimental Psychology, 54*(3), 168–179.

Schnotz, W., & Preuss, A. (1997). Task-dependent construction of mental models as a basis for conceptual change. *European Journal of Psychology of Education, 12*(2), 185–211.

Seel, N. M. (1991). *Weltwissen und mentale Modelle.* Göttingen: Hogrefe.

Seel, N. M. (2003). Model centered learning and instruction. *Technology, Instruction, Cognition and Learning, 1*(1), 59–85.

Seel, N. M. (2006). Mental models and complex problem solving. Instructional effects. In J. Elen & R.E. Clark (Eds.), *Handling complexity in learning environments. Theory and research* (pp. 43–66). Amsterdam: Kluwer.

Seel, N. M., & Dinter, F. R. (1995). Instruction and mental model progression: Learner-dependent effects of teaching strategies on knowledge acquisition and analogical transfer. *Educational Research and Evaluation, 1*(1), 4–35.

Tesla, N. (1919). *My inventions.* Retrieved from http://www.tfcbooks.com/tesla/my_inventions.htm#I.%20My%20Early%20Life

Vosniadou, S., & Brewer, W. F. (1992). Mental models of the earth: A study of conceptual change in childhood. *Cognitive Psychology, 24,* 535–585.

Vosniadou, S., & Brewer, W. F. (1994). Mental models of the day/night cycle. *Cognitive Science, 18*(1), 123–183.

Wallas, G. (1926). *The art of thought.* New York: Harcourt Brace Jovanovich.

Watson, J. D. (1968). *The double helix: A personal account of the discovery of the structure of DNA.* London: Weidenfeld & Nicolson.

Wegner, D. M. (2002). *The illusion of conscious will.* Cambridge, MA: MIT Press.

Wertheimer, M. (1959). *Productive thinking.* New York: Harper.

Wittgenstein, L. (1922). *Tractatus logico-philosophicus.* New York: Harcourt Brace & Company.

Wein, B., Willems, R., & Quanjel, M. (2000). Planspielsimulationen: Ein Konzept für eine integrierte (Re-) Strukturierung von Organisationen. In D. Herz & A. Blätte (Eds.), *Simulation und Planspiel in den Sozialwissenschaften* (pp. 275–299). Münster: Lit.

3 A Practice-Centered Approach to Instructional Design

Brent G. Wilson

Introduction

A defining feature of the field of instructional design (ID) is a commitment to practice. In contrast with educational psychology and the learning sciences, instructional design theories are more explicit in guiding practitioners through the process of creating courses and integrating media. This is in keeping with its origins in the mid-twentieth century, when behavioral psychologists used programmed instruction as a means for implementing scientific advances (Reiser, 2001a). By determining which instructional strategies worked for particular learning objectives, the goal was a comprehensive science of instruction that could also serve as a prescriptive guide for practice (Lumsdaine & Glaser, 1960; also Reigeluth, 1983). Practice in those days referred to an opportunity for students to apply a rule or procedure to a case (as in Rule–Example–Practice sequences).

Improving Practice

Looking at the development of the field, the impulse toward *reform* of practice is never far from the surface. As Reiser (2001b) notes, founders in the twentieth century sought to improve educational practice and enrich education through improved learning interactions and enriching media. Another reform impulse was to fully exploit the learning potential of emerging technologies.

ID theorists often use the word 'prescribe' to talk about guidance to the practitioner. In contrast to applying best practices, prescribing in ID terms usually refers to applying a model or theory. *Prescribe* brings to mind a straightforward fix to a well-defined problem. Doctors prescribe a pill when the ailment is diagnosed and a medicine is known to address the symptoms or cure the ailment. We know, though, that education is one of the most complex and intractable problem areas of study – what Berliner (2002) calls the hardest science of all. We have known for a very long time that complex problems are best understood systemically, because a technical fix sends secondary impacts throughout the system, many of them undesirable and unanticipated (Tenner, 1997). Adding an incentive to use social media, for example, can lead to contortions by designers to add social media regardless of its appropriateness to the need. An overly prescriptive mindset runs the danger of leading to overly simplistic approaches to complex, dynamic and atypical problem situations. Our best thinking is needed to negotiate this path – to apply technical solutions to address obvious and compelling problems that demand attention, while at the same time being sensitive to the health of the larger system and mitigating undesirable impacts to that system.

The term 'practice' is also used as a reference point for theory: Theory is the attempt to model or understand practice; practice is where you apply a prescriptive theory to improve outcomes. Since theorists tend to reify their constructs and reduce the complexities of the world merely in terms of those constructs, encounters with messy and complex practice situations can have a humbling effect, reminding us of what is still unknown and requiring further inquiry. Of course theory construction is itself an important kind of practice, which sociologists of knowledge have shown to depend very much on social and cultural conditions.

Practice Theory

Practice theory denotes a family of theories in sociology, anthropology, and organizational studies that examine human practice as a means of understanding human and organizational behavior. Practices, according to John Postill (2010), are "the embodied sets of activities that humans perform with varying degrees of commitment, competency and flair" (p. 1). Sherry Ortner defined practice in its broad sense as pretty much "anything people do" (1984, p. 149), with special attention to activity that is significantly related to power relations. Practice theory includes any theory that "treats practice as a fundamental category, or takes practice as its point of departure" (Stern, 2003, p. 185).

Practice theory has roots in a number of philosophical traditions, including Marx's historical materialism, German hermeneutic and phenomenological movements, American pragmatism, French post-structuralism, and Wittgenstein's later philosophy. We would also include Emmanuel Levinas's notion of confronting the *Other* and honoring that obligation to respond to another person's presence (Child, Williams, Birch, & Boody, 2005). We are already in the world and connected to people who place demands upon us and invite our response.

Practice theory focuses on the complexities of human activity and inhabit a space between social and organizational structures on the one hand, and individual cognitive/neural processes on the other. Practice theory sees human activity as co-constituted by these macro- and micro-level forces, as well as by the *agency* of individual actors within those structures. Activity theory is an example tradition in this middle space, but there are others less well known to instructional designers, such as ethnomethology (Garfinkel, 1967) and Bourdieu's (1977) practice theory emphasizing behavioral dispositions, meaning construction, and power relationships. For accessible overviews of practice theories see Nicolini, Gherardi, and Yanow (2003), Huizing and Cavanagh (2011), and Postill (2010).

My use of 'practice-centered approach' in the context of instructional design is meant to broaden the focus from individual cognition and instructional strategies toward the practices and experiences of people connected to the design of instruction – that is, designers, instructors, and students. My intention is somewhat different from the social theorist however – rather than full-blown theory development, I am trying to generate more space and attention for practice at both theoretical and practical levels. Also note that this chapter does *not* present an instructional theory in the traditional sense. I am not specifying a set of instructional principles or strategies for use in lesson development. Rather I am sketching out another way of seeing the work of instructional design that will lead to fruitful insights and possibilities for improvement.

A Logic Supporting Practice

Looking back on the titles of dissertations or research articles, instructional strategies are clearly a major thrust of research in the field. Instructional strategies refer to the learning activities that are planned and implemented in an instructional development process. Strategies may be selected or developed based on a particular theory of learning, and include such things as delivery system, media use, ordering and sequencing or instructional elements, and specification of learning activities. The focus on instructional strategies continues today, although with greater attention of other mediating variables such as student cognitive processing and individual differences. The so-called great media debate in the 1990s between Robert Kozma (1991) and Richard Clark (1994) about the relative merits of media and instructional strategies underscores the central role assigned to strategies in accounting for learning impacts.

Yet concerns remain about how exactly strategies mediate learning. The cognitive revolution in psychology suggests that it is thinking and cognitive processing, not just strategies, that mediate learning. Only as strategies reliably invoke certain forms of mental processing can they lead to desired learning outcomes. Critics of cognition point to the problem resulting from the cognitive split between thinking and action upon which cognitive theories necessarily rely. Not all action is pre-planned, and cognitive activity should not always be privileged above embodied actions within a material world. So much of life is improvisation based on emerging and dynamic conditions; identifying where, when and how learning happens is often difficult. For example, a management flight simulation game typically involves a series of decisions followed by a simulation of what results from those decisions followed by an opportunity to reflect on the results and formulate and implement a new set of decisions. Players often report that they gained important insights when talking with fellow players during the pauses between runs of the simulation rather when running the simulation. If true, then the unplanned or unscripted interchange of players between simulation runs becomes a significant locus of learning outside the bounds of the planned strategy.[1]

Instructional theories, even as they seek to prescribe, seriously underspecify the decisions and conditions needed to actually implement them in practice settings (Jonassen, Strobel, & Ionas, 2005). That is to say, the theories and models lack rules of correspondence that convert the generalizations into specific actions. In like manner, a *planned* strategy is different from an *enacted* activity. This is parallel to the construct of the enacted curriculum among curriculum theorists (Walker, 1990). Whatever is planned, the particular enactment is often the determining variable in the success of a lesson or program.

The construct of *fidelity of implementation* (FoI) may be of value here. FoI is a measure of how closely the enacted curriculum (or intervention) fits the specifications of the planned curriculum. For a curriculum that has been carefully validated by research to lead to desired outcomes, a delivery that matches up closely would be desirable if those same outcomes are expected. My research with Jamie Hurley (Hurley & Wilson, 2012) indicates, however, that practicing teachers often have very good reasons for straying from a research-based curriculum specifications; they generally make choices based on competing goods and meeting the needs of students based on local conditions.

Figure 3.1 differentiates planned strategies from enacted activities and the lived experience of participants. A planned instructional strategy is typically based on a model of the situation and what is going on in that situation. Strategies reflect the intentions of the strategist: the designer, the sponsor, or the curriculum that itself is a compromise among interest groups. By its

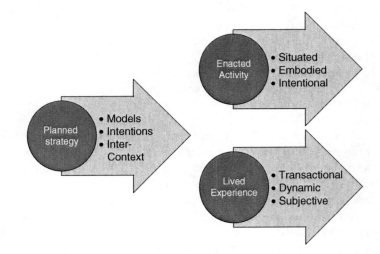

Figure 3.1 A planned instructional strategy can lead to enacted activities and lived experiences on the part of participants.

nature planned strategies separate planning from execution – they transfer intentions from one context to another, across time, space and people.

When enacted, a strategy becomes a completed activity, typically with some variance from the original intention. Under logistical constraints and emerging conditions, participants re-interpret and re-negotiate plans in the completion of tasks and pursuit of conflicting goals. Activity unfolds within a particular time and place as individuals and groups of people pursue various objects and ends. Following Dewey (1997/1938), people undergo *experience* as activities unfold. Experiences are *transactional* in that they are mutually co-constituted by participants and the world they live in as conditions dynamically unfold over time (Parrish, Wilson, & Dunlap, 2011). Students and instructors submit or undergo on the one hand, and engage as active agents on the other, co-determining emergent outcomes, including what is learned from the experience (Wong, 2007). Hence, in contrast to instructional models focusing solely on problem solving (Jonassen, 2011), a practice-centered approach sees value in both active and submitting responses as potentially conducive to learning (Prawat, 1993).

In light of these concerns, the field of ID is challenged to account for the conditions that lead to learning in instructional settings. We know that the choice of instructional strategy makes some difference, yet so many other factors come into play, including instructor and student differences, situational variables, and organizational and cultural background factors. Indeed the *quality* of these things varies significantly across cases – particularly the contributions of designers, instructors, and students. Resources in the form of money, time, and talent are also distributed unevenly across projects and institutions. These situational variables have enormous impact on the quality of instruction and the learning outcomes that result. Our theory bases, however, tend to favor the aggregate instructional strategies and learning processes, which form only part of the picture. What seems to be needed is a broader framework that accounts for more of these quality variables relating to craft, emergence, complexity, implementation, and tradeoffs in resources.

Michael Hannafin's work on grounded design (Hannafin, Hannafin, Land, & Oliver, 1997) takes a somewhat distancing approach to instructional strategies. Different strategies will lead to different outcomes, but achieving a coherence within a program, with design elements fitting within a particular paradigm or theory of learning, can have a cumulative effect contributing toward quality and impact – more than the individual strategy being applied. The way a theory is applied or implemented matters – not just which strategy is applied. Because of the lack of specification of theory, I carry this line of thinking further. Programs indeed need coherence, but not necessarily around a theory of learning or instruction. Rather, coherence can be achieved in configuring an elegant response to a learning need, a problem of practice, or curriculum goal. Design elements may borrow eclectically from different theories, in pastiche or bricolage form, similar to how a bird fashions a nest based on available sticks and twigs and wires.

The coherence and elegance of design does not reflect theoretical purity or consistency of origins, but rather in how elements hang together and support a coherent experience for learners (see Wilson, 1999). Practice-oriented designers face the same complexity in the situation, but they are more open to the paths and solutions afforded by the situation, not dictated by theory or ideology.

What happens *after* a plan is made, after the curriculum is developed, is increasingly of interest to educators and policymakers (e.g. Hung, 2011). *Implementation science* is a term describing a domain in the health professions that examines how evidence-based practices are implemented in the field. Bill Penuel and colleagues (Penuel, Fischman, Haugan Cheng, & Sabelli, 2011) develop a similar construct for education, framing their approach as an expansion on design-based research. While my emphasis is more on emergent practices and lived experience, their work illustrates the need for more attention to the details of implementation in the field.

Activity and Experience

For our purposes a practice-centered approach to ID may be defined as a view of ID work framed in technical, craft, and critical terms, involving activity mediated by tools and situation, where opportunities for innovation emerge from new technologies, ideas, and systemic tensions, as well as the craftsmanship, character, and agency of participants.

Our approach draws heavily on a construct of craftsmanship (Sennett, 2008). People who master a craft show "a sustained dedication to excellence requiring a honing of skill and cultivation of wisdom based on professional experience" (Sennett, p. 9). Instructional design is a domain where craftsmanship plays a role, particularly in collaborative teamwork and the improvement of instruction over time. Other key elements of a practice-based approach are briefly discussed below.

Activity Mediated in Context

Learning is construed in practice terms as *change through activity and accumulated experience over time*. And all of this happens within a rich performative context. Practice-based approaches study how people use tools and resources and rules to envision, make sense of, and accomplish their work. The tools and resources and rules thus *mediate* the activity. The *context* of action is fully considered, including the social, embodied, and temporal/ historical contingencies of action. The *meaning* of activity is based on its context – so activity should always be examined with respect to its unique circumstances.

Narrative is the primary means by which this context can be told (Friesen, 2009; Power, 2009). Narrative implies development over time – as a plot unfolds, so activity evolves over time, based on people's choices and the constraints they face in working together. Practice theorists are prone to use the gerund form of verbs – doing, becoming, acting, developing – to suggest the ongoing dynamic nature of engaged activity. Thus, activity can be seen both in stable, structural terms, and also as an emergent process, which serves as a test-bed for innovation and change (Davis, Sumara, & Luce-Kapler, 2000).

Activity is mediated by the natural world, but also by culture and human relationships. Some practice theories (e.g. the educational theory of Holland, Lachicotte, Skinner, & Cain, 1998) stress the formation of identity through engaged action with the material world but also in collaboration with others. Wenger's (1998) work further illustrates how community forms and gives shape to human interactions.

Participant Experience

John Dewey was the chief advocate for an experiential approach to educa-tion (Dewey, 1997/1938). Indeed "learn by doing," the phrase associated with Dewey's progressive education movement, could very well describe a practice-based pedagogy. Robert Horn (1972) was among the first to talk about *experiential* learning objectives – where the goal of instruction is to provide a certain kind of experience to learners. Experience is the inward way of looking at activity – similar to how the inward looking construct of culture is different from the outward looking construct of society (Wilber, 1996). Experience as a construct is useful because of its relevance to educa-tion – and because of its mystery and undefined, subjective nature. A vocab-ulary that includes "experience" opens the door for aesthetic considerations such as ritual, myth, dramatic pacing of learning experiences, and so forth – which are increasingly important in today's mediated worlds (Wilson & Parrish, 2011).

Aesthetic design plays an important role with new media, but also with traditional instruction. I recently visited Thailand and learned that students place high value on the formal bestowal of certificates of completion, not only for degrees and programs but also individual courses. Such ceremonies, complete with picture-taking, serve as a rite of passage for students, show-ing that they have acquired the expertise contained in the course. Sennett (2008) argues for ritual-like repetitive learning experiences:

> Rote learning is not in itself the enemy. Practice sessions can be made interesting through creating an internal rhythm for them, no matter how short ... We do a disservice to those who suffer from attention deficit disorder by asking that they understand before they engage.
>
> (Sennett, 2008, p. 177)

Narrative becomes doubly important when considering experience, because much experience is patterned or even archetypically based on established forms and scripts. The rituals of life can help convey special meaning to activity, through a consecrating of time and space. As novices face induction into their chosen field, they typically take on a new name, new dress, or new language reflecting their new identity as a skilled or knowledgeable person. This induction happens by a process of submission to authority, sometimes embodied in a trusted master or guide (Steiner, 2003), followed by a semi-scripted adventure requiring all the skills and knowledge (and fortune) available to obtain a life's prize.

Key Levers of Change and Innovation

As mentioned, learning is best construed as change through activity and accumulated experience over time. Hence processes of learning and change are very similar whether at the individual, group, or institutional level. There are certain areas that are especially fertile in creating conditions for productive change. I outline below five points that can be considered levers or hot points where change and innovation are likely to happen.

Exercising Agency

As mentioned, practice theory arose from the tension observed between social or institutional explanations and those emphasizing individual cognition and neural mechanisms. In between the various causative forces – the structures of institutions, cultures, and neural processes – lies the individual agent in the form of the instructor, the student, or the designer. How any individual fills his or her role and engages others in the work can have a huge effect on learning. This is analogous to the *supershrink* effect in psychotherapy, wherein researchers found a significant *therapist* effect independent of the therapy being administered (Bergin & Suinn, 1975). Translating into ID terms, a *master designer* applying a direct-instructional strategy may get better results than an average designer applying a constructivist strategy – even if the constructivist strategy were a more effective method. There is some research in support of the designer having some impact on quality: An experienced designer involved early in the planning process of a large project is more likely to create a realistic scope for the effort resulting in less rework and rescoping later (Grimstad Group, 1995).

   Agency refers to the intentional, embodied capacity to act that is not so easily captured and modeled by theory. It is where the innovation, the disruption, or the surprise tends to happen. Generally, agency is thought to be a human quality, although actor-network theory examines how human and non-human actors are configured into networks within which actions and outcomes unfold. I find the construct of agency very helpful as a marker for the human element in our designs: the difference that a master designer or instructor can make in a course, a program, or within an organization or a working group which achieves a synergy through collaboration, imagination, and effective division of labor (Suchman, 2000). Agency is "the sense that someone or something is not following some pre-established programme of action, is not simply expressing some pre-existing structure" (Middleton & Brown, 2002, as cited in Kaptelinin & Nardi, 2006, p. 207).

An example in Wilson (2012a) illustrates how the agency of a designer or instructor can play a substantial role in learning outcomes. I tell the story of a college professor who pays lip service to a constructivist philosophy, but in reality is leaving students in the lurch with inadequate guidance and support. Students are frustrated and discouraged at the wasted time and effort, and less learning is achieved because of the ostensive adherence to inquiry learning. In this case the instructor, through a lack of commitment to the class or willingness to carefully observe effects, is misreading the situation and misapplying constructivist theory. He is failing to notice and take the appropriate action. That this occurrence is fairly common suggests the importance of the issue. Whether framed in terms of agency, professionalism, character, or commitment – the issue is worthy of serious consideration when looking for impacts of instructional systems.

Tensions in the System

In complex systems, the interface between competing sub-systems, when they come together, can lead to disequilibrium and instability. This interface is a zone between order and disorder where meaning is generated. If everything happens according to plan, the situation is routine and the learning is minimal.[2] Fruitful tension is central to activity theory and fits ID very well because of our focus on learning and development.

The more ill-structured the problem, the greater the opportunity for conflict to arise through unforeseen pairings and border crossings. Such problems are usually not solved; they are managed. Table 3.1 compares static and dynamic systems, showing how dynamic system modeling can better accommodate the complexity found in practice. Each part can potentially affect any other part of the system, and the goal is finding a compatible balance or harmony between elements that is sustainable over time. In reality, though, *all* natural systems exhibit both stasis and change at different points. A general pattern is:

$$Statis > Disruption > Repair > Statis > Etc.$$

Complex systems are more amenable to steering or guidance than full control – a process that Lindblom (1959, 1971) calls "muddling through". We understand complex systems better than we used to, particularly how certain local actions can unexpectedly lead to systemic transformation at critical tipping points (Gladwell, 2000). This is the point of tension between competing systems.

A practice approach also inhabits the world between order and disorder through its critical, often subversive stance toward orthodox practice. To survive, a field must transmit a legacy of effective practices while at the same time integrating new practices that challenge the established order. Thus we are in a constant state of renewal, preserving some things and jettisoning others. Because of its often subversive stance, we would not expect

Table 3.1 Static versus dynamic models of systems

Static model	Dynamic model
Additive causal model (analysis of variance with interactions of variable only inserted individually)	Multiplicative model (if any value approaches zero the output drops to zero)
Linear effects	Non-linear relationships and impacts
Smaller scale, simpler systems	Messier, more complex systems
Optimized performance	Harmony and balance
Consistency and control	Steering toward "satisficing" outputs (Simon, 1969)
Predictable throughput	Impacts vary according to tensions, fissures, and contradictions
Repairing buggy algorithms/routines – restoring to original or proper use	Reconciling relationships and redefining connections – leading to new uses and outcomes

a practice-centered approach to ever dominate the field, bur rather continue as a theme or thread over time, challenging the dominant traditions and encouraging alternative methods when needed.

The willingness to transgress boundaries is associated with progressive positions, but this is not always so. Norm Friesen's (2011) study of the *lecture* as a teaching form subverts common thinking about active and passive learning and shows the resiliency of what many take to be a regressive instructional practice.

Integrating Human Values

I have discussed elsewhere the need for ID professionals to adopt a critical stance toward their work (Wilson, 2012b). Learning designers might think of wearing trifocals, adjusted at three different distances:

(a) *Clients and stakeholders.* What effect will my actions have on interests and concerns of my sponsors, clients, and participants? How can I help them design meaningful solutions to compelling and challenging problems of practice?
(b) *Profession.* How does my work relate to the community of ID professionals and our collective knowledge base? What am I doing and learning that might be of interest to colleagues?
(c) *The world.* How does my work relate to the broader community and the world at large? Am I helping the world be a better place – or what can I do to change my practice to better tune in to those larger concerns?

In the natural division of labor and the pressures of everyday work, most practitioners forget to think of the broader concerns, which is a shame because the foundations of the field suggest that professional knowledge is inseparable from practice. Designers who broaden their focus to attend to larger concerns can be richly rewarded through improved local decisions and solutions. I am thinking, for example, of active bloggers who reach out to other professionals and find their own work enriched through the interaction. Sharing one's everyday concerns with other professionals makes the everyday more meaningful and brings a stronger element of inquiry into one's practice.

One advantage to a practice-centered approach is a more comfortable accommodation of values such as social justice, equity, and inclusion. An instrumentalist, objectives-based view of curriculum design tends toward goals of efficiency and effectiveness, and neglects the moral impacts of the curriculum on participants (Kliebard, 1987). With greater attention to practice and lived experience, values can more easily enter the conversation and be seen as relevant considerations. This can help with our external relations to other currents of educational thought, but also in our efforts to address social-justice concerns in our own practice (Young, 2009).

Reconciling Difference

Aristotle talked about the cooperative arts in contrast to the exploitative or manipulative arts. Sculpture is an exploitative art in that the clay is passive in the sculptor's hands, whereas education and medicine (and animal husbandry) are cooperative because they depend on both artisan and client to work together toward a common end (Komaski, 1987). In that light, the stasis condition in instruction is a trusting, engaged student and a committed, attentive instructor/guide. However, breakdowns from that ideal are common. A mechanism for repair is thus needed, to get the cooperative condition going again. I consider this to be of surprising importance, with much mediocre instruction traceable to failures or breakdowns between instructor and student ('instructor' in the broad sense of the person and the supporting system).

Safety, trust, and learning from failure

The hero's journey, according to Joseph Campbell (1949), typically happens with the assistance of a guru at some point – a wise, mature guide who has been through a similar path with success. If the path were always safe and secure, there would be no learning and no transformation – the traveler would not become a hero. While risk-taking should be encouraged in instruction, safety cannot be guaranteed – otherwise there is no real risk. As Carol Dweck and others have shown, people respond differently to failure than to success, even at the neural level – and differences in how people respond to failure can lead to significantly cumulative differences in learning (Lehrer, 2011). Somehow there needs to be enough trust accumulated through a learning experience that students are willing to follow the instructor down some scary roads and immerse themselves fully in the experience. In that spirit Scott Switzer has developed a framework for accumulating and expending *pedagogical capital*, defined as actionable trust between instructor and instructor, based on their history of interaction together (Wilson & Switzer, 2012). If trust has been successfully established, then the instructor can push students further to take risks and exert themselves down an adventuresome path; if not, then less can be asked and less learning is accomplished.

Breakdowns happen when a mismatch occurs between a student's need and an instructor's guidance – often through professional lapses or limitations, or just the failure of mainstream strategies to meet a particular student's immediate need. At this point the student is left to question the reliability of the guidance and the prospects for success on the journey. Because such breakdowns are inevitable, repair is essential for success. Successful repair can be facilitated by a resilient stance by the student who is slow to take offense and quick to forgive and restart. Instructors can facilitate repair through active and frequent monitoring and observation of student needs, coupled with an instructor's commitment to truth-telling and taking responsibility. Both parties need to stay engaged and avoid ducking out. These qualities are as much a quality of character as they are technique, but again, are critical for the maintenance and restoration of healthy relationships for learning.

My discussion of reconciliation is more focused on the quality of instructor–student relationships than Song, Hannafin, and Hill (2007), but I think we would agree on the need for more theory development in this area of reconciliation in constructivist environments. Kaptelinin and Nardi (2006) emphasize the need for imagination and creativity when systemic breakdowns occur; re-imagining alternative goals, activities, and relationships can open up significant new learning in the face of blockages.

Connecting people

Advocates of *learning communities* tend to stress the nurturing support and safety that communities can provide. But communities can play a normative role in shaping activity that can include enforcing boundaries and encouraging conformity and order. Communities can also be important sources of feedback and guidance that lead to correction. Sennett (2008) referenced the "sharp mutual exchanges" that can occur in a healthy community of practice:

> Caricatures of the Japanese frequently depict them as herd-loving conformists, a stereotype that hardly makes sense of how sharply critical Japanese workers in Toyota, Subaru, and Sony plants could be of one another's efforts.
>
> (Sennett, 2008, p. 31)

Interest in community has risen in those environments where natural human connections have been historically limited: *online learning*. The disembodied nature of an online interaction creates an interesting opportunity to test ideas of embodied cognition (see Li, Clark, & Winchester, 2011, for an introduction to enactivism or embodied cognition). In response, distance-education researchers have advanced the concept of establishing *presence* online (e.g. the Community of Inquiry model – Garrison, Anderson, & Archer, 2000). As it turns out, *all* human communication must break through the barriers between individuals, a problem acknowledged since Plato (Shuell, 1986). If we actively construct our worlds, then how is it possible that we breach the barriers between ourselves and others, and communicate anything of real substance? In the case of online interactions these barriers can be formidable, but they share many characteristics with face-to-face communication challenges. Heidegger's notion of a simulation's *fidelity* – as the illusion of no mediation – is a useful construct (Saito, 2002) because it highlights the fact that all communication is mediated and requires cutting through some barriers.

Michael Polanyi's (1958, p. 59) notion about the fusion of person and tool also adds perspective on how we interact online. A person striking a hammer does not feel the hammer on the palm of her hand so much as the nail going into the wood. In like manner a person's mobile phone can become so integrated with their thinking and activity that loss of it creates confusion, distress and a temporary incapacity to function! All human activity, online or otherwise, must create conditions that bring people together despite obstacles, differences, and perceived distance. Tools and devices can either get in the way of, or help this goal of bridging the gap, depending on the uses put to them.

Empathic thinking

Patrick Parrish (2006) has noted the importance of emphatic thinking for instructional designers. Sennett (2008) frames the point in terms of the instructor's actions and language:

> The writer of instructional language who makes the effort of sympathy has to retrace, step by step, backward knowledge that has bedded in to routine, and only then can take the reader step by step forward. But as an expert, he or she knows what comes next and where danger lies; the expert guides by anticipating difficulties for the novice; sympathy and prehension combine. This is Julia Child's method.
>
> (Sennett, 2008, p. 186)

Sennett continues by noting different tones of authorial voice:

> The paralyzing tone of authority and certainty in much instructional language betrays a writer's inability to re-imagine vulnerability... When we wish to instruct ... particularly in the fixed medium of print, we have to return emotionally just to the point before [skilled] habits were formed, in order to provide guidance. So for a moment [Julia] Child will imagine holding the knife awkwardly; the cello master will return to

playing wrong notes. This return to vulnerability is the sign of sympathy the instructor gives.

(Sennett, 2008, p. 186)

All of these ideas about human connection have clear relevance to instructional practices. The goal of a practice approach would be to expand our views to accommodate both activity- and experienced-based studies of how people connect and relate to each other in the design of and activity of learning and instruction.

Sharing Practices

I participated on a conference panel recently where a colleague, Dan Morris, talked about ways to support professional development (PD) of K12 teachers engaged in blended learning. "Three recommendations," he said: "Model, model, and model!" Dan heads up eNet Colorado, a fledgling initiative to make PD resources widely available to teachers in the state. He understands the significance of teachers helping teachers, and teaching observing teachers. Technology can afford more modeling and observation of teaching practice. Dan's work reflects two major impacts resulting from the advent of the World-Wide Web:

(a) More convenient access to resources, including learning resources
(b) More use of crowd-sourcing or bottom-up, distributed activity in a variety of areas including prompting political action, making decisions, and determining value.

These trends have affected instructional-design practice as well. We have better windows into each other's work, and hope for even better access. Communities of active bloggers, listserv participants, and department colleagues now engage one another about their practices. These communities divide out in innumerable ways: e-learning, instructional design, corporate training, higher education, K12 technology integration, distance education and so on. Significantly, these trends toward greater transparency and sharing also align to best practices of professional development, which include:

- lifelong commitment to keeping up and improving practice
- on-site, on-demand support (rather than separated like a class)
- socially integrated
- continual reflection and conversation about one's work.

Most ID practitioners receive good initial training, typically in graduate school – but after that, continued professional learning is irregular and sporadic. To achieve consistently good outcomes, the entire field must focus more on sharing promising practices and creating space for new knowledge and innovation to take hold. This is somewhat ironic for a field that understands the value of situated, authentic performance with practice opportunities in rich enrichments.

I am convinced we can do a better job exploiting the expertise held by the master craft-persons among us. Here are some questions I have asked the master craft-persons around me:

- What is it that you seem to know that I don't (about the subject at hand)?
- How did you get that knowledge – in particular, what practices, habits, and resources have been helpful to you?
- How do you manage to stay current, to keep up, and to continue leading and modeling best practices?
- How do you run your shop – especially, how do you train apprentices?
- In what ways do you participate in the larger professional community?

Many master designers are quite aware and articulate about their practice, and willing to share. Those conversations have moved to the web and are becoming more accessible to the profession at large (e.g. the blogs of George Siemens, David Wiley, and Michael Grant). Other ways of sharing include: professional logs or histories (Power, 2009); cases and scenarios (Ertmer, Quinn, & Glazewski, in press); delphi studies (York & Ertmer, 2011); and design showcases. A number of methods can help establish quality, including: design competitions; search rankings; collaborative filtering; citation studies; hit counts and link counts; action research (see Toulmin, 2001); surveys of practice; karma points; and learning analytics (Rogers, McEwen, & Pond, 2010). In the spirit of the Web, determination of quality often happens after the fact rather than the pre-screening peer-review methods common in established academic fields (Neilsen, 2011).

Nearly 20 years ago Steven Tripp presented a paper on the reverse engineering of successful designs (Tripp, 1994). His exemplar case was the teaching of navigational skills among Polynesian sailors through ritualized classes and formal training. The stakes were obviously life and death on the high seas, and the skills conveyed were highly nuanced and sophisticated. I don't know that even the best instructional designer could have fashioned a better system of knowledge transmission. Two current examples are the Khan Academy (a website with instructional video clips in a wide range of subjects) and the flipped classroom (a classroom teaching strategy with video lectures assigned as homework and cases solved in class with peer and instructor support). Both of these initiatives were developed by practitioners. Both, I believe, would not likely have been developed by ID theorists because their theoretical ambitions are modest. Both projects apply simple principles of instruction in creative ways to vexing problems of practice, leading to widespread interest among the broader practitioner community. Reverse engineering (carefully analyzing successful practice in case-study fashion) can highlight elements of these designs-in-use that would be used in future designs.

Concluding Thoughts

A generation ago Reigeluth, Bunderson, and Merrill (1978) contrasted three approaches to designing instruction:

(a) *Artistic* – Using intuition to make design decisions.
(b) *Empirical* – Using tryout data to make design decisions and determine effectiveness of programs.
(c) *Analytic* – Using principles drawn from theory to make design decisions.

They saw science relating to the third, analytic approach. Our practice-centered approach agrees with the authors that every designer applies a combination of these forms of reasoning, but disagrees with their views of science. All three approaches – the artistic, empirical and analytic – have some claim to the production of new knowledge in the field. This is a key claim of this chapter: ID practice involves knowledge production just as doing research does. Art, science, craft, analysis, testing – all have a role for designing good instruction, and all have a role in doing good theory and science. All forms of knowledge production should be valued and recognized for their contributions to our understanding of effective practices. A practice-centered approach seeks to expand the inquiry, theorizing, and embodiment of knowledge to better account for the amazingly wide variety of knowledge needed to succeed in producing good instruction.

Instructional design is a hard, demanding field. People trained at one time will need to be retrained (or professionally renewed in some other way) within a few years, to keep up with advancing theory and emerging technology. There is some need for professionals to feel a calling or vocation (Hillman, 1996), to sustain them through the droughts and low points of a demanding career. Practitioners understand the need for compromise and adaptation, yet the pragmatic skills involved in making things work are often neglected by theorists and researchers. A practice-centered approach aims to restore a measure of credibility to such concerns and seeks to redress the imbalance caused by our near-exclusive focus on cognition and traditional theories of learning and instruction. At the same time, the lessons derived from learning and instructional theories are preserved and integrated as part of our framework. The criterion of value, however, shifts toward the *utility of an idea in practice*. By broadening our scope and focus, we will help the field remain relevant and thriving in a fast-changing world.

Notes

1 My thanks to an anonymous reviewer for this example.
2 Learning here refers to learning of the instructional system. Students may proceed through lessons and learn according to the objectives, but the routine practices of teaching will not be changed.

References

Bergin, A. E., & Suinn, R. M. (1975). Individual psychotherapy and behavior therapy. *Annual Review of Psychology*, 26, 509–556.

Berliner, D. C. (2002). Educational research: The hardest science of all. *Educational Researcher*, 31 (8), 18–20.

Bourdieu, P. (1977). *Outline of a theory of practice.* Cambridge: Cambridge University Press.

Campbell, J. (1949). *The hero with a thousand faces.* Princeton: Princeton University Press.

Campbell, K., Schwier, R. A., & Kenny, R. F. (2005). Agency of the instructional designer: Moral coherence and transformative social practice. *Australasian Journal of Educational Technology*, 21(2), 242–262. Retrieved from: http://www.ascilite.org.au/ajet/ajet21/campbell.html

Child, M., Williams, D. D., Birch, A J., & Boody, R. M. (2005). Autonomy or heteronomy? Levinas's challenge to modernism *and* postmodernism. *Educational Theory*, 45(2), 167–189.

Clark, R.E. (1994). Media will never influence learning. *Educational Technology Research and Development*, 42(2), 21–29.

Davis, A. B., Sumara, D. J., & Luce-Kapler, R. (2000). *Engaging minds: Learning and teaching in a complex world.* Mahwah NJ: Erlbaum.

Dewey, J. (1997/1938). *Experience and education.* New York: Simon & Schuster.

Ertmer, P. A., Quinn, J., & Glazewski, K. (Eds., in press). *The ID Casebook* (4th ed.) Boston, MA: Pearson.

Friesen, N. (2011, April). The lecture as a transmedial pedagogical form: An historical analysis. *Educational Researcher*, 95–102.

Friesen N. (2009). *Re-thinking e-learning research: Foundations, methods, and practices.* New York: Peter Lang.

Garrison, D. R., Anderson, T., & Archer, W. (2000). Critical inquiry in a text-based environment: Computer conferencing in higher education. *The Internet and Higher Education*, 2(2–3), 87–105.

Garfinkel, H. (1967). *Studies in ethnomethodology.* Englewood Cliffs, NJ: Prentice-Hall.

Gladwell, M. (2000). *The tipping point: How little things can make a big difference.* Boston, Little Brown.

Grimstad Group (1995). Applying system dynamics to courseware development. *Computers in Human Behavior*, 11(2), 325–339. (The Grimstad Group consists of P. I. Davidsen, J. J. Gonzalez, D. J. Muraida, J. M. Spector, and R. D. Tennyson.)

Hannafin, M. J., Hannafin, K. M., Land, S. M., & Oliver, K. (1997). Grounded practice and the design of constructivist learning environments. *Educational Technology Research and Development*, 45(3), 101–117.

Hillman, J. (1996). *The soul's code: In search of character and calling.* New York, NY: Random House.

Holland D., Lachicotte W. Jr., Skinner D., & Cain C. (1998). *Identity and agency in cultural worlds.* Cambridge: Harvard University Press.

Horn, R. E. (1972). *In pursuit of the e-objective: A paper exploring those educational objectives often called exposure, experiential, and expressive, or even encounter, explorative, expanding, effort, or epistemological.* Retrieved from: http://www.stanford.edu/~rhorn/a/topic/edu/ARTCLInPursuitofEObject.pdf

Huizing, A., & Cavanagh, M. (2011). Planting contemporary practice theory in the garden of information science. *Information Research*, 16(4) paper 497. Retrieved from: http://InformationR.net/ir/16-4/paper497.html

Hung, W. (2011). Theory to reality: A few issues in implementing problem-based learning. *Educational Technology Research and Development*, 529–552.

Hurley, J. P., & Wilson, B. G. (April 2012). *Development of a grounded theory for teacher decisions to adapt research-based health education curricula.* Presented at the meeting of the American Educational Research Association, Vancouver, BC.

Jonassen, D. H. (2011). *Learning to solve problems: A handbook for designing problem-solving learning environments.* New York: Routledge.

Jonassen, D.H., Strobel, J., & Ionas, I.G. (2005, October). *Crisscrossing: A web environment for authoring cognitive flexibility hypertexts.* Association for Educational Communications and Technology, Orlando, FL.

Kaptelinin, F., & Nardi, B. (2006). *Acting with technology: Activity theory and interaction design.* Cambridge and London: MIT Press.

Kliebard, H. M. (1987). *The struggle for the American curriculum 1893–1958.* New York: Routledge.

Komaski, P. K. (1987). *Educational technology: The closing-in or the opening-out of curriculum and instruction.* Syracuse, NY: ERIC Clearinghouse on Information Resources.

Kozma, R. (1991). Learning with media. *Review of Educational Research,* 61(2), 179–211.

Latour, B. (2005). *Reassembling the social: An introduction to Actor-network theory.* New York: Oxford University Press.

Law, J. (2004). *After method: Mess in social science research.* London and New York: Routledge.

Lehrer, J. (2011, October 29). The art of failing successfully. *Wall Street Journal,* C12. [Column: Head Case.]

Li, Q., Clark, B., & Winchester, I. (2011). Instructional design and technology with enactivism: A shift of paradigm? *British Journal of Educational Technology,* 41(3), 403–419.

Lindblom, C. E. (1959). The science of muddling through. *Public Administration Review,* 19(2), 79–88.

Lindblom, C. E. (1971). Still muddling, not yet through. *Public Administration Review,* 39(6), 517–526.

Lumsdaine, A. A., & Glaser, R. (1960). *Teaching machines and programmed learning.* Washington D. C.: National Educational Association.

Middleton, D., & Brown, S. (2002). The baby as a virtual object: Agency and stability in a neonatal care unit. *Athena Digital,* 1 (Spring), 1–23.

Neilsen, M. (2011, 29 October). The new Einsteins will be those who share: From cancer to cosmology, researchers could race ahead by working together – online and in the open. *Wall Street Journal,* C3.

Nicolini, D., Gherardi, S., & Yanow, D. (2003). Introduction: Toward a practice-based view of knowing and learning in organizations. In D. Nicolini, S. Gherardi, & D. Yanow (Eds.), *Knowing in organizations: A practice-based approach* (pp. 3–31). New York: M.E. Sharpe.

Ortner, S. B. (1984). Theory in anthropology since the Sixties. *Comparative Studies in Society and History,* 26(1), 126–166.

Parrish, P. (2006). Design as storytelling. *TechTrends,* 50(4), 72–82.

Parrish, P., Wilson, B. G., & Dunlap, J. C. (2011). Learning experience as transaction: A framework for instructional design. *Educational Technology,* 51(2), 15–22.

Penuel, W. R., Fishman, B. J., Haugan Cheng, B., & Sabelli, N. (2011). Organizing research and development at the intersection of learning, implementation, and design. *Educational Researcher,* 40(7), 331–337.

Polanyi, M. (1958). *Personal knowledge: Towards a post-critical philosophy.* Chicago: University of Chicago Press.

Postill, J. (2010). Introduction: Theorising media and practice. In B. Bräuchler & J. Postill (Eds.), *Theorising media and practice* (pp. 1–32). Oxford and New York: Berghahn. Draft: https://docs.google.com/Doc?id=dxm64w9_209g9vk47t s&hl=en_GB&pli=1

Power, M. (2009). *A designer's log: Case studies in instructional design.* Athabasca University: AU Press. Retrieved from: http://www.aupress.ca/index.php/books/120161

Prawat, R. S. (1993). The value of ideas: Problems versus possibilities in learning. *Educational Researcher,* 22(6), 5–16.

Reigeluth, C. M. (1983). Instructional design: What is it and why is it? In C. M. Reigeluth (Ed.), *Instructional-design theories and models* (pp. 3–36). Hillsdale, NJ: Lawrence Erlbaum Associates.

Reigeluth, C. M., Bunderson, C. V., & Merrill, M. D. (1978). What is the design science of instruction? *Journal of Instructional Development,* 1(2), 11–16. Online: http://faculty.soe.syr.edu/takoszal/IDE830/IDE830_linked_readings/Readinglist2/2-1_Reigeluth_DesignScience.PDF

Reiser, R. A. (2001a). A history of instructional design and technology Part 2: A history of instructional design. *Educational Technology Research and Development,* 49(2), 57–67.

Reiser, R. A. (2001b). A history of instructional design and technology: Part I: A history of instructional media. *Educational Technology Research and Development,* 49(1), 53–64.

Rogers, P. C., McKewen, M. R., & Pond, S. (2010). The use of web analytics in the design and evaluation of distance education. In G. Veletsianos (Ed.), *Emerging technologies in distance education* (pp. 231–245). Edmonton, AB: Athabasca University Press. Online: http://www.aupress.ca/books/120177/ebook/99Z_Veletsianos_2010-Emerging_Technologies_in_Distance_Education.pdf

Rorty, R. M., & Mendieta, E. (2005). *Take care of freedom and truth will take care of itself: Interviews with Richard Rorty.* Palo Alto, CA: Stanford University Press.

Saito, R. (2002). Anxiety and waiting: A Heideggerian view of instructional computing simulation. *Educational Technology,* 42(1), 56–59.

Sennett, R. (2008). *The craftsman.* New Haven: Yale University Press.

Shuell, T. J. (1986). Cognitive conceptions of learning. *Review of Educational Research,* 56(4), 411–436.

Simon, H. A. (1969). *The sciences of the artificial.* Cambridge MA: The MIT Press.

Song, L., Hannafin, M. J., & Hill, J. R. (2007). Reconciling beliefs and practices in teaching and learning. *Educational Technology Research and Development,* 55(1), 27–50.

Steiner, G. (2003). *Lessons of the masters: The Charles Eliot Norton Lectures 2001–2002.* Cambridge MA: Harvard University Press.

Stern, D. G. (2003). The practical turn. In S. P. Turner & P. A. Roth (Eds.), *The Blackwell guide to the philosophy of the social sciences* (pp. 185–206). Malden, MA: Blackwell.

Suchman, L. (2003) Organizational alignment: The case of bridge-building. In D. Nicolini, S. Gherardi, & D. Yanow (Eds.), *Knowing in organizations: A practice-based approach* (pp. 187–203). New York: M. E. Sharpe.

Tenner, E. (1997). *Why things bite back: Technology and the revenge of unintended consequences.* New York: Alfred A. Knopf.

Toulmin, S. (2001). *Return to reason.* Cambridge, MA: Harvard University Press.

Tripp, S. (1994, February). *Reverse engineering the "Stone Canoe" (learning from successful designs).* Paper presented at the meeting of the Association for Educational Communications and Technology, Nashville TN.

Walker, D. F. (1990). *Fundamentals of curriculum.* Fort Worth: Harcourt Brace College.

Wang, M. C., Walberg, H. J., & Haertel, G. D. (December 1993–January 1994). What helps students learn? *Educational Leadership,* 41(4), 74–79.

Wenger, E. (1998). *Communities of practice: Learning, meaning, and identity.* New York: Cambridge University Press.

Wilber, K. (1996). *A brief history of everything.* Boston MA: Shambhala.

Wilson, B. G. (2012a). Constructivism in practical and historical context. In R. Reiser & J. Dempsey (Eds.), *Current trends in instructional design and technology* (3rd ed.) (pp. 45–52). Upper Saddle River, NJ: Pearson Prentice-Hall.

Wilson, B. G. (2012b). Developing a critical stance as an e-learning specialist: A primer for new professionals. In S. Fee & B. Belland (Eds.), *The role of criticism in understanding problem solving* (pp. 57–68). New York: Springer.

Wilson, B. G. (1999). *The dangers of theory-based design.* Instructional Technology Forum Paper No. 31. Retrieved from: http://itech1.coe.uga.edu/itforum/paper31/paper31.html

Wilson, B. G., and Parrish, P. (2011). Transformative learning experience: Aim higher, gain more. *Educational Technology,* 51(2), 10–15.

Wilson, B. G., and Switzer, S. (2012, June) *Pedagogical capital: Understanding and leveraging trusting relationships in online courses.* Paper presented at Ed-Media, Denver.

Wong, E. D. (2007). Beyond control and rationality: Dewey, aesthetics, motivation, and educative experiences. *Teachers College Record,* 109(1), 192–220. Online: http://www.msu.edu/~dwong/publications/Wong-TCRBeyondControl.pdf

York, C. S., & Ertmer, P. A. (2011). Toward an understanding of instructional design heuristics: An exploratory Delphi study. *Educational Technology Research and Development,* 59, 841–863.

Young, P. A. (2009). Instructional design frameworks and intercultural models. Hershey, PA: IGI Global.

4 Experiential Learning and Cognitive Tools

The Impact of Simulations on Conceptual Change in Continuing Healthcare Education

Thomas C. Reeves, Patricia M. Reeves, and Susan E. McKenney

Introduction

Professor David H. Jonassen has made, and continues to make, an enormous contribution to multiple fields including educational technology (Jonassen, 2004a), instructional design (Jonassen, 2004b), and the learning sciences (Jonassen, 2011). His unique characterization of *mindtools* as well as his consistent focus on conceptual change as an important outcome of meaningful learning have influenced the thinking and work of researchers and practitioners at all levels and across all forms of education and training.

Among his academic peers, Jonassen is noted for being direct in stating the implications of his research. For example, in his 2006 book, *Modeling with Technology: Mindtools for Conceptual Change*, he wrote: "The goal of learning should be conceptual change and development" (p. xiv). Jonassen, Strobel, and Gottdenker (2005) defined conceptual change as "changes in conceptual frameworks (mental models or personal theories) that learners construct to comprehend phenomena" (p. 15). Jonassen (2006) contended that conceptual change is critical to problem-solving and decision-making in all professional fields. Conceptual change, especially the development of robust mental models of complex phenomena and the capacity for decisive decision making under duress, is absolutely essential in healthcare fields such as medicine, nursing, public health, and social work.

The primary purpose of this chapter is to review the evidence that continuing healthcare education using simulations as cognitive tools (mindtools) instantiates experiential learning, and, in turn, fosters conceptual change. This review is important because, although conceptual change is often one of the most desirable outcomes of continuing healthcare education, such change is also one of the most difficult goals to accomplish. This chapter concludes with a call for more widespread pursuit of educational design research by members of the global continuing healthcare education community.

Background

Medical practitioners such as physicians, nurses, public health officers, and social workers often resist conceptual change even when faced with compelling evidence of the need to change a foundational mental model underlying treatment decisions. Millard (2011) described in excruciating detail the extraordinary suffering that President James A. Garfield endured for nearly 90 days after being shot by an assassin in July 1881. Garfield's physicians, despite having been strongly advised to use the disinfection procedures developed by Joseph Lister 20 years earlier, continued to probe the President's wound with unclean fingers and unsterilized instruments, thereby introducing the massive blood infection to which President Garfield eventually succumbed.

Despite the evidence-based movement in medicine and healthcare (Sackett, Straus, Richardson, Rosenberg, & Haynes, 2000), the challenges that physicians and other healthcare practitioners face when they need to engage in conceptual change are still evident today. For example, Gawande (2009) documented the difficulties he has confronted in convincing fellow surgeons to adopt a simple checklist that could prevent tragic errors that are all too common in operating theaters. Thagard and Zhu (2003) revealed how Western physicians, especially in the USA, have struggled to give acupuncture, a practice derived from traditional Chinese medicine, a fair evaluation because of the perceived incommensurability of the different world views of medical practice in the East and West. More recently, Jonas, Walter, Fritts, and Niemtzow (2011) detailed the difficulties they have experienced as American military physicians getting other healthcare practitioners who treat wounded American soldiers returning from Iraq and Afghanistan to accept the positive results they have found in relieving pain with acupuncture.

Continuing education for healthcare professionals often has conceptual change as one of its major goals. Unfortunately, continuing healthcare education continues to be inadequate around the world, even in the wealthiest counties. For example, a recent report from the Institute of Medicine (2011) in the USA concluded that:

> Every segment of the healthcare workforce must comprise professionals who provide high-quality health care and assure patient safety. However, the nation lacks a comprehensive, effective system of continuing education in the health professions, and this gap contributes to knowledge and performance deficiencies at the individual and system levels.
>
> (Institute of Medicine, 2011, p. 39)

The inadequacies of continuing healthcare education in the still-developing countries are even more alarming. Consider something as basic as hand washing. Although Gawande (2008) warned that the failure to sterilize hands before interacting with patients is a serious problem in even the most advanced hospitals in the USA and Europe, it is a major cause of death in the developing world where the proportion of patients infected by their caregivers frequently exceeds 25 percent (Pittet Allegranzi, Storr, Bagheri Nejad, Dziekan, Leotsakos, & Donaldson, 2008). Allegranzi and Pittet (2009) wrote:

> Healthcare workers' hands are the most common vehicle for the trans-mission of healthcare-associated pathogens from patient to patient and within the healthcare environment. Hand hygiene is the leading mea-sure for preventing the spread of antimicrobial resistance and reducing healthcare-associated infections (HCAIs), but healthcare worker com-pliance with optimal practices remains low in most settings.
> (Allegranzi and Pittet, 2009, p. 209)

In light of such reports from the World Health Organization and other public health agencies, it seems like many healthcare practitioners have not progressed sufficiently beyond the unclean habits of the eminent physicians who arguably killed President Garfield in 1881. In this and other areas of healthcare practice, the need for conceptual change among healthcare pro-fessionals is clear.

Experiential Learning through Simulations

How can continuing healthcare education foster conceptual change more effectively? The U.S. Institute of Medicine (2010) and others (cf. Vesper, Kartoğlu, Bishara, & Reeves, 2010) have recommended increased adoption of experiential learning as a pedagogical strategy that can foster meaningful learning. Kolb (1984) defined experiential learning as "... the process whereby knowledge is created through the transformation of experience" (p. 38). Experiential learning may be categorized into two different types: one that is personal and informal (e.g. learning from experience that one should always begin a patient interaction by addressing the patient by name to establish rapport), and another type that is a designed event encompass-ing learning opportunities to which people are intentionally exposed (e.g. a continuing nursing education seminar focused on advanced disinfection techniques).

Interactive simulations have been demonstrated to be effective vehicles for enabling experiential learning within the context of continuing health-care education (Kneebone, Arora, King, Bello, Sevdalis, Kassab, Aggarwal, & Darzi, 2010; Levine, Schwartz, Bryson, & DeMaria Jr, 2012; Rogers, 2011). According to McGaghie, Siddall, Mazmanian, and Myers (2009), "A growing body of research evidence documents the utility of simulation technology for educating healthcare professionals" (p. 62). However, they go on to note that "simulation has not been widely endorsed or used for continuing medical education (CME)" (p. 62).

The low level of use of simulations in continuing healthcare education is alarming given that the link between interactive simulation and experiential learning is often stated in the literature. For example, writing in the *Journal of Continuing Education in Nursing*, Decker, Sportsman, Puetz, and Billings, (2008) stated that "Simulation offers a unique mode for experiential learning" (p. 74). Carron, Trueb, and Yersin (2011) wrote:

> Simulation is a promising pedagogical tool in the area of medical education. High-fidelity simulators can reproduce realistic environments or clinical situations. This allows for the practice of teamwork and communication skills, thereby enhancing reflective reasoning and experiential learning.
>
> (Carron, Trueb, and Yersin, 2011, n.p.; online article)

Similarly, in the context of developing high fidelity healthcare simulations for teaching and learning, Carron (2011) stated that "Attaining the appropriate level of realism [in a healthcare simulation] will help participants engage in the scenario by making unprompted actions and hence benefit from experiential learning" (p. 9). It would seem that embracing the use of simulations in continuing healthcare education is itself a conceptual change within the profession that has yet to take hold. This may be tied to the complexity of creating high quality simulations.

For experiential learning to be activated within a simulation, some degree of authenticity must be attained. Regarding the use of simulations in nursing education, Campbell and Daley (2009) wrote: "In order for a transfer of knowledge to occur, the student's role in the simulation must be as authentic as possible" (p. 5). However, authenticity is a complex issue in the design and implementation of learning simulations. Authenticity, like beauty, is often in the mind of the beholder. In this light, Barab, Squire and Dueber (2000) claimed that authenticity occurs "not in the learner, the task, or the environment, but in the dynamic interactions among these various components... authenticity is manifest in the flow itself, and is not an objective feature of any one component in isolation" (p. 38).

Herrington, Reeves, and Oliver (2010) argued that for an e-learning environment, including an interactive simulation, to be authentic, some degree of "suspension of disbelief is required" (p. 92) on the part of the learners. People regularly suspend their disbelief when they watch a film or read a novel, becoming so cognitively and emotionally engaged that they forget that they are just watching and reading rather than actually experiencing what is happening. Instructional designers and educators in the health professions must strive to develop interactive simulations in ways that allow healthcare personnel to engage in similar levels of suspension of disbelief so that as learners they can "immerse themselves in a learning experience that most closely matches that encountered in real life" (Cheng Duff, Grant, Kissoon, & Grant 2007, p. 466), and, hence, become engaged in experiential learning. In a chapter focused on simulations, Jonassen (2011) highlighted the importance of learner engagement when he wrote that "as I have pointed out repeatedly, without engagement, there is no meaningful learning" (p. 233).

The Effectiveness of Simulations

Determining the effectiveness of learning simulations is not as straightforward as it might first seem. As described above, the nature of authenticity and how to foster its perception are challenging design problems. Another complicating issue relates to the amount of *scaffolding* that learners need, or are given, within an instructional simulation. Scaffolding, in the context of a learning environment, refers to the assistance provided to learners so that they can accomplish something that they would not be able to do easily without help. In a comprehensive review of the instructional effectiveness of simulations, de Jong (2011) wrote:

> The overall conclusion is that simulation-based inquiry learning can be effective if the learners have adequate knowledge and skills to work in such an open and demanding environment and if they are provided with the appropriate scaffolds and tools. In those cases where adequate support is given, simulation-based learning may lead to better results than direct instruction or laboratory based exercises.
>
> (de Jong, 2011, p. 459)

However, providing too much scaffolding can turn what it is purported to be a simulation into an elaborate tutorial, thus contravening the intended experiential nature of the interactive learning environment (Jonassen, 1996). The learning theory foundations of medical simulations include constructivism, reflective practice, and situated learning (Bradley, 2006). These theoretical perspectives position the learner with more autonomy than a learner typically experiences in direct instruction (Kirschner, Sweller, & Clark, 2006; Kuhn, 2007). Finding the right mix of "support, feedback, and scaffolding that is provided to students" (Rawson, Dispensa, Goldstein, Nicholson, & Korf Vidal, 2009, p. 207) in simulations for continuing healthcare education is a research challenge that continues to go unresolved (Tobias & Duffy, 2009).

Some educational researchers have devoted themselves to searching for the precise mix of multimedia features to incorporate into interactive learning environments such as simulations (Mayer & Alexander, 2011), but definitive one-size-fits-all prescriptions have not been found. Perhaps this search is ill-advised (Reeves, 2011). The authenticity of a learning simulation largely depends on individual differences such as motivation, readiness, and previous knowledge. Mehlenbacher (2010) reminded researchers and practitioners alike that "we should always remember that [authentic] tasks have both an objective dimension and a subjective one, where the latter represents the learner's perceived experience of the task, whether as simple, dull, complex, or highly engaging" (pp. 234–235). Ultimately the search for universal multimedia design principles may be less successful than the creative crafting of simulation designs, guided by relevant heuristic design principles when available, that are subsequently refined through rigorous cycles of formative evaluation (Harteveld, Thij & Marinka, 2011).

This is essentially what educational design researchers strived to do (McKenney & Reeves, 2012).

Educational Design Research for Simulation Development

Over the last 20 years, a genre of research known variously as "design-based research" (Kelly, 2003), "design experiments" (Brown, 1992; Collins, 1992; Reinking & Bradley, 2008), educational design research (van den Akker, Gravemeijer, McKenney, & Nieveen, 2006; Kelly, Lesh, & Baek, 2008; McKenney & Reeves, 2012), "engineering research" (Burkhardt, 2006), and "formative research" (Newman, 1990) has emerged. Anderson and Shattuck's (2012) analysis of the past decade of design-based research studies led them:

> to concur with Dede, Ketelhut, Whitehouse, Breit, and McCloskey's (2009) claim that "DBR offers a 'best practice' stance that has proved useful in complex learning environments, where formative evaluation plays a significant role, and this methodology incorporates both evaluation and empirical analyses and provides multiple entry points for various scholarly endeavors" (p. 16). However, as promising as the methodology is, much more effort in this and other areas of education research is needed to propel the type of education innovation that many of us feel is required.
>
> (Anderson and Shattuck, 2012, p. 24)

If simulations are to play a major role in fostering conceptual change and others types of higher order learning in continuing healthcare education, they must become the focus of large-scale development initiatives employing educational design research strategies (McKenney & Reeves, 2012). Traditional instructional design approaches (Branch, 2009) whereby developers attempt to apply isolated multimedia design principles derived from experimental studies are insufficient for dealing with the complexity inherent in the types of learning simulations that are capable of fostering profound conceptual change among healthcare professionals. Jonassen, Cernusca, and Ionas (2007) delineated the limitations of instructional design as commonly practiced and went on to describe how they conducted design research in developing web-based simulations that help biology students comprehend "the effects of environmental perturbations on gene flow between two populations" (p. 51). The authors stated that whereas formative evaluation within the context of instructional design focuses only on the instructional materials, the formative experiments that characterize educational design research make more of an effort to "consider the process and the context in which learning takes place" (p. 48).

This consideration of process and context noted by Jonassen et al. (2007) is pertinent to the major outcomes of educational design research: an intervention (in this case, simulations) and theoretical understanding. Educational design research begins with the identification of a significant educational problem in need of a creative solution and which is appropriate for scientific inquiry. Enhancing the conceptual knowledge of healthcare professionals represents precisely the kind of challenge that educational design research is intended to tackle. While the scope of any given research initiative can vary, the intention of educational design research is to produce two main outcomes. First, it enables the conceptualization, design, prototyping, and refinement of a practical solution to the complex challenge with which the research project began (Bereiter, 2002; Edelson, 2001). Second, it leads to the development of enhanced theoretical understanding, often in the form of design principles (Bell, 2004; Kali, 2008). Ideally, and in many documented cases, participating in educational design research also fosters professional development for all involved (e.g. researchers, teachers, subject-matter experts, and others (Bannan-Ritland, 2008; Reinking & Bradley, 2008).

Educational design researchers can also probe the reasons why, despite substantial evidence of their effectiveness, simulations have not been more widely adopted within the context of continuing healthcare education (McGaghie et al., 2009). Dornan, Scherpbier, and Spencer (2008) called for more research "to promote the transfer of simulation education to practice settings" (p. 562). This requires a solid on-the-ground understanding of the factors that influence adoption and uptake of new ideas and resources, such as simulations. McKenney and Reeves (2012) offer detailed guidelines for educational design researchers to help them attend to implementation and spread from the onset of an educational design research initiative (see Figure 4.1).

McKenney and Reeves (2012) defined implementation as the process of adopting, enacting and sustaining interventions within the context for which they are developed, and spread as the process of disseminating and diffusing interventions and insights for use in other contexts. Issenberg and Scalese (2009) identified curricular integration as one of the challenges that anyone involved in developing or deploying simulations in healthcare education must address. According to McKenney and Reeves (2012), a key consideration is

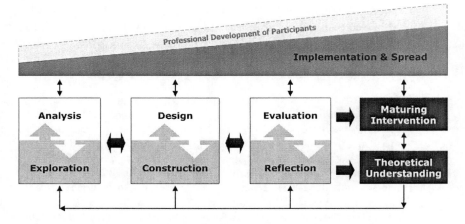

Figure 4.1 Educational design research model (modified and adapted from the generic model in McKenney & Reeves, 2012).

acknowledging that implementation does not come after design, but even influences the final product. As they state:

> Even though actual implementation and spread cannot take place until an intervention has been constructed, researchers and practitioners jointly anticipate and plan for it from the very first stage of analysis and exploration, e.g. by tempering idealist goals with realistic assessments of what is possible; by taking practitioner concerns seriously; and by studying what intrinsic motives and natural opportunities are already present in the target setting".
>
> (McKenney and Reeves, 2012, p. 159)

McKenney and Reeves (2012) also offer multiple practical strategies that educational design researchers can use to address curricular integration in particular, and implementation and spread in general. These specific strategies, as well as the overall design research approach, provide highly relevant starting points for creating simulations for continuing healthcare education that stand to be taken up and used by practising professionals.

The Contributions of David H. Jonassen

Although many hurdles must be overcome before simulations are adequately adopted by the continuing healthcare education community, Jonassen has established many of the benchmarks that must be met as well as establishing several critical signposts on what will inevitably be an arduous journey. For example, his work has established conceptual change as a paramount outcome of CHE (cf. Jonassen, 2006). In addition, his research has defined and refined many of the theoretical constructs underlying the design of interactive simulations for CHE (e.g. constructivism as a philosophy that informs and shapes the pedagogical strategies found in effective learning simulations). He has highlighted the merits of design research as an alternative to traditional instructional design in efforts to develop robust learning simulations (cf. Jonassen et al., 2007). Perhaps above all else he has set the standard for rigorous scholarship that all educational researchers who seek to engage in socially responsible research should emulate (Jonassen, 2011).

References

Alinier, G. (2011). Developing high-fidelity health care simulation scenarios: A guide for educators and professionals. *Simulation and Gaming, 42*(1), 9–26.

Allegranzi, B., & Pittet, D. (2009). Role of hand hygiene in healthcare-associated infection prevention. *Journal of Hospital Infection, 73*(4), 305–315.

Anderson, T., & Shattuck, J. (2012). Design-based research: A decade of progress in education research? *Educational Researcher, 41*(1), 16–25.

Bannan-Ritland, B. (2008). Teacher design research: An emerging paradigm for teachers' professional development. In A. E. Kelly, R. A. Lesh, & J. Y. Baek (Eds.), *Handbook of design research methods in education: Innovations in science, technology, engineering, and mathematics learning and teaching* (pp. 246–262). London: Routledge.

Barab, S. A., Squire, K. D., & Dueber, W. (2000). A co-evolutionary model for supporting the emergence of authenticity. *Educational Technology Research and Development, 48*(2), 37–62.

Bell, P. (2004). On the theoretical breadth of design-based research in education. *Educational Psychologist, 39*(4), 243–253.

Bereiter, C. (2002). Design research for sustained innovation. *Cognitive Studies, Bulletin of the Japanese Cognitive Science Society, 9*(3), 321–327.

Bradley, P. (2006). The history of simulation in medical education and possible future directions. *Medical Education, 40*(3), 254–262.

Branch, R. M. (2009). *Instructional design: The ADDIE approach*. New York: Springer.

Brown, A. L. (1992). Design experiments: Theoretical and methodological challenges in creating complex interventions in classroom settings. *The Journal of the Learning Sciences, 2*(2), 141–178.

Burkhardt, H. (2006). From design research to large-scale impact: Engineering research in education. In J. Van den Akker, K. Gravemeijer, S. McKenney, & N. Nieveen (Eds.), *Educational design research* (pp. 121–150). London: Routledge.

Campbell, S. H., & Daley, K. M. (2009). *Simulation scenarios for nurse educators: Making it real*. New York: Springer.

Carron, P., Trueb, L., & Yersin, B. (2011). High-fidelity simulation in the nonmedical domain: Practices and potential transferable competencies for the medical field. *Advances in Medical Education and Practice, 2*, 149–155.

Cheng, A., Duff, J., Grant, E., Kissoon, N., & Grant, V. J. (2007). Simulation in paediatrics: An educational revolution. *Paediatric Child Health, 12*(6), 465–468.

Collins, A. (1992). Towards a design science of education. In E. Scanlon & T. O'Shea (Eds.), *New directions in educational technology* (pp. 15–22). Berlin: Springer.

Decker, S., Sportsman, S., Puetz, L., & Billings, L. (2008). The evolution of simulation and its contribution to competency. *Journal of Continuing Education in Nursing, 39*(2), 74–80.

de Jong, T. (2011). Instruction based on computer simulations. In R. E. Mayer, & P. A. Alexander (Eds.), *Handbook of research on learning and instruction* (pp. 446–466). New York: Routledge.

Dornan, T., Scherpbier, A., & Spencer, J. (2008). Learning medicine: A continuum from theory to practice. In J. M. Spector, M. D. Merrill, J. J. G. van Merriënboer, & M. P. Driscoll (Eds.), *Handbook of research on educational communications and technology* (3rd ed., pp. 556–566). New York: Lawrence Erlbaum Associates.

Edelson, D. (2001). Learning-for-use: A framework for the design of technology-supported inquiry activities. *Journal of Research in Science Teaching 38*(3), 355–385.

Gawande, A. (2009). *The checklist manifesto: How to get things right*. New York: Metropolitan Books.

Gawande, A. (2008). *Better: A surgeon's notes on performance*. New York: Picador.

Harteveld, C., Thij, E., & Marinka, C. (2011). Design for engaging experience and social interaction. *Simulation & Gaming, 42*(5), 590–595.

Herrington J., Reeves, T. C., & Oliver, R. (2010). *A guide to authentic e-learning*. New York: Routledge.

Institute of Medicine (2011). *Informing the future: Critical issues in health* (6th ed.). Washington, DC: The National Academies Press.

Institute of Medicine (2010). *Redesigning continuing education in the health professions*. Washington, DC: The National Academies Press.

Issenberg, S. B. & Scalese, R. J. (2008). Simulation in health care education. *Perspectives in Biology and Medicine*, 51(1), 31–46.

Jonas, W. B., Walter, J. A. G., Fritts, M., & Niemtzow, R. C. (2011). Acupuncture for the trauma spectrum response: Scientific foundations, challenges to implementation, *Medical Acupuncture*, 23(4), 249–262.

Jonassen, D. (1996). Scaffolding diagnostic reasoning in case-based-learning environments. *Journal of Computing in Higher Education*, 8(1), 48–68.

Jonassen, D. H. (Ed.), (2004a). *Handbook of research on educational communications and technology* (2nd ed.). Mahwah, NJ: Lawrence Erlbaum Associates.

Jonassen, D. H. (2004b). *Learning to solve problems: An instructional design guide*. San Francisco, CA: Pfeiffer/Jossey-Bass.

Jonassen, D. H. (2006). *Modeling with technology: Mindtools for conceptual change* (3rd ed.). Columbus, OH: Merrill/Prentice-Hall.

Jonassen, D. H. (2011). *Learning to solve problems: A handbook for designing problem-solving learning environments*. New York: Routledge.

Jonassen, D. H., Cernusca, D., & Ionas, I. G. (2007). Constructivism and instructional design: The emergence of the learning sciences and design research. In R. A. Reiser, & J. V. Dempsey (Eds.), *Trends and issues in instructional design and technology* (2nd edn, pp. 45–52). Upper Saddle River, NJ: Pearson Education.

Jonassen, D. H., Strobel, J., & Gottdenker, J. (2005). Model building for conceptual change. *Interactive Learning Environments*, 13(1–2), 15–37.

Kali, Y. (2008). The Design Principles Database as means for promoting design-based research. In A. E. Kelly, R. A. Lesh, & J. Y. Baek (Eds.), *Handbook of design research methods in education* (pp. 423–438). London: Routledge.

Kelly, A. E. (2003), Research as design. *Educational Researcher*, 32(1), 3–4.

Kelly, A. E., Lesh, R., & Baek, J. (Eds.) (2008). *Handbook of design research methods in education*. New York: Routledge.

Kelly, A. E., Lesh, R. A., & Baek, J. Y. (Eds.) (2008). *Handbook of design research methods in education: Innovations in science, technology, engineering, and mathematics learning and teaching*. London: Routledge.

Kirschner, P. A., Sweller, J., & Clark, R. E. (2006). Why minimal guidance during instruction does not work: An analysis of the failure of constructivist, discovery, problem-based, experiential, and inquiry based teaching. *Educational Psychologist*, 41(2), 75–86.

Kneebone, R., Arora, S., King, D., Bello, F., Sevdalis, N., Kassab, E., Aggarwal, R., & Darzi, A. (2010). Distributed simulation – Accessible immersive training. *Medical Teacher*, 32(1), 65–70.

Kolb, D. A. (1984). *Experiential learning: Experience as the source of learning and development*. Englewood Cliffs, NJ: Prentice-Hall.

Kuhn, D. (2007). Is direct instruction the answer to the right question? *Educational Psychologist*, 42(2), 109–113.

Levine, A. I., Schwartz, A. D., Bryson, E. O., & DeMaria Jr, S. (2012). Role of simulation in US physician licensure and certification. *Mount Sinai Journal Of Medicine*, 79(1), 140–153.

Mayer, R. E., & Alexander, P. A. (Eds.), (2011). *Handbook of research on learning and instruction*. New York: Routledge.

McGaghie, W. C., Siddall, V. J., Mazmanian, P. E., & Myers, J. (2009). Lessons for continuing medical education from simulation research in undergraduate and graduate medical education: effectiveness of continuing medical education:

American College of Chest Physicians evidence-based educational guidelines. *Chest Journal, 135*(Suppl 3), 62–68.

McKenney, S. E., & Reeves, T. C. (2012). *Conducting educational design research.* New York: Routledge.

Mehlenbacher, B. (2010). *Instruction and technology: Designs for everyday learning.* Cambridge, MA: The MIT Press.

Millard, C. (2011). *Destiny of the republic: A tale of madness, medicine and the murder of a president.* New York: Doubleday.

Newman, D. (1990). Opportunities for research on the organizational impact of school computers. *Educational Researcher, 19*(3), 8–13.

Pittet, D., Allegranzi, B., Storr, J., Bagheri Nejad, S., Dziekan, G., Leotsakos, A., & Donaldson, L. (2008). Infection control as a major World Health Organization priority for developing countries. *Journal of Hospital Infection, 68*(4), 285–292.

Rawson, R. E., Dispensa, M. E., Goldstein, R. E., Nicholson, K. W., & Korf Vidal, N. (2009). A simulation for teaching the basic and clinical science of fluid therapy. *Advances in Physiology Education, 33*(3), 202–208.

Reeves, T. C. (2011). Can educational research be both rigorous and relevant? *Educational Designer: Journal of the International Society for Design and Development in Education, 1*(4). Retrieved from http://www.educationaldesigner.org/ed/volume1/issue4/

Reinking, D., & Bradley, B. A. (2008). *Formative and design experiments: Approaches to language and literacy research.* New York: Teachers College Press.

Rogers, L. (2011). Developing simulations in multi-user virtual environments to enhance healthcare education. *British Journal of Educational Technology, 42*(4), 608–615.

Sackett, D. L., Straus, S. E., Richardson, W. S., Rosenberg, W., & Haynes, R. B. (2000). Evidence-based medicine: How to practice and teach EBM (2nd ed.). Edinburgh, Scotland: Churchill Livingstone.

Thagard, P. & Zhu, R. (2003). Acupuncture, incommensurability, and conceptual change. In G. M. Sinatra, & P. L. Pintrich (Eds.), *Intentional conceptual change* (pp. 81–104). Mahwah, NJ: Lawrence Erlbaum.

Tobias, S., & Duffy, T. M. (2009). *Constructivist instruction: Success or failure.* New York: Routledge.

van den Akker, J., Gravemeijer, K., McKenney, S., & Nieveen, N. (2006). *Educational design research.* New York: Routledge.

Vesper, J., Kartoğlu, Ü., Bishara, R., & Reeves, T. C. (2010). A case study in experiential learning: "Pharmaceutical Cold Chain Management on Wheels." *Journal of Continuing Education in the Health Professions, 30*(4), 229–236.

5 Simulations, Games, and Virtual Worlds as Mindtools

Scott J. Warren and Jenny S. Wakefield

Introduction

Imagine the following scenes from two virtual worlds:

> You arrive in town by way of an old Chevy Camaro and the scene coalesces in your field of vision. It is filled with trees, crumbling buildings, and a winding river that settles into a crystal lake. Climbing from the rusting car, the cracked leather pops and separates into rivulets of feathered gray stuffing. A wooden sign stands quietly before you reading:
> *Welcome to Anytown: A friendly place to call home.*
> You turn towards the building that is the reason you came: The Anytown News. Walking inside, the wooden floors flex underfoot. Before you can proceed, acrid smoke outside redirects your attention to a log cabin in flames. The roof suddenly collapses, spraying ashes onto an obscured historic marker. A blue-suited sheriff stands nearby, badge gleaming, spitting conflagrations laughing cruelly with each breath of wind. You venture back out and approach him. With a fraying garden hose, he silences the guttering sparks that singe a nearby store. You inquire about the blaze and the officer states that without a fire department in town, he cannot investigate. "I have some leads," the lawman tells you. "But the evidence will be gone before I can get to it. Will you help?"
>
> ...
>
> Much further away, in a locale not so ordinary, two men walk through a small room towards the balcony door. They hear masses of people outside eagerly awaiting the speech they know is to come. As the balcony door slides open the noise grows louder. They now see people cheering, whistling, and waving flags. The cobblestone plaza outside the hotel is filled to the brim with adherents, all there to greet, listen to, and get a glimpse of, their leader. Momentarily waiting by the balcony railing, the shorter of the two men stands looking out over the crowd in his army green outfit and cap on his head. A couple of feet behind him, his brother steps to the side. They know this procedure by now. They have done this many times together. The man by the railing slowly lifts his arm and with his hand makes the gesture and the masses

immediately fall silent in anticipation of what is to come. Clearing his throat he begins: "Workers, farmers, students, all Cubans ... these are the questions we should ask ourselves ..." The people listen eagerly. Here is the man who will help them past their troubled times – here, finally is their hope for a better future.

These two scenes illustrate a learner's experiences as they enter game and virtual world spaces created in the last decade to support student knowledge building. The first, *Anytown*, is an example of a naturalistic problem in a story-driven game used to engage students in learning through play. It was designed for elementary and middle schools, students to immerse them in reading and writing activities that were both active and practical, tying their constructed solutions to fictional writing problems and authentic, real world work (Warren, Stein, Dondlinger, & Barab, 2009). The second scene, from a virtual world *role play* called *Castro Salvado*, was developed by students in a higher education history course. Students engaged in active learning through role-playing in a constructivist learning environment. The role play which included perspectives for and against the Castro regime was captured on *machinima* (see http://www.machinima.com/) for later classroom viewing and discourse. Constative classroom communication about the learning experience and expressions of intersubjective understanding of the complex events leading up to the Cuban Revolution, contributed to students' higher-level understanding of the real-world events (Wakefield, Mills, Warren, Rankin, & Gratch, 2012). We shall return to the Anytown and Castro Salvado scenes later in the chapter.

The goal of our chapter is to illustrate how digital constructs associated with the concept of *mindtools* function as tools to support cognition and conceptual change. Each example incorporates *at least* the core mindtool elements of modeling, coaching, scaffolding, means of assessment, and the support for the instructor as they seek shared understanding along with their students. It is through these core mindtool elements that students are supported as they construct knowledge individually and in groups. Specifically, these allow the instructor, peers, and experts to provide learners necessary feedback to challenge poorly developed concepts. We begin with a brief general background and then provide an overview of how simulations, games, and virtual worlds function as mindtools through specific, illuminative examples taken from our own work.

Mindtool Use in Education

> Humans have a need to solve problems
> (Bransford, Brown, & Cocking, 2000, p. 102)

It has long been a desire to guide undergraduate education away from lecture-based learning in which the instructor functions as a disseminator of knowledge toward an educational form that is more cognitively engaging for learners (Duch, Groh, & Allen, 2001) and to construct learning environments and tasks that meaningfully engage all learners. *Mindtools*, or *thinking tools* as described by Jonassen, Mayes, and McAleese (1993) are technology systems or tools that help learners intellectually; they occupy and assist learners in knowledge construction tasks, thereby they also aid in cognitive learning process. Jonassen's conception is that computer applications function as mindtools in that they support and engage students with critical thinking on the topic under study (Jonassen, Carr, & Yueh, 1998; Jonassen, 2006) and thereby assist learners with solving problems. The development of constructivist learning environments (CLEs) has shaped learning with computer tools and has allowed the landscape of learning with games, simulations, and virtual worlds to grow as supported by constructivist learning theories. Any curriculum designed under this conceptual framework largely dispenses with instructor as lecturer, provider of fixed knowledge, or the thought that students are blank slates upon which to be written by the teacher.

Constructivist Learning

Learning experiences designed following constructivist learning theory begin with the concept that individuals construct their own knowledge and that this is built on pre-existing experiences, beliefs, and mental models, thus making learning individualistic. However, this radical conception of constructivism is differentiated from social constructivism that recognizes not only the prominence of the individual in the process, but the fact that a learner's "thinking is grounded in perception of physical and social experiences, which can then be comprehended by the mind. What the mind produces are mental models that explain to the knower what he or she has perceived" (Jonassen, 1991, p. 10). It is this conception that drives CLEs to offer genuine engagement and predicaments to learners allowing them to ponder and confront problems that are closely related to real-world problems (Savery & Duffy, 1995). In these situated environments, problems or questions are posed to learners so as to engage them in meaning-making and problem-solving activities likely to result in knowledge construction (Jonassen, 1999); these activities are scaffolded by embedded and/or interactive feedback provided *constatively*. This social reality construction is realized through interactive communication in which cognition is partly subjective along with the shared representations and consensus of group members (Kriz, 2010).

Harold Barrows (1986) distilled the core concepts of problem-based learning (PBL). This pedagogical model shifted the focus of education from lecture towards practical, hands-on learning activities tied to real-life situations. PBL activities aim to improve student learning while they are collaboratively and actively working in small groups or teams solving "new, complex, and ill-structured real-life problems" (Sluijsmans, Moerkerke, van Merriënboer, & Dochy, 2001, p. 153). The PBL model thus focuses on improving student learning "by requiring students to learn content while solving problems" (Jonassen, 2011b, p. 154). This learning model can be motivating because it can give students a practical reason to develop knowledge and skills. What was missing from early PBL and CLE environments was the inclusion of cognitive support that would help ensure that learners would learn from their interactions with problems.

Mindtools Then and Now

In order to address this gap, Jonassen (1996) conceived that technology tools could function as *mindtools,* which he described as:

> computer-based tools and learning environments that have been adapted or developed to function as intellectual partners with the learner in order to engage and facilitate critical thinking and higher order training ... [they] are extensions of humans [that can] extend cognitive functioning during learning ... while constructing knowledge to engage learners in cognitive operations they would not otherwise have been capable.
>
> (Jonassen, 1996, p. 10)

Since this definition, Jonassen's conception of mindtools has evolved to include interactive simulations and related tools:

> When students use these tools to construct models, they are learning *with* the computer, not *from* it. Computers become intellectual partners ... by helping learners to articulate and represent what they know (not what the teacher knows) and for reflecting on what they have learned and how they came to know.
>
> (Jonassen, 2011b, pp. 306–307)

This later conception of mindtool lends itself more clearly to viewing games, simulations, virtual worlds, and similar technologies that model authentic systems as mindtools. Mindtools are not *productivity* tools; instead, they support cognition by *extending learner thinking* beyond what they may be able to do ordinarily without support. What Jonassen et al. (1998) meant when they said computers become *intellectual partners* is that they allow the learner to achieve when they might not when alone, functioning to guide problem solving through "more capable peers" (Vygotsky, 1978, p. 86).

Constructing Learning: Digital Tools as Today's Scaffolds

During the last decade, pedagogical methods have increasingly leveraged technologies to provide what Brush and Saye (2001) called *hard scaffolds* (i.e. digitally embedded resources that allow students to engage in the abstract critical and creative thinking required in complex areas such as writing (Warren, Barab, & Dondlinger, 2008) and science (Barab, Goldstone, Zuiker, Warren, & Ingram-Goble, 2007; Kafai, Quintero, & Feldon, 2010)). Hard scaffolds include embedded directions, visual depictions of information, and other similar tools that provide general feedback and learner support. These supports free the instructor to challenge learners' poor knowledge constructions and give individualized guidance to students.

As mentioned earlier, the challenge for educators has been to construct learning environments and tasks that meaningfully engage all learners. This task is complicated by a need to concurrently provide aids to learner-centered exploration of problems and both individual and group knowledge construction. Howland, Jonassen, and Marra (2012) suggested that tools such as simulations, virtual worlds, and games are one possible solution to achieve such environments.

Learning Simulations

Howland, Jonassen, and Marra (2012) defined simulations as "imitations of some real thing, state of affairs, or process ... allowing learners to manipulate key characteristics or variables within a physical or abstract system" (p. 58). *Realism* and *relevance* are two characteristics of simulations that have been posited to make them effective tools to support learning goals (Braun, Fernlund, & White, 1998). Braun and colleagues found that the *realism* affordance allows simulations to portray real-life situations reflecting true-to-life experiences that better prepare students for what they will later encounter. The *relevance* characteristic is that it helps provide "meaningful experiences, so students are able to identify with and relate to projects that have a significant bearing on their everyday lives" (Braun, Fernlund, & White, 1998, p. 88).

Simulations, Games, and Virtual Worlds as Mindtools

Since the late 1990s, simulations, games, and virtual worlds have been designed to provide learners with an opportunity "to apply prior learning" and an "opportunity for discovery" (Parry, 1980, p. 103). When integrated into a curriculum along with embedded problem-solving components and social interactions, games, simulations, and virtual worlds can provide deeper learning (Steinkuehler & Johnson, 2009). Learning games, simulations, and virtual worlds include the core mindtools elements: features of modeling, coaching, scaffolding, assessment, and support for instructors as they seek to guide and challenge learner knowledge constructions. In Anytown, students were immersed in reading and writing activities within a simulated town. This location acted as both problem space and scaffold to support cognition and provided learners with practice. The situated conflicts were active and based on practical problems.

These ill-structured challenges required students to tie their constructed solutions to both the game's fictional writing problems and their future authentic writing (Warren, Stein, Dondlinger, & Barab, 2009). Instructor supports included formal trainings to prepare the instructor for the social constructivist methods, just-in-time scaffolding from the instructional designer when the instructor had cognitive conflict about implementing the simulation game as designed, as well as a formal job aid that provided the instructor with background information and daily directions related to what to expect from the digital space and activities. With the aid of the instructor, Anytown was designed to challenge students to reflect on their activities and assignments, think more deeply about what they had learned, as well as on what they could improve. This is in keeping with the concept in Jonassen (2011b) that technologies should function as *knowledge construction tools* letting students learn *with* them rather than *from* them.

Digital Simulations for Building Knowledge

Simulations are commonly viewed as the bedrock upon which games and virtual worlds are built, though the three constructs are often perceived as indiscriminate from one another (Becker & Parker, 2009; Cubitt, 2001). It is important, however, to convey what the primary similarities and differences among games, simulations, and virtual worlds are. While the visible structure of each may appear dissimilar, the mechanism that supports learning in each is the same: *accurate physical or cognitive models* of a system, phenomena, or object(s). In an educational simulation, there is a "dynamic and reciprocal relationship between [a learner's] internal mental models and the external models that students construct" (Jonassen, 2011b, p. 311), or interact with. Educational games also include these representations, but further *layer in* motivating aspects such as an artificial *conflict* to drive play, an interactive *rule set* governing this play, and a *condition* that allows a player to win the game. Virtual worlds have different affordances depending on their core technologies and media affordances. Some virtual spaces provide tools that allow teachers or designers to build static or interactive models of real world phenomena that they want students to internalize (Warren & Wakefield, 2011). Others enable learners to build external representations of their mental models, which allows for critique by instructor and peers with the goal of improving their individual knowledge construction. Today's digital simulations are generally created using computer software to create models that either imitate or represent how something works or lets the user observe how something would work under various conditions. Simulations provide a safe space in which to explore models, experiment with practices too expensive or dangerous to engage with otherwise, such as manipulating objects, but also for practicing problem solving.

Simulations, games, and virtual worlds are malleable. They allow either the instructor or students to construct problem spaces or solutions using the tools themselves. For example, a virtual world design may replicate a complex social environment within which students are challenged to interact towards a goal of constructing understanding and developing possible solutions to an ill-structured problem. Such construction tools allow students not only to interact with simulations built *for* them, but also to build spaces that act as representative evidence of their individually or collaboratively constructed knowledge.

Core Mindtool Elements of a Simulation

Jonassen (1996) identified several affordances of mindtools that have clear connections with simulations, whether they are static representations or interactive models, complex games, or virtual worlds and their accompanying construction tools. Mindtools can be used to represent what learners know; they also engage them in various critical, creative, and complex thinking processes (e.g. analyzing, evaluating, connecting, elaborating, synthesizing, imagining, designing, problem solving, decision making, etc.) (Jonassen 1996, as cited in Jonassen & Carr, 2000).

In keeping with this idea, simulations provide learners with the ability to interact with models or generate their own representations of what they know and also share the representations for peer and expert critique towards a goal of improving their knowledge constructions. These systems can be built to include a number of different mindtools, or as mindtools themselves.

Modeling Reality

The natural learning affordance of simulations is that they model a reality that the instructor seeks to have the learner encounter. The representation need not be visually perfect; instead, providing a clear depiction or experience of applying the skills may be sufficient if one accepts Baudrillard's (1994) concept of *equivalence* in which the "sign and the real" are the same in a pragmatic sense. For example, practicing difficult landings on a flight simulator allows a learner to engage in the actions that they will carry out in a physical plane, such as adjusting flaps and throttle, receiving clearance from the tower, braking, and taxiing. They are not flying a real plane; however, the trainee can reasonably be expected to learn to land a plane if the simulated activities accurately model landing a plane in the physical world.

Coaching and Not Teaching

While not all simulations provide specific feedback, many include software agents which comment on, and help to guide learner performance. Such systems may provide instant responses in the form of visual, auditory, textual, and other relevant performance advice. This may also be supplemented by critique from an outside observer regarding the learner's simulated performance. For instance, returning to the flight simulator example, the simulation can change the wind speed and this may impact the ability to land the plane. If the learner crashes the plane, the system can provide directions about how to improve future performance by noting how best to adjust for changes in wind speeds.

Scaffolding Learning

A simulation can be seen as a case study in which the user applies knowledge and skills and receives immediate feedback on performance and behavior.

The feedback is provided by the system and either supports or contradicts the learner's understanding. Simulations are safe environments in which the learner can practice and refine skills without serious consequences. The feedback is immediate and helps learners prioritize and set realistic goals (Jonassen, 2011a; Parry, 1980). For example, preparation for more advanced flying activities such as air conflict, can be and is, partially, trained using simulations.

Assessing Learning in Complex Digital Environments

Assessment should require "Students to use higher-order thinking skills to solve and analyze problems instead of memorizing facts and solving well structured, decontextualized problems" (Sluijsmans, Moerkerke, van Merriënboer, & Dochy, 2001, pp. 153–154). Ways to assess higher-order skills include *self-* and *peer-assessment* as it has been suggested that these methods allow students a stake in, and responsibility for, assessment (Sluijsmans et al., 2001). These assessment types "encourage[s] students to engage continuously and foster a deep approach to learning" (Dochy & McDowell, 1997, p. 279).

Jonassen (2011b, pp. 354–356) suggest using four different assessment types to improve students' understanding and increase their mental capabilities. We provide some brief examples for each.

- *Assess student problem schema*: For example, weekly readings may provide students with points of view expressed from both sides of an international conflict. When students are asked to reason from both perspectives during classroom discussions they may be asked to specify if the readings contained sufficient or missing information.
- *Assess student problem-solving ability:* Using rubrics to assess a student's developed models helps measure student problem-solving ability. For example, Firaxis' *Civilization* simulation games evaluate a player's performance based on several criteria. This includes items such as how accurately they solved a problem (e.g. building the United Nations), how quickly it was done, and how completely they did so. At the conclusion of the game, a summative ranking is assigned to their performance relative to competing players.
- *Assess the cognitive skills required to solve problems:* Many learning simulations and games test a player's ability to complete particular tasks prior to allowing them to engage with more challenging problems. In an air combat simulator, the system assesses the learner's existing skills and knowledge as a basic pilot. As the learner masters simpler skills, the system increases the level of difficulty. To this, the system will commonly assess several cognitive abilities by requiring the player to complete a series of linked activities within the simulation. For example, the simulation tests memory by requiring a player to remember multiple goals while being attacked (e.g. bomb three different locations) and their ability to sustain their attention on a task. Once players have

mastered simpler cognitive skills, they are asked to interact with more complex ill-structured problems.

• *Assess students' ability to construct arguments in support of solutions:* Expressing one's reasoning is a powerful form of assessment as it allows for confirmatory evidence of a student's ability to problem-solve (Jonassen, 2011b). Open classroom discussions in which students engage in *constative* communication – in a give and take of validity claims – expressing their intersubjectively interpreted truths is a powerful way to share understandings and find consensus.

Learning Simulations as Mindtools

Simulations have long been used for training purposes in military and business situations (Greenblat & Duke, 1981; Horn, 1977). As behaviorist and information processing learning models gave way to situated learning and constructivism, the how and why questions about simulations also changed. In this next section, we review some of the important constructs that most influenced our own work and clearly leveraged mindtools, problem-based learning, and constructivist learning environments. One of the first was the Cognition and Technology Group at Vanderbilt's *Jasper Woodbury.*

Jasper Woodbury: Anchoring Science Learning
in Authentic Problems

John Bransford was part of the development and testing of an early research-based technology-supported simulation activity, the Jasper Woodbury simulation environment, a series of twelve episodes with a narrative constructed around the simulated daily activities of the protagonist, Jasper (Cognition and Technology Group at Vanderbilt (CTGV), 1992). The series is grounded in anchored instruction where learning is based on situated and cognitive learning theory, resides in problem-rich environments, and allows for learner exploration (CTGV, 1990). Jasper Woodbury was designed to teach mathematics, geometry, and statistics through problem-solving detective-like stories.

Each adventure is built on problem finding, problem solving, reasoning, and communication concepts. The intent was to increase students' ability to a holistic picture of problems and improve transfer. Problems are designed following standards from the National Council of Teachers of Mathematics (NCTM). The success in this kind of learning lies in "student ownership of the problem" (Jonassen, 2011b, p. 162). The activities provide a means of cognitive partnership, asking students to construct new knowledge and generate their own ideas about how to solve the problem. Its minimal scaffolding requires students to be active participants in the processing of information and each part of the story is cumulative, building new skills upon both the last activity as well as on what students already know. As described by

Jonassen (1996), these are key theoretical components of mindtools. The influence of this early, situated learning environment can be seen in both the commercial and academic simulations that followed.

River City: Seeking Solutions Through Simulated Scientific Inquiry

The River City project at Harvard University focused on the development and use of a multi-user virtual environment (MUVE) to aid student learning through problem solving. The project challenged students to explore an imaginary city in the nineteenth century as scientists were seeking a solution to health problems besieging the citizens there. In this simulated constructivist space, learners investigated scientific questions while seeking possible reasons for the citizen's illnesses (Harvard University, 2004). By locating multiple casual factors such as tacit clues from virtual agents, monitoring water for bacteria, and measuring the number of bugs in the environment, students were able to generate defensible hypotheses regarding underlying causes of the citizen's illnesses and recommend solutions (Dede, Ketelhut, & Ruess, 2002).

Taiga: A Virtual World Simulation for Collaborative Inquiry

Using the same ActiveWorlds virtual world construction tool as River City, Quest Atlantis' *Taiga* simulation similarly was aimed at supporting scientific reasoning (Barab et al., 2007). The simulation was designed to engage students in science inquiry-based learning activities that would help them understand the abstract formalisms that underlie chemical processes and environmental influences such as erosion, farm run-off, and over-fishing. Taiga included multiple tools such as chat, e-mail, and discussion forums to support discourse for active learning experiences with peers at a distance. As with River City, Taiga also contained embedded scaffolds such as fictional characters and signposts, and simulation elements that visually presented problems (Barab, Warren, & Ingram-Goble, 2008). The simulation also included tools to support student experiments. Further, they could organize their knowledge and evidence using tools embedded in the Taiga environment such as word processors and spreadsheets (Barab, Scott, Siyahhan, Goldstone, Ingram-Goble, Zuiker, & Warren, 2009).

Anytown: Literacy through motivated practice

The Anytown environment was developed as a case problem-based learning environment (PBLE) for fourth grade students to improve writing skills (Warren, Barab, & Dondlinger, 2008) within Quest Atlantis. Anytown allowed students to interact with a simulation in which students acted as reporters with a goal of improving their writing skills. Within Anytown, students sought evidence to solve various ill-structured problems, which were framed as mysterious events tied to social and scientific problems with no clear answer. Game characters asked learners to seek out the complex, underlying causes of the events and write about their findings. This challenged learners to view cases as analogous, develop multiple perspectives, rely on prior experiences, and interact with the simulation to support a solution (Jonassen, 2011b).

To depict a more complete view of how Jonassen's conceptions of mindtools, constructivist learning environments, and problem-based learning have influenced the design and development of simulations, games, and virtual worlds, we provide two elaborated examples in what follows.

Illuminative examples

We next illustrate the mindtool concepts using two of our own designs. The first is a virtual world simulation, *Castro Salvado*. The second, *Broken Window,* involves students playing and designing a *transmedia* game that simulated aspects of the real world of work.

Example 1: Virtual world simulation: Castro Salvado

As noted earlier, mindtools function as tools to support cognition and conceptual change. In this first illuminative example we explain how the core mindtool elements modeling, coaching, scaffolding, means of assessment, and the support for instructor were in place in a history course and how the elements supported students in their knowledge construction both individually and as a group:

> Stories help us negotiate meaning, learn about the past, understand human actions and intentions, create an identity, and understand our experiences in the world.
>
> (Jonassen, 2004, p. 93)

In the chapter introduction, we experienced a scene from a *machinima* called *Castro Salvado*, scripted and role-played in the virtual world of Second Life® by higher education history course students. Students studied the Cuban Revolution, its causes and aftereffects. Wakefield, Mills, Warren, Rankin, and Gratch (2012) described how this role play took place using PBL instructional methodology and the learning and teaching as communicative actions theory (Warren & Stein, 2008; Wakefield, Warren & Alsobrook, 2011) as a theoretical framework. Ill-structured problems, inquiry, critical thinking, communicative actions, role play, reflective activities, and mindtools to aid in the cognitive learning process were all part of the learning process.

Initially, students were provided weekly readings in the form of primary and secondary source materials, which were discussed weekly in classroom sessions through constative communicative acts. Facilitated by the instructor, learners shared and refined their knowledge about the Cuban Revolution with a focus on the events leading up to the revolution, the associated problems, and the multi-level international challenges involved. Students were then presented with the ill-structured task of working collaboratively in small groups taking a side for or against the Castro regime producing scripts for short role plays. The expert instructor provided students with feedback and pre-approval of their role play scripts. Setting their scenes with descriptive narrative during a specific time period of the revolution students then started drafting their stories. Stories, Jonassen (2004) noted, are of use "as instructional support systems" (p. 93) and aid learners in problem solving. Student scripts formed the basis for their role play in Second Life®. Coaching by the instructor in this sense took place outside of the virtual world as a critique of students' scripts, helping learners see what relevant role play realistically could be conducted in the virtual realm.

Modeling

The virtual world of Second Life® allows for elaborate and realistic environment design as well as design of persona models called avatars, that is to say as virtual representations of self or a character of choice. These affordances make the environment well suited for role play. Using a model such as avatar role play and the virtual world as a mindtool helped simulate the actions and reactions of the stakeholders in the real-world historical events contributing to a as close realistic event as possible, also making the experience memorable (Wakefield et al., 2012) (see Figure 5.1).

Figure 5.1 The balcony scene in the Castro Salvado role play.

Scaffolding and Coaching

Having the virtual world environment pre-designed (but according to students' descriptions) allowed students to focus on their narratives and their avatar designs rather than having to spend time on learning the techniques to construct things in Second Life® which can be intimidating for learners (Warren & Wakefield, 2011) as the learning curve may be steep as with learners unfamiliar with the use of new technology. Having the environment pre-designed thus removed a large obstacle for students, allowing them to "have fun" while also being supported in their role play assignment by a technology specialist. This technology specialist, a more advanced peer from a technology program, provided coaching for students in the virtual world: the help, guidance, and encouragement students needed to be successful. Students customized the appearance of their avatars, playing with the embedded tools to animate their characters and allow them to speak using their voices through the help of connected microphones. They practiced moving their avatars and rehearsed for the role play, and when ready, their play was captured on machinima by the more experienced peer for later classroom viewing and group debriefing.

Assessment

Following Sluijsmans' and colleagues' (2001) advice to tie learning and assessment to context, students on this course were challenged to acquire knowledge and understanding not only about specific Latin American historical events, but also about the many interacting systems that were in place during the Cuban Revolution. This helped contribute to a deeper, more holistic picture of ongoing world events. By studying related and interacting systems rather than specifics, learners develop "a more integrated view of the world" (Jonassen, 2006, p. 17). On this course, the instructor's goal was to increase students' conceptual understanding and critical thinking of the narrative of the revolution, its causes and consequences. While writing papers may be the more traditional assessment means in a history course, it does not allow for assessment past an individual level of understanding. Mindtools employ learners in critical thinking. However, critical thinking is hard to assess and context specific (Jonassen, 2006).

Jonassen (2004) noted that "[r]eflection is necessary for regulating learning and constructing meaning based on intentions and actions" (p. 137). The constative and dramaturgical communicative actions of the LTCA theory, specifically the constative speech acts which include the exchange of validity claims in search for truth and the dramaturgical communicative actions where students express their intersubjective mutual understandings through such artistic means as virtual role play, function as such reflective activities. They allow for a means to assess what Jonassen (2006) called

students' model construction. Specifically, the classroom constative communicative act of questioning which offers the instructor the opportunity to
engage students in discourse by asking questions such as "How should the
American presidents have dealt with Castro's decision to associate with the
Russians?," "How could confrontations have been avoided?," "Why did
the Castro assassinations fail over and over again?" Such questions contribute to position taking and analysis from multiple perspectives and are complex and multi-faceted (Jonassen, 2011a) and foster argumentation. Further,
the dramaturgical role play was critiqued and validated through discourse
after classroom viewing of the machinimas which provided a means for
the instructor to assess student comprehension and cognitive growth.
Constative communicative action, as originally described by Habermas
(1998), include such discursive activities as sharing learning experiences
with the classroom community, revisiting problems, generating hypotheses,
providing arguments, and rejecting other's students' validity claims, and
then generating intersubjective, shared truths.

Support for Instructor

In order to promote learning it is essential to provide students with the freedom to shape their own stories, critically think about historical events, and
reflect upon their thinking, their role play stories, and their peers' stories.
The assignment required the instructor to seek out help with technology to
be able to implement the role play activity into her lesson plan. Having
access to such a support systems, allowed the history instructor to blend in
technology and story elements into a lecture course providing students with
an opportunity to learn not only through lecture but also through stories,
role play, and with mindtools. Jonassen (2006) noted that "[s]tories are
the oldest and most natural form of sense making" (p. 18). It is through
stories that we "negotiate meaning, learn about the past, understand human
actions and intentions, create identity, and understand our experiences of
the world" (Jonassen, 2004, p. 93). When coupled with the communicative
actions of the LTCA theory and collaborative work, students in this course
had the opportunity to tell their stories, view different perspectives and
arrive at mutual understanding through discourse.

"Stories are marvelous means of summarizing experiences, of capturing
an event and the surrounding context that seems essential. Stories are important cognitive events, for they encapsulate, into one compact package, information, knowledge, context, and emotion" (Norman, 1993, p. 129). Using
the immersive virtual world role play as a basis for critical and deep thinking around ill-structured problems, Wakefield et al. (2012) found that students, through their role-playing and classroom discourse, developed a
higher-level appreciation and understanding of the multifaceted events
occurring during the Cuban revolution by analyzing views for and against
Castro's government.

Example 2. Simulation as game: Broken Window

In our first example, *Castro Salvado*, the virtual world functioned as mind-tool – an intellectual partner – in that students were able to place themselves in the shoes of virtual characters simulating through role play real-world people and creating representations of real-world historical events. Through this experience students were able to create external representations of their internal mental models. Post-play debriefing through constative classroom discourse with peers and instructor – a necessary final step of role play (van Ments, 1983) – further helped students validate their cognition of learned concepts and express their intersubjective understanding.

Our next example is a game that included opportunities for student to interact with accurate, external models, construct their own internal models, and then represent them externally for critique by peers and instructor. This was enabled by a learning game design called *Broken Window*.

Transmedia Model

The Broken Window design sought to support undergraduates knowledge acquisition and construction on the subject of basic computer applications, Internet tools, and hardware and software structures by leveraging ill-structured problem solving along with game structures as motivating contexts for learning (Warren, 2010a, b; Warren & Dondlinger, 2009). Thus, the design leveraged a distributed transmedia model in which information and scaffolding resources, learning activities, and game play were distributed throughout including Internet tools such as blogs, YouTube videos, Twitter, and virtual worlds. Students crisscrossed various platforms in a transmedia-simulated way, acting as detectives. By distributing resources and challenging students to locate them, follow clues, seek solutions, and externally represent their own mental models, learners encountered multiple problems that would drive play that concurrently engendered the types of cognitive conflict that would drive learning.

Learning and Teaching as Communicative Actions (LTCA)

In order to ensure the transmedia creation supported the educational goals of the project, Broken Window was guided by the pragmatic theory of learning and teaching as communicative actions (LTCA) that claims that human communication towards goals is central to learning (Wakefield, Warren, & Alsobrook., 2011). As such, four particular communicative actions identified by Habermas (1998) are necessary for an educational experience to be sufficiently comprehensive to be viewed as valid: (a) normative communication that specifies the explicit or underlying rules and understandings that govern learner interactions; (b) strategic communication or directives generally made by an instructor; (c) constative communication in which learners engage in argumentation regarding claims to truth or knowledge towards a goal of agreement on valid knowledge; and

(d) dramaturgical communications in which learners make claims about their identities through external representations that are open to critique by instructor, peers, or experts. The following were the four learning goals established for the design of Broken Window (Warren, 2010a, b):

- *Normative action:* communicate with peers and group towards a goal of understanding norms, roles, and appropriate functioning as a either in class or in the real world.
- *Strategic action:* communicate effectively in a manner that allows for successfully completing personal objectives.
- *Constative action:* communicate the validity of their truth claims in a manner that allows for peers and client to accept this validity towards allowing design action.
- *Dramaturgical action:* communicate through self-expression that allow for others to critique based on elements of individual and group identities that emerge from the communicative process.

Table 5.1 presents the LTCA structures as designed into *Broken Window*.

To incorporate these communicative actions, the game-based course was designed with two main parts, the first lasting six weeks and the latter taking students through the end of the sixteen-week semester. Learners were immersed in an alternate reality game called *Broken Window* that was created *for students* by the instructor and an instructional designer and included intensive interactions and explicit connections between game tasks and learning goals. This alternate reality game included distributed game challenges, tasks, and rewards through a narrative that immersed students in a story that often included not one correct solution (Warren et al., 2011). Students were required to play the game to be successful at reaching the learning objectives.

Structuring the Game

As a contextualized, story-driven game, *Broken Window* started players in a learning management system (LMS) that included game play and educational resources. It acted as the main portal through which game characters could communicate relevant information and it provided the necessary scaffolds. As the game began, a researcher was kidnapped and the other story characters went into hiding, fearing for their safety. A warning note, signed by a villain, *c0d4,* was posted (see Figure 5.2). As learners progressed through the game, clues and resources were provided on the course blog and in the LMS by the professors that were in hiding. These clues included still photos with codes and a podcast from the kidnapped researcher.

The resources challenged learners to think more deeply about the bigger picture and challenged them to engage in interdisciplinary inquiry in areas such as scientific thinking, logic, computer security, and forensic analysis. Thus, the game provided learners a space in which to play and experiment

Table 5.1 Learning and teaching as communicative actions in *Broken Window*

Communicative action	Broken Window *enactments*
Normative	1. Syllabus contained basic outline of class participation expectations (i.e. attendance, discussions, appropriate tools)
	2. Rules for game participation that could be changed or broken by learners
	3. Expectations for group member roles and participation
Strategic	1. Directions and hard scaffolds were embedded in the LMS and websites
	2. Characters role-played by instructor provided directives to act in e-mail, etc.
	3. Directions from the instructor in LMS and forums during game construction
Constative	1. Claims and counter-claims made by fictional characters drove learner discourse towards shared understandings about problems, problem solutions, and approaches to game play
	2. Group tasks required collaborative work and discourse regarding the nature of their game construction for the second half of the course to meet course requirements
	3. Critiques by instructor and peers on solutions and final products spurred argumentation geared towards meeting shared understandings of what the games should achieve and were expected to engender cognitive conflict
Dramaturgical	1. Final game products included individual and group claims to truth about the quality of the game, its effectiveness for learning, and their knowledge of what such a game should contain and what form it should take
	2. Learner solutions included learner values regarding the projects themselves, their personal identity as an investigator, and how well they participated in constructing knowledge

There will be more kidnappings if you continue.

We have Rybickin. Aubichon-Saenz is next.

Leonard has a message for you here

Figure 5.2 c0d4's warning to *Broken Window* players.

with ideas, while still providing, at times, explicit scaffolds (e.g. a description of expected activities within a particular time frame), and at other times scaffolds emerge from social discourses with peers and characters. As students struggled during the game, the instructor scaffolded through the LMS with posts that would, for example, include a short list of helpful hints. The instructor, too, was supported by the formal scaffold of a detailed job aid that explained how to scaffold student learning each week, appropriate means of role-playing characters, and suggestions for dealing with expected student struggles. Further, as the course was taught in several course sections the group of instructors teaching also had regular access to the instructional game designer who would answer questions and update the job aid and even the game space as necessary.

Student interactions in the game provided clues that, combined with students' critical thinking, helped them generate their own creative, defensible solutions to a problem, with no single correct answer. Table 5.2 provides an

Table 5.2 Broken Window's mindtool elements

Mindtool	Broken Window *implementation*
Social support tools	Online forums, synchronous class meetings, group activities
Contextual support tools	The game itself acted as a problem manipulation and representation space
Information resources	Embedded in learning management system (LMS) with connections to Internet resources; also, included instructions on using search engines to locate their own resources
Static and dynamic models	*Broken Window* itself acted as a model for the game students would later create and changed dynamically in response to student actions
Conversation and collaboration tools	Numerous digital communication tools were used including e-mail, Skype, Twitter, text messaging
Scaffolding	Supports and mild directives were embedded in the distributed game components (e.g. LMS itself, entries, interactions with characters and instructor)
Modeling	Characters modeled appropriate forms of communication, types of game play; instructor modeled game management; game itself modeled appropriate game format
Coaching	The instructor provided coaching support to learners both as herself and as the characters in the game, providing cognitive challenge where needed and scaffolding as necessary
Assessment	Learning was assessed using rubrics completed by the instructor, peer students (within and outside of game construction groups), graders that role played particular characters, and the learners completed evaluations of their own participation and work

overview of the characteristics and the elements of *Broken Window* and how each functioned as a mindtool element.

In the Broken Window instructional model, students were expected to learn not *from the game* but *through their individual and group struggles* to generate solutions to the ill-structured problems framed within the game narrative in the give and take of conflict among competing truth claims shared by group members. It is this process that generates shared understandings and it emerges through argument and constructed social agreement: constative communicative acts. As such, they received specific feedback from peers, instructor, and in-game characters that would challenge and help revise their existing knowledge constructions. This course challenged students to solve problems using computer applications, knowledge of computer hardware and software, proper Internet use (i.e. online security, netiquette, Boolean searches, etc.). In addition, the game components required students to learn and use high levels of self-regulation skills such as organization, planning, preparing students for future academic studies, with the long-term curriculum goal of increased retention and lowered drop rates.

If students were successful, they received rewards from the characters or instructor such as exclusive clues and additional resources. However, to truly be successful as learners, an individual, and as a group game play or construction had to meet the expectations of their peers, the game characters, and the instructor. The most successful group at playing the game and developing their own solution to the global problem sought help from a number of different sources. They contacted faculty at several internationally renowned universities, located large numbers of resources not found in the game, and wound up generating a 75-page report detailing how their solution addressed the problem with logical evidence supporting their ideas taken from real data that they analyzed, synthesized, and presented not only in text, but also visually. The game they developed required the players to use the provided data and cross-reference it with real outside sites through Boolean searches, watch short videos by characters that led them towards working on ill-structured problems, and developing their solutions using additional information from fictional wikis, related UN Millennium development goal sites, and other online spaces with necessary information and data. This was all in a fictional narrative that included a good deal of humor, because of the incompetence of the villains that sought to thwart the players. This was a true example of traversing or crisscrossing the Internet in search of answers and using the tools under study to express the knowledge constructed.

Conclusion

David Jonassen has greatly influenced how simulations, games, and virtual worlds are used today in education. While these instruments have become increasingly prevalent in classrooms today, it has been his ideas regarding the use of internal and external models in situated, constructivist learning environments, and the use of mindtools to extend student critical thinking that has provided the pedagogical support for educators. Mindtools provide justification for the implementation of learning games, simulations, and virtual worlds as classroom assignments. Such learning spaces help situate learning in ways that aid student learning transfer and supports learner cognition in complex settings. As Jonassen's conception of mindtools has been highly influential in our own work and that of many others, we believe that it will continue to have a major impact in the field on the use of simulations, games, and virtual worlds for learning.

References

Barab, S., Scott, B., Siyahhan, S., Goldstone, R., Ingram-Goble, A., Zuiker, S., & Warren, S. (2009). Transformational play as a curricular scaffold: Using videogames to support science education. *Journal of Science Education and Technology.* 18(4), 305–320.

Barab, S. A., Scott, B., Goldstone, R., Zuiker, S., Warren, S. J., & Ingram-Goble, A. (2007, April). *Scaffolding to facilitate higher order skills.* Paper presented at the American Educational Research Association Annual Meeting, Chicago, IL.

Barab, S., Warren, S., & Ingram-Goble, A. (2008). Conceptual play spaces. In R. Fertig (Ed.), *Handbook of research on effective electronic gaming in education* (pp. 989–1009). Hershey, PA: Idea Group Reference: IGI Global.

Barrows, H. S. (1986). A taxonomy of problem-based learning methods. *Medical Education, 20,* 481–486.

Baudrillard, J. (1994). *Simulacra and simulation (The body, in theory: Histories of cultural materialism).* (S. F. Glaser, Trans.). Ann Arbor: University of Michigan Press.

Becker, K., & Parker, J. (2009). A simulation primer. In D. Gibson & Y. Baek (Eds.), *Digital simulations for improving education* (pp. 1–24). Hershey, PA: Information Science Reference.

Brush, T., & Saye, J. (2001). The use of embedded scaffolds with hypermedia-supported student-centered learning. *Journal of Educational Multimedia and Hypermedia, 10*(4), 333–356.

Bransford, J. D., Brown A. L., & Cocking, R. R. (2000). *How people learn: Brain, mind, experience, and school.* Washington, D.C: National Academy Press.

Braun, J. A., Fernlund P., & White, C. S. (1998). *Technology tools in the social studies curriculum.* Wilsonville, OR: Franklin, Beedele and Associates Incorporated.

Cognition and Technology Group at Vanderbilt – CTGV. (1990). Anchored instruction and its relationship to situated cognition. *Educational Researcher. 19*(6), 2–10.

Cognition and Technology Group at Vanderbilt – CTGV. (1992). The Jasper experiment: An exploration of issues in learning and instructional design. *Educational Technology Research and Development. 40*(1), 65–80.

Cubitt, S. (2001). *Simulation and Social Theory* (1st ed.). London: Sage Publications.

Dede, C., Ketelhut, D., & Ruess, K. (2002). Designing for motivation and usability in a museum-based multi-user virtual environment. In P. Bell, R. Stevens, & T. Satwicz (Eds.), *Keeping Learning Complex: The Proceedings of the Fifth International Conference of the Learning Sciences (ICLS).* Mahwah, NJ: Erlbaum.

Dochy, F. J. R. C., & McDowell, L. (1997). Introduction assessment as a tool for learning. *Studies in Educational Evaluation 23*(4), 279–298.

Duch, B. J., Groh, S. E., & Allen, D. E. (2001). Why problem-based learning? A case study of institutional change in undergraduate education. In B. Duch, S. Groh, & D. Allen (Eds.). *The power of problem-based learning* (pp. 3–11). Sterling, VA: Stylus.

Greenblat, C. S., & Duke, R. (1981). *Principles and practices of gaming-simulation.* Beverly Hills: Sage Publications.

Habermas, J. (1998). *On the pragmatics of communication.* Cambridge, MA: The MIT Press.

Harvard University. (2004). The river city project. A multi-user virtual environment for learning scientific inquiry and 21st century skills. Retrieved from http://muve.gse.harvard.edu/rivercityproject/

Horn, R. (Ed.), (1977). *The guide to simulations/games for education and training* (Vol. 1). Crawford, New Jersey: Didactic Systems.

Howland, J. L., Jonassen, D. H., & Marra, R. M. (2012). *Meaningful learning with technology* (4th ed). Boston, MA: Pearson.

Jonassen, D. H. (1991). Objectivism versus constructivism: Do we need a new philosophical paradigm? *Educational Technology Research and Development 39*(3), 5–14.

Jonassen, D. H. (1996). *Computers in the classroom: Mindtools for critical thinking.* Columbus, OH: Merrill/Prentice-Hall.

Jonassen, D. H. (1999). Designing constructivist learning environments. In C. M Reigeluth (Ed.), *Instructional-design theories and models. A new paradigm of instructional theory, Vol. II* (pp. 217–239). Mahwah, NJ: Lawrence Erlbaum Associates, Inc.

Jonassen, D. H. (2004). *Learning to solve problems. An instructional design guide.* San Francisco, CA: Pfeiffer.

Jonassen, D. H. (2006). *Modeling with technology. Mindtools for conceptual change.* (3rd ed.). Upper Saddle River, NJ: Pearson/Merrill Prentice Hall.

Jonassen, D. (2011a) Supporting problem solving in PBL. *Interdisciplinary Journal of Problem-based Learning. 5*(2), 95–119.

Jonassen, D. H. (2011b). *Learning to solve problems. A handbook for designing problem-solving learning environments.* New York, NY: Routledge.

Jonassen, D. H., & Carr, C. S. (2000). Mindtools: Affording multiple knowledge representations for learning. In S. P. Lajoie (Ed.), *Computers as cognitive tools, Volume 2: No more walls* (pp. 165–195). Mahwah, NJ: Lawrence Erlbaum Associates.

Jonassen, D. H, Carr, C., & Yueh, H-P. (1998). Computers as Mindtools for engaging learners in critical thinking. *TechTrends. 43*(2), 24–32.

Jonassen, D., Mayes, T., & McAleese, R. (1993). A manifesto for a constructivist approach to uses of technology in higher education. In T. M. Duffy, J. Lowyck, J., & D. H. Jonassen (Eds.), *Designing environments for constructive learning* (pp. 231–247). Heidelberg, Germany: Springer-Verlag Berlin.

Kafai, Y., Quintero, M., & Feldon, D. (2010). Investigating the "Why" in Whypox: Casual and systematic explorations of a virtual epidemic. *Games and Culture, 5*(1), 116–135.

Kriz, W. C. (2010). A systemic-constructivist approach to the facilitation and debriefing of simulations and games. *Simulation Gaming. 41*(5), 663–680.

Norman, D. A. (1993). *Things that make us smart: Defending human attributes in the age of the machine.* United States: Perseus Books.

Parry, S. B. (1980). The name of the game ... is simulation. *Training and Development Journal. 34*(6), 99–105.

Savery, J. R., & Duffy, T. M. (1995). Problem-Based Learning: An instructional model and its constructivist framework. *Educational Technology (35),* 31–38.

Sluijsmans, D. M. A., Moerkerke, G., van Merriënboer, J. J. G., & Dochy, F. J. R. C. (2001). Peer assessment in problem based learning. *Studies in Educational Evaluation 27,* 153–173.

Steinkuehler, C., & Johnson, B. Z. (2009). Computational literacy in online games: The social life of mods. *International Journal of Gaming and Computer-Mediated Simulations, 1*(1), 53–65.

Van Ments, M. (1983). *The effective use of role-play. A handbook for teachers and trainers.* Worcester, UK: Billing and Sons Limited.

Vygotsky, L.S. (1978). *Mind in society: The development of higher psychological processes.* Cambridge, MA: Harvard University Press.

Wakefield, J. S., Mills, L. A., Warren, S. J., Rankin, M., & Gratch, J. S. (2012, April). *Design, play, communicate, and learn: Examining the value of learning history through avatar role play.* Paper presented at the annual meeting of American Educational Research Association, Vancouver, Canada, April, 2012.

Wakefield, J. S., Warren, S. J., & Alsobrook, M. (2011). Learning and teaching as communicative actions: A mixed-methods Twitter study. *Knowledge Management and E-Learning. 3*(4), 563–584.

Warren, S. J. (2010a). Broken Window Codex (3rd edn, Vol. 2). Denton, TX: ThinkTankTwo@UNT.

Warren, S. (2010b). *From The Door, to Broken Window, to now: Design process, research, and lessons learned.* Paper presented at the Next Generation Course Redesign Project, University of North Texas, Denton, Texas, April, 2010.

Warren, S. J., Barab, S., & Dondlinger, M. (2008). A MUVE towards PBL writing: Effects of a digital learning environment designed to improve elementary student writing. *Journal of Research on Technology in Education, 41*(1), 53–79.

Warren, S. J., & Dondlinger, M. J. (2009, October). *Examining four games for learning: Research-based lessons learned from five years of learning game design and development.* Paper presented at the meeting of the Association for Educational Communications and Technology, Louisville, KY.

Warren, S. J., & Stein, R. (2008). Simulating teaching experience with role-play. In D. Gibson & Y. Baek (Eds.), *Digital simulations for improving education: Learning through artificial teaching environments* (pp. 273–288). Hershey, PA: IGI Global.

Warren, S. J., Stein, R., Dondlinger, M., & Barab, S. (2009). A look inside a design process: Blending instructional design and game principles to target writing skills. *Journal of Educational Computing Research, 40*(3), 295–301.

Warren, S. J., & Wakefield, J. S. (2011). Instructional design frameworks for Second Life virtual learning. In R. Hinrichs & C. Wankel. (Eds.), *Transforming virtual world learning. Cutting-edge technologies in higher education* (pp. 113–161). Bingley, UK: Emerald Group Publishing Limited.

6 Do You Know the Way to...Web 2.0?

Paul A. Kirschner and
Iwan G. J. H. Wopereis

Begin at the Beginning: Some Definitions

Millennials

Marc Prensky (2001) coined the term *digital native* to refer to a group of young people who have been immersed in technology all their lives, giving them distinct and unique characteristics that set them apart from previous generations. They have sophisticated technical skills and learning preferences for which traditional education is unprepared. He coined the term not based on research into this generation, but rather by rationalizing phenomena that he observed (e.g. he saw kids "surrounded by and using computers, videogames, digital music players, video cams, cell phones, and all the other toys and tools of the digital age" (2001, p. 1) and assumed (a) that they understood what they were doing, (b) that they were using the artifacts effectively and efficiently, and (c) that it's good to design education where they can do this. Veen and Vrakking (2006) followed suit, introducing the term *homo zappiens* to refer to a new generation of learners who learn in a significantly different way than their predecessors.

These terms are comparable to others given to a generation that has never known a world without computers, mobile phones and the Internet such as the Net generation (Oblinger & Oblinger, 2005; Tapscott, 1997), Generation I or iGeneration (Rosen, 2007), Google® Generation (Rowlands, Nicholas, Williams, Huntington, Fieldhouse, Gunter, Withey, Jamali, Dobrowolski, & Tenopir 2008), and so forth. The most generic term for this group is possibly the *millennial generation*, which does not denote a specific age group, but rather a generation characterized by high level use of, and familiarity with, communications, media, and digital technologies. According to Veen and Vrakking (2006), children of this generation develop – on their own and without instruction – the metacognitive skills necessary for enquiry-based, discovery-based, networked, experiential, collaborative, and active learning along with self organization, self-regulation, and problem-solving skills, and who are capable of making their own implicit (i.e. tacit) and explicit knowledge explicit to others.

Unfortunately, research has shown that this information technology-savvy generation really does not exist, at least with respect to learning, learning tools, and mindtools. Margaryan, Littlejohn, and Vojt (2011), for example, reported that university students (i.e. millennials) use a limited range of technologies for learning and socialization: "… the tools these students used were largely established technologies, in particular mobile phones, media player, Google®, and Wikipedia®. The use of handheld computers as well as gaming, social networking sites, blogs and other emergent social technologies was very low" (p. 438). A number of research studies (Bullen, Morgan, Belfer, & Qayyum, 2008; Ebner, Schiefner, & Nagler, 2008; Kennedy, Dalgarno, Gray, Judd, Waycott, Bennett, Maton, Krause, Bishop, Chang, & Churchward, 2007; Kvavik, 2005) in different countries (e.g. Austria, Australia, Canada, Switzerland, the United States) question whether the homo zappiens and/or digital native really exists. These researchers found that university students do not really have deep knowledge of technology, but that this is often limited to basic office suite skills, emailing, text messaging, Facebook® and surfing the Internet. According to Bullen et al., "… it appears they [university students] do not recognize the enhanced functionality of the applications they own and use" (p. 77) and that significant further training in how technology can be used for learning and problem-solving is needed. When used for learning, this was mostly for passive consumption of information (e.g. Wikipedia®) or for downloading lecture notes. A report commissioned by the British library and JISC (Williams and Rowlands, 2007) also overturns the common assumption that the Google generation is the most web-literate. Rowlands et al. (2008) conclude: "… the main findings are that much professional commentary, popular writing and PowerPoint presentations overestimate the impact of ICTs (information and communications technologies) on the young, and that the ubiquitous presence of technology in their lives has not resulted in improved information retrieval, information seeking or evaluation skills" (p. 308).

Related to this, a recent study by Valtonen Pontinen, Kukkonen, Dillon, Väisänen, and Hacklin (2011) under what they called Finnish Net Generation student teachers (i.e. student teachers born in the period 1984–1989) showed "that the technological knowledge of student teachers is not what would be expected for representatives of the Net Generation" (pp.13–14). In the study, they explored the technological pedagogical knowledge which they defined as "an understanding of the benefits and disadvantages of various technologies related to different pedagogical aims and practices" (p. 7). While it was expected that these Net Generation students would be adept at learning through discovery and thinking in a hypertext-like manner (Oblinger & Oblinger, 2005; Prensky, 2001) and that they would be able to transfer those skills to their teaching practices upon entering the teaching profession (Prensky), the results showed, just as those of Margaryan et al. (2011) and Bullen et al. (2008), that the range of software used was very limited and that, for example, social media was used as a passive source of information, not to actively create content, interact with others, and share resources. Valtonen et al. (2011) conclude that the expectations and assumptions about this group of "student teachers' abilities to adopt and adapt ICT in their teaching are highly questionable" (p. 1).

Mindtools

According to David Jonassen (2000) mindtools are "computer-based tools and learning environments that have been adapted or developed to function as intellectual partners with the learner in order to engage and facilitate critical thinking and higher order learning" (p. 9).

Learners constantly use applications such as databases, spreadsheets, search engines, visualization tools, and conversation environments which have been developed both as aids in the execution of work and to make users more productive. These tools are called productivity tools. When used as a mindtool, databases – for example – can help learners integrate and interrelate discrete bits of content, making them both more meaningful and more memorable. Building a database requires learners to organize information by identifying relevant content dimensions. In using a spreadsheet, learners can design, use, and fill in values and formulas requiring them to use existing rules and generate new rules to describe relationships and organize information, thus engaging critical thinking, forcing them to think more deeply (Blignaut, 1999; Jonassen & Carr, 2000). In this situation such applications have also been referred to as cognitive technologies (Pea, 1985), technologies of the mind (Salomon, Perkins, & Globerson, 1991), cognitive tools (Jonassen & Reeves, 1996; Lajoie, 2000) or tools for thinking/tool[s] for thoughts (Williamson Shaffer, 2009).

We broaden the scope in this chapter to include the facilitation of work by knowledge workers such as teachers and aspirant teachers. Since critical thinking and higher order learning also are necessary in their work, mindtools are also intellectual partners with these professionals whose working and learning are intertwined. Teachers must continuously develop themselves and learn and mindtools can play an important role in this learning process. Teachers and aspirant teachers must learn how to use mindtools, both as a means to encourage constructive learning in the classroom and as a tool for their own professional growth.

Web 2.0

Since its introduction in the early 1990s, the World Wide Web or "web" has developed from a static set of reference pages into a dynamic programming and application hosting environment. Terms like "Web 1.0" (Cormode & Krishnamurthy, 2008), "Web 1.5" (Dron & Anderson, 2009), "Web 2.0" (O'Reilly, 2007), "Web 3.0" (Morris, 2011) and "Web Squared" (O'Reilly & Battelle, 2009) underline the progressive nature of the evolving Web, even suggesting some kind of evolutionary stage model. Although there is a lot of criticism of this "software versioning" way of denoting Web development (since its inception, the Web has not been updated in a technological sense), we cannot neglect this terminology, simply because of its widespread use in all kinds of information and communication sources. A traditional Google search on the aforementioned terms performed on January 10,

2012, for instance yielded approximately 3,060,000 (Web 1.0), 766,000 (Web 1.5), 117,000,000 (Web 2.0), 4,500,000 (Web 3.0), and 120,000 (Web Squared) hits respectively. Based on these results it is obvious that the contemporary world is essentially dealing with second generation Web tools and applications. It is the crowd that talks the talk; we will walk the walk and describe the second generation technologies in the context of learning and professional development.

According to Wikipedia®, the term Web 2.0 is "associated with web applications that facilitate participatory information sharing, interoperability, user-centered design, and collaboration on the World Wide Web." It is often referred to as "read/write Web" for so-called "prosumers" (producer-consumers) to emphasize easy-to-use services regarding the creation and publication of content on the Web (as opposed to the preceding read-only Web for consumers; cf. Greenhow, Robelia, & Hughes, 2009). Also the term "social Web" is frequently linked to Web 2.0 as it stresses the opportunities to co-create and share knowledge and meaning with others in a social way (Boulos & Wheeler, 2007; Kim, Jeong, & Lee, 2010).

Dede (2009) analyzed the proliferating collection of Web 2.0 applications with respect to purpose, resulting in a three-group classification. He distinguishes between applications for:

(a) sharing, including applications for communal bookmarking, photo and video sharing, social networking, and writers' workshops and fan fiction;
(b) thinking, including applications like weblogs, podcasts, and online discussion forums; and
(c) co-creating, including applications like wikis and collaborative file creation, mash-ups and collective media creation, and collaborative social change communities.

According to Dede, this categorization by purpose can be helpful for assessing the differential utility of applications in formal learning contexts and beyond. This is necessary, since education is struggling with the implementation of Web 2.0 technologies in the classroom. Ravenscroft (2009) for instance signifies an interesting paradox, "levering around the notion that we are trying to incorporate the open, opportunistic and radical into a set of broader practices that are highly structured, time-constrained and quite traditional" (p. 2).

For Web 2.0 to be successful in education, traditional views on pedagogy must change (Brown, 2012). Some believe that Web 2.0 drives a desired paradigm shift in pedagogy necessary for riding the wave of technological and societal change (Brown, 2012). The term "Pedagogy 2.0" (McLoughlin & Lee, 2008) points to serious efforts to enhance learning with new technologies. Examples provided by aforementioned scholars make clear that Web 2.0 technologies affording interconnectivity, content creation and remixing, and interactivity can be successful on condition that learners are not left to their own devices (Kirschner, Sweller, & Clarke, 2006). Thus, for educators it will be a challenge to fully embrace Web 2.0 philosophies like openness, collective intelligence, and transparency. The least one can do is to design adequate support for learning (cf. Jonassen, 1999) and additionally focus on the development of new literacies that feature terms like "digital, pluralized, hybridized, intertextual, immediate, spontaneous, abbreviated, informal, collaborative, productive, interactive, hyperlinked, dialogic, and linguistically diverse" (Mills, 2010, p. 255).

Characteristics of Mindtools

David Jonassen (2000) distinguished five *characteristics* of mindtools. Perhaps a better term is *affordances* of mindtools; the perceived properties of a thing in reference to a user that influences how it is used (Kirschner, 2002). Originally proposed by James Gibson in 1977 (and refined in 1979), an affordance refers to the relationship between an object's physical properties (artifacts) and the characteristics of an agent (user) that enables particular interactions between agent and object. Affordances, thus offer the user opportunities to do something; whether the opportunity is seized depends on the user.

First, mindtools afford *cognitive amplification and reorganization* allowing the user to exceed the limitations of the human mind by doing things more accurately and at a higher speed. Engelbart (1962) spoke of augmenting human intellect:

> Increasing the capability of a man [*sic*] to approach a complex problem situation, to gain comprehension to suit his particular needs, and to derive solutions to problems. Increased capability in this respect is taken to mean a mixture of the following: more-rapid comprehension, better comprehension, the possibility of gaining a useful degree of comprehension in a situation that previously was too complex, speedier solutions, better solutions, and the possibility of finding solutions to problems that before seemed insolvable.
>
> (Engelbart, 1962, p. 1)

Using the term "intelligence amplification," Kirschner and Wopereis (2003) described this as the humans and machines working together to do things neither could do alone. It does not make things easier, but rather makes things possible.

Second, mindtools are *generalizable* and can be used in various settings and domains to engage and facilitate cognitive processing. They are not specific to any one purpose nor do they reduce information processing. They do not make processing easier, but afford it/allow it to occur. This also means that users have to think harder since to think more deeply costs more effort.

Third, mindtools can afford *critical thinking*, helping users think for themselves, make new connections between concepts, and create new knowledge. This is similar to what Crombag, Chang, Drift, and Moonen, (1979) referred to as carrying out operations on knowledge as opposed to operations with knowledge.

Mindtools are also *intellectual partners* in the learning of working process. As such, they are responsible for that which they can perform best. Computers should calculate and store and retrieve information, while the user of the tool should be responsible for recognizing and judging patterns of information and its organization.

Finally, a mindtool is a *concept*. It is a way of thinking about and using ICT, other technology, the learning environment, or intentional and incidental learning activity/opportunity (constructivist in nature) so that the users of these tools can represent, manipulate, and reflect on what they know instead of reproducing what others tell them.

The distinction between productivity tools and mindtools is comparable to Salomon's (1995) distinction between effects *with* technology and effects *of* technology. Effects *with* technology and/or tools relate to what happens while one is engaged in working with ICT and/or while she/he is busy with the tools. An example of effects with technology can be seen as the changed quality of problem analysis and solution as a result of either working with a group decision support system with others or that a specific project is delivered on time because of the use of project planning software. They are short-term changes induced by and/or effects of the technology or technology tool. Effects *of* technology and/or technology-tools on the other hand are those longer lasting changes that are a result of working with technology or are the result of having made use of the tools. An example of the effect of technology could be the skill of asking more exact and explicit questions because of the experiences working with the group decision support system. An effect of the planning software could be that the person becomes better able to plan and execute a project (i.e. that she/he plans and works more effectively and efficiently at a later date and without the tool) due to earlier use of and experience with the project planning software. Salomon argues that education should emphasize attaining effects of and not just effects with tools.

Used as productivity tools, we speak of the effects obtained with a program or application. Used as a mindtool, we speak of the effects of the program or application.

Teacher Communities of Practice

Teaching is a strange profession for a number of reasons. First, though the teaching profession is dedicated to education and learning, it strangely enough does not have a universal policy of continuing certification. Once you have become a teacher and receive your permanent certification, you no longer need to recertify. Second, though the profession itself is segmented into natural communities (e.g. school districts, schools, school types and levels, subject areas, and so forth) teachers tend to work in a solitary way (e.g. each teacher rules her or his little kingdom). Finally, they are possibly the only knowledge professionals who do not have their own personal space at their place of work. They share their classrooms with their pupils, often do not have their own desk with a computer, and lack the "down time" in the course of the working day (i.e. their "free time" during the day is usually filled with administrative or other school-related duties). There is, however, a mindtool that may help here: the *community of practice* (CoP).

Many people might not think of a CoP as a mindtool, but CoPs actually conform to all of the characteristics. First, a CoP affords *cognitive amplification and reorganization* in that the sum of its participants far exceeds the limitations of a single human mind. Second, CoPs are *generalizable*. A CoP can be set up and used in many settings and is not domain specific (e.g. anywhere from baking to ADHD to quantum astrophysics) to engage and facilitate cognitive processing. CoPs also can afford *critical thinking* in that they can help users think for themselves, make new connections between concepts, and create new knowledge. CoPs can also be considered to be *intellectual partners* in the learning of working process. Persons in CoPs assume different roles in different situations (as one moment a student teacher can be a learner and at another moment can advise another) with participants taking responsibility for that which they can perform best. Finally, a CoP is a *concept*. It is a way of thinking about and using the knowledge and experience of others so that members of the CoP can represent, manipulate, and reflect on what they know and not just reproduce what others say.

Communities of practice are groups of people who share similar goals and interests (CoVis). In pursuit of these goals and interests, they make use of common practices, use the same tools and express themselves in a common language. Through such common activity, they come to hold similar beliefs and value systems. Teachers belong to a large community of practice (the worldwide community of teachers) and almost always to one or more sub-communities such as the community of teachers in Iowa or the Netherlands, the community of science teachers, the community of elementary school teachers, the community of special educators or even the community of teacher educators.

According to CoVis (adapted from Lave & Wenger, 1991; Edelson, Pea, & Gomez, 1996):

> [P]art of belonging to a community of practice is being aware of the range of goals and beliefs held, as well as techniques used, by community members at large. Some of these will be part of the practice and belief system of a large number of the community members. Some will belong to a minority of the membership, or "fringe" groups. Awareness of the community debates and contentions is as important a part of community membership as awareness of what is common to most, or all. It is not unusual in some communities for such debates and contentions to be a key component of what drives community activity and the evolution of that activity over time.
>
> (CoVis, 2002, p. 4)

Schaap, de Bruijn, van der Schaaf, and Kirschner (2009) refer, in this respect, to the individual development of a Personal Professional Theory of the profession and note that this needs to be tuned to the Group Professional Theory. In this, communication and conversation with other members of the community and its sub-communities is of the utmost importance.

According to Barnett (2002), network-based technologies have had an impact on teachers' professional development in that it has reduced teacher isolation, has supported sharing, and has fostered reflection on practice. To this end, it has influenced actual practice and played a role in the creation of a CoP. These technologies allow pre-service and novice teachers to access a distributed expertise from more experienced teachers, teacher trainers and university faculties. In a CoP, network-based technologies can make sustained support available to these teachers, even after they themselves have become experienced teachers (i.e. in a CoP there are no general experts; each participant can be a learner in one situation and an expert in another). They allow teachers to share teaching experiences and techniques with others, get feedback so that they can modify their actions, methods and curricula, and hear of, and learn from, the experiences of others, and learn of new techniques (e.g. strong points, weak points, and implementation problems). Such interaction, according to Schlager, Fusco, and Schank (1999), can play a key role in innovating education.

In the following section we will present the role of conversation tools in these communities and illustrate how this can be learnt based upon examples of good practice in teacher training.

Conversation Tools as Mindtools

Conversation tools encourage and support discussion and discourse, allowing meaningful conversations that can lead to knowledge co-construction. These tools can be synchronous (communication with others within the community at the same time and in real-time as in Skype® or a chat tool such as MSN Messenger®) or asynchronous (communication with others within a community at different times as in e-mail or a discussion board). The first category allows people to share information (different types of data, thoughts, ideas, et cetera) with each other, process it, and discuss it at the same time. Asynchronous communication involves delayed communication where only one person can communicate at any one time and there can be a considerable delay between communications of the different users. Jonassen (2000) distinguished three types of asynchronous conferencing:

- one-to-one communication as in e-mail (though e-mail also allows for one-to-many communication),
- one-to-many communication as in bulletin boards (special-purpose computer programs that enable individuals to post messages to a bulletin board or read messages and copy them to a computer), and
- many-to-many communication as in computer conferences (asynchronous discussions, debates, and collaborative efforts among a group of people who share an interest in the topic).

Conversation tools can support communities or networks for the professional development of (aspirant) teachers. These communities for the professional development of teachers can differ with respect to a number of variables and these differences will manifest themselves in the use of different types of conversation tools. Three major differences are: the size of a community, the setting where the community operates and the composition of a community. Biology teachers, for example, who want to make use of mindtools in their teaching may form a special-interest discussion group in a news group. These teachers can be regarded to be a relatively small homogenous discourse community. This same topic (mindtool use in biology) may also be the subject of discourse in a learning community with aspiring biology teachers (i.e. student teachers), teacher educators, and experienced biology teachers. In such a community, the group is larger and also heterogeneous with respect to both expertise and domain of professional specialization. Size and heterogeneity could be further increased when domain experts (e.g. biologists, biomedical researchers, members of allied fields, et cetera) are added to the community of practice where biology is binding factor.

An example of a widely used and mature community of practice that makes use of network-based technologies is *La Main à la Pâte* (Hands-on Work), in which a community of practice for science teachers is formed throughout France (see Figure 6.1). This community won the 2001 eSchola prize for best initiative for teachers.

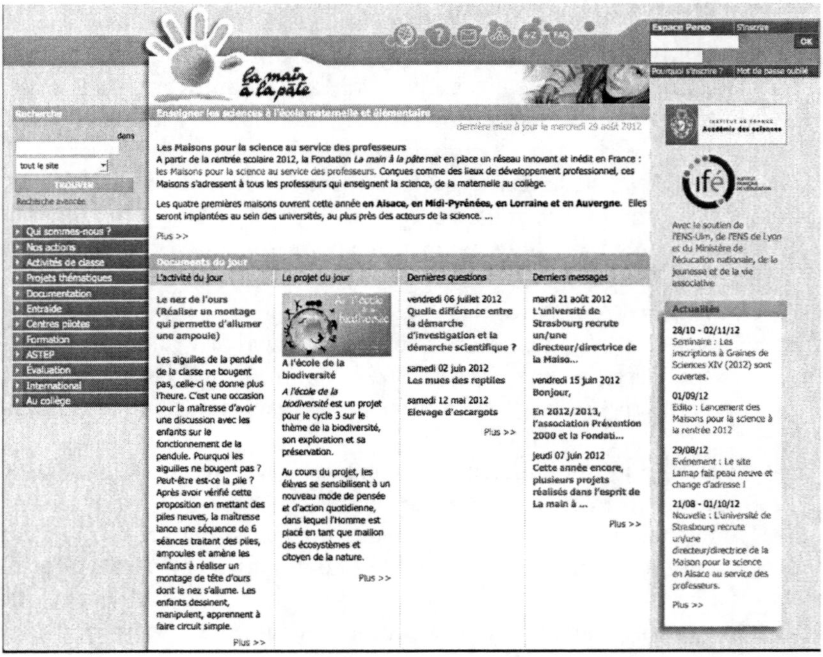

Figure 6.1 Opening page of La Main à la Pâte (http://www.lamap.fr/).

Initiated in 1996 by Georges Charpak, Nobel prize winner for physics in 1992, this community is managed by the French Academy of Science. It is based on teachers networking their skills to create effective synergy with external actors, inspectors and educational advisers, College of Education Training Staff, teaching specialists in science and other subjects, scientists, researchers, engineers, students from science universities or from the national colleges, and parents. In April 1998, an Internet site was opened offering teachers an information section on the structure and history of the project, a resource section containing class activities, scientific documents, and educational documents, and an exchange section with access to training and scientist networks, to (sub)sites of the *La main à la pâte* network, and to archives of a distribution list.

The networks are set up to foster exchange and cooperation between the different actors involved in the teaching of science, inter-teachers dialogue, and teacher–teacher assistance. Two important networks within the exchange section are the scientific consultant network and the teaching specialist network. Dialogue within these networks is achieved through asynchronous, built-in conversation tools with the results classified by both topic and resource-form. The scientific consultant network is a constantly expanding network made up of researchers and engineers who are willing to help (i.e. act as a resource or sounding board) teachers. They, in their own area of competence, reply to science-related queries by teachers preparing or implementing an activity. Replies are generally received within 48 hours. The teaching specialist network is made up of trainers and researchers skilled in the teaching of an academic subject (i.e. the pedagogical content knowledge of a certain area). These community members aid teachers to solve those problems encountered when preparing or conducting science activities.

Weblogs as Mindtools

A *weblog* or "*blog*" is a frequently updated personal website with dated entries displayed in reverse chronological order (i.e. newest/most recent first). Such entries or "posts" can easily be commented on, offering opportunities for discussion and feedback. As a weblog "grows," older posts and accompanying comments gradually disappear from the main page into an archive. Access to this archive is guaranteed, since each post has a unique resource locator called a "permalink." In addition, *tags* (i.e. non-hierarchical keywords or terms given to a piece of information that makes them easier to find) can be added to posts, aiding categorization and retrieval of content. Both weblog readers and writers (bloggers) can easily search through this (categorized) content by means of hyperlink navigation and keyword search. Further, when readers make use of web syndication technology (e.g. RSS: Really Simple Syndication), they are notified when weblogs are updated, allowing both knowledge of and adequate responses to new content.

The aforementioned functionalities, combined with technological features that enable tool ownership and user-friendliness, make weblogs popular tools for recording, sharing, and discussing information. Although not as trendy as in the previous decade, weblogs can still be regarded as mainstream Web 2.0 tools. On January 11, 2012 BlogPulse Stats identified 182,297,340 weblogs world-wide, including 100,897 new weblogs that had been established in the preceding 24 hours. Based on its popularity as a leisure tool, it is not surprising that educators consider implementing weblogs in formal education. Luehmann (2008) identified several affordances of weblogs for formal learning. According to her, weblogs (a) allow for self-direction, (b) provide rich opportunities for reflection and meta-cognition, (c) invite perspective making and taking through interacting with an audience, (d) allow for knowledge brokering, and (e) support identity development. These affordances strongly relate to the results of a literature review on weblog use in higher education conducted by Sim and Hew (2010). They identified six uses of weblogs from which instances can come across concurrently in a single weblog. They found that weblogs were mainly employed as:

(a)   learning journals or knowledge logs for gathering relevant information and ideas pertained to specific topics;
(b)   tools for recording personal and everyday life;
(c)   tools for expressing emotions or feelings;
(d)   instruments to interact or communicate with fellow students or teacher;
(e)   tools for (formative) assessment of learning; and
(f)   tools for task management.

We consider weblogs to be mindtools, especially when they are used as learning journals or knowledge logs. Although not mentioned as such in the work of Jonassen (1996, 2000, 2006), we are of the opinion that weblogs can be regarded intellectual partners that facilitate critical thinking and higher order learning (see also Boulos, Maramba, & Wheeler, 2006). Weblogs defined as mindtools include collections of posts and comments that reflect someone's history of learning. Weblog users can act on this content, discuss it, reflect on it, and compare it with other (expert) knowledge in order to continue learning. In other words, they can be used as/are tools to allow teachers either to be, or become, reflective practitioners. The effect of these activities will be enhanced when weblogs are situated in a larger community where the "wisdom of the crowd", and/or – even better – the "wisdom of experts" can be tapped. In his latest book on mindtools, Jonassen (2006) emphasizes that they should focus on the process of conceptual change, a mechanism underlying meaningful learning. According to him "[o]ne of the most powerful strategies that support meaningful learning is learners constructing models of what they are learning" (p. xiv). The kinds of phenomena that can be modeled using different modeling tools are (a) domain knowledge, (b) systems, (c) problems, (d) experiences, and (e) thinking (Jonassen, 2000; 2006). Weblogs are well-suited instruments for modeling experiences (i.e. for capturing, indexing, and making stories and experiences available for reflection on and enhancement of by others). The next example which stems from the domain of teacher education explains why.

In the teacher training domain, a growing number of studies address the added value of weblog use for learning. These studies cover both weblog use in initial education (e.g. Granberg, 2010; Shoffner, 2009; Top, Yukselturk, & Inan, 2010) and subsequent professional development (e.g. Killeavy & Moloney, 2010; Luehmann, 2008). We present a project here where three groups of student teachers used weblogs for reflective practice during their apprenticeship – student-teaching – period (Wopereis, Sloep, & Poortman, 2010). Within each group, weblogs of student teachers and teacher trainers were connected to each other by means of hyperlinks and web syndication, creating a blog community. In order to promote ownership, customization features were offered to the students. Two other important features of each weblog were the possibility for students to protect each reflection contribution with a password and the option to categorize each post.

During the project, student teachers were asked to reflect on their actions in the classroom and provide feedback to their fellows. In order to aid

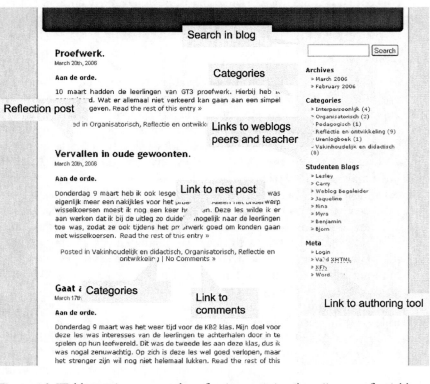

Figure 6.2 Weblogs as instruments for reflection on action (http://www.reflectieblogs.info).

reflective storytelling, the student teachers were asked to post structured entries. These structured posts mirrored the phases of the ALACT-model for reflective practice of Korthagen (1999; Action; Looking back on the action; Awareness of essential aspects; Creating alternative methods of action; Trial). By means of structured writing, student teachers were forced to better focus on learning-specific teacher knowledge in a cyclic manner (see Mishra & Koehler, 2006 for an in-depth analysis of types of teacher knowledge). It was hypothesized that when student teachers record their reflections on action in a consistent and structured way, this would result in deeper reflection and consequently to more and more meaningful conceptual change. The student teachers capitalized on the possibility to read the feedback on their posts as well as to read the other student teachers' weblogs (Boud, 1999). Seeing and thinking about multiple solutions for problems enriched the developing teaching knowledge base of the student teachers (Lin, Hmelo, Kinzer, & Secules. 1999).

Dede (2009) classified weblogs as Web 2.0 applications for thinking. We see them as mindtools as well, provided the content is recorded in a well-structured way and that there is ample opportunity to interact with it. Multiple perspectives on the content, obtained by reading and discussing feedback, as well as the availability of experts may further help achieve conceptual change, the cornerstone of meaningful learning and a necessity for teachers in these quickly changing times.

Conclusion

Teacher education (i.e. pre-service teacher training and education) should not have as its goal the transmission of subject matter knowledge, pedagogical content knowledge and the current set of teaching tools to a new generation of teacher for the rest of their careers. The goal of in-service teacher education and training should not be simply the transmission of new knowledge either in the teacher's subject-matter domain or as *how to* training in the use of new technologies. The goal of both of these forms of teacher education should be, at the very least, the gaining/acquisition of those competencies which allow student teachers and in-service teachers to become and remain teachers who are reflective of the decisions that they make and who are able to interact with their ever-changing environments in a meaningful and responsive way. This means that they need to become competent life-long learners. Things are moving and changing too quickly, and life is becoming so complex, that courses cannot be made quickly enough and in great enough numbers to meet this need and many teachers will struggle to follow all of these courses.

Communities of Practice (CoPs) and weblogs can be the mindtools that can alleviate this problem. These are examples of good practice (we have presented two), but they are sparse and in the early stages of development and use. Teachers are still busy trying to obtain the necessary instrumental skills and schools still see information and communication technologies as productivity tools. The key is not initial education and continuing education at universities and teacher colleges. It is rather continuous (and ubiquitous) learning in communities of practice (including communities of interest and communities of expertise) and weblogs in and between schools, at teacher-training institutions, and in society in general. CoPs and blogs as mindtools can be the key needed to unlock a bright future.

References

Barnett, M. (2002, April). *Issues and trends concerning new technologies for teacher professional development: A review of the literature.* Paper presented at the annual meeting of the American Educational Research Association 2002, New Orleans, LA.

Blignaut, A. S. (1999). *The use of computer-based mindtools in teaching and learning.* University of Pretoria, Department of Didactics. Retrieved from http://hagar.up.ac.za/cie/med/modules/oro800_2000/resources/theory/spreadsheet.html

Boud, D. (1999). Situated academic development in professional work: using peer learning. *International Journal for Academic Development, 4,* 3–10.

Boulos, M., Maramba, I., & Wheeler, S. (2006). Wikis, blogs and podcasts: a new generation of Web-based tools for virtual collaborative clinical practice and education. *BMC Medical Education, 6*(41). Retrieved from http://www.biomedcentral.com/1472-6920/6/41

Boulos, M., & Wheeler, S. (2007). The emerging Web 2.0 social software: an enabling suite of sociable technologies in health and health care education. *Health Informatics and Libraries Journal, 24,* 2–23.

Brown, S. A. (2012). Seeing Web 2.0 in context: A study of academic perceptions. *Internet and Higher Education, 15,* 50–57.

Bullen, M., Morgan, T., Belfer, K., & Qayyum, A. (2008). *The digital learner at BCIT and implications for an e-strategy.* Paper presented at the 2008 Research Workshop of the European Distance Education Network (EDEN), "Researching and promoting access to education and training: The role of distance education and e-learning in technology-enhanced environments," Paris, France, October 20–22.

Cormode, G., & Krishnamurthy, B. (2008). Key differences between Web 1.0 and Web 2.0. *First Monday, 13*(6). Retrieved from: http://firstmonday.org/htbin/cgiwrap/bin/ojs/index.php/fm/article/viewArticle/2125/1972

CoVis. Communities of Practice. Retrieved November 13, 2002, from the World Wide Web: http://www.covis.nwu.edu/info/philosophy/communities-of-practice.html#definition

Crombag, H. F., Chang, T. M., Drift, K. D. J. M. van der, & Moonen, J. M. (1979). *Onderwijsmiddelen van de open universiteit: functies en kosten* [Educational materials for the open university: Functions and costs]. Ministry of Education and Sciences, The Hague.

Dede, C. (2009). Technologies that facilitate generating knowledge and possibly wisdom. *Educational Researcher, 38,* 260–263.

Dron, J., & Anderson, T. (2009). Lost in social space: Information retrieval issues in Web 1.5. *Journal of Digital Computing, 10*(2). Retrieved from http://journals.tdl.org/jodi/article/view/443/280

Ebner, M., Schiefner, M., & Nagler, W. (2008). Has the Net-Generation arrived at the university? – oder der Student von Heute, ein Digital Native? [or Contemporary student – a Digital Native?]. In S. Zauchner, P. Baumgartner, E. Blaschitz, &

A. Weissenbäck (Eds.), *Medien in der Wissenschaft [Media in science]* (Vol. 48) (pp. 113–123). Muenster, Germany: Waxmann Verlag.

Edelson, D. C., Pea, R. D., & Gomez, L. (1996). Constructivism in collaboratory. In B. G. Wilson (Ed.), *Constructivist learning environments: Case studies in instructional design* (pp. 151–164). Englewood Cliffs, NJ: Educational Technology.

Engelbart, D. C. (1962). *Augmenting human intellect: A conceptual framework*. Summary Report AFOSR-3233, Stanford Research Institute, Menlo Park, CA.

Gibson, J. J. (1977). The theory of affordances. In R. Shaw & J. Bransford (Eds.), *Perceiving, Acting and Knowing* (pp. 67–82). Hillsdale, NJ: Erlbaum.

Gibson, J. J. (1979). *The ecological approach to visual perception*. New York, NY: Houghton Mifflin.

Granberg, C. (2010). Social software for reflective dialogue: Questions about reflection and dialogue in student teachers' blogs. *Technology, Pedagogy, and Education, 19*, 345–360.

Greenhow, C., Robelia, B., & Hughes, J. E. (2009). Learning, teaching, and scholarship in a digital age: Web 2.0 and classroom research: What path should we take now? *Educational Researcher, 38*, 246–259.

Jonassen, D. (1999). Designing constructivist learning environments. In C. M. Reigeluth (Ed.), *Instructional-design theories and models: A new paradigm of instructional theory* (Vol. 2) (pp. 215–239). Mahwah, NJ: Lawrence Erlbaum Associates.

Jonassen, D. H. (2000). *Computers as mindtools for schools: Engaging critical thinking* (2nd ed.). Upper Saddle River, NJ: Prentice Hall.

Jonassen, D. H. (2006). *Modeling with technology: Mindtools for conceptual change* (3rd ed.). Upper Saddle River, NJ: Pearson Education.

Jonassen, D. H. & Carr, C. (2000). Mindtools: Affording multiple knowledge representations for learning. In S. Lajoie (Ed.), *Computers as cognitive tools Volume II: No more walls* (pp. 165–196). Lawrence Erlbaum: New Jersey.

Jonassen, D. H., & Reeves, T. C. (1996). Learning with technology: Using computers as cognitive tools. In D. H. Jonassen (Ed.), *Handbook of research for educational communications and technology* (pp. 693–719). New York: Macmillan.

Kennedy, G., Dalgarno, B., Gray, K., Judd, T., Waycott, J., Bennett, S., Maton, K., Krause, K.-L., Bishop, A., Chang, R., & Churchward, A. (2007). The net generation are not big users of Web 2.0 technologies: Preliminary findings. In R. J. Atkinson, C. McBeath, S. K. A. Soong, & C. Cheers (Eds.), *ICT: Providing choices for learners and learning. Proceedings of ASCILITE 2007 Conference.* Centre for Educational Development, Nanyang Technological University, Singapore. Retrieved from http://www.ascilite.org.au/conferences/singapore07/procs/kennedy.pdf

Killeavy, M., & Moloney, A. (2010). Reflection in a social space; Can blogging support reflective practice for beginning teachers? *Teaching and Teacher Education, 26*, 1070–1076.

Kim, W., Jeong, O.-K., & Lee, S.-W. (2010). On social Web sites. *Information Systems, 35*, 215–236.

Kirschner, P. A. (2002). Can we afford CSCL? Educational, social and technological affordances for learning. In P. Kirschner (Ed.), *Three worlds of CSCL: Can we support CSCL.* Inaugural address, Open University of the Netherlands.

Kirschner, P. A., Sweller, J., & Clark, R. E. (2006). Why minimal guidance during instruction does not work: An analysis of the failure of constructivist, discovery, problem-based, experiential, and inquiry-based teaching. *Educational Psychologist, 41*, 75–86.

Kirschner, P. A., & Wopereis, I. G. J. H. (2003). Mindtools for teacher communities: A European perspective. *Technology, Pedagogy and Education, 12, 107–126.*

Korthagen, F. A. J. (1999). Linking reflection and technical competence: The logbook as an instrument in teacher education. *European Journal of Teacher Education, 22,* 191–207.

Kvavik, R. (2005). Convenience, communications, and control: How students use technology. In D. Oblinger & J. Oblinger (Eds.), *Educating the Net Generation (Chapter 7)* [e-book]. Retrieved from http://www.educause.edu/educatingthenetgen/5989

Lave, J., & Wenger, E. (1991). *Situated learning: Legitimate peripheral participation.* Cambridge, UK: Cambridge University Press.

Lin, X., Hmelo, C., Kinzer, C. K., & Secules, T. J. (1999). Designing technology to support reflection. *Educational Technology, Research* & Development, 47(3), 43–62.

Luehmann, A. L. (2008). Using blogging in support of teacher professional identity development: A case study. *The Journal of the Learning Sciences, 17,* 287–337.

Margaryan, A., Littlejohn, A., & Vojt, G. (2011). Are digital natives a myth or reality? University students' use of digital technologies. *Computers and Education, 56*(2), 429–440.

McLoughlin, C., & Lee, M. J. W. (2008). The three p's of pedagogy for the networked society: Personalization, participation, and productivity. International *Journal of Teaching and Learning in Higher Education, 20,* 10–27.

Mills, K. A. (2010). A review of the "Digital Turn" in new literacy studies. *Review of Educational Research, 80,* 246–271.

Mishra, P., & Koehler, M. J. (2006). Technological pedagogical content knowledge: A framework for teacher knowledge. *Teachers College Record, 108,* 1017–1054.

Morris, R. D. (2011). Web 3.0: Implications for online learning. *TechTrends, 55*(1), 42–46.

O'Reilly, T. (2007). What is Web 2.0: Design patterns and business models for the next generation of software. *Communications* & *Strategies, 65,* 17–37.

O'Reilly, T., & Battelle, J. (2009). *Web squared: Web 2.0 five years on.* Retrieved from http://assets.en.oreilly.com/1/event/28/web2009_websquared-whitepaper.pdf

Oblinger, D., & Oblinger, J. (Eds.), (2005). *Educating the Net Generation* [e-book]. Retrieved July 31, 2009 from http://www.educause.edu/educatingthenetgen/5989

Pea, R. D. (1985). Beyond amplification: Using the computer to reorganize mental functioning. *Educational Psychologist, 20,* 167–182.

Prensky, M. (2001). Digital natives, digital immigrants. *On the Horizon (*NCB University Press, Vol. 9 No. 5, October 2001).

Ravenscroft, A. (2009). Social software, Web 2.0 and learning: Status and implications of an evolving paradigm. *British Journal of Educational Technology, 25,* 1–5.

Rosen, L. D. (2007). Me, MySpace, and I: Parenting the Net generation. New York: Palgrave Macmillan.

Rowlands, I., Nicholas, D., Williams, P., Huntington, P., Fieldhouse, M., Gunter, B., Withey, R., Jamali, H. R., Dobrowolski, T., & Tenopir, C. (2008). The Google generation: The information behaviour of the researcher of the future. *Aslib Proceedings: New Information Perspectives, 60,* 290–310.

Salomon, G. (1995). What does the design of effective CSCL require and how do we study its effects? In J. L. Schnase & E. L. Cunnius (Eds.), *Proceedings of CSCL '95: The first international conference on computer support for collaborative learning.* Mahwah, NJ: LEA.

Salomon, G., Perkins, D. N., & Globerson, T. (1991). Partners in cognition: Extending human intelligence with intelligent technologies. *Educational Researcher, 20*(3), 2–9.

Schaap, H., De Bruijn, E., Van der Schaaf, M. F., & Kirschner, P. A. (2009). Students' Personal Professional Theories in Competence-based Vocational Education; the Construction of Personal Knowledge through Internalisation and Socialisation. *Journal of Vocational Education and Training, 61*, 481–494.

Schlager, M. S., Fusco. J., Schank, P. (1999). Evolution of an online education community of practice. In K. A. Renninger & W. Shumar (Eds.), *Building virtual communities: Learning and change in cyberspace.* New York: Cambridge University Press.

Shoffner, M. (2009). The place of the personal: Exploring the affective domain through reflection in teacher preparation. *Teaching and Teacher Education, 25*, 783–789.

Sim, J. W. S., & Hew, K. F. (2010). The use of weblogs in higher education settings: A review of empirical research. *Educational Research Review, 5*, 151–163.

Tapscott, D. (1997). Growing up digital: The rise of the net generation. New York: McGraw-Hill.

Top, E., Yukselturk, E., & Inan, F. A. (2010). Reconsidering usage of blogging in preservice teacher education courses. *The Internet and Higher Education, 13*(4), 214–217.

Valtonen, T., Pontinen, S., Kukkonen, J., Dillon, P., Väisänen, P., & Hacklin, S. (2011). Confronting the technological pedagogical knowledge of Finnish Net Generation student teachers. *Technology, Pedagogy and Education, 20*, 3–18.

Veen, W., & Vrakking, B. (2006). *Homo Zappiens: Growing up in a digital age.* London, UK: Network Continuum Education.

Williams, P., & Rowlands, I. (2007). *Information behaviour of the researcher of the future: Work package II.* London, UK: University College London.

Williamson Shaffer, D. W. (2009). Toolsforthought: Reexamining thinking in the digital age. *Mind, Culture, and Activity, 13*, 283–300.

Wopereis, I. G. J. H., Sloep, P. B., & Poortman, S. H. (2010). Weblogs as instruments for reflection on action in teacher education. *Interactive Learning Environments, 18*, 245–261.

7 Virtual Gaming and Learning Environments as Experience-Tools for Learning Through Problem Solving

James M. Laffey, Matthew Schmidt, and Krista Galyen

Introduction to Virtual Experiential Learning: Our Focus and Perspective

The purpose of this chapter is to consider an extension of the mindtools paradigm to include the potential of three-dimensional virtual environments (3D VE). Virtualization of experience makes it possible to envision technology-based learning extending beyond augmenting cognition to also being social, embodied, and even playful.

It is a fool's errand to try to rigidly categorize educational technology. Technologies that were not designed for education can be used in teaching, and learning scenarios and educational technology can be applied in a variety of ways, suggesting that it is usage rather than design that defines educational technology. David Jonassen (1996, 2000) and other leaders in educational technology (Blumenfeld, Soloway, Marx, Krajcik, Guzdial, & Palincsar, 1991; Krajcik, Blumenfeld, Marx, Bass, Fredricks, & Soloway,1998; Pea, 1993; Perkins, 1993) used this insight to develop a framework for educational technology called mindtools. The mindtools framework allowed educators to move beyond seeing computers as simple tutors for computer-assisted instruction (CAI) to viewing the use of computers as part of a process to enable and augment desired cognitive practices. Spreadsheets, databases, semantic networks, and simple micro-worlds can be used for collecting/accessing, organizing, representing and analyzing data to address meaningful problems; these activities fit the constructivist model of instruction.

Another aspect of educational technology that makes categorization a fool's errand is that the rapid advancement of technology enables new possibilities and makes what was once esoteric now commonplace. In the 1980s and 1990s, when the mindtools framework was being developed, the usage paradigm was of a student sitting at a computer using a standalone application such as CAI or a spreadsheet. Today's paradigm includes a multiplicity of devices and interfaces from mobile handheld devices to immersive 3D VE, all of which may come with a high degree of connectivity to other people and resources around the world and which are likely part of a set of multitasking activities. While usage still defines educational technology, we must also address this onrush and the inevitability of new technological capabilities leading to new educational technology possibilities. Newer capabilities include higher bandwidth and nearly ubiquitous networking, which allows students to be connected with others and with resources in ways that are dramatically changing the computing experience. The new capabilities also include increased processing capabilities relentlessly delivered in smaller and cheaper forms. These processing advancements make it possible to envision virtualization of experience through creating computer models of real and realistic contexts that provide a sense of presence and immersion.

Given these new capabilities for virtualization, we see 3D VE as extending the role of technology in learning through problem solving (i.e. mindtools) by creating immersive contexts. Envisioning the potential of 3D VE for learning is especially important for our work and our view of further development in educational technology. Our interests are in distance learning (DL) which is increasingly an option for students, parents and schools. Based on a national survey of school district administrators, the Sloan Consortium estimates that over 1 million K-12 students were engaged in online learning in the 2007–2008 school year (Picciano & Seaman, 2008). This number represents a 47 percent increase from 2005–2006. Using data from the 2009–2010 school year the International Association for K-12 Online (Wicks, 2010) reports that 1.5 million K-12 students are learning online (another 50 percent increase). The range of students opting for online learning spans all communities and includes those seeking Advanced Placement (AP) courses, those with special needs, those choosing home schooling, those needing credit recovery and those who for some reason do not fit well in traditional school settings. The seventh annual *Keeping Pace Report* (Watson, Murin, Vashaw, Gemin, & Rapp 2010) notes that, in 2010, 48 states supported significant DL opportunities for students and estimated that about 50 percent of all school districts are operating or planning DL or blended programs. Our focus is primarily on K-12; however, in higher education the trends toward DL are even further along.

Hypothetically, technology-mediated DL can be superior to the one-teacher-to-many students model that is typical in American classrooms, but in practice this is rarely so. Distance learning is limited by having course management systems (CMS) as the primary technology and by having pedagogical stances based on providing access to content and oversight of course processes, such as ensuring that students contribute to discussion boards and upload work to drop boxes. Our vision of the future of DL includes a broad range of CMS, mobile and virtual learning technologies and multiple pedagogical approaches. We envision 3D VE and complementary pedagogical approaches as powerful tools in the DL repertoire to provide active and meaningful learning experiences that are social, embodied and playful.

Opportunities for Virtual Experiential Learning

Following a constructivist view of learning, the protagonists of mindtools believe that learning experiences needed to be both active and meaningful.

By placing both the learning objectives and the learning process in the context of a problem to be solved, the early visionaries provided the motivation for students to seek and use information to solve a problem, thus building their conceptualization of the problem space through both engaged practice and trial and error. Computers served as scaffolding to make trials more palatable (e.g. changing a few numbers in a spreadsheet versus starting your work all over again) and in representing data in ways that were easier to fit to the problem and stimuli for further thinking (e.g. seeing a trend line on a graph or seeing the results of a simulation). Clever educators completed the pedagogy of these mindtools opportunities by creating a social context for students, such as having them work in teams in the classroom or setting up opportunities to share and compare results and lessons learned (Blumenfeld et al., 1991; Brown, Collins, & Duguid, 1989; Collins, Brown, & Newman, 1989; Resnick, 1987; Scardamalia & Bereiter, 1993). These same educators also looked for ways to embody the problem space by having students collect data (such as collecting water samples or clocking the speeds of toy cars rolling down an incline) and create representations of the data. These *mindtools educators* integrated the social and embodied opportunities that could be managed in the classroom with the cognitive experiences of data which were augmented by the use of technology to create rich constructivist learning experiences. Unfortunately, while the conceptual framework for mindtools makes a great deal of sense, has many great examples, and is no doubt being used by many educators, the potential of educational technology to support constructivist teaching and learning is still largely untapped and its potential to support constructivist learning in DL is just beginning.

The extension that we propose to mindtools is to consider how a 3D VE can be used to support the social nature of learning, to provide embodiment in the learning process, and to do so in ways that are engaging and playful for learners. When we say playful we hearken back to Malone's theory (Malone, 1980) of intrinsically motivating instruction to include challenge, fantasy and curiosity. Fantasy does not simply mean fairytales, but rather draws from Piaget's explanation that play is a release from the demands of external reality. For example, failing at a task is not much of a problem when you can simply restart and try again. We believe this extension of mindtools to 3D VE is necessary to carry the mindtools paradigm forward for DL; this will also augment a teacher's capabilities to support mindtools in classrooms. We call this extension "experience-tools" because, while the use of tools is still envisioned as supporting cognitive functioning, the tools are also seen as supporting other aspects of the learning experience including social and embodiment.

The Social Nature of Learning

Since the beginning of technology-mediated DL, educators have been concerned about how it changes the social nature of learning and often diminishes social ability in learning (Laffey, Lin, & Lin, 2006). These concerns follow from the belief that social practices between teachers and students and among students (such as dialog, modeling, navigation) are fundamental to classroom learning and are constrained in typical DL. While there are many forms of 3D virtual gaming and learning systems, most systems offer support for key social practices and how they are experienced. In this brief review we will discuss support for conversations, identity and co-presence as key elements of the social nature of learning.

Most 3D virtual gaming and learning systems enable synchronous *conversations* among participants. While in the past the main conversation tool was typically text chat (due to bandwidth issues for supporting voice chat) modern gaming systems (e.g. Playstation 3 and Xbox 360) and virtual world platforms (e.g. Open Wonderland and Second Life) can offer immersive audio features including distance attenuation to give a sense of physical distance of speakers mimicking real world conversations. 3D VE also enable the control of one's avatar (e.g. making gestures for greetings or moving closer to a speaker to signify interest). While not common in current 3D VE, some investigators are testing the impacts of including facial expressions in 3D interaction (Fabri, Elouski, & Moore, 2007). Early research results show a benefit to engagement and satisfaction of gestures and facial expressions from avatars, especially as the length of communication grows (Rigas & Gazepidis, 2009; Theonas, Hobbs, & Rigas, 2008).

Students' identities – how they perceive themselves in a context or community – impact how and what they learn (Brown et al., 1989; Wenger, 1998). Wortham (2006) presented compelling case reports showing that social identity and academic learning co-develop and also showing how social identity is used by students to shape their experiences in the curriculum and by others to tacitly shape how the curriculum is provided. Wenger (1998) placed identity as a key function in his social theory of learning by showing that identity is both an outcome of learning practice (we see ourselves and are seen by others as having new forms of participation and contribution as we progress on a learning trajectory) and a part of how we practice (membership and accountability define how we participate and contribute in a community). Thus, how a learning environment supports the representation, sharing and development of identity shapes how it fosters social interaction and dialog. This point is analogous to Dourish's (2001) commentary on the importance of designing interactive systems to support social computing. In a typical CMS, identity representation, sharing and development is done by construction of, or interaction with, artifacts, such as creating profiles or the ways participants present themselves in their discussion forum posts. Thus, there is a growing body of thought and some research findings to support attending to student identity (and probably teacher identity as well) in a learning experience as an important driver of what is to be learned.

Identity representation in 3D games and learning environments can be much more direct and dynamic than in CMS. Avatars can be designed (selected) to mirror the identity the participant wishes to project. In a play on the classic parody of early Internet use involving two dogs at a computer, one says to the other: "On the Internet, nobody knows you're a dog." For a 3D VE parody, the script could read "On the Internet, you can be a dog." In Gee's (2007) classic book on what video games have to teach us about learning and literacy he describes taking the role of Bead Bead (a female elf) which provides him with an ability to play with alternative capabilities and perspectives and shows how taking on, and playing with, identities can shape both experience and learning. Gee's account also shows how power-ful the avatar representation can be in shaping the player's view of what he or she is doing and why. While the use of avatars for presenting one's self in 3D VE can be good or inappropriate, supporting or inhibiting learning, the plasticity and dynamism of avatars in 3D VE provides rich potential for identity representation, sharing and development.

Co-presence refers to a sense of being with others. In a shared 3D VE participants not only have a sense of being there, but can also experience *being there together*. In addition to the sense of representing one's identity that a participant can achieve via the use of an avatar, being engaged with the avatars of others provides a sense of sharing an experience with a teacher or with peers, which can in turn be cooperative or competitive. This sense of togetherness in a 3D VE may not be as multifaceted as a face-to-face personal encounter, but it offers the potential for dynamic channels of com-munication, joint availability of materials and the sense of occupying a shared space for DL. Findings (Schroeder, 2002, 2006) about the role of technology in supporting co-presence suggest that the more immersive the environment the more participants focus on navigation and manipulating objects and the less immersive the more the participants focus on verbal or textual communication. The key functions of a 3D VE that support co-presence are avatars, audio, visible co-activity, occupying the same space and a sense of distance or proximity to others. While video or audio confer-encing offers a robust communication channel, the advantage of 3D VE is to be able to act on materials and do things together with a teacher or peers.

Embodiment in Learning

Dourish (2001) characterizes embodiment as the common and familiar way we encounter physical and social reality in the real world; it means possess-ing and acting through a physical manifestation in the world. In a sense embodiment in learning means that the way our body is a part of an experi-ence with a phenomena impacts how we understand that phenomena and how we will be able to use those understandings. As Dourish notes we find the world meaningful based on how we act within it. The notion of embodi-ment has two manifestations in 3D VE. The first is that a 3D VE experience mediated by an avatar can be more richly embodied than simply reading a passage, looking at a picture or watching a video. For example, if a student is studying the operations of the human heart, we can contrast the experi-ence of watching a video with that of 3D VE engagement. The video includes watching a beating heart and being guided through, or using mouse clicks to interactively choose animated cut outs of the heart for closer inspection. The 3D VE experience includes having the beating heart present in the same space as your avatar and the need to guide your avatar as it walks around the heart for different views. The avatar can also touch parts of the heart for more detailed inspection as well as walking through the heart to get a sense of volume and other physical dimensions. The second manifestation is that 3D VE can take us and our avatars places that are not physically feasible. The example of walking around the human heart or visiting a nuclear plant and inspecting the fuel rods come to mind as examples. Winn (2003) provides another example and a detailed description of connecting the brain to body and to the environment in hard to do ways by describing how a 3D VE allows students to explore how water moves in a virtual Puget Sound.

3D VE such as the Puget Sound example have the potential to tightly couple a student to an interesting environment such that actions of the student impact the environment and actions of the environment impact the student. Winn argues that this coupling can lead to affective as well as cognitive affects and can be directly related to the amount that students learn (Winn, Windschitl, & Hedley 2001; Winn, Windschitl, Fruland, & Lee, 2002). There is still a lot to learn about embodied learning and the role of 3D VE representations as embodiment. Earlier we used the expression 'more richly embodied' to compare 3D VE with other modes of encountering subject matter so as to convey the increased potential for a sense of embodiment, but it is probably more precise to call these instances differently embodied. Even though there is much to learn about how 3D VE serves embodiment in learning, the core point of this section is that 3D VE provides a variety of affordances for how we perceive and relate to phenomena in learning contexts and that these affordances can be used to build meaning for students in new and powerful ways. Some of the key affordances are:

- presence as represented by your avatar in the learning space;
- location in the space;
- availability of and proximity to materials and others in the space;
- visibility of activity being undertaken; and
- status which can be indicated by completion of tasks or changes in the avatar.

Playfulness in Learning

Playfulness is a characterization that we often give to our observation of children as they explore their worlds and seek to gain competency and mastery through a trial and error approach. Playfulness often includes deep engagement with a subject, curiosity and discovery, willingness to take risks and delight or amusement even when a discovery means starting over in the exploration. In a document articulating a framework for moving games forward in education, Klopfer and colleagues (2009) identify five freedoms which are exercised in play: (a) freedom to fail, (b) freedom to experiment, (c) freedom to fashion identities, (d) freedom of effort, and (e) freedom of interpretation. These freedoms characterize a player who is playing on his/her own terms and accepts the game space, rules, constraints and goals defined by the games as worth attempting. It is almost a contradiction to think of harnessing these freedoms for educational purposes, but modern video games have the potential to do just that. Gee (2007) shows how playing videogames has the potential for players to see and act on phenomena in new ways and to develop a sense of agency and consequentiality that builds resources for future learning as well as teaching how to think in various domains. Barab and colleagues (Barab, Gresalfi, & Arici, 2009; Barab, Gresalfi, & Ingram-Goble, 2010) have developed a theory of transformational play based on their decade-long research and design of the game-like 3D VE Quest Atlantis. Transformational play includes the student taking on the role of a protagonist who must use subject matter knowledge to make decisions and take action during play, and that these actions and decisions transform the problem-based situation (e.g, solving an environmental problem of a declining fish population and thus saving a community dependent on fishing). In turn the student's understanding of the subject matter is transformed and so is the student's identity.

Transformational play is a compelling model and suggests that specific design strategies can optimize the potential of games and play to lead to desired learning outcomes. More generally, other game environments for learning take advantage of students' willingness and desire to play by placing them in contexts where their actions have consequences. To the extent that these environments support playfulness students become highly engaged and learn to act and use knowledge in the game contexts. It should be noted that merely creating a context and consequentiality in a 3D VE does not make a game a playful learning experience. Baker (2008) describes how Castronova and colleagues designed a game about the world of William Shakespeare which failed to be an engaging experience and proved to be no fun for the players. Game design for 3D VE is challenging and requires implementing the affordances of 3D VE in a way that provides a gripping experience for the players–learners.

Examples of Virtual Experiential Learning

There is a growing set of examples of 3D virtual experiential learning systems. In this section we will describe three examples as illustrations of the forms, variety and potential of virtual experiential learning as an extension of mindtools.

River City

River City is a multi-user 3D VE developed for middle-school students to learn skills of hypothesis formation and experimental design as well as content related to national standards and assessments in biology and epidemiology (Clarke, Dede, Ketelhut, & Nelson, 2006). The River City world is a historical town in the late 1800s, where residents are becoming ill. The students, typically working in teams using computers in classrooms or lab settings, take on the role of twenty-first century scientists who travel back in time and engage in problem-solving to help the town figure out what is causing the illness. After following a protocol to make observations at various seasonal time points, they then form a hypothesis about the cause of the illness and set up an experiment to test their hypotheses. After undertaking an experiment, such as cleaning up the trash, the students use their observations of the virtual results to evaluate their hypotheses and make recommendations.

A typical student experience in River City includes navigating around the visually rich and interesting world of River City looking for clues and undertaking tasks. Students are represented by their own avatars and often interact with system-based agents, also known as Non-Player Characters (NPC). NPCs populate the world and use pre-scripted dialogs to provide guidance, information and increase the sense of immersion. A common usage of River City would be to have students be members of a class-based team who may all be in the world at the same time and exploring independently and using text chat to communicate about their observations and ideas (Metcalf, Clarke, & Dede, 2009).

Research results show that students in River City gain greater knowledge and skills in scientific inquiry than through conventional instruction or equivalent learning experiences delivered via a board game. The findings indicate that students are deeply and actively engaged in the learning experience and are developing sophisticated problem-finding skills. When compared with a similar, paper-based curriculum that included laboratory experiences, students were more engaged in the immersive interface and learned as much or more (Clarke et al., 2006; Ketelhut, 2006; Ketelhut, Dede, Clarke, & Nelson, 2007). In particular, River City has been effective in motivating students who are usually unengaged and low-performing academically. In a review of immersive learning systems, Dede (2009) notes that many typically academically low performing students in River City do as well as typical high performers on performance tasks and he conjectures that the immersive environment allows them to step out of their real-world identities of poor performers and allows them to act as the successful scientist they are playing in the virtual world.

Quest Atlantis

Quest Atlantis is a set of multi-user 3D VE for knowledge quests and interactive tasks and is designed to implement learning through transformational play. As of 2009, 15 different virtual worlds aligned with academic subject matter have been developed and have been used by thousands of students around the world (Barab, Gresalfi, & Arici, 2009). One example is an aquatic habitat called Taiga Fishkill. Students are hired as environmental scientists to investigate a declining fish population and propose solutions. Before taking on the larger problem, students are given opportunities to build prerequisite knowledge and skills through tasks which are legitimate to their role as novice scientists. Throughout the quest students are encouraged to use knowledge to make decisions and are positioned as experts trying to help solve a problem. Being in a virtual world allows students to see the results of their decisions and builds the consequentiality which is emphasized in Transformational Play Theory (Barab, Gresalfi, & Ingram-Goble, 2009) and the coupling emphasized by Winn et al., (2002) as dynamic adaptation. As with River City, students typically work in teams using computers in classrooms or lab settings.

The innovative design work of Quest Atlantis includes the development of a custom interface between the student in his classroom and the world of Atlantis. Screenshots of this custom interface can be found in several publications including Gresalfi, Barab, Siyahhan, and Christensen (2009). The majority of the screen is filled with the 3D world, which can include multiple avatars controlled by different players. Another part of the screen shows the player's home page which includes messaging, links and information about quests. The typical virtual experience in Quest Atlantis is similar in many ways to River City in that students using avatars navigate a visually interesting virtual space and encounter NPCs. Also similar to River City is that the students are typically working in classroom teams with each member independently exploring the world and periodically using text chat to communicate. Aside from visual worlds and academic subject matter River City and Quest Atlantis differ in the way they implement story lines and structure the learning activities. In each case the storylines and learning activities are set in the context of problem solving, but, for example, Quest Atlantis uses a custom framework of missions and quests. Key to the success of both River City and Quest Atlantis is the consequentiality built into each environment. Barab and colleagues (Barab, Gresalfi, & Ingram-Goble, 2010) describe how this consequentiality plays out in a unit of Quest Atlantis:

> Much of the game play takes place as players click on nonplayer characters that have been scripted to respond in ways that are consistent with the game narrative and which change on the basis of previous player choices and in-game happenings. So, for example, if the player initiated a logging ban, logger characters in the game would become aggressive in their response to the player. As students complete various activities, their game characters also change in both appearance and functionality (i.e. their game characters can perform previously inaccessible behaviors).
>
> (Barab, Gresalfi, & Ingram-Goble, 2010, p. 528)

Research results from a study of the Taiga VE (Arici, 2009) show that students in Quest Atlantis scored equivalently on a standardized science test of water-quality concepts with control students who received their curriculum in traditional fashion directly from a teacher and a textbook. A post-test format showed that both groups showed significant learning gains. However, the Quest Atlantis group significantly outpaced the traditional group on other measures of interpreting data, defining core concepts and a transfer task. Additionally the Quest Atlantis group scored substantially higher on a delayed (8 weeks) post-test. Interestingly, another contrast between the groups showed that 97 percent of the traditional students reported that they did the tasks in order to get a good grade or because the teacher told them to. Whereas, only 36 percent of the Quest Atlantis students reported those reasons while 46 percent of the students reported they were doing the tasks because they wanted to. These findings of learning gains and high levels of engagement with Quest Atlantis have been repeated across numerous settings (Barab, Gresalfi, & Ingram-Goble, 2010; Barab, Dodge, Thomas, Jackson, & Tuzun, 2007).

iSocial

iSocial (Laffey, Schmidt, Stichter, Schmidt, Oprean, Herzog, & Babiuch, 2009; Laffey, Stichter, & Schmidt, 2010; Schmidt, Laffey, & Stichter, 2011; Schmidt, Laffey, Schmidt, Wang, & Stichter, 2012) is a multi-user 3D VE being developed for youth 11 to 14 with Autism Spectrum Disorders to help them build knowledge and skills to improve their social competence. Individuals identified with high functioning autism or Asperger's Syndrome are typically characterized as having a desire to be social (Myles & Simpson, 2002), but lacking sufficient social competencies to do so. Social competence instruction shows promise for remediation of these individuals' social deficits (Stichter, Randolph, Gage, & Schmidt, 2007); however, access to such instruction is limited, and providing access to high quality instruction that conforms closely to specialized approaches demonstrated to be successful can be challenging. Using virtual worlds built on top of Open Wonderland (see http://openwonderland.org/), an open-source toolkit licensed under the GNU General Public License (GPL) v2, the iSocial project seeks to adapt and implement in a 3D VE a clinic-based curriculum with demonstrated impact for improving social competence (Stichter, Herzog, Visovsky, Schmidt, Randolph, Schultz, & Gage, 2010).

The curriculum places students together in small groups of four to six students who are led by an expert instructor through a sequence of activities that are tightly scripted for pedagogical impact. The activities call for a variety of activity types: direct instruction from the instructor, monitoring of student behavior by the instructor, behavior management from the instructor by giving verbal feedback as well as tokens and strikes for student behavior; opportunities for students to express themselves verbally, in text, and with avatar gestures; group discussion; modeling of behavior by members of the group and by use of media; sharing and interpreting facial expressions and cues for recognizing emotions; and a large variety of opportunities to apply understandings and practice skills in settings that range from well structured to more naturalistic practice. The iSocial developers have translated these teaching and learning activities into human-computer interaction and human-to-human via computer interaction that are all mediated and enabled by the 3D VE. This model and implementation allows students from small and rural schools who may have only one or two students who need the curriculum to have access via DL to a proven curriculum and high quality instruction. The iSocial curriculum has five units of instruction implemented as 33 lessons of 45-minute duration.

Figure 7.1 helps illustrate what it is like to participate in iSocial by showing a scene from Unit 2 (Lost at Sea) where the students are learning and practicing how to identify and apply the role of speaker and listener in order to better share ideas. On the left is the ship where students undertake the lesson. On the right, students, Online Teacher and Helper gather in an area on the ship to discuss their roles for the upcoming activity. After having spent several lessons on the ship, students are told that the ship is sinking. Their mission during this lesson is to complete four tasks: (1) decide on which role each member will take, (2) go into the cargo hold and collectively decide on which eight (out of 15) items to take with them, (3) escape to the rescue boat where they will need to negotiate which part of the island they think it is best to go for their survival, and (4) arrive on the chosen part of the island. The lesson is designed to require discussion and negotiation among the students through activities that the online teacher facilitates to build students' social competence accessing targeted curricular-based skills.

iSocial has been developed for special needs learners and a specialized curriculum for developing social competence. Because of these requirements the iSocial developers have created a number of innovations to help shape and manage the experience of the users, support the students as active and social learners, and facilitate the teacher–student relationship. Some notable examples of innovations are:

(a) The Media Board is a whiteboard for displaying and interacting with multiple forms of media in the virtual world. The board includes a function that allows students to take pictures of themselves with a webcam, such as when displaying a particular facial expression, for sharing with the online teacher and peers. The student, online teacher and peers can then discuss the images and arrange them on a continuum so as to give feedback to the student.

(b) Pods, Spaces and Barriers have been developed as behavior management devices to aid the online teacher in managing individual and group behavior during lesson activities. These devices act like furniture to invite students to move to appropriate places and orientations and also can be locked to prevent students from disrupting activities.

(c) Live Images is a device for helping the online teacher manage and facilitate behavior. Before Live Images the online teacher could see avatar movements and listen to the student talk, but did not have any visual cues about physical presence. For example, a still avatar could mean that the student is cognitively engaged and is in the right place for the

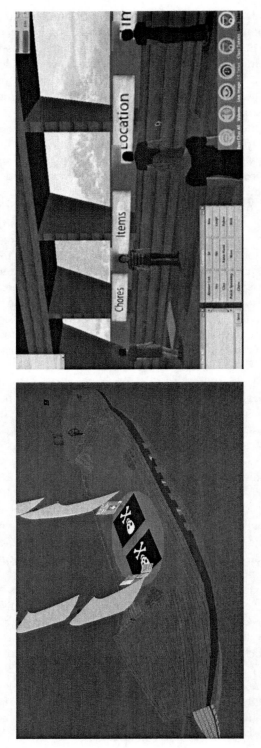

Figure 7.1 iSocial participation scenario.

activity (does not need to move) or that the student is no longer attending to the instruction. Live Images gives the instructor a snapshot of each student every 20 seconds so as to monitor physical behavior. Full video streaming would be too great a drain on network resources but every 20 seconds seems to be a good compromise between technology concerns and behavioral concerns.

The iSocial VE is still in development so it does not have a comparable track record for engagement and achievement as can be reported for River City and Quest Atlantis. However, field testing of units to date has shown that iSocial has fidelity with the successful face-to-face-based instructional program.

Coding of the online behaviors has shown that students in iSocial have equivalent levels to the face-to-face program of access to appropriate materials and teacher guidance, of undertaking similar processes and levels of activity and of receiving equivalent levels of behavior management such as the use of strikes, passes and warnings from the teacher. In addition similar levels of opportunities for and the exercise of verbal feedback were observed between the two instructional modes. Also, evidence from early trials indicates that students are engaged in appropriate learning activity during lessons and that they have positive impressions of learning from iSocial. The average rate of student *on-topic* responses was 1.57 per minute with an average rate *off-topic* of .12 responses per minute. These rates show that students are spending their time on task. On average, 81.1 percent of responses were judged to be correct responses indicating the students were acquiring the content but also indicating that the subject matter was not so scripted that every response was correct. Student ratings of the helpfulness of iSocial for their developing social competence averages 4.58 on a five-point scale. These early findings offer initial evidence that iSocial will be able to support and foster the social, cognitive and behavioral activity at a high and appropriate level, and provide promise for the ability of 3D VE to support DL for special needs learners.

Framework for Virtual Experiential Learning

This section hypothesizes about a framework for understanding the role of 3D VE as an experience-tool for learning through problem solving. We start with the assumption that students primarily think and learn through the experiences they have and the sense they make of them (Clark, 1993, 1997; Gee, 2004, 2008). Learning through the experience of solving ill-defined and ill-structured problems, quests, questions, cases or projects is an important pedagogical approach that is hard to manage and achieve in classrooms and even harder to manage and achieve in DL. The mindtools framework showed how computers can scaffold key cognitive processes of learning through problem solving. The promise of 3D VE is to support a fuller range of the student's experience, including the cognitive, social and embodied nature of acting and learning. 3D VE offers the potential to engage students in active resolution of authentic or at least engaging problems in a context with consequentiality (Barab, Gresalfi, & Ingram-Goble, 2010), and in turn this experience in the problem-solving process encourages ownership and membership in a way of thinking (community of people who solve those sorts of problems) and builds understanding of concepts and how to apply them in realistic contexts. Also, as part of this process, knowledge evolves and becomes more meaningful through social interaction and negotiation. To enable and support these forms of learning experiences, 3D VE offers the potential to design worlds of content and context, to reify structures that support learning and social interaction and to provide just in time supports and functions that cohere with learning activity rather than interrupt it.

Figure 7.2 uses a theory-of-change format to illustrate a framework for how VE can act as a mechanism for learning from problem solving. The example systems provided in the preceding section demonstrate that VE can impact personal, social and academic outcomes of learning through experience in problem solving. River City and Quest Atlantis provide a large base of usage across classrooms and compelling evidence that high quality VE deeply engages students and fosters academic outcomes. These outcomes, as noted in the examples, go beyond simple test results but also show promise for application of knowledge, transfer of knowledge and retention of knowledge. The iSocial example shows a different model for 3D VE instruction and shows promise for engagement and high levels of on task and appropriate learning activity for special needs students learning at a distance.

The mindtools movement showed the power of using computers to shape and support cognitive processes in problem solving in support of learning. The integration of 3D VE and gaming has promise for an extension of the mindtools movement to shaping and supporting a fuller set of the attributes of experience. We see the technology and art of virtualization and the knowledge bases of motivation and pedagogy as conditions that need to be

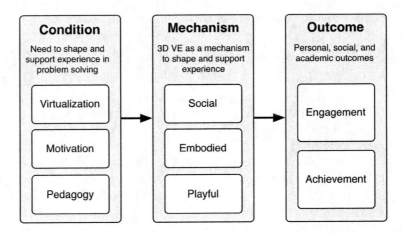

Figure 7.2 Theory of change format for showing an hypothetical view of the key components and mechanisms of VE for learning in problem solving.

accounted for and can be utilized. The technologies of virtualization are high speed networks, powerful processing engines in computers, development environments such as Open Wonderland and ActiveWorlds and advanced input technology (e.g. real world sensors). The art of virtualization is in envisioning worlds and in-world behaviors of individuals and social units, as well as the modeling of these visions to balance the visual and perceptible with the state of the networking and processing capability. When the art and technology come together, elaborate and sophisticated contexts for learning experiences can be developed, as illustrated by River City and Quest Atlantis. By context we mean the space, such as the River City or Taiga, where the learning is situated. The broad potential and flexibility of designing these contexts means that they can hold both content and structure for learning. Content includes the knowledgebase that the students will discover as they work to resolve the problem and the methods of problem solving they will learn and practice during their work. By structure we mean the strategies and pedagogy reified in the environment, such as having the nature of the quest emerge for students as they inspect their environment and interact with NPCs.

The theory of transformational play being developed by Barab and colleagues provides a rich and powerful way of integrating the motivational aspects of gaming with the transformational intentions of a pedagogical framework. In his chapter on "Learning and Games," Gee (2008) provides a Situated Learning Matrix with similar intentions, but with less of a focus on academic learning. Gee says:

> Why do I call this a situated learning matrix? Because content is rooted in experiences a person is having as part and parcel of taking on a specific identity (in terms of goals and norms stemming from a social group, like SWAT team members). Learning is situated in experience, but goal-driven, identity-focused experience.
>
> Learning in video games—learning in terms of the Situated Learning Matrix—is not "anything goes," "just turn the learners loose to do their own thing." There is a good deal of guidance in games: guidance from the game design itself, from the NPCs and the environment, from information given "just in time" and "on demand," from other players in and out of the game, and from the resources of communities of practice built up around the game.
>
> (Gee, 2008, p. 26)

Figure 7.2 also shows social, embodied and playful as key mechanisms for how VE impacts the learning experience. We reviewed these mechanisms earlier in the section on opportunities for virtual experiential learning. The social nature of a virtual experience can be shaped and supported by the functionality available for conversations. The choice and ways of implementing text, audio, and gestures support different forms of communication and a different experience of the other members in conversation. How we choose or are able to communicate also influences what we may try to communicate and how we express ourselves. For example, if the youth with Autism Spectrum Disorders in iSocial were limited to text chat they would struggle to communicate and would have less of a sense of participating and learning about typical social interactions. Choices and ways of implementing avatars will impact both the sense of identity and the sense of co-presence which are enabled in 3D VE.

An embodied approach to learning supports building understanding of the knowledge and skills of a domain by mapping physical interaction with cognitive processing. This view argues that cognition does not operate solely as computations in the brain, but rather by taking the state of the learner and the environment as conditions of learning, having the learner operate in these conditions and seeing transformations in understanding and behavior as outcomes. Creating, supporting and managing learning comes from the interaction and mutual adaptation of the two complex systems (student and environment) (Winn, 2003; Winn, Windschitl, Fruland, & Lee, 2002; Winn, Windschitl, & Hedley, 2001). 3D VE offers near limitless potential to build environments (including content and structures) to enable managed and transformative adaptation of the learner to the environment and of the environment to the learner. There is still much to be learned about how embodiment works as a mechanism in learning and in particular embodiment through a computer interface. For example, Barab et al. (2007) suggest possible distinctions between narrative and perceptual embodiment. However Glenberg and colleagues (Glenberg et al., 2009; Glenberg & Gallese, 2011) through a series of research and development efforts have shown that including manipulation of toys (related to the reading texts) in reading comprehension instruction impacts learning and that when the manipulation of toys was embedded on a computer screen the children benefitted as much as in the physical manipulation. This coupling of the learner in both physical and cognitive ways to the environment in a context of consequentiality is a core mechanism for how 3D VE shapes and support learning and experience.

Numerous models exist for envisioning playful systems. Malone (1980) integrated existing theories of intrinsic motivation with studies of computer game playing to develop a new framework for explaining and potentially developing intrinsic motivation and fun in learning. The framework included three categories: (a) challenge, (b) fantasy, and (c) curiosity. It should be noted that computer games were considerably different in the late 1970s from what they are today especially as relates to their social nature and social opportunities and in how action and cognition can be embodied. Gee (2003) studied modern video game play and noted the approaches to game design which build the learning necessary to advance and succeed in the games. He identifies 36 principles of how games support learning. Principle #6 is called the Psychosocial Moratorium Principle and refers to having learners be able to take risks in a space where real-world consequences are lowered. One function of gaming that supports this principle is allowing gamers to save game states so no matter how bad a next move may turn out they can easily return to the former state and try a new approach. This principle and others align well with the five freedoms that Klopfer, Osterweil and Salen (2009) characterized as important functions of game play.

Another critical insight from Gee's work that applies to making learning environments playful is in his description of how gaming environments provide training modules for novice game players. He states that training modules only give the player enough information and skill to play and learn from the subsequent game episode, and that each episode gets more difficult but in a measured way so that the players are always both playing and learning. Barab et al., (2007) confirm the power of integrating learning and playing. As part of their design research process they noticed that students were not using scientific formalisms to the extent hoped for within their Quest Atlantis activity. In response the unit was redesigned to use gaming strategies to better integrate formalisms with the story narrative. For example, the new story required the students to earn an authorization card in order to proceed. In order to gain the card the students needed to work with the resident technician, an NPC. The technician modeled the processes to be undertaken and used the authentic language of the formalisms. The tighter integration of the domain formalisms with the play activity led to greater usage of scientific formalisms in the quest and indicates the potential of design decisions in the development of playful environments that serve learning objectives.

Conclusions

The purpose of this chapter has been to consider implications for extending the mindtools framework based on reflecting upon a growing body of design experience and research with 3D VE. The new and advancing technologies of 3D VE and the lessons that can be drawn from 3D video-game playing attune us to the potential of learning environments which shape and support a broad range of attributes of experience beyond the current cognitive scaffolding of mindtools. Substantial progress has been made in bringing visions of virtual experiential learning into practice by researchers such as the teams led by Sasha Barab and Chris Dede. New formalisms are being developed, such as the Theory of Transformational Play, which will assist designers and researchers as they take on new and continuing work. The hypothetical view of the key components and mechanisms of VE for learning in problem solving offered in this chapter is an effort to share the experience of our team's work and lessons learned as we envisioned experience tools for youth with special needs and in need of DL (Laffey, Gaylen & Babiuch, 2012). While there is much to be learned to harness the potential of 3D VE and gaming approaches for learning, it is clear that these tools and methods provide educators with new ways to foster learning through problem solving which is social, embodied and playful.

Acknowledgments

The research reported here was supported by the Institute of Education Sciences, U.S. Department of Education, through Grant R324A090197 to the University of Missouri. The opinions expressed are those of the authors and do not represent views of the Institute or the U.S. Department of Education.

References

Arici, A. (2009). *Meeting kids at their own game: A comparison of learning and engagement in traditional and 3D MUVE educational-gaming* contexts. Unpublished doctoral dissertation, Indiana University, Bloomington.

Baker, C. (2008, March 24). Trying to Design a Truly Entertaining Game Can Defeat Even a Certified Genius. Wired, 16(4). Retrieved from http://www.wired.com/gaming/gamingreviews/magazine/16-04/pl_games.

Barab, S.A., Gresalfi, M.S., & Ingram-Goble, A. (2010). Transformational play: Using games to position person, content, and context. *Educational Researcher, 39*(7), 525–536.

Barab, S. A., Gresalfi, M. S., & Arici, A. (2009). Why educators should care about games. *Educational Leadership, 67*(1), 76–80.

Barab, S. A., Dodge, T., Ingram-Goble, A., Pettyjohn, P., Peppler, K., Volk, C., & Solomou, M. (2010). Pedagogical dramas and transformational play: Narratively rich games for learning. *Mind, Culture, and Activity, 17*(3), 235–264.

Barab, S. A., Dodge, T., Thomas, M., Jackson, C., & Tuzun, H. (2007). Our designs and the social agendas they carry. *Journal of the Learning Sciences, 16*(2), 263–305.

Blumenfeld, P. C., Soloway, E., Marx, R. W., Krajcik, J. S., Guzdial, M., & Palincsar, A. (1991). Motivating project-based learning: Sustaining the doing, supporting the learning. *Educational Psychologist, 26*(3 & 4), 369–398.

Brown, J. S., Collins, A., & Duguid, P. (1989). Situated cognition and the culture of learning. *Educational Researcher, 18*(1), 32–42.

Clark, A. (1993). *Associative engines: Connectionism, concepts and Representational change.* Cambridge, MA: MIT Press.

Clark, A. (1997). *Being there: Putting brain, body and world together again.* Cambridge, MA: MIT Press.

Clarke, J., Dede, C., Ketelhut, D. J., & Nelson, B. (2006). A design-based research strategy to promote scalability for educational innovations. *Educational Technology, 46*(3), 27–36.

Collins, A., Brown, J. S., & Newman, S. E. (1989). Cognitive apprenticeship: Teaching the crafts of reading, writing, and mathematics. In L. B. Resnick (Ed.), *Knowing, learning, and instruction: Essays in honor of Robert Glasser* (pp. 453–494). Hillsdale, NJ: Lawrence Erlbaum & Associates, Inc.

Dede, C. (2009). Immersive interfaces for engagement and learning. *Science, 323*(5910), 66–69.

Dourish, P. (2001). *Where the action is: The foundations of embodied interaction.* Cambridge, MA: MIT Press.

Fabri M., Elzouki, S. Y. A., & Moore, D. (2007). Emotionally expressive avatars for chatting, learning and therapeutic intervention. In J. A. Jacko (Ed.), *Lecture Notes and Computer Science: Vol. 4552* (pp. 275–285). Heidelberg: Springer-Verlag.

Gee, J. P. (2003). *What Video Games Have to Teach Us About Learning and Literacy.* New York: Palgrave Macmillan.

Gee, J. P. (2004). *Situated language and learning: A critique of traditional schooling.* London: Routledge.

Gee, J. P. (2008). Learning and Games. In K. Salen (Ed.), *The ecology of games: Connecting youth, games, and learning* (pp. 21–40). Cambridge, MA: The MIT Press.

Glenberg, A. M., Webster, B. J., Mouilso, E., Havas, D. A., & Lindeman, L. M. (2009). Gender, emotion, and the embodiment of language comprehension. *Emotion Review*, *1*(2), 151–161.

Glenberg, A. M., & Gallese, V. (2012). Action-based language: A theory of language acquisition, comprehension, and production. *Cortex*, *48*(7), 905–922.

Gresalfi, M., Barab, S., Siyahhan, S., & Christensen, T. (2009). Virtual worlds, conceptual understanding, and me: designing for consequential engagement. *On the Horizon*, *17*(1), 21–34.

Jonassen, D. H. (1996). *Computers in the classroom: Mindtools for critical thinking*. Englewood Cliffs, NJ: Merrill.

Jonassen, D. H. (2000). *Mindtools for engaging critical thinking in the classroom* (2nd ed.). Columbus, OH: Prentice-Hall.

Ketelhut, D. J. (2006). The impact of student self-efficacy on scientific inquiry skills: An exploratory investigation in River City, a multi-user virtual environment. *Journal of Science Education and Technology*, *16*(1), 99–111.

Ketelhut, D. J., Dede, C., Clarke, J., & Nelson, B. (2007). Studying situated learning in a multi-user virtual environment. In E. Baker, J. Dickieson, W. Wulfeck & H. O'Neil (Eds.), *Assessment of problem solving using simulations* (pp. 37–58). Maywah, NJ: Lawrence Erlbaum Associates.

Klopfer, E., Osterweil, S., & Salen, K. (2009). Moving learning games forward: Obstacles, opportunities & openness. Retrieved from http://education.mit.edu/papers/MovingLearningGames Forward_EdArcade.pdf

Krajcik, J. S., Blumenfeld, P. C., Marx, R. W., Bass, K. M., Fredricks, J., & Soloway, E. (1998). Inquiry in project-based science classrooms: Initial attempts by middle school students. *The Journal of the Learning Sciences*, *7*(3–4), 313–350.

Laffey, J., Lin, G., & Lin, Y. (2006). Assessing social ability in online learning environments. *Journal of Interactive Learning Research*, *17*(2), 166–173.

Laffey, J., Galyen, K., & Babiuch, R. (2012, June). *Guidance in game-based virtual learning: Lessons from developing iSocial*. Paper presented at Immersive Education Initiative Summit, Boston, Massachusetts, June, 2012.

Laffey, J., Schmidt, M., Stichter, J., Schmidt, C., Oprean, D., Herzog, M., & Babiuch, R. (2009). Designing for social interaction and social competence in a 3D-VLE. In D. Russell (Ed.), *Cases on collaboration in virtual learning environments: Processes and interactions.* (pp. 154–169). Hershey, PA: Information Science Reference.

Laffey, J., Stichter, J., & Schmidt, M. (2010). Social orthotics for youth with ASD to learn in a collaborative 3D VLE. In S. Seok, B. Dacosta, & E. L. Meyen (Eds.), *Handbook of research on human cognition and assistive technology: Design, accessibility and transdisciplinary perspectives* (pp. 76–95). New York: Idea Group.

Malone, T. W. (1980). What makes things fun to learn? A study of intrinsically motivating computer games. Technical report no. CIS-7 (SSL-80-11) Palo Alto, CA: Xerox PARC.

Metcalf, S. J., Clarke, J., & Dede, C. (2009). *Virtual worlds for education: River city and EcoMUVE*. Paper presented at the Media in Transition International Conference, MIT, April 24–26, Cambridge, MA.

Myles, B.S., & Simpson, R.L. (2002). Asperger syndrome: An overview of characteristics. *Focus on Autism and other Developmental Disabilities*, *17*(3), 132–137.

Pea, R. D. (1993). Learning scientific concepts through material and social activities: Conversational analysis meets conceptual change. *Educational Psychologist, 28*(3), 265–277.

Perkins, D. N. (1993). Person-plus: A distributed view of thinking and learning. In G. Salomon (Ed.), *Distributed cognitions: Psychological and educational considerations* (pp. 88–110). Cambridge, MA: Cambridge University Press.

Picciano, A. G., & Seaman J. (2009). *K-12 online learning: A 2008 Follow-up of the Survey of U.S. School District Administrators.* Retrieved from http://sloanconsortium.org/publications/survey/k-12online2008

Resnick, L. B. (1987). Learning in school and out. *Educational Researcher, 16*(9), 13–20.

Rigas, D., & Gazepidis, N. (2009). The role of facial expressions and body gestures in avatars for e-commerce interfaces. In I. Maurtua (Ed.), *Human-Computer Interaction* (pp. 223–243). Rijeka, Croatia: InTech.

Scardamalia, M., & Bereiter, C. (1994). Computer support for knowledge-building communities. *The Journal of the Learning Sciences, 3,* 265–283.

Schroeder, R. (2002). Copresence and interaction in virtual environments: An overview of the range of issues. *Presence 2002: Fifth International Workshop,* 274–295.

Schroeder, R. (2006). Being there together and the future of connected presence. *Presence: Teleoperators and Virtual Environments, 15*(4), 438–454.

Schmidt, M., Laffey, J., & Stichter, J. (2011). Virtual social competence instruction for individuals with autism spectrum disorders: Beyond the single-user experience. *Proceedings of CSCL 2011*, Hong Kong, China.

Schmidt, M., Laffey, J., Schmidt, C., Wang, X., & Stichter, J. (2012). Developing methods for understanding social behavior in a 3D virtual learning environment, *Computers in Human Behavior, 28*(2), 405–413.

Stichter, J. P., Randolph, J., Gage, N. & Schmidt, C. (2007). A review of recommended practices in effective social competency programs for students with ASD. *Exceptionality, 15*(4), 219–232.

Stichter, J. P., Herzog, M. J., Visovsky, K., Schmidt, C., Randolph, J., Schultz, T., & Gage, N. (2010). Social competence intervention for youth with Aspergers Syndrome and high functioning autism: An initial investigation. *Journal of Autism and Developmental Disorders, 40,* 1067–1079.

Theonas, G., Hobbs, D., & Rigas, D. (2008). Employing virtual lecturers' facial expressions in virtual educational environments. *International Journal of Virtual Reality, 7*(1), 31–44.

Watson, J., Murin, A., Vashaw, L., Gemin, B., & Rapp, C. (2010). *Keeping pace with K-12 online learning: An annual review of policy and practice.* Evergreen Education Group. Retrieved from http://kpk12.com/reports/

Wenger, E. (1998). *Communities of practice: Learning, meaning, and identity.* Cambridge, MA: Cambridge University Press.

Wicks, M. (2010). *A national primer on K-12 online learning.* International Association for K-12 Online. Retrieved from http://www.inacol.org/research/bookstore/detail.php?id=22

Winn, W. D. (2003). Learning in artificial environments: Embodiment, embeddedness and dynamic adaptation. *Technology, Instruction, Cognition and Learning, 1,* 87–114.

Winn, W. D., Windschitl, M., & Hedley, N.R. (2001, April). *Learning science in an immersive virtual environment.* Presented at American Educational Research Association (AERA) Annual Meeting 2001, Seattle, WA, April, 2001.

Winn, W. D., Windschitl, M., Fruland, R., & Lee, Y.L. (2002). When does immersion in a virtual environment help students construct understanding? In *Proceedings of International Conference of the Learning Societies* (pp. 497–503). Seattle, WA: ICLS.

Wortham, S. (2006). *Learning identity: The joint emergence of social identification and academic learning.* New York: Cambridge University Press.

8 Comprehension Using the Strategic Organization of Text Aided by a Web-Based Intelligent Tutoring System

A Text and Computer-Based Mindtool

Kausalai (Kay) Wijekumar and
Bonnie J. F. Meyer

Introduction

Reading comprehension is an essential component of most human activities. Schools are particularly concerned about content area reading comprehension. State and national assessments of fourth, eighth, and eleventh graders' reading comprehension has shown more than a third of students not understanding at a basic level (NAEP, 2007). Lacking this essential skill affects student performance in all their academic courses and further contributes to life-long challenges in decision making and problem solving.

Comprehension requires the learner to build a coherent mental representation of the text. This relies on the readers' ability to select important ideas and encode them. It also requires them to build a hierarchical organization of the text. Skills that contribute to this will include the ability to read the text, understand the vocabulary, build a cohesive and hierarchically organized representation of the text to incorporate with their prior knowledge, and create associations and pathways to the memory store.

The structure strategy is the only comprehension approach that has focused exclusively on this process. For over 40 years it has consistently shown statistically significant improvements in reading comprehension with all age groups. We present the rationale for describing the structure strategy as a mindtool, followed by the design of a web-based intelligent tutoring system to deliver the structure strategy and finally present accumulating evidence of the efficacy of the structure strategy as well as the intelligent tutoring system to deliver the approach.

The Structure Strategy as a Mindtool

The focus of mindtools has been on engaging students in meaningful thinking by effectively seeking and organizing information, creating effective schemas, and applying their knowledge to solve problems. The structure strategy can be described as the ultimate mindtool initially conceptualized as a method to comprehend expository text. The power of the structure strategy does not end with text but is only the beginning. If one were to look at the basic formulation of the structure strategy it serves as the foundation to seek, organize, and apply text-based information. Further, it serves as an approach to monitor one's own cognition (metacognition) and a framework for solving problems. Each component of the structure strategy is described next using a mindtools lens.

The Structure Strategy

The structure strategy is organized into three basic steps. The first step is to effectively seek information by finding the most important ideas in the text. Identifying the text structure used by the author to organize the passage allows the reader to distil the most important ideas in the passage. Text structure is identified by finding the words in the text that signal its strategic organization. For example, when an author describes the cause of gas prices and the resulting effects on products in the marketplace, the reader should notice that this passage is organized using a cause-and-effect text structure.

The second step of the structure strategy is to select important top-level ideas in the passage and abstracting or chunking these ideas using the strategic main idea pattern. Each text structure uses a specific hierarchical main idea pattern. In Figure 8.1, the top-level ideas are about the causes and effects of the gas prices. The main idea pattern for the cause and effect structure is: *the cause is ____ and the effect is _____.* The secondary ideas are

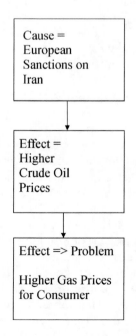

Figure 8.1 Cause-and-effect passage example with hierarchical main idea.

related to solving the problems caused by the high gas prices by increasing the drilling for oil. The main idea pattern for each structure serves as a foundation for building a carefully linked set of ideas. The written version is the external representation that also helps construct a mental representation of the text.

The last step of the structure strategy is connecting the ideas in a meaningful manner and creating a hierarchical mental representation of the full text. This approach is similar to chunking described in expertise literature (Chi, Feltovich, & Glaser, 1981). Strategically linking the highest level ideas in a cause-and-effect pattern allows the reader to chunk the ideas and create a top-level structure from which further links are created to subordinate ideas in the text. This type of organization allows the reader to efficiently focus their attention to the top nodes of their knowledge tree and link these to the branches and leaves containing ideas that support the main ideas. This allows for a more organized mental representation that also aids in recall and flexibility of use.

Justification for Describing the Structure Strategy as a Mindtool

The focus of mindtools is to create learning environments that allow the learner to create representations of data (through tools such as databases, spreadsheets, concept maps, and modeling software), understand the relationships between concepts in the problem-solving environment, and build abstracted mental representations and schema that allow flexible recall and application of the knowledge. A constructive learner processes information in an intentional and meaningful manner, integrates information with prior knowledge, and creates flexible and easily accessible mental representations (Jonassen, 1996). Chunked and correctly organized information is linked to expertise and results in efficient and highly-effective problem-solving skills (Wijekumar & Jonassen, 2007).

As students learn the structure strategy they can learn causes and effects, problems and solutions, and comparisons of alternative solutions. They can also trace the antecedents to any problem (usually the cause of the problem) and analyze alternative solutions using a structured format. For example, they can compare the solution alternatives on three or four characteristics or factors. These types of strategies are more powerful than the listing approach that most students use. In studies with both middle grade and high school students, Meyer, Brandt, and Bluth (1980) found that most recall text by loosely listing whatever ideas pop into their mind as they write. Meyer (2003) reported that over 70 percent of fifth graders completely missed the solution part of a newspaper article organized using the problem-and-solution text structure. Unless students understand how text structure is used, their recall lacks any hierarchical organization and their mental representations follow that same list-like pattern. This approach, resulting in loosely organized lists of ideas, is an inefficient and ineffective organization for their memory of text and lacks utility.

Mindtools are also designed to engender metacognition and monitoring of problem solving. This is one of the hardest parts of the learning environment for novices. They are unable to reflect on what they know and how well they know it. They are also uncertain about where and when to apply the different problem-solving approaches and usually attempt many different approaches with little thought to planning and imposing any structure to the problem at hand. The loosely organized listing structure described in the previous paragraph further lacks any systematic framework for monitoring understanding, an essential skill in metacognition, other than simply asking oneself: "What else do I remember (to add to my disjointed list)?"

A structure strategy based organization-to-lesson content (whether acquired via text or other medium) can serve as an effective organizing framework. The framework allows the learner to focus their attention to the most important factors, abstract the ideas in a strategic manner, and use their abstracted knowledge flexibly when needed. It also allows the learner to monitor their understanding by using the text structure to make connections to ideas that otherwise may have not been incorporated into their memory. For example, when the learner organizes their memory using the problem-and-solution text structure, it will focus their attention on identifying the problem and the possible solutions. Further, it links that knowledge to the causes of the problem and even provides a framework for comparing the solution alternatives depicted in Figure 8.1. In this situation the text structure can serve as a comprehension-monitoring tool. The structure strategy also can speed up the chunking and organizing of ideas in a hierarchical manner more similar to those of experts.

Examples of the Use of Structure Strategy in the Science Classroom

Teachers in two school districts actively using the structure strategy have recently instituted two approaches into their biology, physics, and chemistry classrooms. The first approach requires students to use a structure strategy framework for organizing their note-taking. Students take notes while reading their textbook and also while listening to lectures or conducting laboratory observations. Students focus their attention to problems and solutions, comparing alternative solutions based on specific criteria, and also noting possible causes to the effects manifested in the laboratory activity.

This method was introduced to the curriculum after the structure strategy team conducting a large scale efficacy study observed that the AP Biology textbook was poorly organized and teachers noted that most students were not able to read and understand the textbook content. Two teachers also reported that they had created summaries of each chapter to help the students' comprehend the unwieldy text. Focusing students' attention on creating tables to compare the different forms respiration and species allowed the students to extract the most important ideas in the text.

The second approach was to write the laboratory reports using the structure strategy. Again, these reports now explicitly asked the student to note problems and solutions, causes of the problems, and comparisons of solution alternatives. The conclusions drawn from the laboratory activities also required justifications using some form of text structure based organization, such as explanation (a variation of the cause and effect structure; Meyer, 1975; 1985).

Instruction on the Structure Strategy

The structure strategy was designed in the early 1970s by Bonnie Meyer and was delivered to students of all ages by trained personnel. Five text structures (comparison, problem and solution, cause and effect, sequence, and description) were presented to learners with example passages. Each passage was organized using one or more of the text structures and contained signaling words to clue the reader about which text structure was used to organize the passage. Throughout the last 40 years, there have been variations to the delivery of the structure strategy training to learners in the form of the number of text structures presented, sequencing of the text structures presented, and medium of presentation. The 1970s to the 1990s were dominated by paper and pencil presentations delivered by trained personnel to middle-grade students to older adults (e.g. Meyer & Poon, 2001; Meyer, Young, & Bartlett, 1989). During the late 1990s the shift was made to use the WWW as a tool to present the lesson contents to fifth-grade learners (Meyer, Middlemiss, Theodorou, Brezinski, McDougall, & Bartlett 2002). This method used retired teachers and professionals as tutors who read responses transmitted to them by the website and gave students feedback on their usage of the structure strategy. By the year 2002 the static web page presentation was becoming outdated and had other problems like a lack of immediate feedback to the learner. Training a large number of tutors was also a daunting task.

The idea of a web-based intelligent tutoring system to deliver the structure strategy (ITSS) to a wide audience was conceived in 2002 and proceeded to full design and development by 2003 (funded by the U.S. Department of Education, Institute of Education Sciences, Meyer, Wijekumar, Middlemiss, & vanHorn 2003–2007). The design of ITSS focused on four themes – effective multimedia use (Mayer, 2001), metacognition (Aleven & Koedinger, 2002), memory, and motivation.

Multimedia Use in ITSS

With the advances in multimedia capabilities comes the responsibility of differentiating the gimmicks from the tools that can facilitate active learning. ITSS was designed by carefully separating the wheat from the chaff and focusing on the best tools to show children in grades four through eight how experts use the structure strategy to read and comprehend text. We facilitate mindful learning by concentrating on modeling best practices, allowing the learner to practice the tasks, providing immediate assessment and feedback, and scaffolding the learning by varying the complexity of the readings as well as breaking up the tasks into meaningful units (e.g. finding signaling words, writing a main idea, and writing a full recall).

Multimedia use was limited to creating the correct tone and setting (Mayer, 2001) for a student to read from a book helped by an animated pedagogical agent playing the part of a teacher named IT (Intelligent Tutor). All the modeled segments were created by in-service and retired teachers who assisted in developing the lessons by thinking aloud during their use of the structure strategy.

Figure 8.2 shows the book-like interface without any pictures or peripherally related images. All the texts and instructions were narrated by a teenage male whose voice was preferred by almost all participants in an initial pilot study. The use of real human voice to narrate the contents fosters social agency within multimedia learning environments (Atkinson, Mayer, & Merrill, 2005).

Student behavior patterns were noted from the previous research and also from other research on engagement and gaming in multimedia learning environments. Based on that research, students were not allowed to transition to the next page of the lesson until IT finished narrating the page's contents. Additionally, the numbers of tries for each activity varied from lesson to lesson so that students did not take advantage of the expected help

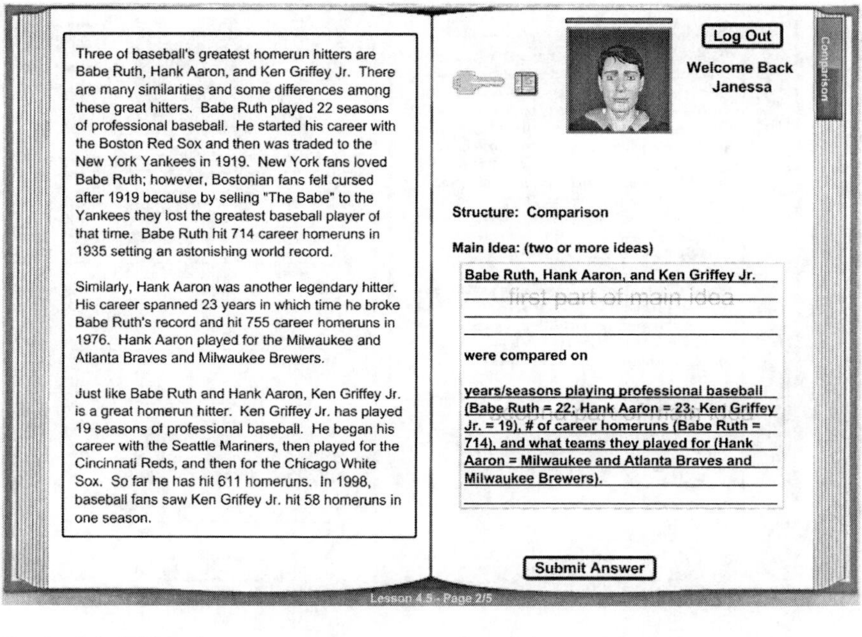

Figure 8.2 ITSS screen – comparison main idea with a text-based pattern.

after a limited number of tries. For example, if students noted that after the third try they always received a complete answer to the question, they may be tempted to game the system by typing nonsense answers for tries 1 and 2, thereby not engaging their minds and waiting for the system to provide the correct answer. By varying the numbers of tries for each question, students could not anticipate an expected pattern.

Metacognition in ITSS

Students' ability to monitor their comprehension by practicing their skills and reflecting on their structure strategy efficacy are an integral part of ITSS. Students self-assess their work during the practice tasks and assess sample writings from other sources. As part of the step-by-step approach to building memory of text using the strategic organization of the passage, students also learn to use different formats for organizing the passage. For example, the main idea passage for a comparison text structure is initially presented to the learner as ____ and ____ were compared on ____, ____, and ____ as shown in Figure 8.3. As they proceed through the lessons, they are introduced to a matrix style presentation of the same ideas shown in Figure 8.4 where who or what is being compared are the columns and what basis they are being compared are the rows. Another presentation option is a tree-style concept map that allows the learner to view the parallel structures shown in Figure 8.5.

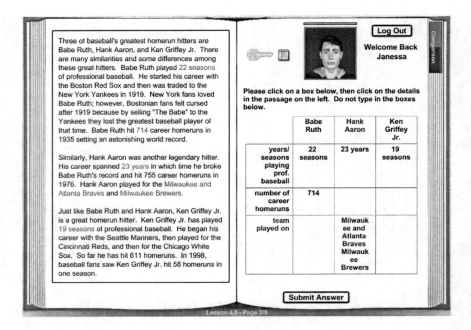

Figure 8.3 Comparison main idea presented in matrix format.

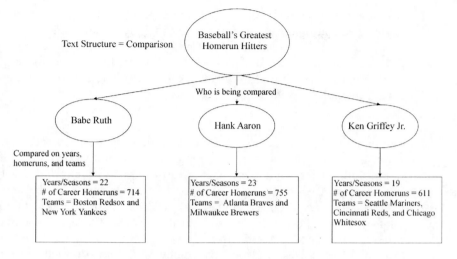

Figure 8.4 Comparison main idea presented in graphical format.

Memory in ITSS

Students learn to create hierarchically organized memories of the text; they read by identifying the text structure used to organize the passage. They begin to create associations by writing a main idea while the passage is in view. They further strengthen their memory and organization by writing a full recall without the passage being visible. They are reminded to organize their full recall using the correct text structure and by consulting their main idea as needed. They can also consult the pop-up windows showing signaling words and main idea patterns. Before IT assesses their work, the student is asked to review and revise their work using the structure strategy framework, allowing time for reflection and self-assessment.

ITSS learning activities focus on writing main ideas, constructing comparison matrices, and other tasks designed to build coherent memory representations and avoid multiple-choice tests. Additionally, we focus on showcasing how each text structure can be applied to many different domains instead of presenting examples in a single domain. These examples allow the learners to transfer their skill to any domain showcasing how memory organization can be similar regardless of the content.

Motivation in ITSS

One of the most powerful statements by David Jonassen (1996) is the following excerpt from his book, *Computers in the Classroom*:

> Learners are poorly motivated. I believe that the most pandemic, yet most insidious, cause for underachievement in schools is lower expectations on the part of teachers, which reduces expectations of students

and parents, which further erodes the expectations of teachers and the entire educational system. Salomon and Globerson also refer to factors such as learned helplessness, poor perceived self-efficacy, and improper attribution of success or failure. In the USA, people frequently litigate personal responsibility. Students ask for help before investing significant mental effort in solving problems.

(David Jonassen, 1996, p. 258)

Mindful activity is the goal of ITSS with students engaged in reading and creating effective mental and external representations of their organized information. Both intrinsic and extrinsic motivational factors are included within the system. To develop their self-efficacy and efficacy for applying the strategy students receive advanced, elaborated feedback from IT as well as histograms of stars that show how well they performed each task. The learning activities are designed to encourage effortful reasoning with scaffolding to help students build their skills. Students are reminded to reflect on their work and self-assess prior to submitting their work for assessment. Feedback is detailed and focuses their attention toward important parts of their writing. If students fail to update their writing sufficiently after receiving elaborated feedback to warrant moving to the next stage, they are asked to consult the teacher for help. Scaffolding is gradually removed as students become proficient in using the structure strategy to seek, organize, and utilize the information.

Justification for describing ITSS as a mindtool

Through the selective use of web-based technologies we have developed an intelligent tutoring system that uses the best ideas for constructive learning. ITSS focuses on mindful learning, self-regulation, and representation of knowledge. ITSS also showcases how the strategy works in many different domains, engages the learner in critical thinking, and formalizes the learner's comprehension through written summaries and recalls.

Our goal in designing ITSS was to limit the reliance on teachers to understand how the structure strategy should be used. Instead, ITSS would instruct both students and their teachers about the structure strategy. Then, teachers could take a lead in helping students to apply the knowledge about strategically using text structure in classroom content areas. Jonassen (1996) notes that teachers can foster the integration of mindtools by modeling, coaching, articulation, reflection, and scaffolding. We believe that ITSS is quite useful in teaching the teachers as well as the students.

We have observed that some teachers initially have a superficial knowledge of the structure strategy and piece together ideas from different comprehension strategies without understanding how they can all be used together in their classrooms. For example, teachers' frequently used summarizing and underlining as comprehension strategies in their classrooms. These strategies were also the primary approaches mentioned in the textbooks. Many teachers noted that students with poor comprehension skills underlined almost all the concepts in the reading and their summaries did not contain the most important ideas. The same teachers noted that they understood signal words and would mention knowing problem and solution and compare/contrast text structures. During professional development conducted by the ITSS team, we would bring to their attention the five text structures presented in ITSS and also the need for the main idea patterns. We would then showcase how the structure strategy approach results in improved summaries and underlining of important ideas.

Another example from our school-based outreach for ITSS was about writing with text structure. One vocal teacher was adamant that his approach to writing using the 4-square approach was far superior to any other method. Additionally, he stated that the text structure approach did not apply to his classroom. As shown in Figure 8.5, the 4-square approach can be significantly enhanced with the use of text structure. Without understanding text structure, students using the 4-square approach are led to use the listing approach to writing, reinforcing poor organization to their written text as well as memory structures.

As these examples show, there is an urgent need to expand access to the structure strategy to a wider audience. One of the most efficient methods to achieve this goal was to create an intelligent tutoring system that focuses on applying the best available tools to help students seek and organize information, effectively apply their skills to solve problems, and self-monitor and improve their self-efficacy.

ITSS lessons use different representations of the text data. For example, main idea formats used include a fill in the blank, matrix, and graphical representation similar to concept maps, but with relational links. Students learn how to extract the most important ideas in the text by first identifying

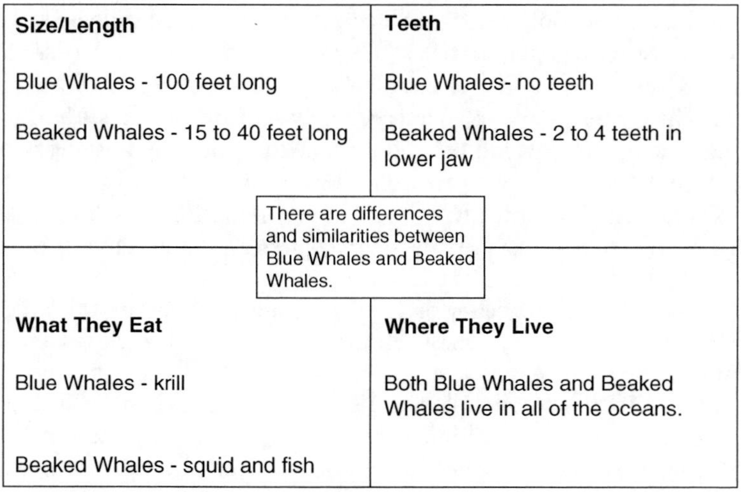

Size/Length	Teeth
Blue Whales - 100 feet long	Blue Whales- no teeth
Beaked Whales - 15 to 40 feet long	Beaked Whales - 2 to 4 teeth in lower jaw

There are differences and similarities between Blue Whales and Beaked Whales.

What They Eat	Where They Live
Blue Whales - krill	Both Blue Whales and Beaked Whales live in all of the oceans.
Beaked Whales - squid and fish	

Figure 8.5 4-square approach organized using the comparison structure.

the text structure and then constructing the main idea for the passage. The main idea task allows students to reflect on their work, receive feedback from the system to improve their organization, and finally reminders for the learner to construct their memory with this framework. When students write about a topic, they use both the text structure and the main idea to organize their writing. By using the text structure during writing they learn how to traverse their hierarchical knowledge tree to recall more information. Thus, by using the reading, learning activities, and writing, the ITSS system allows the learner to seek information, organize, create hierarchical memory structures, and monitor their understanding.

The intelligent tutoring system also goes much further in achieving the learning goals by providing modeling of the strategy using flash animations. Narrations accompany almost all the text freeing up the visual channel of the reader to concentrate on the reading. These narrations, combined with highlighting words, focuses readers' attention on the text. The tutor reminds the students to reflect on their learning and provides scaffolding to the learners, which is faded away as students become more proficient.

Assessment and feedback are important components of ITSS. Our approach uses the hierarchical tree structure of the text with synonyms and spell-checking to provide detailed feedback to the learner. Teachers actively monitor the students' performance through reports and through comments from IT to the learner. Students are asked to consult the teacher prior to proceeding with their lesson if they have not been successful in representing their understanding of the text.

Efficacy of ITSS

The web-based intelligent tutoring system to deliver the structure strategy was initially developed and tested in a study with fifth and seventh graders within one school district (Meyer, Wijekumar, Middlemiss, Higley, Lei, Meier, & Spielvogel, 2010). The research study measured student performance on the Gray Silent Reading Test (GSRT), a standardized reading comprehension test as well as researcher designed measures of comprehension (e.g. recall, strategy competence). Procedures included pre-tests, 90-minutes of weekly use of ITSS for the school year, followed by immediate post-tests, and delayed post-tests after the summer break. Results showed large effects from pre- to post-tests on all the measures and maintenance of strategy use through the summer to the fall delayed post-test.

Research on the efficacy of ITSS continues with large-scale efficacy studies with suburban and rural fourth- through eighth-grade classrooms (Wijekumar, Meyer, & Lei, 2008–2012). These studies were designed as fully randomized controlled trials (i.e. 128 participating fifth-grade classrooms) and hierarchical linear models for data analyses. Wijekumar, et al. (2011), reported that the fifth-grade ITSS classrooms statistically significantly outperformed their control counterparts on the GSRT and researcher-designed post-test measures. There were no differences in performance of rural and suburban students. Results also indicated that ITSS had a significant direct effect on post-test scores for reading self-efficacy and structure strategy self-efficacy with the participating fifth graders.

Wijekumar, Meyer, and Lei (2012) report on the randomized controlled trial with 130 fourth-grade classrooms. The fourth-grade students received an abridged version of ITSS because they were unable to type efficiently on the keyboard. Therefore, fourth-grade classrooms received lessons on identifying signaling words and writing main ideas only. The full-recall task was eliminated from each fourth-grade lesson. In spite of this reduced version, fourth-grade ITSS classrooms outperformed their control counterparts on the GSRT as well as the researcher-designed measures. The effect sizes were smaller than those of the fifth-grade students as was expected due to the limited practice they received on the structure strategy.

Conclusion

The growing research evidence supports the expansion of access to the structure strategy. The efficacy of the ITSS delivery of the strategy to a wide audience is being confirmed through the continuing research studies. Teachers participating in the recent studies are noting marked improvements in their students' writing quality in addition to improved comprehension. As noted earlier, content area teachers are also adopting the structure strategy framework for their learning activities. Schools are beginning to appreciate the utility of the structure strategy in their curriculum. Most importantly, students are able to think about text in a meaningful way, and also know how to represent their knowledge using the powerful structure strategy.

In conclusion, the structure strategy and its implementation within ITSS support the development of powerful comprehension strategies for learners. The focus of our approach is about non-fiction or content area learning *with* intelligent tutoring computer systems. The system allows students to seek and organize information, create effective memory representations, and utilize their hierarchically organized knowledge effectively. The structure strategy with its computer delivery can provide an important mindtool in the classroom.

References

Aleven, V. A., & Koedinger, K. R. (2002). An effective metacognitive strategy: Learning by doing and explaining with a computer-based cognitive tutor. *Cognitive Science, 26*, 147–179.

Atkinson, R. K., Mayer, R. E., and Merrill, M. M. (2005). Fostering social agency in multimedia learning: Examining the impact of an animated agent's voice. *Contemporary Educational Psychology, 30*(1), 117–139.

Chi, M. T. H., Feltovich, P. J., & Glaser, R. (1981). Categorization and representation of physics problems by experts and novices. *Cognitive Science, 5,* 121–52.

Jonassen, D. H. (1996). *Computers in the classroom: Mindtools for critical thinking.* Englewood Cliffs, New Jersey, US: Prentice Hall.

Mayer, R. E. (2001). *Multimedia learning.* New York, NY, US: Cambridge University Press.

Meyer, B. J. F. (1975). *The organization of prose and its effects on memory.* Amsterdam: North-Holland.

Meyer, B. J. F. (2003). Text coherence and readability. *Topics in Language Disorders, 23,* 204–224.

Meyer, B. J. F., Brandt, D. M., & Bluth, G. J. (1980). Use of the top-level structure in text: Key for reading comprehension of ninth-grade students. *Reading Research Quarterly, 16,* 72–103.

Meyer, B. J. F., & Poon, L. W. (2001). Effects of structure strategy training and signaling on recall of text. *Journal of Educational Psychology, 93,* 141–159.

Meyer, B. J. F., & Rice, G. E. (1989). Prose processing in adulthood: The text, the reader, and the task. In L. W. Poon, D. C. Rubin, & B. A. Wilson (Eds.), *Everyday cognition in adulthood and later life* (pp. 157–194). New York, NY: Cambridge University Press.

Meyer, B. J. F., & Wijekumar, K. (2007). A web-based tutoring system for the structure strategy: Theoretical background, design, and findings. In D. S. McNamara (Ed.), *Reading comprehension strategies: Theories, interventions, and technologies* (pp. 347–375). Mahwah, NJ: Lawrence Erlbaum Associates.

Meyer, B. J. F., Middlemiss, W., Theodorou, E., Brezinski, K. L., McDougall, J., & Bartlett, B. J. (2002). Effects of structure strategy instruction delivered to fifth-grade children using the internet with and without the aid of older adult tutors. *Journal of Educational Psychology, 94,* 486–519.

Meyer, B. J. F., Wijekumar, K., Middlemiss, W., & VanHorn, B. (2003–2007). Intelligent tutoring using the structure strategy to improve reading comprehension of middle school students. Washington, DC: United States Department of Education, Institute of Education Sciences.

Meyer, B. J. F., Wijekumar, K., Middlemiss, W., Higley, K., Lei, P., Meier, C., & Spielvogel, J. (2010). Web-based tutoring of the structure strategy with or without elaborated feedback or choice for fifth- and seventh-grade readers. *Reading Research Quarterly, 41,* 62–92.

Wijekumar, K., & Jonassen, D. H. (2007). The effects of tool expertise on ill-structured problem solving, *Computers in Human Behavior, 23*(1), 664–704.

Wijekumar, K., Meyer, B. J. F., & Lei, P. (2008–2012). Efficacy and replication research on the intelligent tutoring system for the structure strategy – Rural and suburban schools grades 4, 5, 7 and 8. Report # R305A080133. Washington, DC: US Department of Education, Institute of Education Sciences.

Wijekumar, K., Meyer, B. J. F., & Lei, P. (2012). Multisite randomized controlled trial examining intelligent tutoring of the structure strategy for 4th-grade readers. *Journal of Educational Technology Research and Development.* Paper submitted for publication.

Wijekumar, K., Meyer, B. J. F., Lei, P., Lin, Y., Johnson, L.A., Shurmatz, K., & Spielvogel, J. (2011). Improving reading comprehension for 5th-grade readers in rural and suburban schools using Web-based intelligent tutoring systems. *Journal of Educational Psychology.* Paper submitted for publication.

9 Alternative Pathways for Research and Instructional Design on Technology-Supported Group Problem Solving

Seng-Chee Tan

Introduction

This chapter focuses on research and instructional design on the use of educational technologies to support group problem solving. David Jonassen's (2000a) seminal paper on the design theory of problem solving initiated an important research agenda in the field of instructional design and technology. Building on his past research work – constructivist learning environments (Jonassen, 1999), structuredness of problems (Jonassen, 1997), knowledge representation (Jonassen, Beisnner, & Yacci, 1993) and individual differences (Jonassen & Grabowski, 1993) – he proposed a design theory of problem solving by examining problem types, problem representations, and individual differences, with the goal of generating instructional theory on developing problem-solving skills among learners. One way of rationalizing the roles of technologies in supporting problem solving is from the perspective of using computers as mindtools (Jonassen, 1996, 2000b), which represents another major research track of Jonassen. In essence, as mindtools, computers are used for knowledge representation by learners rather than as a repository of knowledge or as a surrogate tutor. In other words, students learn *with* computers rather than *from* computers.

Coincidentally, at around the same time, similar development was emerging in the field of computer-supported collaborative learning (CSCL) and learning sciences. Koschmann, Kelson, Feltovich, and Barrows (1996), for example, illustrated a principled approach toward the development of computer-supported problem-based learning by examining theories of learning, classroom practices and affordances of technology. Though seemingly working towards similar goal of supporting group problem solving with technologies, some researchers in the field of CSCL based their work on different theories, for example, collaborative knowing by Stahl (2004) and knowledge building by Scardamalia and Bereiter (2006). Different research methodologies are also favored in the field of learning sciences and CSCL. For example, design experiment was advocated among researchers in learning sciences (Brown, 1992). These differences in theoretical frameworks culminate in variations in methodologies and instructional design practices.

In this chapter, I discuss ways to move forward with research and to inform instructional design on the use of technologies to support learning in problem-based learning environments. The discussion focuses on two broad approaches, one based on traditional experimental approach and the other based on design experiment. These approaches were compared for their convergence and differences, and the consequent implications for the design and implementation of learning environments and activities that aim at improving solving challenging problems in a group setting.

Design Theory of Problem Solving and Group Problem Solving

This section reviews Jonassen's design theory of problem solving (2000a) and his notion of computers as mindtools (1996, 2000b), which form the foundation for making decisions on the design of a technology-supported problem-based learning environment.

Problem Solving

To Jonassen (2000a), a *problem* has two important attributes, one is related to the problem situation and the other is associated with the characteristics of a potential problem solver. First, a problem is a situation to a person where there is a gap between the goal state and the current state, and the path from the current state to the goal state is not immediately recognized. Second, the person must perceive a need and values to pursue the solution to the problem. Problem solving refers to the process of finding the unknown, which could even include defining the problem space, not just finding the solution. Consistent to this definition, Jonassen identified three important groups of factors that could affect a person's ability to solve a problem: Problem variations, problem representation, and individual differences. In short:

Problem-solving ability of a person = f (problem variations, problem representation, individual differences)

Problem variations refer to the nature of the problem, which include the structuredness of a problem (how much of the problem situation is known), the complexity (the number of variables and relationships among them), and domain specificity (how much of domain-specific knowledge and skills are required). Problem representation refers to the way that the problem is being presented or represented by the instructional designer and how it is perceived by the problem solver, which could include decisions on how many contextual cues to include and the fidelity of the problem compared with a real life problem. An instructional designer needs to be cognizant of the individual differences in order to make decisions about the problem representation when designing a learning environment. The individual differences include the problem solver's knowledge (e.g. domain knowledge, structural knowledge, and procedural knowledge) and the problem solver's affective and conative attributes (e.g. attitudes toward the problem and persistence toward problem-solving task). Details on each of these factors can be found in several publications (Jonassen, 1997, 2000a, 2004).

There are at least two points to note about Jonassen's theory of problem solving. First, it is positioned as a design theory, which means its ultimate goal is to illuminate instructional design of a problem-based learning activity or environment. Nevertheless, it is based on analysis of problems in the real world. Besides acting as a prescriptive theory (Reigeluth, 1999) for instructional design, it does contain elements of a descriptive theory that explains processes of problem solving and factors affecting problem solving. Second, it is more encompassing that the problem-based learning model (Barrows & Tamblyn, 1980) that has its genesis in medical education. Jonassen (2004) held that the medical model of problem-based learning represents only one model of problem solving and it is fraught with the transferability of its applications to contexts other than medical education.

Group Problem Solving

In this chapter, research approaches to studying problem solving in a group setting will be contrasted. It is thus pertinent to elaborate on Jonassen's (1997) model of ill-structured problem solving, which sheds some light on the group problem-solving processes. First, Jonassen held that compared with well-structured problems, real-world problems are often complex and ill-structured and thus require different skills to develop effective solutions. In contrast, classroom instruction often engages students in solving well-structured problems, typified by those presented in textbooks. Well-structured problems are well defined in that all elements and processes needed to solve the problems are present; they have single, correct, convergent answers and preferred solution processes, and they engage a limited number of rules and principles. Ill-structured problems, on the other hand, have the following properties:

(a) they are ill-defined with one or more aspects of the problem situations not specified or without the information needed to solve the problem being contained in the problem statements;
(b) they have vaguely defined goal states;
(c) they engage more than general rules or principles;
(d) they possess multiple solutions, multiple ways of solving the problems or sometimes no definite solution; and
(e) they require problem solvers to express personal opinions and beliefs and to make and defend judgments about the problem.

The nature of ill-structured problems necessitates different problem-solving processes. Jonassen (1997) proposed the following sequence of actions:

(1) *Identification of problem space.* There is a need to identify problem space and contextual constraints because ill-structured problems are domain or context dependent.

(2) *Clarify alternative perspectives.* A problem solver needs to identify and clarify alternative perspectives of the possible stakeholders involved because they could have different definitions of the problem space or different representations of the problem. Solving ill-structured problems involves the reconciliation of conflicting conceptualizations of the problem so as to identify and decide on the problem schema that is most relevant and useful for solving the problem.

(3) *Generate possible solutions.* After identifying the problem space and alternative positions, possible solutions can be generated by inferring how people, holding different perspectives, would solve the problem.

(4) *Assess the validity of solutions.* Since there is typically no single, best solution, the preferred solution could be justified with arguments grounded on relevant and sufficient evidence and backed up with supportive facts or conjectures.

(5) *Monitor problem space and solution options.* Ill-structured problem solving requires not only metacognitive strategies of planning and comprehension, but also epistemic monitoring of the truth-value of alternate problem representations and solutions. This means recognizing an individual's limits of knowing and certainty of knowledge in order to judge the validity of various problem representations and solutions. This monitoring process occurs throughout the first four steps and leads to iterative refinement of the mental model of the problem space and solutions.

(6) *Implement and monitor the solution.* In real life, the solution could be put to test and its effectiveness can be assessed based on the outcomes of the implementation.

(7) *Adapt the solution.* The problem solver can adjust and adapt the solution based on feedback. Often, ill-structured problem solving involves an iterative process of monitoring and adapting the solution as the problem is not easily solved in a single attempt.

The multiplicity of perspectives on defining problem space, alternative solutions, and assessment of viability of solutions demand social interactions among learners. Thus, group problem solving becomes a necessary condition for solving an ill-structured problem, not a nice-to-have. Note that Jonassen (1997) emphasized the use of argumentation as a key strategy for social negotiation among learners. From the perspective of distributed cognition (Hutchins & Klausen, 1996; Pea, 1993), cognitive activities of individuals are dependent on the social and material setting, which also brings in the influence of culture, context, and history on learning. It highlights the importance of social interaction in the learning process, as well as the choice of technologies that could weave the distributed expertise and knowledge resources. The following review of the concept of computers as mindtools (Jonassen, 1996, 2000b) illustrates how technologies can be used to support such group problem solving.

Computers as Mindtools

Using the design theory of problem solving as a framework, the important role of technologies in supporting problem solving is evident (Jonassen, Howland, Moore, & Marra, 2003). For example, the Tutorials-in-Problem-Solving (TiPs) program could be used to support learners in solving well-structured story problems by scaffolding the conceptual modeling of the task (Wisconsin Center for Education Research, 1996). On the other hand, a multimedia computer program like *The Nardoo River* (Interactive Multimedia Pty Ltd, n.d.) provides a suite of tools that allow students to design investigations and make decisions based on simulated outcomes.

This chapter focuses on a specific way of using technologies: using computers as mindtools (Jonassen, 1996, 2000b) to support group problem solving. There are several key attributes of a mindtool. First, mindtools are applications of computer-based tools or learning environments, which could include such things as a spreadsheet, semantic networking tools, and online discussion forums. Unlike computer tutorial programs that act as a tutor to conduct instruction, a mindtool is not hard-wired with domain knowledge. Instead, it affords an environment for a learner to work on, yet constrains the learner to represent his or her knowledge in a specific formalism. For example, an online discussion forum with suggested sentence openers constrain a learner on the ways to think about and present an idea on a topic; but the content knowledge in the forum is provided by the learner, not programmed in the computer.

Second, the main goal of using these tools is to engage a learner in complex thinking. Jonassen adopted the Integrated Thinking Model proposed by Iowa Department of Education (1989), which includes processes like problem solving, decision making, designing, analyzing, evaluating, and synthesizing. In short, the goal of using a mindtool is to engage a learner in higher order thinking. Technologies are not used for facilitating the administrative or logistic processes that are subsidiary to learning, but for mindful engagement of learners in knowledge construction. In other words, mindtools are computer-based applications that engage learners in constructivist learning (Duffy & Jonassen, 1992), rather than as instructivist tools.

Third, mindtools are cognitive tools which are "technologies, tangible or intangible, that enhance the cognitive powers of human beings during thinking, problem solving, and learning" (Jonassen & Reeves, 1996, p. 693). The applications of mindtools aim to achieve the effects of learning *with* and learning *of* technology (Salomon, Perkins, & Globerson, 1991). As an *intellectual partner* that a person learns *with*, a computer-based tool affords the learner a learning space to perform actions that would otherwise be impossible or difficult to achieve. For example, a computer-supported collaborative argumentation tool (e.g. QuestMap™) allows multiple users to work on and expand some arguments collaboratively. In this partnership, the computer plays the role in rapid digital calculations to connect, represent and visualize the learner's arguments, while the learner is engaged in higher order thinking about the quality of an argument. Another important reason for using this mindtool is the effect of its use, which can be the development of improved skills and mastery of problem-solving strategies (Salomon, Perkins, & Globerson, 1991). In other words, the learner could eventually perform the higher order thinking without the support of the tool. A mindtool thus acts as a scaffold, supporting a learner to achieve a higher level task. In a way, it extends Vygotskian concepts of scaffolding, which traditionally involves people, either adults or more capable peers, who provide guidance and support to the learner. In this case, technology provides support to a learner, empowering the learner to perform more complex tasks and enabling them to develop skills (effects with technology) such that they would be able to perform the tasks independently (effects of technology).

Alternative Pathways Forward

Jonassen's design theory of problem solving and concepts of mindtools provide the foundation for research and instructional design on learning environments that support problem solving. Scanning the literature, Jonassen's theoretical frameworks could be systematically studied in numerous ways with various research foci; the frameworks could be used to organize extant studies. For example, Lauenbacher et al. (1997) and Orrill (2002) studied technological tools that support distributed problem solving; Zumbach, Hillers, and Reimann (2003) and Zumbach and Reimann (1999) examined approaches of supporting distributed problem solving in an online environment, through the use of feedback mechanisms and through collaborative argumentation; whereas Kapur and Kinzer (2009) and Kapur, Voiklis and Kinzer (2008) analyzed group interactional behaviors in a synchronous CSCL environment. In this chapter, rather than reviewing various research studies, I focus on the approaches of research and their respective implications on instructional design.

Theory Constrained Research Design and Instructional Design

This section illustrates how theoretical frameworks for problem solving and mindtools could be used for research and instructional design, using deductive reasoning. Several research papers seem to have adopted this approach, including Cho and Jonassen (2002), Ge and Land (2003), Tan (2000), and Wijekumar and Jonassen (2007). I will illustrate this approach using the paper by Oh and Jonassen (2007), beginning with a synopsis of the study.

In the study by Oh and Jonassen (2007), 58 undergraduates in a Teacher Development Program were engaged in solving classroom management problems, which were categorized as diagnosis-solution problem. Two main independent variables were identified: the effect of constraint-based argumentation scaffolds and students' epistemological beliefs. The dependent variables included students' online argumentation behaviors, argumentation skills and their problem-solving processes. The transfer of argumentation skills and the impact of epistemological belief in individual problem-solving performances were also examined. Three treatment conditions were compared, including two types of scaffolded online discussion (constraint-based versus threaded discussion) and no online discussion (control group). For the constraint-based forum, Future Learning Environments (FLE), a computer-supported collaborative argumentation tool, was used to provide a hard scaffold in the form of six message types that represent various argumentation sentence openers. Among other findings, it was found that the scaffolded (FLE) group generated more evidence message than the threaded group, whereas the converse was true for verification notes. The authors inferred that the scaffolded group was engaged in generating grounds (evidence) in argumentation whereas the threaded discussion group was more engaged in meaning making. No significant difference was found for rebuttal, indicating the reluctance among the students to challenge alternative perspectives. In terms of online problem-solving behaviors, the scaffolded group had significantly higher occurrences of comments on problem space, hypotheses, and testing of hypotheses. In terms of epistemological beliefs, students' belief in simple knowledge was the strongest predictor for their online argumentation performance. In sum, the study revealed the positive effects of scaffolding on online argumentation and problem solving, though there was a need to guide the students to be more engaged in rebuttal and elaboration. The study also provided some evidence on the relationships among students' epistemological beliefs, their argumentation behaviors and problem-solving performance.

I will now attempt to infer the underlying thought processes and logic in the previous study, which are not explicitly stated in the report. At a macrolevel, the contextual conditions and the design theory of problem solving influence what is to be studied. Specifically, the context of the study involves designing classroom management instruction in a teacher education program and problems within this specific discipline are identified. The categorization of classroom management problems as ill-structured diagnosis problems is apparently guided by the problem variations in Jonassen's design theory (2000a). Subsequently, the *diagnosis* problem forms the context of the study while the research questions focus on the effect of scaffolding students for this type of problem solving.

More specifically, the intervention approach is likely to be guided by the theory of solving ill-structured problem, where argumentation in a group setting is one of the key processes. It is thus important to consider how to scaffold the argumentation skills among learners. It was decided to impose constraints in the form of argumentation sentence openers. FLE, a mindtool that supports collaborative argumentation, was selected because of its affordances in providing a networked communication platform that could provide the necessary scaffolds.

The research design and methods are guided by theories of educational research methodologies as well as theory on mindtools and design theory of problem solving. The design theory of problem solving is used to inform how the problem-solving performance could be assessed. Likewise, literature on epistemological beliefs provides the framework to select an appropriate instrument. The study of problem-solving behaviors is an examination of the effects *with* the mindtool (FLE) whereas the investigation of retention of learning is an examination of the effects *of* the mindtool.

Discussion and interpretation of the findings are constrained by the design theory of problem-solving and theory of mindtools. For example, there are implicit hypotheses that challenging alternative perspectives should occur more frequently and scaffolded group should perform better in problem solving. The findings that scaffolded group did not perform better in overall problem-solving assessment was explained by instructor's effect. Likewise, alternative explanation (cultural influence) was invoked for the unexpected low occurrence of rebuttal in students' argumentation. The paper suggests that constraint-based collaborative argumentation is effective to some extent, but there is a need to provide more scaffold to university students in solving ill-structured problems, particularly in the area of elaboration and rebuttal. Educators need to be cognizant of the culture that shapes student's epistemological beliefs.

In short, the underlying epistemological stance of the research study is that of deductive reasoning. The design theory of problem solving, mindtools, argumentation and students' epistemological beliefs constrain and guide the study, from conceptualizing the study to deriving inferences from the findings. The findings serve to validate the theories. Unexpected findings are regarded as inconclusive and alternative mediating factors are invoked to provide possible explanations. In the next section, I will describe an alternative approach to advance the research agenda in technology-supported group problem solving.

Design Experiment: Integrated Research and Design

An alternative approach to the deductive logic in research and instructional design is *design experiment*, which is favored by researchers in the field of learning sciences. Jonassen, Cernusca, and Ionas (2007) suggest learning sciences as an alternative to the instructional science. To them, learning sciences is a discipline that is multitheoretical and multidisciplinary; it draws upon a range of theoretical perspectives that are grounded in constructivism, including cognitive anthropology, situated learning, distributed cognition, social cognition, activity theory, and Deweyian pragmatism. In contrast, traditional instructional design is premised on information processing theory. In learning sciences, the focus of the learning activities is engaging learners to solve complex and authentic problems typically in a collaborative environment supported or mediated by technology. The goals are not acquisition of facts and procedures but learners' ability to engage in knowledge building, conceptual change learning, reflective and collaborative meaning making. Jonassen, Cernusca, and Ionas (2007) described the research practice of learning sciences as "the integration of design and research" (p. 47).

Currently, there is apparently no design experiment study that declares its influence by Jonassen's design theory of problem solving and mindtools. In this chapter, to illustrate what it might look like and to discuss its potential, I relate a study that involves the use of a networked technology for group problem solving. Yeo (2008) conducted a design experiment in a Singaporean high school that attempted to implement problem-based learning pedagogy. More details could be found in Yeo and Tan (2010, 2011) and Yeo, Tan and Lee (in press), which were reports derived from Yeo's study (2008).

Yeo's study (2008) examined learning of physics among three groups of Grade 9 Singaporean students over three cycles of design, implementation and evaluation. The main foci of investigation included how PBL was enacted in the high school classroom and how students' scientific conceptions progressed during the PBL process. A computer-supported collaborative learning (CSCL) tool, known as the Knowledge Constructor, was developed to support problem-solving processes. The main sources of data included video and online discussion data. The analysis framework that combined cultural-historical activity theory or CHAT (Engeström, 1999) and systemic functional linguistics provided the tools for analyzing the classroom activity system and the meaning making process enacted in the three research cycles. Findings from one research cycle were used to inform the intervention of the next cycle.

In the first cycle (see Table 9.1), a team of physics teachers in the school espoused the goal of implementing the medical model of problem-based learning. They developed a problem-based learning (PBL) framework, which was used to guide their development and implementation of the physics lessons. In this cycle, the researchers (including the author) focused on ethnographic observation of the lesson implementation. Using CHAT as a framework of analysis, among other findings, we found the following contradiction in the system: the reversal of tool and object in the activity system. Specifically, the espoused motive of implementing PBL was not enacted; rather, the underlying and hidden motive of the teacher was on imparting knowledge. Thus, the problems were used as a mediating tool to achieve the object of teaching the content knowledge. Using a widely cited model of PBL offered by Savery (2006) and Savery and Duffy (1996) as a reference, we suggested changes to the design strategy, which was to focus on problem solving as the object of the activity system.

The second intervention (see Table 9.1), however, revealed yet another problem: The students were too obsessed with getting the right answers to the problems and some of them resorted to solving the problems with simple heuristics and trial-and-error method, rather than to systematically tackling the problems with the relevant physics principles. In short, the students were task-focused, yet at the expense of their learning. This also exposed one of the weaknesses of transferring the medical model of PBL to a high school. In a medical school, the interns go through intensive courses focusing on disciplinary knowledge. PBL could engage them to apply their knowledge in diagnosing complex and authentic medical cases. In a high school, the students

Table 9.1 The three iterations of intervention study on designing a
problem-based learning environment

	Research cycle 1	Research cycle 2	Research cycle 3
Nature of study	Ethnographic	Intervention based on findings from Cycle 1. Rationalization of tool and object in the activity system.	Intervention based on findings from Cycle 2. Integration of knowledge building into PBL.
Theoretical basis	PBL (Savery, 2006)	PBL (Savery, 2006)	PBL (Savery, 2006) + Knowledge Building (Scardamalia and Bereiter, 2006)
Intervention design	Teachers' design based on their interpretation of PBL	Co-design based on researchers' interpretation of PBL	Co-design based on researchers' suggestion to integrate PBL and knowledge building
Key findings	Problem was used as the *tool*, the manifested *object* was physics content knowledge, the outcome was mastery of this knowledge.	Knowledge is the *tool* and problem is the *object*. Students found solution without using the knowledge specified in the formal curriculum.	Evidence of achievement of dual goals – mastery of content knowledge and effective problem solution.

are expected to gain the necessary knowledge and engage in the problem solving at the same time. That means greater extent of scaffolding is needed.

In the third intervention (see Table 9.1), the researchers and the teachers revisited the PBL theory and incorporated knowledge building (Scardamalia & Bereiter, 2006) in the process. Instead of a single phase problem solving, after defining the problem space and their knowledge gaps, the students engaged in knowledge building to develop deeper understanding of the physics concepts, theories, and principles that they identified to be useful in solving the problems. This process was supported by Knowledge Constructor, a CSCL platform that was designed by the school and developed by a commercial vendor. In essence, Knowledge Constructor is an online discussion forum with a graphical interface; icons, representing different types of ideas, help to constrain the ways ideas can be represented and discussed. Consequently, in this third intervention, there was a better balance between the dual goal of achieving better understanding of subject knowledge and developing the students' problem-solving skills.

Overall, among other findings, the theory of PBL was examined. We saw correspondence of learning in the three cycles of research with the three metaphors of learning (Paavola & Hakkarainen, 2005; Sfard, 1998): knowledge acquisition, learning through participation, and knowledge creation.

In the first phase of the research cycle, knowledge was treated as commodity that could be transferred from the teacher to the students through didactic instruction. In the second phase, learning through participation in a community was assumed. The validity of this assumption was later questioned because the community of learners was different from a community of practitioners. In the third phase, learning through knowledge creation was integrated with learning through participation, which engaged the students in developing conceptual understanding of domain knowledge and later problem solving. We concluded that in a high school setting, situating PBL in a knowledge creation paradigm supported science meaning making more effectively than in an acquisition or a participation paradigm. Therefore, a PBL framework that is based on knowledge creation paradigm, where there is a co-dependence between problem solving and knowledge building, is proposed for supporting the process of science meaning making in a high school.

Comparisons of the Two Approaches

The two approaches bear several similarities. First, theories are used to guide the research and design practices. We have illustrated the influence of design theory of problem solving, as well as other theories like collaborative argumentation, throughout various phases of research in the study by Oh and Jonassen (2007). In the study by Yeo (2008), the medical model of PBL and knowledge building guided the research intervention and analyses. Second, mindtools, in the form of a network technology to support interactions among learners, were used in both studies. The key affordances are similar: providing a platform that affords communication among learners, yet constrains the interactions with sentence openers or types of ideas. The main strategy underlying this approach is scaffolding with computers as an intellectual partner. It imposes constraints on the ways students write their messages (effect with technology) with the ultimate goal that such thinking habits or strategies for problem solving will be developed in students (effect of technology). Both approaches rely on reifying and capturing students' ideas in the form of text or graphics, which are stored in the forum database to be revisited, revised and improved upon. The process engages the students in reflective thinking and idea improvement.

On the other hand, there are differences between the two approaches, which are labeled as Approach A and Approach B in Table 9.2.

The Role of Design Theory

It is important to clarify that in this section, theory refers to design theory that could guide research and instructional design. In the words of Cobb, Confrey, deSessa, Lehrer, & Schauble (2003), the theory "must do real work" (p. 10) in guiding design of the intervention. Thus, we are talking specifically about design theory rather than grand theories like constructivism that are too remote to practical applications. In Approach A, the design theory

Table 9.2 Differences between the two research approaches

	Approach A: Theory constrained approach	Approach B: Design experiment
The roles of a theory	Theory is assumed to be valid, which constrains and guides research and instructional design.	Theory can be examined in the research process; it is regarded as a foundation and a launch pad for research.
	Theory informs research and instructional design.	Theory evolves with research and instructional design.
Relationships among theory, research and instructional design	Research to validate hypothesis generated from the theory.	Research to improve practice and design theory.
	Evaluation findings within instructional design process is program specific, not transferable.	Research yield findings that are program specific and information that is transferable to some extent.
	Iterative research cycles are optional and could be treated as discrete projects.	Design experiment approach using iterative improvement; Iterative research cycles are necessary.
Relationships among researchers, instructional designers and participants	Researchers are likely to be different from instructional designers; however, both tend to take control of the design of the learning environment.	Researchers take on the roles of instructional designers
	Participants follow the specified learning pathway; they provide feedback about the intervention from their performance or their reflection.	Participants could be co-designer of the learning situation and could play active role in the analysis.

adopted is assumed to be valid. For the study by Oh and Jonassen (2007), I have discussed the influence of theory in various phases of research. Theory improvement, however, was not featured. There is an implicit assumption that the theories adopted are valid; findings that do not cohere with the hypotheses are deemed inconclusive and other mediating factors are offered as possible explanations for the deviation. In Approach B, on the other hand, the initial design theory employed was the medical model of problem-based learning. This theory, however, was examined when unexpected finding was uncovered in the second iteration. A new theory was sought to guide the design, which culminated in an integrative approach that incorporates a knowledge building phase within the problem-solving framework. Incidentally, Bereiter and Scardamalia (2000) contrasted knowledge building with the medical model of problem-based learning. They regarded knowledge building as a process of working on problems of understanding; and the goal of knowledge building is not to reach a conclusion, but to advance collective understanding of participants. Thus, in Approach B, theory is treated as a foundation and improvement of the design theory is an intentional goal. Cobb et al. (2003) highlighted the "prospective and reflective" (p. 10) faces of design experiments: the reflective side uses theory to design the intervention, and the prospective side capitalizes on the emergent pathways and alternative to improve the design theory.

Taking Approach A, it means that design theory of problem solving could be regarded as a framework upon which numerous combinations of factors could be evaluated for design of problem-based learning environments. Improvement to this design theory will require a separate and dedicated attempt to scan the literature and to rationalize the theory. Approach B, however, takes the current design theory as a version of theory that could be examined and fine-tuned in the research cycles. Thus, rather than treating design theory as the *ceiling*, limiting what can be and should be done, theory is used as the *launch pad* that could lead to improved theory and practice.

Relationships among Theory, Research, and Instructional Design

Following the above analysis, the purpose of Approach A is to validate the theory and its applications in a specific context. Findings that cohere with the theory enhance the confidence of its applications in instructional design; otherwise, instructional designers need to be cognizant about possible mediating factors. Details about these mediating factors could be illuminated with future studies. In other words, the research provides instructional designers with information about the confidence level of using the theory in guiding the design and implementation of a problem-based learning environment. Thus, theory precedes research and instructional design, but there is no absolute necessity for instructional design to be informed by research. Instructional design guidelines could be derived logically from the theory. For example, Jonassen (2002) provided examples of potential architectures for designing online problem-based learning for story problems and troubleshooting problems, based solely on his design theory. The traditional instructional design process could be conducted independent of the research process because it usually includes evaluation as a component that serves the purpose of providing feedback to the instructional designer about the effectiveness of the instructional design process.

Approach B has dual goals of improving the design theory as well as the instructional design practice through the iterative process. Cobb et al. (2003) described the dual purpose of a design experiment: "to develop a class of theories about both the process of learning" as well as to develop "the means that are designed to support that learning" (p. 9). Rather than controlling variables, a design experiment reflects the "messiness" of a real life learning situation where there is interplay of multiple variables

(Collins, Joseph, & Bielaczyc, 2004, p. 20). More explicitly, Jonassen, Cernusca, and Ionas (2007) explicated the integrative nature of research and design, which means that instructional design is an integral part of a design experiment. This has further implications on the generic instructional design process and suggests a re-examination of the role of evaluation in the instructional design process. Even though an evaluation study could share similar data collection and analysis methods as research, the key difference from research lies in its program specificity: it is intended to inform the practice of a particular program or object of evaluation. A research study, on the other hand, carries some degree of transferability. Design experiment serves the dual purpose of advancing domain specific design theory, yet at the same time, improving the practices. Thus, rather than segregating the processes of improving theory, conducting research and designing instruction, these three processes could now be integrated.

In Approach A, each research study is a discrete project. From a macro perspective, each research project could be influenced by the past studies and they could engender future studies, but there are weak links among the various iterations of projects. That means the projects need not strictly follow the same theoretical arguments or similar goals. In Approach B, having iterative cycles is an essential feature of a design experiment. Such a methodology could potentially yield better practices, though it demands greater amount of resources.

The above examples also highlight the profound influence of epistemological assumptions of the design theory on the research methodologies, although this is not an inherent effect of the research approach.

As a strong advocate of constructivist learning (Jonassen, 1990, 1999), Jonassen's design theory on problem solving (2000a) is strongly influenced by cognitivist perspectives of learning. This is perhaps most evident in the various factors related to individual differences (Jonassen & Grabowski, 1993), including cognitive control and metacognition. According to Greeno, Collins, and Resnick (1996), a cognitive perspective on learning as the view that "treats knowing as having structures of information and processes that recognize and construct patterns of symbols to understand concepts and exhibit general abilities, such as reasoning, solving problems, and using and understanding language" (p. 18). Consequently, in the study by Oh and Jonassen (2007), the unit of analysis focuses on individuals; individual's argumentation skills and problem-solving performance were analyzed.

Yeo (2008), on the other hand, adopted a situative perspective toward learning, where knowing is "an activity that takes place among individuals, the tools and artifacts that they use, and the communities and practices in which they participate" (Greeno, Collins, & Resnick, 1996, p. 20). Consequently, the focus of analysis was on the class as an activity system, rather than individuals; discourse analysis was also employed to analyze interactions among the learners, rather than to assess the performance of individuals. In other words, the unit of analysis is a group and the emphasis is on the processes, rather than individual outcomes.

Relationships Among Researchers, Instructional Designers and Participants

In Approach A, researchers and instructional designers are usually not the same people. In fact, they assume very different identities. A researcher's role focuses on academic work that is valued for theory contribution. An instructional designer is regarded as a practitioner who applies the knowledge of instructional design theories to design learning environment for real life applications. Both researchers and instructional designers tend to take control of the design of the learning environment, while participants need only to follow the designed pathway of learning. Feedback about effectiveness of the learning environment could be obtained by observing the participants, interviewing them or assessing their performance. In short, there was clear division of roles and identities of researchers, instructional designers and learners.

In Approach B, the design nature of the experiment compels the researcher to act also as an instructional designer. Such role could be augmented by co-designing the learning environment with some participants (e.g. a teacher). In the study by Yeo (2000), the researchers co-designed the problem-based learning lessons with the teachers in Phase 2 and 3 of the study. The participants also played more active roles in the analysis of data (Collins, Joseph, & Bielaczyc, 2004). In another study that involved design experiment, Marton and Pang (2006) illustrated an approach that leveraged the distributed expertise of teachers and researchers in a community, which also transformed the traditional working relationship between researchers and teachers: from that of an expert-practitioner relationship to that of a co-designer and co-researcher of a classroom environment. With such a structure and social arrangement, researchers could focus on validating theories while practitioners test their tacit knowledge about possible interventional approaches. Incidentally, drawing ideas from some industry research and development sectors, a similar approach, known as networked improvement community (Bryk, Gomez, & Grunow, 2010), is emerging. It is an approach of using a network of researchers, instructional designers and practitioners as agents to produce rapid iterative cycles of design, prototyping, and testing.

Conclusion

Among many contributions David Jonassen has made to the field of instructional design and technologies, he has pioneered the use of computers as mindtools and offered a design theory of problem solving, thus providing a framework that could guide researchers and instructional designers in designing problem-based learning environments. This chapter contrasts two broad approaches in advancing research agenda and instructional practices on group problem solving, supported by the use of networked communication technologies as a mindtool. One approach regards the theory as a framework that guides research and instructional design processes; as a valid framework, the theory imposes constrains on these processes and remains unchallenged. Research and instructional design are discrete activities that could be independent of each other. The other approach, the design experiment approach, aims to improve both the theory and practice, and integrates research and instructional design. It also restructures the relationships among researchers, instructional designers and participants.

By comparing and discussing the two approaches, this chapter does not intend to assess or to make a judgment on which approach is superior. Rather, it serves as a reflection on our assumptions about theory, method and instructional design (cf. Wilson, 2005). It aims to reveal alternative paradigms of our beliefs and values about design theory, research and instructional design, which could lead to alternative pathways of agenda of supporting problem-based learning environment with mindtools. It presents different ways of research methods and instructional design, and non-traditional ways of embracing practitioner's voices or leveraging insider's perspectives for research and instructional design. This diversity in approaches could enrich the field of research and instructional design practices, and would likely benefit a wider group of participants.

As a researcher or an instructional designer who is interested in participating in this agenda of designing technology-supported problem-based learning environment, what are your underlying beliefs and ideologies? How would you conduct your research and instructional design practices? How would you contribute to this field?

References

Barrows, H., & Tamblyn, R. (1980). *Problem-based learning: An approach to medical education.* New York, NY: Springer Pub Co.

Bereiter, C., & Scardamalia, M. (2000). Process and product in Problem-Based Learning (PBL) research. In D. H. Evensen & C. E. Hmelo (Eds.), *Problem-based learning: A research perspective on learning interactions* (pp. 185–195). Mahwah, NJ: Lawrence Erlbaum Associates.

Brown, A. L. (1992). Design experiments: Theoretical and methodological challenges in creating complex interventions. *Journal of the Learning Sciences, 2* (2), 141–178.

Bryk, A. S., Gomez, L. M., & Grunow, A. (2010). *Getting ideas into action: Building networked improvement communities in education.* Stanford, CA: Carnegie Foundation for the Advancement of Teaching. (Essay). Retrieved from http://www.carnegiefoundation.org/spotlight/webinar-bryk-gomez-building-networkedimprovement-communities-in-education

Cho, K. L., & Jonassen, D. H. (2002). The effects of argumentation scaffolds on argumentation and problem solving. *Educational Technology Research and Development, 50*(3), 5–22.

Cobb, P., Confrey, J., deSessa, A., Lehrer, R., & Schauble, L. (2003). Design experiments in educational research. *Educational Researcher, 32*(1), 9–13.

Collins, A., Joseph, D., & Bielaczyc, K. (2004). Design research: Theoretical and methodological issues. *Journal of the Learning Sciences, 13*(1), 15–42.

Duffy, T., & Jonassen, D. H. (Eds.), (1992). *Constructivism and the Technology of Instruction: A Conversation.* Hillsdale, NJ: Lawrence Erlbaum Associates.

Engestrom, Y. (1999). Activity theory and individual and social transformation. In Y. Engrestrom, R. Miettinen, & R-L. Punamaki (Eds.), *Perspectives on activity theory* (pp. 19–38). Cambridge: Cambridge University Press.

Ge, X., & Land, S. M. (2003). Scaffolding students' problem-solving processes in an ill-structured task using question prompts and peer interactions. *Educational Technology Research and Development, 51*(1), 21–38.

Greeno, J. G., Collins, A. M., & Resnick, L. B. (1996). Cognition and learning. In D. C. Berliner & R. C. Calfee (Eds.), *Handbook of educational psychology* (pp. 15–46). New York, NY: Macmillan.

Hutchins, E., & Klausen, T. (1996). Distributed cognition in an airline cockpit. In D. Middleton & Y. Engeström (Eds.), *Communication & cognition at work* (pp. 15–34). Cambridge, UK: Cambridge University Press.

Interactive Multimedia Pty Ltd. (n.d.) Exploring the Nardoo. Retrieved from http://www.impty.com/nardoo.htm#rev1

Iowa Department of Education. (1989). A guide to developing higher order thinking across the curriculum. Des Moines, IA: Department of Education. Retrieved from http://www.eric.ed.gov/PDFS/ED306550.pdf

Jonassen, D. H. (1990). Toward a constructivistic conception of instructional design. *Educational Technology, 30*(9), 32–34.

Jonassen, D. H. (1996). *Computers in the classroom: Mindtools for critical thinking.* Columbus, OH: Merrill/Prentice-Hall.

Jonassen, D. H. (1997). Instructional design model for well-structured and ill-structured problem-solving learning outcomes. *Educational Technology Research and Development, 45*(1), 65–95.

Jonassen, D. H. (1999). Designing constructivist learning environments. In C. M. Reigeluth, (Ed.), *Instructional design theories and models: A new paradigm of instructional technology,* Vol. 2 (pp. 215–240). Mahwah, NJ: Lawrence Erlbaum Associates.

Jonassen, D. H. (2000a). Toward a design theory of problem solving. *Educational Technology Research and Development, 48*(4), 63–85.

Jonassen, D. H. (2000b). *Computers as mindtools for schools: Engaging critical thinking.* Columbus, OH: Prentice-Hall.

Jonassen, D. H. (2002). Engaging and supporting problem solving in online learning. *The Quarterly Review of Distance Education, 3*(1), 1–13.

Jonassen, D. H. (2004). *Learning to solve problems: An instructional design guide.* San Francisco, CA: Pfeiffer/Jossey-Bass.

Jonassen, D. H., & Grabowski, B. L. (1993). *Handbook of individual differences, learning and instruction.* Hillsdale, NJ: Lawrence Erlbaum Associates.

Jonassen, D. H., & Reeves, T. C. (1996). Learning with technology: Using computers as cognitive tools. In D. H. Jonassen (Ed.), *Handbook of research for educational communications and technology* (pp. 693–719). New York: Macmillan.

Jonassen, D. H., Beissner, K., & Yacci, M. A. (1993). *Structural knowledge: Techniques for representing, assessing, and acquiring structural knowledge.* Hillsdale, NJ: Lawrence Erlbaum Associates.

Jonassen, D. H., Cernusca, D., & Ionas, G. (2007). Constructivism and instructional design: The emergence of the learning sciences and design research. In R. A. Reiser & J. V. Dempsey (Eds.), *Trends and issues in instructional design and technology* (2nd ed.) (pp. 45–61). Upper Saddle River, N.J.: Merrill/Prentice Hall.

Jonassen, D. H., Howland, J., Moore, J., & Marra, R. M. (2003) *Learning to solve problems with technology: A constructivist perspective* (2nd ed.). Columbus, OH: Merrill/Prentice-Hall.

Kapur, M., & Kinzer, C. K. (2009). Productive failure in CSCL groups. *International Journal of CSCL, 4*(1), 21–46.

Kapur, M., Voiklis, J., & Kinzer, C. (2008). Sensitivities to early exchange in synchronous computer-supported collaborative learning (CSCL) groups. *Computers and Education, 51,* 54–66.

Koschmann, T., Kelson, A. C., Feltovich, P. J., & Barrows, H. S. (1996). Computer-supported problem-based learning: A principled approach to the use of computers in collaborative learning. In T. Koschmann (Ed.), *CSCL: Theory and practice of an emerging paradigm* (pp. 83–124). Hillsdale, NJ: Lawrence Erlbaum Associates.

Lauenbacher, G. E., Campbell, J. D., Sorrows, B. B., & Mahling, D. E. (1997). Supporting collaborative, problem-based learning through information system technology. *Proceedings of Frontiers in Education Conference at the 27th Annual Conference Teaching and learning in an Era of Change,* Vol. 3, 1252–1256.

Marton F., & Pang, M. F. (2006). On some necessary conditions of learning. *The Journal of the Learning Sciences, 15,* 193–220.

Oh, S. C., & Jonassen, D. H. (2007). Scaffolding argumentation during problem solving. *Journal of Computer Assisted Learning, 23*(2), 95–105.

Orrill, C. H. (2002). Supporting online PBL: Design considerations for supporting distributed problem solving. *Distance Education, 23*(1), 41–57.

Paavola, S., & Hakkarainen, K. (2005). The knowledge creation metaphor – An emergent epistemological approach to learning. *Science & Education, 14,* 535–557.

Pea, R. (1993). Practices of distributed intelligence and designs for education. In G. Salomon (Ed.), *Distributed Cognitions: Psychological and Educational Considerations* (pp. 47–87). Cambridge: Cambridge University Press.

Reigeluth, C. M. (Ed.), (1999). *Instructional-design theories and models. A new paradigm of instructional theory,* Vol. II. Mahwah, NJ: Lawrence Erlbaum Associates.

Salomon, G., Perkins, D. N., & Globerson, T. (1991). Partners in cognition: Extending human intelligences with intelligent technologies. *Educational Researcher,* 2–9.

Savery, J. R. (2006). Overview of problem-based learning: definitions and distinctions. *The Interdisciplinary Journal of Problem-based Learning.* Retrieved from http://docs.lib.purdue.edu/cgi/viewcontent.cgi?article=1002&context=ijpbl.

Savery, J. R., & Duffy, T. M. (1996). Problem-based learning: An instructional model and its constructivist framework. In B. Wilson (Ed.), *Constructivist learning environments: Case studies in instructional design* (pp. 135–148). Englewood Cliffs, NJ: Educational Technological Publications.

Scardamalia, M., & Bereiter, C. (2006). Knowledge building: Theory, pedagogy, and technology. In Sawyer, R. K. (Ed.), *The Cambridge Handbook of the Learning Sciences* (pp. 97–118). NY: Cambridge University Press.

Stahl, G. (2004). Building collaborative knowing: Elements of a social theory of CSCL. In J. W. Strijbos, P. A. Kirschner, & R. L. Martens (Eds.), *What we know about CSCL: And implementing it in higher education* (pp. 53–86). The Netherlands: Kluwer Academic Publishers.

Sfard, A. (1998). On two metaphors for learning and the dangers of choosing just one. *Educational Researcher, 27*(2), 4–13.

Tan, O. S. (2000). Thinking skills, creativity and problem-based learning. Paper presented at the 2nd Asia Pacific Conference on Problem-Based Learning: Education Across Disciplines. Singapore, December 4–7, 2000.

Yeo, J. (2008). *Orchestrating talk for science meaning making in a problem-based learning classroom mediated by computer-supported collaborative learning.* (Unpublished doctoral dissertation). National Institute of Education, Nanyang Technological University, Singapore.

Yeo, J., & Tan, S. C. (2010). Constructive use of authoritative sources in science meaning making. *International Journal of Science Education, 32*(13), 1739–1754.

Yeo, J., & Tan, S. C. (2011). How groups learn: Implications for collaborative work in science. *The Asia-Pacific Education Researcher, 20*(2), 231–245.

Yeo, J., Tan, S. C., & Lee, Y. J. (in press). A learning journey in problem-based learning in a physics classroom. *The Asia-Pacific Education Researcher.*

Wijekumar, K. K., & Jonassen, D. H. (2007). The role of computer tools in experts' solving ill-structured problems. *Computers in Human Behavior, 23*, 664–704.

Wilson, B. G. (2005). Theory and method as tools: Reflections on research on the pedagogical uses of ICT in education. *Computers in Human Behavior, 21*, 541–546.

Wisconsin Center for Education Research. (1996). *WCER Highlights, 8*(1), 1–3. Retrieved from http://www.wcer.wisc.edu/publications/highlights/v8n1.pdf

Zumbach, J., & Reimann, P. (1999). Combining computer supported collaborative argumentation and problem-based learning: An approach for designing online learning environments. Workshop on Computer Supported Collaborative Argumentation conducted at the CSCL99 Conference, Stanford, California.

Zumbach, J., Hillers, A., & Reimann, P. (2003). Supporting distributed problem-based learning: The Use of feedback in online learning. In T. Roberts (Ed.), *Online collaborative learning: Theory and practice* (pp. 86–102). Hershey, PA: Idea Group.

10 Reconsidering Epistemology, Learning and Design

Michael J. Hannafin

Introduction

Designers face varied, often competing, demands across different disciplines and clients. This has stimulated significant but divergent demands from social scientists, professional educators, training professionals, basic scientists, and K12 and post-secondary educators. While prospects appear unlimited, the approach needed to address these design challenges continues to be disputed. Disagreements concerning the role and influence of differing theoretical, philosophical, epistemological and pedagogical perspectives on design have been debated for more than a century, but with little resolution (see, e.g. R.E. Clark, 1983; Kozma, 1991; Sheehan & Johnson, 2012). Constructivists, for example, define learning as "a change in social activity that integrates what is known with how one came to know it" (Tobias & Duffy, 2009, p. 8). They present evidence that different approaches facilitate learning, especially for ill-structured problems and in ill-structured domains. Critics, however, question the basis for these assertions as well as the implications for associated design practices. Criticisms have been levied against a range of learning approaches including discovery, problem-based, experiential, and inquiry-based teaching. While the debates often center on constructivism versus objectivism, I argue that the design issues require close examination of underlying theories, epistemologies and research appropriate for directed versus non-directed approaches to support learning.

Fundamental questions are apparent: Can (or should) design requirements reflect presumed underlying epistemological beliefs and values? This chapter compares perspectives advanced by supporters and critics of non-directed learning environments in learning and design, and how non-directed learning approaches influence design. My intent is not to repeat arguments that have already been debated exhaustively, but rather to clarify contentions that underscore the implications for non-directed approaches to design.

Epistemology, Theory and Design

According to Jonassen (2008), students "attribute too much truth-value to theories ... accept theories ... without questioning the meaning or veracity ...

are unable to adequately criticize or evaluate the utility of theories [and] often misinterpret and misapply them. If we expect our students to base research and design decisions on theories, then we must teach students to treat them differently" (p. 45). He then stated, "The proper study of theories is rooted in epistemology, the branch of philosophy that deals with the nature of knowledge and truth. Epistemology is concerned with fundamental questions, such as: What is knowledge? What do people know? How is that knowledge acquired?" (p. 46).

Nearly a century ago Dewey (1916) described user-centered learning as "that reconstruction or reorganization of experience which adds to the meaning of experience, and which increases ability to direct the course of subsequent experience" (p. 76). Human reasoning, in effect, involves self-action, interaction, and transaction; individuals initiate or act differently according to context-specific circumstances. Dewey (1938) subsequently advocated providing students opportunities to test hypotheses and explore issues critically, which lie at the heart of non-directed learning design. Similar beliefs are now evident across diverse learning environments including discovery learning, problem-based learning, and inquiry-based learning.

Emerging Differences in Learning and Design

Recent research confirms wide variations in philosophies and methods among instructional designers (Sheehan & Johnson, 2012). Unlike "mere vehicles," Winn (1992) suggested distinctions between design as delivery of content and design as tools, or shells, that embody epistemic and learning assumptions differently. The tool metaphor offers an alternative view as neither the product nor object, but rather as enabling designer shells that rely less on hierarchical content organizers but as the means through which designs are dynamically constructed.

Other important, but largely overlooked differences exist between the values, beliefs and practices across disciplines (Stroble, Cernusca, & Jonassen, 2004). Increasingly, educators strive to immerse students in the everyday culture and practices in mathematics, history, science, law, medical education and engineering. Significant advances have been spearheaded largely by scholars outside the IT (instructional technology) design traditions, who have pushed the forefront of design. It is designers who determine how much or how little we enhance the disciplines we presume to support. The needs of clients have expanded and evolved, as has the instructional designers preparing to support those needs; we risk becoming insulated from important developments and further isolated from those we would otherwise support" (Clark & Hannafin, 2011).

Boling and Smith (2011) also described basic differences in design foci – some built upon validated design principles, others on problem-solving. Not all learning environments can successfully apply the same principles to address vastly different design requirements. Tam (2000) noted that the design task requires providing a rich context within which meaning can be negotiated and ways of understanding can emerge and develop. She concluded that the debate among scholars and practitioners is essential for clarifying foundations and assumptions as well as for promoting understanding of the value of different perspectives and methods. There is no single way to conceptualize learning or instructional systems.

Jonassen (2008) characterized design as iterative decision-making. Designers weigh constraints and functional specifications to determine design requirements (materials, functionality, style, medium, etc.) based on emergent problem constraints and personal biases. "Decisions represent a moderately ill-structured kind of problem in which the problem solver evaluates two or more optional outcomes and commits to an option ... Decisions may be simple, or they may be complex, involving multiple options, multiple criteria, along with numerous perspectives on each criteria" (Jonassen, 2012, p. 341). Similarly, Marston and Mistree (1997) noted, "The principal role of the designer is to make decisions. Decisions help to bridge the gaps between idea and reality, decisions serve as markers to identify the progression of the design from initiation to implementation to termination" (p. 1).

Self-Directed, Self-Regulated Learning (SRL)

Methodological differences need to account for fundamentally different theories, epistemologies, and assumptions about learning (Jonassen, 2008). Design demands, therefore, are rapidly changing; strategies must vary according to shifting learning goals, contexts, and requirements. Critical differences are evident in the nature of and goals for learning. Alternatives are needed to guide and support individual sense-making and reasoning; alternatives do not direct learning to specific defined outcomes uniform across learners, but rather support the individual's negotiation of meaning base on individual goals and needs.

SRL (self-regulated learning) approaches often share epistemological and theoretical foundations. Collectively, their focus encompasses a range of SRL approaches including problem-based learning (Dochy et al., 2003; Savery, 2006), project-based learning (Blumenfeld et al., 1991), student-centered, open learning environments (Hannafin et al., in press), case-based learning (Erskine et al., 1998), cognitive apprenticeships (Collins, Brown, & Newman, 1989), and anchored instruction (Cognition and Technology Group at Vanderbilt, 1992). According to Kuhn (2007), student inquiry skills and strategies have become increasingly critical to contemporary, dynamic, education at all levels. Individuals pursue resolution to ill-defined issues, formulate and test hypotheses, design plans, collect and analyze information, and generate and evaluate solutions or artifacts of their understanding. SRL designers nurture and guide the pursuit of deep understanding via self-directed activity. Individuals are scaffolded and guided individually as they learn; they rarely engage in pure discovery as characterized by Mayer. In a recent debate contrasting perspectives on learning and design, I argued that: "No single design methodology is sufficiently robust to address the diversity and complexity of all learning goals" (Clark & Hannafin, 2011, p. 377).

Appropriate methodologies do not simply separate objectivists from relativists but guide the disciplined study of any research questions that reveals appropriate design strategies. Where research questions can be well-addressed via "gold standard" experimental rigor, such methods are warranted and necessary; to the extent they cannot be appropriately addressed by such methods, however, the methodology must vary accordingly. Kuhn (2007) suggested that direct instruction research and associated design strategies fail to answer the questions posed by SRL advocates. She suggests that typical SRL research and design questions require methods that differ in focus and intent to gold-standard methods advocated by critics. Similarly, Hmelo-Silver et al. (2007) analyzed findings from a range of PBL and inquiry learning studies which provided empirical support for SRL. Land, Hannafin, and Oliver (2011) also reported numerous student-centered efforts with compelling evidence for effects and impacts, as well as issues and concerns for both researchers and designers.

The potential and applicability of student-centered approaches has been well-supported, but persistent questions remain. If traditional experimental methodologies do not adequately address SRL learning and design questions, which methods are needed? Research supporting SRL design has documented effects for knowledge acquisition and application, problem solving, critical thinking, decision making, collaboration, and communication skills. Flynn and Klein (2001) reported that college students who engage in collaborative, case-based learning are more highly motivated and learn more effectively than those working independently. Meta-analyses indicated that PBL offers significant benefits over traditional methods of education (Gijbels et al., 2005; Vernon & Blake, 1993; Walker & Leary, 2009). PBL students gained slightly less knowledge, but retained the knowledge over longer periods of time and applied the knowledge and skills more effectively that those receiving direct instruction (Dochy et al., 2003). PBL improvements were also reported for thinking and problem-solving skills, effective communication skills, and for their own learning (Lieux, 1996).

Several researchers have documented both effective and ineffective SRL approaches. Case-based learning, for example, immerses learners in authentic contexts that require examination of alternative solutions (Erskine et al., 1998; Levin, 1995). Meta-analyses indicated that PBL offers significant benefits over traditional methods of education (Gijbels et al., 2005; Vernon & Blake, 1993; Walker & Leary, 2009). Students in PBL gained slightly less knowledge, but retained it over longer periods of time and tended to apply the knowledge and skills more effectively than those receiving direct instruction (Dochy et al., 2003). PBL students also developed stronger thinking and problem-solving skills, more effective communication skills, and a greater sense of personal autonomy than did students who received direct instruction (Lieux, 1996). Project-based learning researchers have documented similar benefits for both professional and academic purposes. Engineering students confronted open-ended, real-world problems that required the application of engineering concepts and interactions with outside clients. Employers reported that those who addressed real-world tasks were "more mature, had greater communication skills, and had a greater understanding of working with clients" (Chinowsky et al., 2006, p. 123). Charney et al. (2007), while teaching science as inquiry, reported that apprenticing high school students with university scientists improved students' hypotheses generation, considered alternative hypotheses, provided appropriate models and logical arguments, connected ideas, extended concepts, and posed relevant questions. According to Eskrootchi and Oskrochi (2010), middle-schoolers who participated in project simulations comprehended domain content knowledge, improved attitudes toward science and learning, and invested additional time and effort in their studies.

Still, while evidence is promising, SRL strategies do not universally support all types of learning for all learners. Schwartz and Bransford (1998), influential in developing and validating the Jasper Woodbury mathematics series, reported that didactic instruction was needed to provide essential domain knowledge for young students with limited prior knowledge. Hill and Hannafin (1997) noted that limited domain knowledge and technology facility can confound the implementation of support strategies. Similarly, Şendağ and Odabaşı (2009) reported that online PBL did not improve mathematics content knowledge appreciably, although critical thinking skills increased. Medical students with limited prior science knowledge reported greater difficulty when encountering embedded domain content within PBL, while those who completed individual prerequisite courses did not (Tedman et al. 2011). Many students lack the background and metacognitive wherewithal to regulate their learning (Hannafin & Land, 1997) and require significant support. Thus, fundamental design questions remain as to which strategies are most appropriate for different priorities and contextual assumptions

Design for Self-Regulated Learning

For self-directed, online learning, Song and Hill (2008) noted that instructors need to align their own epistemological beliefs with the practice of instructional design that is explicitly student centered. Can we support individually different goals, needs, and demands across diverse learners? Using grounded design, consider how we may clarify contextually specific epistemological perspectives, support associated learning goals and needs, and align epistemology, methodology, and assessment.

We have applied underlying assumptions for learning environments and integrated grounded design practices (see Hannafin, Lee & Chang, in press). The recognition of a client's values and goals is critical to assessing implications for design. Designers recognize similarities to, and differences between, personal perspectives and the client's values and goals for learning. Unfortunately, the failure to acknowledge such differences, or to one's views to the exclusion of, or detriment to, the client's perspectives, mismatches the over-arching frame of the product or service. This is evident independent of the designer's particular views; designs that are not consonant with and support the client's goals and needs provide fixed solutions to undefined learning goals and needs.

Grounded design also involves recognizing the assumptions attendant to given learning goals. Clients may espouse relativist learning goals seeking to promote individual reasoning over canonical "correctness" of domain content. For example, a client's goal may be to examine scientific discoveries from different cultural perspectives to compare perspectives, evaluate individual differences, and recognize how events are documented in different regions of the world. The foundation may draw psychologically from situated cognition theory rather than behavioral theory to demonstrate the influence of situated thinking.

The pedagogical design requirements need to support, and be consistent with, the associated perspectives and foundations. Assuming the above epistemological and psychological assumptions, some design strategies are better aligned than others. In the ongoing example, the designer seeks validated strategies for similar learning goals. Given the situated cognition frame, anchored instruction may well promote the desired while examining different documents, but the context may also involve competing priorities such as evident in accountability-oriented which emphasize performance on standardized assessments. To address McCaslin and Good's (1992) concerns for *compliant cognition*, the designer may emphasize examples of where various aspects are documented differently.

Technological, cultural and pragmatic foundations must also be weighed in planning and implementing appropriately grounded designs for learning. Given contextual availability and constraints, the designer may include threaded discussion boards to highlight similarities and differences in individual or group interpretations, provide learning objects comprising collections of different accounts, provide an in-house blog to support students in organizing and representing differences in perceptions, sharing of interpretations, and exchanging comments. Students may seek further Web documentation beyond the repository to catalog editorial opinions as they co-construct positions and opinions, and collaboratively document shared knowledge in a wiki. Assessments might focus on individual and group artifacts documenting positions and justifications, revised position papers with supporting argumentation, and presentations demonstrating changes in student reasoning as documented over time.

Criticisms of SRL

Clearly, authorities have raised serious questions regarding the credibility and wisdom of SRL and its underlying assumptions. Critics have challenged the validity of the current shifts in theory, epistemology, and practices that guide self-directed designs. Are epistemological shifts unprecedented and unwarranted, as suggested by Merrill, Drake, Lacy, Pratt, and the ID_2 Research Group (1996)?

> Too much of the structure of educational technology is built upon the sand of relativism, rather than the rock of science. When winds of new paradigms blow and the sands of old paradigms shift; then the structure of educational technology slides toward the sea of pseudo-science and mythology. We stand firm against the shifting sands of new paradigms and "realities" … We boldly reclaim the technology of instructional design that is built upon the rock of instructional science.
>
> (Merrill, Drake, Lacy, Pratt, and the ID2 Research Group, 1996, p. 7)

Clark (in Clark & Hannafin, 2011) note that:

> "Solid evidence, collected by many researchers over the past half century clearly indicates that many of our popular design strategies and enthusiasms are groundless or worse. We avoid evidence that some of these opinion-based strategies can cause people to become more ignorant than they were before they tried to learn something".
>
> (Clark & Hannafin, 2011, p. 375)

He speculated that interest in constructivism may be fueled by lack of "motivation or training necessary to invest the effort to carefully review complex research on learning and instruction … ambivalence about research training…optimal guidance for external goals is also optimal for self-chosen goals" (p. 375). Clark also suggested that while individuals may prefer to pursue individual goals but questioned whether self-regulation was warranted: "What I want to find (and so what I value most) is fully guided instruction…optimal guidance for external goals is also optimal for self-chosen goals" (p. 375).

Clark's (1983) often-cited, classic criticism of media comparison research provided sound and well-reasoned arguments that underscored flaws in traditional, but widely disseminated, media research. It also, however, stimulated critical distinctions between those who focus on learning *with* versus learning *from* media. Kozma (1991), who advocated for reconsidering media as tools rather than delivery devices, challenged Clark's position as an "unnecessary schism between medium and method" as he distinguished learning *from* media from learning *with* media: "Ultimately, our ability to take advantage of the power of emerging technologies will depend on the creativity of designers, their ability to exploit the capabilities of the media, and our understanding of the relationship between these capabilities and learning" (pp. 457).

Critics also contend that many children lack the cognitive capabilities to think and act like adult experts; hence, they require accurate and complete information as well as demonstrations of how and when learning tasks are processed and performed and question the empirical basis of constructivist's assumptions. Mayer (2004) analyzed 50 years of research that supports direct instruction but noted little support for pure discovery learning. R. C. Clark and Mayer's (2011a) chapter, "Using Rich Media Wisely" detailed empirically-based design guidelines that refuted, and often contradicted, current alternative foundations and associated design strategies (Clark & Mayer, 2011b). Kirschner, Sweller, and R. E. Clark (2006) argued: "After a half century of advocacy associated with instruction using minimal guidance ... there is no body of research supporting the technique ... evidence from controlled studies almost uniformly supports direct, strong instructional guidance rather than constructivist-based minimal guidance [for] novice to intermediate learners" (pp. 83–84). These views were recently reinforced by Azevedo and colleagues (Azevedo, Moos, Greene, Winters, & Cromley, 2008; Azevedo, Behnagh, Duffy, Harley, & Trevors, 2012).

Similar criticisms stem from disagreements as to what constitutes valid evidence to support claims and conclusions, that is, what does (and does not) constitute "gold standard" research methodology. Sweller, Kirschner and R.E. Clark (2006) suggest that "randomized, controlled tests of competing instructional processes" are needed where individual moderating variables are "properly controlled" (p. 115) to validate constructivists' assertions.

The Challenges Ahead: Re-framing the Debate

It is clear that the debate over which perspective is right or correct has not yet yielded solutions to diverse learning requirements. Arguably, neither die-hard direct instruction nor SRL enthusiasts have provided sufficient evidence to warrant the guidelines needed for self-directed learning. Neither advocates nor critics appear able to acknowledge legitimate limitations and reservations for design. While some promising avenues have been broached, SRL enthusiasts require better documented, convincing evidence to guide and replicate successful design strategies. The following issues require both reasonable, appropriate research methods for inquiry, as well as associated implications for design.

Scaffolding SRL

Scaffolding research has been reported for decades, but support for SRL design is only emerging. Since prior knowledge, goals, and intent often cannot be known in advance and can vary dramatically across learners, scaffolding often focuses on general cognitive support. Research is needed to refine our understanding of the scaffolding needed, how those supports vary, and the extent to which individual goals and intents are addressed effectively.

Evaluating Available Resources

While the Internet has dramatically increased access to information, resource quality varies in terms of accuracy, authority, and completeness. Often, Web resources contain naïve and ill-informed information, some of which may intentionally impart biased propaganda. Since naïve students attempt to address individual needs, but typically lack metacognitive abilities to monitor and regulate understanding effectively, we need to examine how perceptions of different resources influence students' evaluations and interpretations.

Providing Adaptive vs. Fixed Scaffolds

While the potential to adapt to individual differences holds promise, fixed scaffolds have proven largely applicable to formal procedures and generic reasoning, research suggests that soft (adaptive) scaffolds have the potential to address individual needs dynamically. Adaptive scaffolding by teachers, peers and other "human" resources is better able to accommodate real-time, dynamic changes in learner needs and cognitive demands. However, limited evidence has been published to indicate that adaptive supports perform comparably when technologically mediated. Given the rapid growth in technology-facilitated SRL, the potential of electronically-mediated supports warrants further study.

Negotiating Meaning

Some resources may appear to address learning needs effectively, but many will not. Understanding is enhanced comparing individual resources containing partial, potentially contradictory information. Meaning must be interpreted, inferred, and derived through individual scrutiny. Research is needed to gauge that meaning is derived differentially based on unique needs and goals, and the extent to which individual needs are addressed.

Utilizing Prior Knowledge

Familiarity with browser tools may predict success more accurately than prior domain knowledge and experience alone. Remillard (2005) indicated that teachers' prior knowledge and experience influenced and often dominated how SRL activities were enacted in classroom settings. In Hill and Hannafin's (1997) study, teachers located Internet content for grade-appropriate materials for a subject of their choosing. Prior tool expertise facilitated learning more than prior domain knowledge or experience:

Teachers with previous browser experience were more successful and reported greater confidence independent of prior teaching experiences. While familiarity with browser technology will undoubtedly increase across users, the influence of system experience during SRL may well be underestimated.

Reconciling Meaning

SRL environments emphasize the value of personal investigation, hypothesis formation and testing. In Land and Zembal-Saul's (2003) studies, college-age participants obtained and documented evidence during experiments in portfolios, and generated hypotheses to orient future inquiries. While some groups benefited from computer-assisted inquiry, others fell back on faulty prior experiments which misdirected future inquiries even when confronting contradictory evidence. SRL functioned as expected only when students had adequate background knowledge, evaluated their knowledge limitations, critical questioned and clarified, and evaluated faulty explanations. According to the "situated learning paradox" (Land & Hannafin, 2000), prior knowledge needed to orient and guide sense-making often reflects incomplete and inaccurate misconceptions. Without scaffolded reconciliation, misinformation and disinformation may go undetected, as misunderstandings become reified rather than reconciled.

Guiding or to Telling?

Hard scaffolds characteristically have been applied to support shared needs across students. The instructor, then, provides on-demand, contextually sensitive support for individual needs. Azevedo and Hadwin's (2005) scaffolds were presented dynamically to support specific types of learning, tools, and individual needs. Conceptual scaffolds identify information relevant to the learning context (Brush & Saye, 2000, 2001). Research indicates that soft (adaptive) scaffolding technologies may address the varied needs of individual student-centered learners (Saye & Brush, 2007). Kim, Hannafin, and Bryan's (2007) scaffolding framework outlines interplay between and among technology, teachers and students in SRL contexts. The scaffolding provided by "human" resources is believed to accommodate real-time, dynamic changes in learner needs and cognitive demands. Again, however, research findings documenting these effects have proven equivocal. Technology supports during multimedia instruction yielded higher scores on basic information, but not the transfer presumed for SRL (Jamet, Gavota & Quaireau, 2008).

Reconciling Attitudes, Beliefs and Practices

In an effort to deepen understanding of mathematics through investigation, Orrill's (2006) website included open-ended investigations, a dictionary, discussion board, and electronic portfolios. Teachers explored available resources, selected problems, and identified individually-relevant instructional paths (in conjunction with face-to-face workshops). Improvements in mathematics skills and depth of knowledge were expected, but teachers instead focused on technology skills, not on their understanding or skills. Research is needed to examine how supports are actually utilized and negotiated, and meaning is differentiated based on individual needs and goals.

Managing Cognitive Load

Disorientation has become increasingly problematic in rich, student-centered, learning environments as learners identify, select, and evaluate available resources based on unique goals. Web resources are numerous and largely unregulated, with quality varying widely in terms of accuracy, authority, and completeness. Eveland and Dunwoody (2001) compared students assigned to browse a website with different hyperlinking and navigation structures with those using only a paper-only guide. The paper-based control group outperformed the online group, suggesting that hyperlinking may increase extraneous cognitive load. Thus, nonlinear websites may increase germane load for some types of learning, but increase extraneous load for others (Eveland and Dunwoody, 2001). In contrast, while students learned factual content best from linear websites designed to optimize germane load, they understood relationships better from nonlinear sites (Eveland et al., 2004). Given the varied learning demands associated with student-centered, web-based learning, optimizing cognitive load differentially will be essential for effective online students. Research is needed to examine how students' evaluate and adapt understanding based on the perceived relevance as well as complimentary versus contradictory nature of available contents.

Monitoring Prerequisite vs. Emergent Learning

Students who have developed metacognitive strategies, or develop them while engaging SRL, perform more successfully than those who do not. Smidt and Heigelheimer (2004), upon interviewing adult learners to detect web-learning strategies, reported that only advanced learners used metacognitive strategies actively while middle- and low-performing students relied mainly on basic cognitive strategies. Their findings suggest that advanced metacognitive abilities are critical, but may be either requisite to, or a consequence of, effective online learning. We need to clarify which strategies learners possess in advance, require advance training in preparation for, or develop while monitoring their progress.

Summary and Conclusions

While we clearly require stronger rigor in SRL research, the problems studies and questions posed necessitate appropriately differentiated methodologies not just experimental rigor. We cannot simply apply methods and standards that fail to adequately and appropriately address relevant questions. The National Science Foundation has published a series of reports designed to promote rigorous qualitative inquiry, as well as design research methods to address shifts in teaching-learning paradigms. Self-regulated learning promotes outcomes and processes that differ from those of direct instruction, thus the methods needed to investigate associated effects and impacts must vary accordingly.

Hannafin, Hannafin, and Gabbitas (2009) distinguished the cognitive demands of direct instruction from student-centered learning related to prior knowledge, allocation and management of cognitive load, beliefs and dispositions, and scaffolding. "Rather than imposing a canonical perspective to supplant initial conceptions, student-centered approaches guide the learners in challenging their initial assumptions as they test and refine initial conceptions" (p. 772). Similarly, Land (2000) concluded that "strategies are needed to help learners ... construct coherent explanations and self-regulate when they have little background knowledge" (p.76). Learner variables must be accounted for.

Can we reasonably apply strategies proven effective for outcome-based instruction to learning that is not as self-directed learning critics propose? That is not feasible or appropriate. Rather, we need to determine which approaches are responsive and appropriate to support challenging, and often fundamentally different, perspectives on the nature of teaching and learning.

References

Azevedo, R., Moos, D., Greene, J., Winters, F., & Cromley, J. (2008). Why is externally-facilitated regulated learning more effective that self-regulated learning with hypermedia? *Educational Technology Research & Development, 56*(1), 45–72.

Azevedo, R., Behnagh, R., Duffy, M., Harley, J., & Trevors, G. (2012). Metacognition and self-regulated learning in student-centered learning environments. In D. H. Jonassen & S. M. Land (Eds.), *Theoretical foundations of learning environments* (2nd ed.) (pp. 171–197). New York: Routledge.

Blumenfeld, P., Soloway, E., Marx, R., Krajcik, J., Guzdial, M., & Palincsar, A. (1991). Motivating project-based learning: Sustaining the doing, supporting the learning. *Educational Psychologist, 26*(3, 4), 369–398.

Boling, E., & Smith, K. (2011). The changing nature of design. In R. Reiser & J. Dempsey (Eds), *Trends and issues in instructional design and technology* (3rd ed.) (pp. 358–366). Upper Saddle River, NJ: Merrill/Prentice-Hall.

Charney, J., Hmelo-Silver, C. E., Sofer, W., Neigeborn, L., Coletta, S., & Nemeroff, M. (2007). Cognitive apprenticeship in science through immersion in laboratory practices. *International Journal of Science Education, 29*, 195–213.

Chinowsky, P., Brown, H., Szajnman, A., & Realph, A. (2006). Developing knowledge landscapes through project-based learning. *Journal of Professional Issues in Engineering Issues and Practice, 132*(2), 118–124.

Clark R. C., & Mayer, R.E. (2011a). Using rich media wisely. In R. Reiser & J. Dempsey (Eds.), *Trends and issues in instructional design and technology* (3rd ed.) (pp. 309–320)). Upper Saddle River, NJ: Merrill/Prentice-Hall.

Clark, R. C., & Mayer, R. E. (2011b). *E-Learning and the science of instruction: Proven guidelines for consumers and designers of multimedia learning.* New York: John Wiley & Sons.

Clark, R. E. (1983). Reconsidering research on learning from media. *Review of Educational Research, 53*, 445–459.

Clark, R. E., & Hannafin, M. J. (2011). Debate about the benefits of different levels of instructional guidance. In R. Reiser & J. Dempsey (Eds.), *Trends and issues in instructional design and technology* (3rd ed.) (pp. 367–382). Upper Saddle River, NJ: Merrill/Prentice-Hall.

Diggelen, W-v. (2009). Grounded design: Design patterns as the link between theory and practice. *Computers in Human Behavior, 25*(5), 1056–1966.

Dochy, F., Segers, M., van den Bosche, P., & Gijbels, D. (2003). Effects of problem-based learning: A meta-analysis. *Learning and Instruction, 13*(5), 553–568.

Duffy, T., & Jonassen, D. H. (Eds.), (1992). *Constructivism and the technology of instruction: A conversation.* Hillsdale, NJ: Lawrence Erlbaum Associates.

Duffy, T. M., Lowyck, J., & Jonassen, D. H. (Eds.), (1993). *The design of constructivistic learning environments: Implications for instructional design and the use of technology.* Heidelburg, FRG: Springer-Verlag.

Erskine, J. A., Leenders, M. R., & Mauffette-Leenders, L. A. (1998). *Teaching with cases* (2nd ed.). London: Ivey Publishing.

Eskrootchi, R., & Oskrochi, G. R. (2010). *Educational Technology & Society, 13*(1), 236–245.

Eveland, W. P., & Dunwoody, S. (2001). User control and structural isomorphism or disorientation and cognitive load? Learning from the Web versus print. *Communication Research, 28*(1), 48–78.

Eveland, W. P., Jr., Cortese, J., Park, H., & Dunwoody, S. (2004). How Web site organization influences free recall, factual knowledge, and knowledge structure. *Human Communication Research, 30*, 208–233.

Gijbels, D., Dochy, P., van den Bossche, P., & Segers, M. (2005). Effects of problem-based learning: A meta-analysis from the angle of assessment. *Review of Educational Research, 75*(1), 27–61.

Hannafin, M. J., Hannafin, K. M., & Gabbitas, B. (2009). Reexamining cognition during student-centered, web-based learning. *Educational Technology Research and Development, 57*, 767–785.

Hannafin, M. J., Hannafin, K. M., Land, S. M., & Oliver, K. (1997). Grounded practice and the design of constructivist learning environments. *Educational Technology Research & Development, 45*(3), 101–117.

Hannafin, M. J., Hill, J. R., Land, S. M., & Lee, E. (in press). Student-centered, open learning environments: Research, theory and practice. In J. M. Spector, M. D. Merrill, J. Elen, & M. J. Bishop (Eds.), *Handbook of research on educational communications and technology* (4th ed.). New York: Springer.

Hannafin, M. J., & Land, S. M. (1997). The foundations and assumptions of technology-enhanced student-centered learning environments. *Instructional Science, 25*(3), 167.

Hannafin, M. J., Lee, E., & Chang, Y. (in press). Philosophical and epistemological differences in design: The case for alignment among foundations, models, and frameworks. In R. Luckin, P. Goodyear, B. Grabowski, S. Puntambeker, J. Underwood, & N. Winters (Eds.), *Handbook on design in educational technology*. New York: Routledge.

Hannafin, M. J., West, R., & Shepherd, C. (2009). The cognitive demands of student-centered, web-based multimedia: Current and emerging perspectives. In R. Zheng (Ed.), *Cognitive effects of multimedia learning* (pp. 194–216). New York: Information Science References.

Hill, J., & Hannafin, M. J. (1997). Cognitive strategies and learning from the World-Wide Web. *Educational Technology Research & Development, 45*(4), 37–64.

Hmelo-Silver, C. E., Duncan, R. G., & Chinn, C. A. (2007). Scaffolding and achievement in problem-based and inquiry learning: A response to Kirschner, Sweller, & Clark (2006). *Educational Psychologist, 42*(2), 99–107.

Jamet, E., Gavota, M., & Quaireau, C. (2008) Attention guiding in multimedia learning. *Learning and instruction, 18*(2), 135–145.

Jonassen, D. H. (1991). Objectivism versus constructivism: Do we need a new philosophical paradigm? *Educational Technology Research & Development, 39*(3), 5–14.

Jonassen, D. H. (1997). Instructional design model for well-structured and ill-structured problem-solving learning outcomes. *Educational Technology Research & Development, 45*(1), 65–95.

Jonassen, D. H. (2003). The vain quest for a unified theory of learning? *Educational Technology, 43*(4), 5–8.

Jonassen, D. H. (2008). It's just a theory. *Educational Technology, Nov–Dec*, 45–48.

Jonassen, D. H. (2011). *Learning to solve problems: A handbook for designing problem-solving learning environments.* New York: Routledge.

Jonassen, D. H. (2012). Designing for decision making. *Educational Technology Research and Development*, 341–359.

Kim, M., Hannafin, M.J., & Bryan, L. (2007). Technology-enhanced inquiry tools in science education: An emerging pedagogical framework for classroom practice. *Science Education, 96*(6), 1010–1030.

Kirschner, P. A., Sweller, J., & Clark, R. E. (2006). Why minimal guidance during instruction does not work: An analysis of the failure of constructivist, discovery, problem-based, experiential, and inquiry-based teaching. *Educational Psychologist, 41*(2), 75–86.

Kozma, R. (1991). Learning with media. *Review of Educational Research, 61*(2), 179–211.

Kuhn, D. (2007). Is direct instruction an answer to the right question? *Educational Psychologist, 42*(2), 109–113.

Land, S. (2000). Cognitive requirements for learning with open-ended learning environments. *Educational Technology Research & Development, 48*(3), 61–78.

Land, S. M., Hannafin, M. J., & Oliver, K. (2012). Student-centered learning environments: Foundations, assumptions and design. In D. Jonassen & S. M. Land (Eds.), *Theoretical foundations of learning environments* (2nd ed.). (pp. 3–25). New York: Routledge.

Land, S. M., & Zembal-Saul, C. (2003). Scaffolding reflection and articulation of scientific explanations in a data-rich, project-based learning environment: An investigation of Progress Portfolio. *Educational Technology Research & Development, 51*(4), 65–84.

Lieux, E. M. (1996). A comparative study of learning in lecture vs. problem-based format. Retrieved May 12, 2011 from http://www.udel.edu/pbl/cte/spr96-nutr.html.

Mayer, R. E. (2004). Should there be a three-strikes rule against pure discovery learning? The case for guided methods of instruction. *American Psychologist, 59*(1), 14–19.

Mayer, R. E., Heiser, J., & Lonn, S. (2001). Cognitive constraints on multimedia learning: When presenting more material results in less understanding. *Journal of Educational Psychology, 93*(1), 187–198.

McCaslin, M., & Good, T. (1992). Compliant cognition: The misalliance of management and instructional goals in current school reform. *Educational Researcher, 21*(3), 4–17.

Merrill, M. D., Drake, L., Lacy, M., Pratt, J., & the ID_2 Research Group (1996). Reclaiming instructional design. *Educational Technology, 36*(5), 5–7.

Nelson, B. C. (2007). Exploring the use of individualized, reflective guidance in an educational Multi-User Virtual Environment. *Journal of Science Education & Technology, 16*(1), 83–97.

Northrup, P. (2001). A framework for designing interactivity into web-based instruction. In A. Rossett, (Ed.), *The ASTD e-learning handbook: Best practices, strategies, and case studies for an emerging field* (pp. 127–138). New York: McGraw-Hill.

Remillard, J. T. (2005). Examining key concepts in research on teachers' use of mathematics curricula. *Review of Educational Research, 75*(2), 211–246.

Saye, J. W., & Brush, T. A. (2007). Using technology-enhanced learning environments to support problem-based historical inquiry in seconday school classroooms. *Theory and Research in Social Education, 35*(2), 196–230.

Schwartz, D. L., & Bransford, J. D. (1998). A time for telling. *Cognition & Instruction, 16*(4), 475–522.

Sheehan, M., & Johnson, R. (2012). Philosophical and methodological beliefs of instructional design faculty and professionals. *Educational Technology Research & Development, 60*(1), 131–153.

Smidt, E., & Hegelheimer, V. (2004). Effects of online academic lectures on ESL listening comprehension, incidental vocabulary acquisition, and strategy use. *Computer Assisted Language Learning, 17*(5), 517–556.

Song, L., & Hill, J. (2008). A conceptual model for understanding self-directed learning in online environments. *Journal of Interactive Online Learning, 6*(1), 27–41.

Strobel, J., Cernusca, D., & Jonassen, D. H. (2004). Different majors – different epistemological beliefs? *Academic Exchange Quarterly*, 208–212.

Tam, M. (2000). Constructivism, instructional design, and technology: Implications for transforming distance learning. *Educational Technology & Society, 3*(2) 2000. [Available at: http://www.ifets.info/journals/3_2/tam.html]

Tedman, R. A., Alexander, H., Massa, H., Moses, D. (2011). Student perception of a new integrated anatomy practical program: Does students' prior learning make a difference? *Clinical Anatomy. 24*(5), 664–670.

Tobias, S., & Duffy, T. M. (Eds.), (2009). *Constructivism theory applied to instruction: Success or failure?* New York: Routledge.

Winn, W. (1992). The assumptions of constructivism and instructional design. In Duffy, T. & Jonassen, D. H. (Eds.), *Constructivism and the technology of instruction: A conversation* (pp. 177–182). Hillsdale, NJ: Lawrence Erlbaum Associates.

11 Conceptualizing Problems in Problem-Based Learning

Its Role and Cognitive Tools

Woei Hung

Introduction

Problem-based learning (PBL) is an innovative instructional method for better preparing students for real-world challenges. It was first conceived in medical education in the 1950s in response to the students' unsatisfactory clinical performance (Barrows, 1996; Barrows & Tamblyn, 1980). This deficiency was attributed to students' ill-established clinical problem-solving and lack of lifelong learning skills (Albanese & Mitchell, 1993; Barrows, 1996). Its implementation began in medical education (Barrows & Tamblyn, 1980; Schmidt, 1983). Currently, approximately 80 percent of medical schools in the US and the majority of medical schools in Canada implement pure PBL or hybrid PBL curricula (Karimi, 2011). With the positive results from implementing PBL in medical education, it has also been embraced by numerous disciplines in higher education (see, for example, Arts, Gijselaers, & Segers, 2002; Woods, 1996; Bridges & Hallinger, 1996). Furthermore, in introducing PBL into K-12 education, Barrows and Kelson (1993) systematically developed PBL curricula and teacher-training programs for all high school core subjects. Since then, PBL has been implemented to enhance K-12 students' problem-solving skills, higher order thinking, collaborative learning skills, and ability to apply various subject content knowledge (for example, Barrows, 2000; Cognition and Technology Group at Vanderbilt (CTGV), 1993; Linn, Shear, Bell, & Slotta, 1999; Kolodner, Camp, Crismond, Fasse, Gray, Holbrook, Puntambekar, & Ryan, 2003; Jacobsen & Spiro, 1994; Maxwell, Mergendoller, & Bellisimo, 2005; Gallagher, Stepien, & Rosenthal, 1992; Torp & Sage, 2002).

Problem-Based Learning – Goals and Process

The goals of PBL have been described as to help students develop (1) problem-solving and reasoning skills, (2) contextualized knowledge structure, (3) self-directed learning skills, (4) motivation to learn, and (5) collaborative skills (Barrows, 1986, Hmelo-Silver, 2004; Norman & Schmidt, 1992). These goals are first realized by the format of PBL in which the content is problem-structured, learning is problem-initiated, and instruction is problem-driven.

During PBL instruction, students actively pursue and collaboratively direct their own learning in small groups with facilitation provided from the instructor (Hung, Jonassen, & Liu, 2008). Then, the process of PBL operationalizes these goals into a series of learning stages and tasks. The first and foremost important goal of PBL is to help students establish their scientific problem-solving skills schema. Therefore, the process of PBL targets the cultivation of such a skill set. At the same time, the specific learning tasks (e.g. defining problem, determining what needs to be known, self-directed researching of necessary information, or managing teamwork) are incorporated into the PBL process to help students develop self-directed learning skills, acquire content knowledge, and practice collaborative learning proficiency. Therefore, the problem-solving process in PBL is the vehicle for affording the development of the other four learning goals in PBL. Thus, although these learning objectives are equally important, problem-solving skills may be deemed as the most vital target skills that students need to develop.

Some PBL implementations structure students' learning with a step-specific PBL process to guide the students to engage in necessary cognitive activities in a scientific problem-solving process. Barrows and Myers' (1993) PBL process and Schmidt's (1983) 7-Jump PBL process are two examples that are widely used in the PBL field (see Table 11.1). Other PBL implementations follow similar processes but may not divide the process into distinctive steps. Regardless of specific steps or the general process utilized, these PBL processes mimic the scientific problem-solving process in order to help students follow a scientific problem-solving process and develop this skills set and schema, rather than rely on intuitive problem-solving habits.

Inadequate Problem Conceptualization during a PBL Process

One of the issues emerging after a few decades of implementation is that students tend to overlook, downplay, or even skip the first four steps of the

Table 11.1 Two examples of PBL process

Barrows and Myers' PBL process	Schmidt's 7-Jump PBL process
1. Set the problem	1. Understand the problem
2. Bring the problem home	2. Define the problem
3. Describe the product/performance required	3. Brainstorming
4. Assign tasks	4. Elaboration: Develop personal "theory"
5. Reasoning through the problem	5. Formulate learning objectives
6. Commitment as to probable outcome	6. Self-study
7. Learning issue shaping/assignment	7. Collaborative learning and reflection
8. Resource identification	
9. Schedule follow-up	

Note: Problem starting, follow-up, presentation, and reflection steps for Barrows and Myers' PBL process are not included here.

PBL process (in 7-Jump process's terms) and go straight to the solution-seeking process. For example, in surveying how students actually solve problems in PBL, Kenny, Bullen, and Loftus (2006) conducted a study investigating undergraduate agricultural sciences students' problem formulation and resolution processes. They analyzed the students' postings from their online discussions to profile the students' general problem-solving approach. They found that approximately only 5 percent of the postings during their PBL sessions were devoted to defining the problem to be solved. This problem-solving habit and approach is likely to result in an incomplete understanding of the problem. Also, Dolmans and her colleagues (Dolmans, Wolfhagen, van der Vleuten, & Wijnen, 2001) observed student behaviors such as coming to tutorials unprepared and spending insufficient time and discussion about understanding the problem before formulating their learning objectives, hypotheses, and solutions, which were indicators of inadequate problem conceptualization. Moreover, Moust, Berkel, and Schmidt's (2005) campus-level evaluation of PBL implementations across programs and curricula at Maastricht University reported similar findings, such as skipping brainstorming and elaboration during group discussions. Similarly, Taylor and Miflin (2008) reported that students preferred to be given learning objectives, rather than go through the process of understanding and conceptualizing the problem in order to generate their own learning objectives. These reports signal a concern that students either do not understand or ignore the importance of problem conceptualization in their PBL processes.

The Role of Problem Conceptualization in PBL

What could happen if students downplay or skip the steps of problem conceptualization in the PBL process? Problem-solving researchers agree that understanding and conceptualizing problems is the first and most critical step for a scientific problem-solving process to take place (Bransford & Stein, 1984; Polya, 1957). In this step, the problem solver constructs the problem space (Newell & Simon, 1972), which serves as the foundation for determining how to approach the problem. In PBL, this process is especially crucial. At first glance, conceptualizing problems appears to be only related to students' development of problem-solving skills. In fact, the results of this conceptualization process have a direct impact on the students' development of self-directed learning skills, content acquisition, as well as collaborative skills.

Self-directed Learning

Self-directed learning in PBL does not equate to free inquiry that the students can decide whatever they would like to study. In fact, PBL curriculum has specific learning goals and objectives for the students to achieve by completing a series of PBL problem modules. Thus, it is important that the students are able to self-direct their problem solving and learning toward the reasoning and practical skills as well as the content knowledge for which the module is designed. Also, self-directed learning is not only about the students' skills for searching relevant information for solving the problem (and therefore acquiring content knowledge), but more importantly, their ability to identify what needs to be learned to reach the goal state of the problem solving. This is a very specific skill that PBL aims to enhance in students for their lifelong learning skills. In order to *effectively* and *independently* determine what knowledge or skills need to be learned, or what information needs to be known, students need a well-constructed problem space. Without a clear and complete understanding of the problem (discrepancy between the current state and goal state of the problem, what is known and unknown, and the constraints), effective self-directed learning is less likely to occur.

Content Knowledge Acquisition

In PBL, content knowledge is acquired by means of solving the problem (Barrows, 1996). The knowledge students acquired through the problem-solving process is applicable knowledge, rather than inert knowledge. Not only do they have to obtain the knowledge (know what), but they also have to apply it to solve the problem (know how). How do students effectively and accurately identify the target content knowledge and skills that meet the curriculum? The key lies in effective self-directed learning processes and skills. PBL students determine what information, knowledge, or skills are necessary for connecting the dots in the path to the solution based on the problem space that they construct, and then conduct further research on this targeted information (and therefore the intended content knowledge). Therefore, a self-directed learning process is the mechanism that determines the content and quality of the knowledge acquired by the students in the PBL process.

Collaborative Learning

This component of PBL functions to reduce individual students' cognitive load (Schmidt, Loyens, van Gog, & Paas, 2007), as well as serving as a platform for students to hone their social, communication, and teamwork skills. In order to work effectively as a team, the cognitive load needs to be effectively distributed to its members to avoid overlapping or missing tasks. More importantly, by identifying the nature of necessary tasks for solving the problem, the team can assign the tasks to the appropriate members based on their background or expertise for optimal team problem-solving performance (Cooke, Salas, Kiekel, & Bell, 2004). Furthermore, effective collaborative problem solving and learning depends on effective teamwork. In PBL, because of the format of small group learning, self-directed learning not only refers to individual students but also the team as a whole. The team collectively self-directs its own problem solving and learning as well as content knowledge acquisition. Therefore, it is important for the team members to work collectively as a cognitive system (Curseu, & Rus, 2005) for the team's self-directed learning to be effective. For this to occur, a collective understanding of the problem is a prerequisite. If there is no consensus from individual students' understanding about the problem, group self-directed learning is unlikely to be effective. When that happens, the collaborative learning in PBL is likely to be just simply a division of labor, rather than an interactive, argumentation process that challenges and therefore refines and fuses individual members' understanding about the problem into a collective problem space.

From the discussion above, it is clear that problem conceptualization is the first step in a scientific problem-solving process, and it is also a premise for the learning activities (problem-solving process, self-directed learning, content knowledge acquisition, and collaborative learning) to be effective in the PBL process and in turn, work together inter-supportively to enhance student' learning outcomes.

Why Students Skip Problem Conceptualization Process

Why do students skip the problem conceptualization process when studying under PBL? There are a number of possibilities. First of all, it has been documented that students tend to use a naïve, intuitive problem-solving approach, rather than a scientific problem-solving process. Several studies (for example, Chi, Feltovich, & Glaser, 1981; deKleer, 1985; Johnson, Flesher, Jehng, & Ferej, 1993) have suggested that a distinct difference between expert and novice problem solvers is that experts tend to qualitatively analyze the problem (that is, conceptualize the problem and construct a problem space) when first faced with a problem, while novices are apt to seek out solutions immediately in their first attempt. When an intuitive problem-solving approach is utilized, the focus of the problem-solving process is to identify *a* working solution, rather than understanding the problem conceptually so that the most effective or viable solution can be devised. Secondly, motivation is a difficult issue faced in most educational settings. Even though PBL is theoretically supposed to motivate students to be active in the learning process by the intrinsic motivation to solve problems (Barrows, 1986), after studying under a PBL format for a while and the process becomes routine, students' motivation starts to subside (Taylor & Miflin, 2008).

It is understandable that students may not possess sophisticated scientific problem-solving skills (knowing the proper process). However, the PBL process provides students with the steps that comprise the scientific problem-solving process to follow. Why do they still choose to skip the conceptualization step? Moreover, if lack of motivation is the problem, why is it the step of problem conceptualization that most students choose to downplay or skip, but not other steps in PBL process? In a typical PBL process, learning objectives (or called learning issues) and delivery of solution in forms of presentations or papers are the two main artifacts that the students have to produce to satisfy the course requirements. Students naturally pay more attention and allocate more time and effort to engaging in and to complete the tasks that are product-based and likely to be graded (e.g. papers or presentations) than the tasks that are process-based and harder to grade (e.g. discussion or brainstorming). Furthermore, compared to traditional curriculum, PBL is more time consuming and heavier in workload (Vardi & Ciccarelli, 2008). When students are not able to allocate an adequate amount of time to complete the learning tasks, some of the steps in the PBL process would have to be downplayed or even skipped. Also, most students are assessment-driven (Perrenet, Bouhuijs, & Smits, 2000). When no specific, tangible products or performance are required as part of their grades, students are likely to downplay the task. Lastly, conceptualization of a problem entails higher order thinking skills as well as high demands on cognitive processing. It requires the students to identify the most critical variables, their inter-causal relationships, as well as the mechanism governing the relationships. This analysis is a difficult cognitive task. Without appropriate tools to support the cognitive processing, as well as high motivation, the difficulty of the task may deter the students from engaging in the process. When any of the these possibilities occur, the process-based learning tasks are more likely to be sacrificed or skipped altogether, which, in the case of PBL, is the step of problem conceptualization and problem space construction.

External Mental Representations and Problem Conceptualization

While there are a number of instructional approaches such as eSTEP (Derry, 2005), case-based reasoning (Kolodner et al., 1993), or scaffolding with question prompts (Ge & Land, 2003) that could help address the issue of skipping problem conceptualization, another possible instructional intervention is visual external representation. First and foremost, construction of a visual external representation produces tangible artifacts. A requirement of producing a visual representation of the problem under study is to convert the problem conceptualization steps in the PBL process from a process-based only task to a process/product-based task which, in turn, could help students more mindfully engage in this learning process. Furthermore, visual representations can facilitate students' problem-conceptualizing processes by reducing cognitive processing load. When students can visualize a complex problem, the sense of being cognitively overwhelmed could be reduced, and as a result, encourage students to engage in the process. Moreover, external representation helps students visualize the inter-causal relationships among the variables in the problem, which enables them to more effectively identify the cause of the problem and the solution path (Sterman, 1994).

Moreover, to facilitate students to mindfully engage in problem conceptualization steps in the PBL process, incorporating construction of external mental representation of the problem provides an explicit learning structure.

Having students brainstorm about what is known, what is unknown, and what could be the underlying cause of the problem (Dolmans & Schmidt, 1994) through an unstructured discussion could result in an ineffective problem conceptualization process, and consequently, ineffective self-directed learning. Also, problem conceptualization is a personal theory construction (Barrows & Myers' PBL process, 1993). The theory needs to be validated through intra-personal (within individual students themselves) and inter-personal (among the students) validation process (Hung, 2009). This effectiveness of the validation process would depend on a well-constructed problem space. External representations of the problem could realistically enable group members to capture the abstract collective cognition into a visual map, and therefore, elevate the effectiveness of collaborative learning in PBL.

Concept map, influence diagrams, and system modeling are three visual representation tools that can help an individual or a group of members visually represent his/her or their mental model about a subject under study. These tools are commonly used for facilitating conceptualization of physical, psychological, social, or political phenomena that are complex and beyond an individual's working memory and cognitive capacity. These three tools all provide basic functions for depicting conceptual representation of a given problem. However, each tool also has its own slightly different emphasis and focus, and therefore provides different specific functions and different levels of conceptualization techniques as well. In the following, I will discuss these tools in terms of their functions and strengths and weaknesses in relation to facilitating students' problem conceptualization processes.

Concept Maps

Jonassen (2006) described the concept map as "a spatial representation of concepts and their interrelationships that simulate the knowledge structures that humans store in their mind" (p. 101) This cognitive tool was developed based on the cognitivist theories explaining how humans structure and organize their knowledge. Rather than storing knowledge in a raw form as it is first received, humans process the information through an encoding process and store the newly acquired information by its semantic relationships with the existing knowledge base (See Figure 11.1). All pieces of information stored in the brain are interlinked into meaningful propositions or complex schemas, which provide the basic structure of human knowledge base (Rumelhart & Norman, 1988; Shiffrin & Schneider, 1980). Concept mapping has been widely utilized in K-12 and higher education, as well as the corporate world (Coffey, Eskridge, & Sanchez, 2004). It has been confirmed that it has very positive effects on facilitating conceptualization process related tasks, such as mental model building (Stout, Cannon-Bowers, Salas, & Milanovich, 1999), meta-cognition (Stoyanov, 1997), self-regulated learning (Tan, Dawson, & Venville, 2008), and conceptual change (Novak, 1998; Trowbridge & Wandersee, 1998).

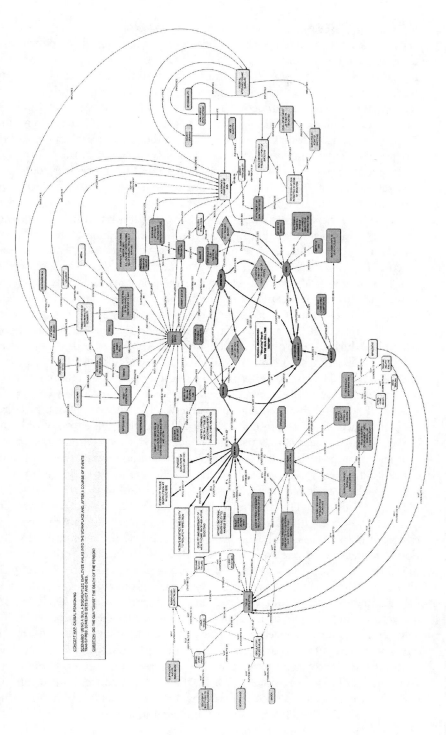

Figure 11.1 Concept map example (relationships among nodes).

Concept Maps in PBL

Though the concept map has been used in various disciplines and educational levels in helping students organize and integrate the concepts learned, the utilization of concept maps is still rare in PBL implementations. A few pioneers have incorporated concept maps as an instructional cognitive tool to help students' learning processes in PBL settings. For example, Eitel and Steiner (1999) incorporated concept maps to help medical students visualize the problem space during the understanding and defining problem stage of the PBL process. They found that the process of concept mapping the information in the problem and the evidence students gathered from literature enhanced their self-efficacy and therefore, more confidence in the hypothetical deductive reasoning process. Also, Hsu (2004) utilized concept maps in a PBL nursing course to help the students engage in higher order thinking during discussion sessions. It was concluded that by constructing concept maps, students' problem-solving skills and critical thinking abilities were elevated. These learning outcomes were evidenced in the students' increased abilities to identify key concepts, understanding cause–effect interrelationships among the concepts as well as part–whole relationships. Concept maps also helped the students validate or revise the concept structures of their personal "theory" (represented in the concept map) with the evidence and further information researched during the problem-solving process. Another case of using concept maps in a PBL nursing program conducted by Tseng, Chou, Wang, Ko, Jian, and Weng (2011) also showed a promising result of concept mapping enhancing nursing students' self-directed learning skills. As discussed earlier, the effectiveness of self-directed learning largely relies on a well-conceptualized problem space. Thus, the result of this study provided evidence not only that the process of concept map construction facilitated the students' problem conceptualization in PBL, but also confirmed the foundational role of problem conceptualization for the core learning activities and process (i.e. problem solving, self-directed learning, knowledge acquisition) to occur.

Hung (2006, 2011) has argued that students' cognitive readiness and familiarity with the PBL process vary due to age, cognitive maturity, or experience with PBL courses. The levels of self-directed learning and tutor facilitation are inter-causally related aspects in PBL. With students' different levels of self-directed learning skills, the construction process of a concept map can also be adjusted to meet the need for different levels of facilitation. For example, Rendas, Fonseca, and Pinto (2006) used partially completed concept maps to facilitate students in the problem conceptualization process in PBL. They constructed 36 concept maps for the problems that were used for their existing PBL courses. To scaffold the students' construction of problem space, the students were provided with a concept map with a number of key concepts having been removed. During the problem conceptualization process, the students would need to fill in the missing concepts and relationships in the map. This is an effective scaffolding technique that has been applied in many educational settings for providing students with an appropriate level of scaffolding when using concept maps as a cognitive tool for facilitating students' concept learning process (e.g. Cañas, Coffey, Carnot, Feltovich, Hoffman, Feltovich, & Novak, 2003; Chang, Sung, & Chen, 2001).

Concept Mapping to Conceptualize Problems in PBL process

The problem conceptualization process in PBL occurs primarily during the first four steps (if using 7-Jump PBL process), which are (1) understanding the problem, (2) defining the problem, (3) brainstorming, and (4) elaboration: develop personal "theory" about the problem. Thus, in Step 1, the students have to identify what the situation is that needs amendment (Step 1). In Step 2, they need to determine what the root of the "problem" is that causes the unsatisfactory situation. In other words, what is the underlying problem(s) that causes the symptoms? In Step 3, students brainstorm what the main variables are involved in the problem and their basic relationships, what the goal state is of the situation to be achieved, and what the scope is of the problem with which can be reasonably dealt within the timeframe and resources. In Step 4, through discussion, elaboration, hypothesis-deductive reasoning, and argumentation, the students develop their theory that explains the mechanism of the problem.

With the aid of the concept map, students can visually construct the problem space by listing the key points (or symptoms, faults) in the problem (Step 1); identify variables related to the key points (Step 2) and visually represent their relationships on the map. In Step 3, with these initial understandings of the problem, students can start to articulate the causal relationships among the key points and the variables, the boundary of the problem space, as well as the goal state of the problem space on the concept map. In Step 4, the concept map can be used as a foundation for the students to develop the "theory" or the mechanism for the cause of the problem by scrutinizing, debating, and validating (or invalidating) the logic of the causal reasoning path of the theory on the concept map. Also, utilizing concept maps in the problem conceptualization process in PBL is especially beneficial for facilitating group problem solving and learning. A collectively constructed concept map can help reduce miscommunication or ineffective communication.

The basic uses of concept map, influence diagrams, and systems modeling in facilitating students' problem conceptualization in the PBL process is similar. Therefore, I will discuss only the basic functions and features of influence diagrams and systems modeling, and not repeat their uses in specific steps in the PBL process. Then I will provide a comparison of these three tools in their capabilities of facilitating students' problem conceptualization process during the PBL process.

Influence Diagrams

An influence diagram is one of the diagrammatical tools that enable problem solvers to conceptualize complex inter-causal relationships in a problem or a system. It is a graphic representational tool developed from two predecessors. First is Forrester's (1968) work on representing causal loop feedback. The other one is Howard and Matheson's (1989) decision-making problem-solving analysis. Influence diagrams can be used to create a visual representation that describes the probabilistic dependency between/among the key variables in a decision analysis (Howard & Matheson, 1989). By analyzing the probabilistic dependency (or in reverse direction, influence or causal power), a complex problem or system (e.g. wildlife management, a student behavioral problem, or a natural phenomenon) can be graphically and conceptually represented with a diagram. This diagram illustrates the cause variables, intermediate variables, the effect variables, and the casual (or dependency) relationships among these variables in the problem being analyzed (Kros, 2001).

Influence diagrams can be used to represent a problem space as well as conceptual framework of a given problem to be solved or a subject under study (Kros, 2001). A number of different diagraming systems have been developed in constructing influence diagrams (e.g. Howard & Matheson, 2005; Kros, 2001). Depending upon the nature of the problem to be conceptualized, a variety of different causal relationships and complexity levels can be concisely yet explicitly and clearly described in influence diagrams (see Figure 11.2). For example, a simple causal relationship may consist of a pair of variables who have a direct cause-effect relationship. However, a complex causal relationship could consist of a number of intermediate variables in between the cause (attribute variable) and the effect variable. Other types of variables or relationships could include decision variables, intermediate variables, attribute (cause) variables, effect variable, or chance (probability) variables, as well as certain influence, uncertain influence, informational influence, or conditioning influence (Howard & Matheson, 2005; Kros, 2001). Thus, by identifying and articulate the causal-chain relationship among the involved variables, the problem space provides a more comprehensive and precise depiction of the problem.

Influence diagrams can help PBL students perform the problem conceptualization process by enabling them to construct a structural overview of the problem and the conceptual framework so that they do not lose sight of some variables while examining the others (Shapiro, van den Broek, & Fletcher, 1995). This conceptual framework serves as the foundation for the students to identify what they already know and what they need to know in order to solve the problem (Dolmans & Schmidt, 1994). The former is used to activate the relevant prior knowledge for the problem-solving process (Schmidt, 1993). The latter is the base for determining the learning objectives. Moreover, since PBL problems are real life, complex problems in most cases, influence diagrams provide the students with a more sophisticated tool to facilitate students' problem conceptualization process by unloading some of the cognitive processing demand from their working memory to the graphic representation of the problem. Thus, an influence diagram can be a useful cognitive and instructional tool for facilitating students in constructing

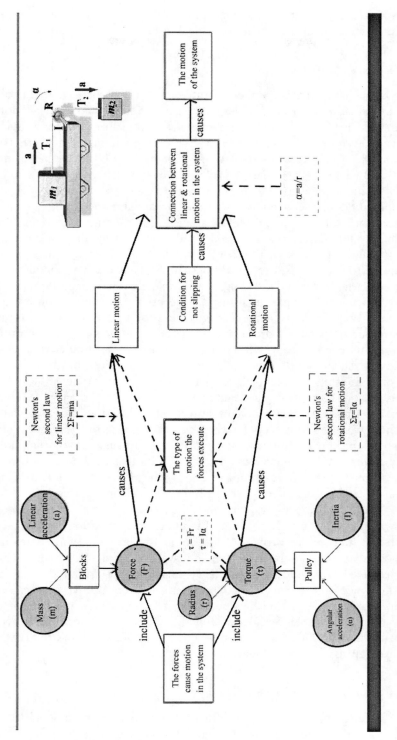

Figure 11.2 Influence diagram example (pulley problem in physics).

a visual problem space that conceptualizes more complex mechanism-based inter-causal relationships in a problem in PBL process.

Systems Modeling

Systems modeling is another cognitive tool useful for a problem solver to conceptualize a problem or system (Jonassen, 2006; Mandinach, Thorpe, & Lahart, 1988). It is a tool that allows a problem solver to describe a problem at an even more complex level by considering additional variables (such as time delay, feedback loop effect, reinforcing loop effect, or balancing loop effect) where concept map and influence diagrams fall short. This additional capability empowers systems modeling to be a cognitive tool that is not only able to do what concept maps and influence diagrams do, but also to make prediction of how the problem may behave in the future. Systems modeling has been utilized as an instructional and conceptual aid in interactive learning environments (Alessi, 2000, 2009; Funke, 2001) fostering analogical reasoning (Carney, Forbus, Ureel, & Fisher, 2009), facilitating reasoning processes, (Jonassen, 2009), and assessing learning in complex domains (Spector, 2009).

Systems modeling helps students conceptualize complex, non-linear inter-causal relationships embedded in the problem. PBL problems are ill-structured, complex problems. To understand these types of problems, students need to deal with complex non-linear, accumulative inter-causal relationships as well. These relationships could include feedback loop, reinforcing loop, or balancing loop relationships and they induce different effects on their related elements and the system where the problem is taking place. Understanding problems systemically, the students will have to take these variables into account when conceptualizing the problem. Equipped with sophisticated understanding about the domain and reasoning skills, the students will be capable of constructing a more accurate and holistic problem space. The more complete and sophisticated the students' problem space is, the more effective the PBL problem-solving process will be.

Additionally, using systems modeling to construct an external conceptual representation of the problem, PBL students are creating a testable mental model (deKleer & Brown, 1981) about the problem. This is realized by constructing a simulation to model a system that describes the problem to be solved (see Figure 11.3). This construction requires students to understand not only the individual parts and their respective inter-causal and feedback loop relationships, but also the underlying mechanism of the system as a whole. Simulation functions in systems modeling provide the students with an opportunity to evaluate the accuracy and the representative nature of their problem space.

A Comparison of the Three Tools

A concept map can be a useful tool for facilitating students to engage in identifying related variables and the nature of relationships between

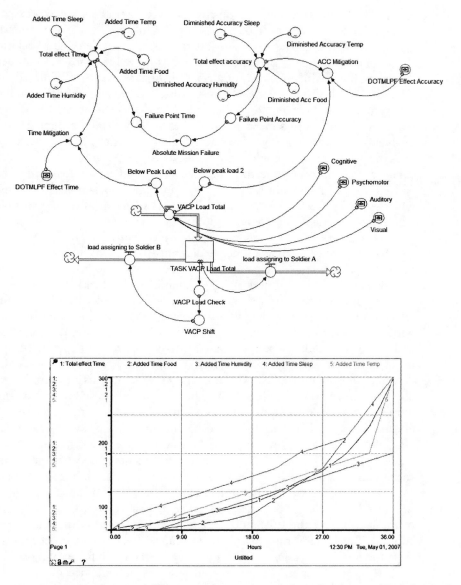

Figure 11.3 Systems modeling example (stock and flow diagram and a behavior
graph).

variables during the problem conceptualization process in the PBL process.
It helps students process the information and conceptualize problems that
some students find difficult to do mentally without cognitive support. A
concept map is effective in describing simple and linear types of relationships, however, falls short in communicating more complex relationships or
effects, for example, types of causality, multi-directional effects, or time

effect. This is because the relationships between variables are expressed as propositional statement in concept maps, while influence diagrams and systems modeling have their own sets of specific complex causal relationships notations. The propositional relationship expressions help students describe all types of propositional relationships between two immediately related variables, while influence diagrams and systems modeling do not offer this capability and flexibility. However, this advantage of concept maps would turn into a disadvantage when it comes to describing complex problems. Because of this characteristic of concept maps, though it is possible to describe complex problems or systems, when doing so, the concept map may become too complex and cumbersome to read. Thus, concept maps may be more suitable for conceptualizing simpler problems or when studying detailed interrelationships between variables in a problem when this is the learning goal of the PBL module.

For a problem that has more complex inter-causal relationships, more sophisticated tools such as influence diagrams or systems modeling may be needed for helping students articulate and conceptualize such complex causal relationships and underlying mechanisms. With the more advanced diagram notation system, a number of specific types of variables or causal effects can be easily described with influence diagrams or systems modeling without having to use extra variables or labels. Therefore, influence diagrams and systems modeling enable problem solvers to clearly depict a complex problem more efficiently. These diagram notation systems allow students to describe more complex relationships and effects, such as probability variables or informational influence in influence diagrams. Moreover, systems modeling provides highly sophisticated functions to describe accumulative effects such as reinforcing loop and balancing loop, as well as time delay effects that are commonly seen in real life complex problems. Yet, again, an efficient diagram notation system may allow students to construct a problem space more efficiently and at a more sophisticated level, but it sacrifices the capability to describe detailed relationships between variables. In general, when understanding a complex cause-effect chain relationship is the target of the learning of the PBL module, the influence diagram may be a better choice, while systems modeling may be a more effective tool for conceptualizing the underlying conceptual framework or the mechanism of a problem.

Lastly, the advanced functions and features of influence diagrams and systems modeling present a challenge for students who use the tools (see Table 11.2). These sophisticated features are designed based on specific causality concepts and systems thinking concepts. Therefore, the students will also have to learn these concepts in order to master the tools. However, Sterman (2002) has suggested that some of the concepts of systems thinking and modeling are counterintuitive. These concepts are not difficult to comprehend. However, their actual application for constructing a model (representation) of a problem is difficult (Hung, 2008), for example, the relationships among inflow, stock, and outflow in systems modeling. A steep learning curve for using systems modeling may be expected with a majority of students.

Table 11.2 A comparison of concept map, influence diagrams, and systems modeling

Cognitive tools	Describing the nature of relationships	Depicting underlying mechanism	Differentiating types of variables	Types of relationship	Types of effects	Learning to use the tool	Make inference/ prediction	Best for depicting
Concept map	Excellent	Fair	No (or on a case-by-case basis)	Simple, linear	Simple, propositional	Easy	No	Simple, linear relationships between/among variables
Influence diagram	Good	Good	Yes (e.g. probability, attribute)	Complex, bi or multi-directional	Complex (e.g. informational influence, conditioning influence)	Intermediate	Yes (with software)	Complex causal relationships
Systems modeling	Fair	Excellent	Yes (e.g. stocks, flow, variables)	Complex, multi-directional, or close-loop (feedback)	Complex, accumulative (e.g. reinforcing loop, balancing loop, time delay)	Difficult	Yes (with software)	Underlying mechanism of a problem/ system

Moreover, for constructing a testable/runnable model with influence diagrams or systems modeling for making inferences or predictions, a computer-based modeling software is required. The use of this software also necessitates a certain amount of training. Therefore, though influence diagrams and systems modeling are powerful cognitive/conceptualization tools, utilization of these tools will require a comprehensive instructional evaluation and design process to ensure the supporting instruction and materials are in place.

Conclusion

In response to traditional instruction's deficiency in educating students to be independent, proactive problem solvers and lifelong learners, PBL has made a definite mark in the field of education. Four decades after its first implementation, the adoption of PBL has not slowed down. Instead, the growth of PBL is accelerating. It is worth celebrating that this contemporary educational philosophy has not only been translated into a practical and implementable instructional method but also embraced by educators, refinement of the instructional method is a lifelong process. As helping students make connections between abstract conceptual content knowledge and its practical application is one of its instructional goals, this is also true for the development of PBL itself. In the past few decades, PBL research has mainly focused on the exploration of its practicality, the overall structure of the instructional method, as well as the end results. That is, the effectiveness of facilitating students to achieve the learning goals. Now, PBL research has arrived at the refining stage that should focus on the process where a great deal of variables could influence the end results. Students' insufficient or lack of effort exerted in the problem conceptualization step during the PBL process is one of the deficiencies identified in the previous PBL research. This chapter has discussed the possible causes and suggested externalization of the problem conceptualization process as an instructional remedy. Concept mapping, influence diagrams, and systems modeling are some of the concept externalization/visualization tools that could be implemented as a remedy in the PBL process. The use of these tools in PBL for helping students mindfully engage in the problem conceptualization step is still in its infancy. More systematic research is needed to shed light in this area and provide PBL educators with practical insights for refining PBL implementations.

References

Albanese, M. A., & Mitchell, S. (1993). Problem-based learning: A review of literature on its outcomes and implementation issues. *Academic Medicine, 68*, 52–81.

Alessi, S. (2000). Designing educational support in system-dynamics-based interactive learning environments. *Simulation & Gaming, 31*(2), 178–196.

Alessi, S. (2009). Modeling a system and teaching a system: Enhancing what students learn from modeling. In P. Blumschein, W. Hung, D. H. Jonassen, & J. Strobel (Eds.), *Model-based approaches to learning: Using systems models and simulations to improve understanding and problem solving in complex domains* (pp. 199–214). Rotterdam, the Netherlands: Sense Publishers.

Arts, J. A. R., Gijselaers, W. H., & Segers, M. S. R. (2002). Cognitive effects of an authentic computer-supported problem-based learning environment. *Instructional Science, 30,* 465–495.

Barrows, H. S. (1986). A taxonomy of problem-based learning methods. *Medical Education, 20,* 481–486.

Barrows, H. S. (1996). Problem-based learning in medicine and beyond: A brief overview. *New Direction for Teaching and Learning, 68,* 3–12.

Barrows, H. S. (2000). *Problem-based learning applied to medical education.* Springfield, IL: Southern Illinois University School of Medicine.

Barrows H. S., & Kelson, A. (1993). *Problem-based learning in secondary education and the Problem-Based Learning Institute* (Monograph). Springfield, IL: Southern Illinois University School of Medicine.

Barrows, H. S., & Myers, A. C. (1993). *Problem-based learning in secondary schools* [unpublished monograph]. Springfield, IL: Problem-Based Learning Institute, Lanphier High School, and Southern Illinois University Medical School.

Barrows, H. S., & Tamblyn, R. (1980). *Problem-based learning.* New York: Springer.

Bransford, J. D., & Stein, B. S. (1984). *The IDEAL problem solver.* New York: W. H. Freeman.

Bridges, E. M., & Hallinger, P. (1996). Problem-based learning in leadership education. In L. Wilkerson & W. H. Gijselaers (Eds.), *Bringing problem-based learning into higher education: Theory and practice.* San Francisco, CA: Jossey-Bass Publishers.

Cañas, A. J., Coffey, J. W., Carnot, M. J., Feltovich, P., Hoffman, R. R., Feltovich, J., & Novak, J. D. (2003). *A summary of literature pertaining to the use of concept mapping techniques and technologies for education and performance support.* IHMC Technical Report prepared for The Chief of Naval Education and Training, Pensacola, FL.

Carney, K., Forbus, K. D., Ureel, L. C. II., & Fisher, D. (2009). Can modeling foster analogical reasoning? In P. Blumschein, W. Hung, D. H. Jonassen, & J. Strobel (Eds.), *Model-based approaches to learning: Using systems models and simulations to improve understanding and problem solving in somplex domains* (pp. 73–109). Rotterdam, The Netherlands: Sense Publishers.

Chang, K. E., Sung, Y. T., & Chen, S. F. (2001). Learning through computer-based concept mapping with scaffolding aid. *Journal of Computer Assisted Learning, 17*(1), 21–33.

Chi, M. T. H., Feltovich, P., & Glaser, R. (1981). Categorization and representation of physics problems by experts and novices. *Cognitive Science, 5,* 121–152.

Coffey, J., Eskridge, T.C., & Sanchez, D. P. (2004). A case study in knowledge elicitation for institutional memory preservation using concept maps. In A. J. Cañas, J. D. Novak, & F. M. González (Eds.), *Concept maps: Theory, methodology, technology, Proceedings of the 1st international conference on concept mapping.* Pamplona, Spain: Universidad Pública de Navarra.

Cognition and Technology Group at Vanderbilt. (1993). Anchored instruction and situated cognition revisited. *Educational Technology, 33*(3), 52–70.

Cooke, N. J., Salas, E., Kiekel, P. A., & Bell, B. (2004). Advances in measuring team cognition. In E. Salas, & S. M. Fiore (Eds.), *Team cognition: understanding the factors that drive process and performance* (pp. 83–106). Washington, DC: American Psychological Association.

Curseu, P. L., & Rus, D. (2005). The cognitive complexity of groups: A critical look at team cognition research. *Cognitie, Creier, Comportament, 9*(4), 681–710.

deKleer, J. (1985). How circuits work. In D. G. Bobrow (Ed.), *Qualitative reasoning about physical systems* (pp. 205–280). Cambridge, MA: MIT Press.

deKleer, J., & Brown, J. S. (1981). Mental models of physical mechanisms and their acquisition. In J. R. Anderson (Ed.), *Cognitive skills and their acquisition* (pp. 285–309). Hillsdale, NJ: Erlbaum.

Derry, S. J. (2005). eSTEP as a case of theory-based Web course design. In A. M. O'Donnell, C. E. Hmelo-Silver, & G. Erkens (Eds.), *Collaborative reasoning, learning, and technology*, (pp. 171–196). Mahwah, NJ: Erlbaum.

Dolmans, D. H. J. M., & Schmidt, H. G. (1994). What drives the student in problem-based learning? *Medical Education, 28*, 372–380.

Dolmans, D. H. J. M., Wolfhagen, I. H. A. P., van der Vleuten, C. P. M., & Wijnen, W. H. F. W. (2001). Solving problems with group work in problem-based learning: Hold on to the philosophy. *Medical Education, 35*, 884–889.

Eitel, F., & Steiner, S. (1999). Evidence-based learning. *Medical Teacher, 21*(5), 506–512.

Forrester, J. W. (1968). *Principles of systems.* Waltham, MA: Pegasus Communications.

Funke, J. (2001). Dynamic systems as tools for analyzing human judgment. *Thinking and Reasoning, 7*(1), 69–89.

Gallagher, S. A., Stepien, W. J., & Rosenthal, H. (1992). The effects of problem-based learning on problem solving. *Gifted Child Quarterly, 36*(4), 195–200.

Ge, X., & Land, S. M. (2003). Scaffolding students' problem-solving processes in an ill-structured task using question prompts and peer interactions. *Educational Technology Research & Development, 51*(1), 21–38.

Hmelo-Silver, C. E. (2004). Problem-based learning: What and how do students learn? *Educational Psychology Review, 16*(3), 235–266.

Howard, R. A., & Matheson, J. E. (1989). Influence diagrams. In R. A. Howard, & J. E. Matheson (Eds.), *Readings on the principles and applications of decision analysis* (pp. 721–762). Menlo Park, CA: Strategic Decisions Group.

Howard, R. A., & Matheson, J. E. (2005). Influence diagrams. *Decision Analysis, 2*(3), 127–143.

Hsu, L. –L. (2004). Developing concept maps from problem-based learning scenario discussions. *Journal of Advanced Nursing, 48*(5), 510–518.

Hung, W. (2006). The 3C3R model: A conceptual framework for designing problems in PBL. *Interdisciplinary Journal of Problem-based Learning, 1*(1), 55–77.

Hung, W. (2008). Enhancing systems-thinking skills with modeling. *British Journal of Educational Technology, 39*(6), 1099–1120.

Hung, W. (2009). Utilizing system modeling to enhance students' construction of problem representations in problem solving. In Blumschein, P., Hung, W., Jonassen, D. H., & Strobel, J. (Eds.), *Model-based approaches to learning: Using systems models and simulations to improve understanding and problem solving in complex domains* (pp. 41–57). Rotterdam, The Netherlands: Sense Publishers.

Hung, W. (2011). Theory to reality: A few issues in implementing problem-based learning. *Educational Technology Research & Development, 59*(4), 529–552.

Hung, W., Jonassen, D. H., & Liu, R. (2008). Problem-based learning. In J. M. Spector, M. D. Merrill, J. J. G. van Merrienböer, & M. P. Driscoll (Eds.), *Handbook of research on educational communications and technology* (3rd ed.) (pp. 485–506). New York: Erlbaum.

Jacobsen, M., & Spiro, R. (1994). A framework for the contextual analysis of technology-based learning environments. *Journal of Computing in Higher Education*, 5(2), 2–32.

Johnson, S. D., Flesher, J. W., Jehng, J. -C. J., & Ferej, A. (1993). Enhancing electrical troubleshooting skills in computer-coached practice environment. *Interactive Learning Environments*, 3(3), 199–214.

Jonassen, D. H. (2006). *Modeling with technology: Mindtools for conceptual change*. Upper Saddle River, NJ: Pearson.

Jonassen, D. H. (2009). Modeling thinking processes by building cognitive simulations. In P. Blumschein, W. Hung, D. H. Jonassen, & J. Strobel (2009, Eds.), *Model-based approaches to learning: Using systems models and simulations to improve understanding and problem solving in complex domains* (pp. 61–71). Rotterdam, the Netherlands: Sense Publishers.

Karimi, R. (2011). Interface between problem-based learning and a learner-centered paradigm. *Advances in Medical Education & Practice*, 2, 117–125.

Kenny, R. F., Bullen, M., & Loftus, J. (2006). Problem formulation and resolution in online problem-based learning. *International Review of Research in Open and Distance Learning*, 7(3), 1–20.

Kolodner, J. L., Camp, P. J., Crismond, D., Fasse, B., Gray, J., Holbrook, J., Puntambekar, S., & Ryan, M. (2003). Problem-based learning meets case-based reasoning in the middle-school science classroom: Putting learning by Design™ into practice. *The Journal of the Learning Sciences*, 12(4), 495–547.

Kros, J. F. (2001). *Making effective business decisions: Using spreadsheet models and quantitative problems solving techniques* (2nd ed.). Burr Ridge, IL: McGraw-Hill.

Linn, M., Shear, L., Bell, P., & Slotta, J. D. (1999). Organizing principles for science education partnerships: Case studies of students' learning about 'rats in space' and 'deformed frogs'. *Educational Technology, Research & Development*, 47(2), 61–84.

Mandinach, E. B., Thorpe, M. E., & Lahart, C. M. (1988). *The impact of the systems thinking approach on teaching and learning activities*. ERIC No. ED 305 928.

Maxwell, N., Mergendoller, J. R., & Bellisimo, Y. (2005). Problem-Based Learning and high school macroeconomics: A comparative study of instructional methods. *The Journal of Economic Education*, 36(4), 315–331.

Moust, J. H. C., van Berkel, H. J. M., & Schmidt, H. G. (2005). Signs of erosion: Reflections on three decades of problem-based learning at Maastricht University. *Higher Education*, 50(4), 665–683.

Newell, A., & Simon, H. A. (1972). *Human problem solving*. Englewood Cliffs, NJ: Prentice Hall.

Norman, G., & Schmidt, H. G. (1992). The psychological basis of problem-based learning: A review of the evidence. *Academic Medicine*, 67(9), 557–565.

Novak, J. D. (1998) *Learning, creating and using knowledge: Concept maps as facilitative tools in schools and corporations*. Mahwah, NJ: Erlbaum.

Perrenet, J. C., Bouhuijs, P. A. J., & Smits, J. G. M. M. (2000). The suitability of problem-based learning for engineering education: Theory and practice. *Teaching in Higher Education*, 5(3), 345–358.

Polya, G. (1957). *How to solve it: A new aspect of mathematical method*. Princeton, NJ: Princeton University Press.

Rendas, A. B., Fonseca, M., & Pinto, P. R. (2006). Toward meaningful learning in undergraduate medical education using concept maps in a PBL pathophysiology course. *Advance in Physiology Education*, 30, 23–29.

Rumelhart, D. E., & Norman, D. A. (1988). Representation in memory. In R. C. Atkinson, R. J. Herrnstein, G. Lindzey, & R. D. Luce (Eds.), *Steven's handbook of experimental psychology: Vol. 2. Learning and cognition* (2nd ed., pp. 511–587). New York: John Wiley & Sons.

Schmidt, H. G. (1983). Problem-based learning: Rationale and description. *Medical Education, 17*, 11–16.

Schmidt, H. G. (1993). Foundations of problem-based learning: Some explanatory notes. *Medical Education, 27*, 422–432.

Schmidt, H. G., Loyens, S. M. M., van Gog, T., & Paas, F. (2007). Problem-based learning is compatible with human cognitive architecture: Commentary on Kirschner, Sweller, & Clark (2006). *Educational Psychologist, 42*(2), 91–97.

Shiffrin, R. M., & Schneider, W. (1980). Controlled and automatic human information processing: II perceptual learning, automatic attending, and a general theory. In J. G. Seamon (Ed.), *Human memory: Contemporary readings* (pp. 24–41). New York: Oxford University Press.

Spector, J. M. (2009). A modeling methodology for assessing learning in complex domains. In P. Blumschein, W. Hung, D. H. Jonassen, & J. Strobel (Eds.), *Model-based approaches to learning: Using systems models and simulations to improve understanding and problem solving in complex domains* (pp. 163–177). Rotterdam, the Netherlands: Sense Publishers.

Shapiro, B. R., van den Broek, P., & Fletcher, C. R. (1995). Using story-based causal diagrams to analyze disagreements about complex events. *Discourse Processes, 20*, 51–77.

Sterman, J. D. (1994). Learning in and about complex systems. *System Dynamics Review, 10*(2–3), 291–330.

Sterman, J. D. (2002). All models are wrong: Reflections on becoming a systems scientist. *System Dynamics Review, 18*(4), 501–531.

Stout, R. J., Cannon-Bowers, J. A., Salas, E., & Milanovich, D. M. (1999). Planning, shared mental models, and coordinated performance: An empirical link is established. *Human Factors, 41*(1), 61–71.

Stoyanov, S. (1997) Cognitive mapping as a learning method in hypermedia design. *Journal of Interactive Learning Research, 8*, 3/4, 309–325.

Tan, K., Dawson, V., & Venville, G. (2008). Use of cognitive organisers as a self regulated learning strategy. *Issues in Education Research, 18*(2), 183–207.

Taylor, D., & Miflin, B. (2008). Problem-based learning: Where are we now? *Medical Teacher, 30*, 742–763.

Torp, L., & Sage, S. (1998). *Problems as possibilities: Problem-based learning for K-12 education*. Alexandria, VA: Association for Supervision and Curriculum Development.

Trowbridge, J. E., & Wandersee, J. H. (1998). Theory-driven graphic organizers. In J. J. Mintzes, J. H. Wandersee, & J. D. Novak (Eds.), *Teaching science* (pp. 95–131). San Diego, CA: Academic Press.

Tseng, H.-C., Chou, F.-H., Wang, H.-H., Ko, H.-H., Jian, S.-Y., & Weng, W.-C. (2011). The effectiveness of problem-based learning and concept mapping among Taiwanese registered nursing students. *Nurse Education Today, 31*, e41–e46.

Vardi, I., & Ciccarelli, M. (2008). Overcoming problems in problem-based learning: A trial of strategies in an undergraduate unit. *Innovations in Education and Teaching International, 45*(4), 345–354.

Woods, D. R. (1996). Problem-based learning for large classes in chemical engineering. *New Directions for Teaching and Learning, 68*, 91–99.

12 Problem Solving for Conceptual Change

Chwee Beng Lee and
Karen Murcia

Introduction

Conceptual change theories explain how learners revise or change their conceptual framework and belief systems as a result of some form of educational intervention. Although conceptual change is defined differently among researchers (see Murphy & Alexander, 2008), most would agree that conceptual change can take a variety of forms, from more ordinary change, such as weak restructuring (Vosniadou, 2008), to more radical change, which usually requires change across ontological categories (Carey, 1985; Chi, 1992; Tyson, Venville, Harrsion, & Treagust, 1997). Despite the variation in defining conceptual change, most researchers defend their conceptions by interpreting the kinds of change they define. In general, science education researchers in the conceptual change tradition tend to agree that conceptual change is a process through which students' initial understanding or beliefs are modified or refined to become more aligned with dominant scientific understandings.

Research on conceptual change has been a key focus in education over the past few decades and it has generated a large volume of research. Such efforts aim to address gaps in student learning caused by misconceptions (also known as naïve theories, alternative conceptions or informal knowledge) that are deeply rooted in daily life experiences and are continuously reinforced by such experiences and the coherent explanatory structure they provide (Duit, 1999; Vosniadou, 1999). Over the decades, important issues that are central to conceptual change such as hot-versus-cold conceptual change (Sinatra, 2005), cognitive versus socio-cultural perspectives (Mason, 2007; Murphy, 2007; Vosniadou, 2007a), and the implications of the conceptual change approach for the design of instruction and curricula (Duit, Treagust, & Widodo, 2008; Jonassen, 2008; Leach & Scott, 2008; Lee, Jonassen, & Teo, 2011; Linn, 2008; Sinatra, Brem, & Evans, 2008; White & Gunstone, 2008; Scott, P., Asoko, H., & Leach, J. 2007), have been discussed and debated extensively. These efforts attempted to provide better descriptions and explanations of the theories of conceptual change.

In recent years, Vosniadou (2007a; 2007b) has conceptualized a constructivist and domain-specific approach to address previous limitations raised by conceptual change researchers. In her work, Vosniadou (2007b) proposed using instruction-induced conceptual change to achieve more significant changes in learning, rather than bottom-up implicit additive mechanisms which may produce synthetic models of understanding that combine both everyday and scientific descriptions of phenomena. While the bottom-up additive approach assumes that new information is added to the existing explanatory framework through participation in socio-cultural activities, the instruction-induced approach assumes systematic instruction is required by learners in order to understand the complex counter-intuitive scientific theory which has a different explanatory framework to their naïve theories. Specifically, problem solving as a learning strategy can increase students' awareness of the inconsistencies between their naïve theories and those that are scientifically accepted. It can also create intentional learning opportunities that arguably avoid the development of confused synthetic models (Lee, 2010). Most research related to conceptual change and problem solving focuses on using problem solving as an intervention to foster or induce conceptual change. The underlying assumption behind this kind of relationship is that problem solving is a process that may bring about the ultimate outcome – conceptual change.

In this chapter, we will discuss the issues and considerations emerging from our review of recent literature in the area of problem solving for conceptual change. We then use the literature review to frame our argument that there is an interdependent relationship between conceptual change and problem solving. We propose that conceptual change and problem solving are two dynamic processes, which constantly interact with each other and generate synergy in a cyclical knowledge acquisition process. In other words, solving an ill-structured contextually rich problem requires students to formulate and test hypotheses, self-question, check and revisit their initial conceptual understandings. During this cyclic process, students are likely to encounter information that challenges them to significantly reorganize or restructure their conceptual framework. This evoked meta-conceptual awareness can also require aspects of the problem situation to be re-thought and restructured to achieve feasible solutions. In this interdependent relationship, problem solving and conceptual change are themselves both process and outcome.

Problem Solving in Conceptual Change

Problem solving rightly plays a central role in education, as it is arguably one of the most important cognitive processes in our everyday life. It aims to achieve a goal when the solution method is unclear to the problem solver (Mayer, 1992; Schoenfeld, 1985). Researchers have established the importance and the benefits of using problem solving as a teaching and learning intervention for conceptual development or change (Duschl & Gitomer, 1997; Limon, 2003; Vosniadou, 1994). For instance, Tarhan, Ayar-Kayali, Urek, and Acar (2008) found that problem-based learning is effective in

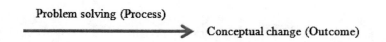

Figure 12.1 Problem solving as the process to induce conceptual change.

helping students to achieve a better understanding of intermolecular forces and for remedying alternative conceptions.

However, very few research studies have explored or established the relationship between conceptual change and problem solving. Studies that have explored the relationship were largely grounded on problem-based learning and typically viewed problem solving as a vehicle or process to bring about conceptual change. Such a relationship is depicted in Figure 12.1.

In this section, we discuss some of the key issues that emerged from our literature review of approximately 30 recent journal articles on using problem solving as a process to bring about conceptual change. We identified various studies examining the impact of teaching and learning approaches for inducing conceptual change that highlighted the influences of contextual factors, and the individuals' epistemological beliefs, structural and prior knowledge in the change process and achievement of learning outcomes.

Epistemological Beliefs

In recent years, an emphasis has been placed on identifying and explaining the influence of epistemological beliefs in conceptual change (e.g. Mason, 2002; Qian & Alvermann, 1995; Sinatra, Southerland, McConaghy, & Demastes, 2003; Vosniadou, 2007b; Windschitl & Andre, 1998). It was frequently reported in the literature that students' alternative conceptions or misconceptions were not changed even after targeted instruction. This suggests that traditional and didactic teaching may not be sufficient to change learners' belief systems, especially when the concepts involved are abstract. A commonly reported reason for the resilience of alternate conceptions to change was that they were intertwined with the learners' epistemological beliefs and were deeply rooted in their explanatory framework. As the term "epistemological belief" is defined differently by various researchers, for conceptual clarity, we will use it to refer to beliefs that people hold about knowledge and knowing (Hofer, 2002). To elaborate, Kitchner (1983) proposed that *epistemic cognition* enabled individuals to consider the "limits of knowing, the certainty of knowing, and the criteria for knowing" (p. 222). Such cognition is critical as individuals engage in solving complex and ill-structured problems.

In the context of problem solving, Muis (2008) and Muis and Franco (2010) found that learners focused more on aspects of the content that were consonant with their own epistemic beliefs. This finding was also evident in a recent study conducted by Bell and Trundle (2008) on early childhood pre-service teachers' learning of standards-based lunar concepts taught via inquiry-based instruction utilizing computer simulation. The researchers noted that participants' with prior experiences in astronomy courses did not do any better on the research's pre-intervention assessment of moon phase concepts. This result implied that even with a targeted curriculum on astronomy, these pre-service teachers had not refined or change their conceptual framework. For example, the pre-service teachers typically drew non-scientific shapes consistent with the view that the Earth's shadow caused moon phases rather than the scientific explanation that the moon reflects sunlight towards the Earth.

However, the researchers later found that using computer simulation in their inquiry-based instruction improved the learners' scientific knowledge of moon phases. Specifically, through their intervention, participants experienced the nature of science and the inquiry process that generates new knowledge. The participants used the computer simulation program *Starry Night Backyard* to gather, record, and share moon observations, analyze their data by looking for, and discussing patterns, and then modeled the cause of the moon phases. The problem-solving tasks coupled with the manipulation of computer simulation as a problem representation tool arguably shifted the learners' epistemological beliefs.

In addition, the findings of this study aligned with what was reported in Tarhan, Ayay-Kayali, Urek, and Acar's (2008) study, which examined the effectiveness of problem-based learning on developing 9th-grade students' understanding of chemistry concepts. The researchers reported that students who had experienced the problem-based learning (PBL) approach acquired more scientific and crucial ideas, whereas those who had not gone through a similar intervention still held many alternate conceptions about intermolecular forces. What was most intriguing was that the students indicated that they were aware that PBL ensured increased student learning, creative and critical thinking, researching and sharing knowledge, using relevant and varied resources, and working collaboratively. Such a constructive approach effectively challenged and changed the way the students perceived knowledge and knowing.

Structural Knowledge

Another theme that emerged from our literature review was the importance of structural knowledge in problem solving for conceptual change. Structural knowledge is being used here to refer to the knowledge of how concepts within a domain are interrelated (Diekhoff, 1983; Jonassen, Beissner, & Yacci, 1993). By nature, problem-solving activities are situated and dependent on the context. Hence, domain-specific knowledge is influential in the way learners solve problems and achieve conceptual change. However, simply applying a set of constrained rules to attempt to solve ill-structured problems is clearly inadequate. Supporting this assertion, Robertson (1990) found that learners' semantic networks were a strong predictor of how well they solved transfer problems in physics. The meaning of a concept held by the learner was found to be defined by the relationship it held to other concepts. The knowledge drawn on for physics problem solving was based on a set of concepts that related to one another. Similarly, Liu (2004) found that concept mapping instruction with high school students promoted structural knowledge and facilitated relational conceptual change. To transfer problem-solving skills, students must learn to construct structural knowledge of concepts and understand how problems relate to domain knowledge (Jonassen, 1997; Smith, 1992). Activating domain-specific knowledge when solving ill-structured problems requires problem solvers to organize concepts and strategies in a meaningful, accessible, and integrated way; this requires structural knowledge.

To illustrate, a recent study conducted by Marbach-Ad, Rotbain, and Stavy (2008) to examine the influence of computer simulation and illustration activities on student achievement in molecular genetics, found that students from the experimental group who participated in the computer-based activities improved their knowledge of genetics concepts beyond the level demonstrated by the control group. What was significant about the results was that through computer simulation, which required students to make explicit and refine their structural knowledge of the problem, the students built better conceptual knowledge. Supporting this finding, a student from the experimental group explained: "Yes, the computer animation helped me very much. It demonstrated the process, since you can't really see it … it was like I could see it in front of my eyes, and so I could connect between things." Similarly, Taasoobshirazi and Glynn (2009) found in their study of college students solving of chemistry problems that learners who used schemas to assist in recognizing and mentally classifying the problems meaningful were more successful in finding appropriate solutions.

Problem solving is a highly complex process that requires learners to activate various levels of cognition to achieve the most logical and suitable solution in a given context. This is especially true when problems vary in their dynamicity, structure and complexity (Jonassen, 2004). When integrated appropriately into the learning environment, especially with technology as a problem representation tool, problem solving can serve to perturb the learners' thinking and challenge them to reconsider their existing frameworks. Structural knowledge plays a prominent role in facilitating this process but at the same time, problem-solving activity enables the learners to build stronger structural knowledge that can lead to enhanced conceptual understanding.

Prior Knowledge

Traditionally, researchers have tended to treat students' misconceptions as unfavorable and as needing to be "repaired" or "removed". However, in recent years, this perspective of students' naïve theories has changed. From a more constructivist paradigm, students' non-scientific notions arguably have value in helping them to develop sophisticated scientific understandings.

There are two key principles related to naïve theories from this re-framed perspective (Vosniadou, 2007a, 2007b). First, what requires change is not the isolated misconceptions per se, but the "naïve, intuitive, domain-specific theories in early childhood, (*formed*) on the basis of everyday experiences" (Vosniadou, 2007b, p. 4). In other words, misconceptions cannot be treated as faulty isolated alternative conceptions, but as naïve theories that possess a coherent body of domain-specific and structural knowledge, which forms the basis of students' explanations and predictions. Second, students' intuitive ideas about science anchor their conceptions and are the starting point for development (Clement, Brown, & Zietsman, 1989; Karmiloff-Smith, 1992). Such a perspective is closely aligned with the work of Vosniadou (2007a) who identified a complex theory-like structure to conceptual knowledge and Thagard's (1990) who also took a theory-based view of concepts. Anchoring the learning process to students prior structural and conceptual understanding enables naïve theories to be refined and leads to a more complex and integrative view of a scientific phenomenon. In this regard, constructivist approaches such as problem solving offers an avenue for students to change their naïve theories rather than to 'correct' isolated misconceptions.

For example, in a study examining the role of intuitive knowledge in physics problem solving, Sherin (2006) found that intuitive physics knowledge played a significant role as it provided a context for interpretation. For instance, the researcher noted that students actively used their intuitive knowledge as they worked on solving the 'Shoved Block' problem. Instead of immediately writing the formal physics equations, the students started off by stating their intuitions concerning the outcome. It was also suggested that the competing intuitive knowledge of collaborating students provided motivation in the problem-solving context. Similarly, Chang, Wu, Weng, and Sung (2012) conducted a study with fifth graders to understand the effect of a problem-posing system on elementary students' achievement of learning outcomes. The researchers designed a computational system that was structured by four problem-posing phases: posing a problem, planning, solving the problem, and finally looking back, in which students used game-scenarios to connect back to the problem-posing stage. They found that to succeed in problem-solving activities, the participating students had to integrate their own everyday experiences with conceptual knowledge. In fact, the problem-posing system encouraged students to concentrate on materials they had already encountered, apply suitable strategies during the process, and in addition they related better to the relevant mathematical representations of target concepts.

Interactions Between Problem Solving and Conceptual Change

While problem solving may induce conceptual change by perturbing learners' cognitive structure and creating learners' awareness of the need to construct a coherent and scientifically supported conceptual framework, it is also an engaging process that requires a high level of cognitive understanding as it stimulates students to discover inconsistencies in their thinking (Biemans and Simons, 1999). Solving problems that are ill-structured and complex challenges the learner to question their own hypotheses, and to externalize the problem by going through a series of repeated testing and revising cycles (Lesh & Harel, 2003). Moreover, when learners build problem concrete representations to externalize their mental representations, the abstract understanding of certain concepts is made explicit. Constructing the representation helps the learner to reflect upon their knowledge structure and to potentially identify their own learning need or problem gap which, in turn, involves conceptual change for the problem solver to reconcile his or her problem representation. The process of problem solving requires the elements of the problem situation to be reorganized and restructured in a new way to solve the problem (Mayer, 1992). In other words, problem solvers must be able to actively search for new ways to externalize their problems to generate a coherent problem representation. In this sense, restructuring or reorganizing the elements of problems can be regarded as a state of conceptual change. De Grave, Boshuizen, and Schmidt (1996) showed that, during the process of analysing a set of medical problems, students demonstrated traces of conceptual change. The students in this study were observed going through a process of hypothesis questioning, checking, and revising their initial conceptual understandings during problem solving. Similarly, Vosniadou and Brewer (1994) implicitly referred to such interaction when they discovered elementary school students had constructed synthetic theoretical models of the structure of the Earth by combining their explanations of everyday experiences with more scientific descriptions. These young students were actually attempting to synthesize two inconsistent pieces of information, and were searching for a solution or explanation to construct a coherent understanding.

Education research has demonstrated that problem solving involves conceptual change processes (Nersessian, 2008). Furthermore, we propose that when problem solving is employed to induce conceptual change, it necessarily invokes the learner to embark on a series of conceptual change processes which contributes to more effective problem solving. This suggests that to improve students' learning outcomes there is a need to examine the dynamic interaction between problem solving and conceptual change processes. However, from our literature review, we have found that little effort has been put into examining such relationships. In this section of our chapter, we seek to describe the interaction between conceptual change and problem solving through some related studies. The relationship is depicted in Figure 12.2.

Although some studies (Furio, Calatayud, Barcena, & Padilla, 2000) have suggested that conceptual change not only involves the restructuring of concepts, but also the way learners reason, most of the related studies assume that the various instructional approaches are simply processes to bring

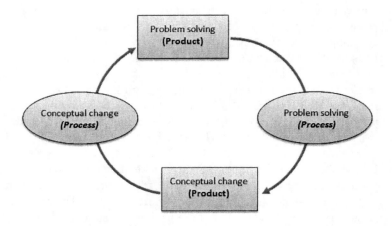

Figure 12.2 Interactions between problem solving and conceptual change.

about conceptual change as the outcome. Few efforts have been made to understand the change process itself, which is complex and often unpredictable.

The Interaction Between Problem Solving and Conceptual Change

We will now describe in relative detail a recent study which investigated the relationship between problem solving and conceptual change. This illustrative study was conducted by Lee (2010) and aimed to explain the interaction observed between problem solving and conceptual change as a group of 35 Fifth-grade students learned about the water cycle in science. The main purpose of the study was to understand conceptual change in the context of problem solving using system modeling as a problem representation tool. System dynamic modeling is a highly challenging and engaging activity (Bravo, Joolingen, & de Jong, 2009) which requires learners to analyze, synthesize, and evaluate their domain-specific knowledge to create a model that supports their conceptual understanding of the system they are working on (Stratford, Krajcik, & Soloway, 1998). The students in this study used a system modeling tool named *Model-It*. This tool uses accumulations and flows to enable the learner to describe rules related to populations of entities. To build a model in *Model-It*, students are required to identify the measurable, quantifiable factors that are used to predict the outcome they are simulating. Each factor is described in terms of its measurement units, initial values, minimum, average, and maximum values in the Factor Editor. From factor maps, students define the relationships between the factors using the Relationship Editor. When the model is complete, students can test their models with the results shown in a graph; they can then refine their hypotheses accordingly and re-run the models.

Largely using a qualitative analysis approach the researcher articulated a theoretical model, which explained the interaction of problem solving and conceptual change in the process of learning science with *Model-It* software. Prior to the beginning of the study, students were taught how to use the Model-It software. The research program, including data collection, then ran for approximately ten weeks. To determine students' starting conceptions a pre-intervention Knowledge Test (KTI) was administered to the class of participating students. In addition face-to-face interviews were carried out with ten selected students, each lasting approximately 40 minutes. The whole class of participating students then went through four sessions of system modeling of problems in the computer lab after school hours. During those 90-minute sessions, students modeled the given problem using the Model-It software. They constructed their own models and were told that they could revise and refine their model throughout the four sessions. At the end of each session, their models were saved electronically and kept by the researcher. A reflection log was provided to guide students' reflections about how their models were working. Students could use the reflection log to state their primary prediction, list down what they have learned from running their models, and elaborate on how they had derived the results. At the end of the fourth session, the post-KTI was administered, and follow-up face-to-face interviews were conducted with the ten-student focus group.

The researchers analyzed students' interview transcripts to identify their prior knowledge of the water cycle using the grounded theory approach. Classroom observation field notes and reflection logs were used as supplementary evidence to support the analyses. The students' problem representations, which they built using Model-It, and knowledge test results (KTI) were also quantitatively analyzed to provide supporting evidence during the theory-generation phase of the research project. The KTI was designed to assess the students' understanding of evaporation and condensation, and it was assessed in two ways. First, one point was awarded for a correct response on the multiple-choice items (a total of 14 points for 14 items). Second, the students provided a short justification for their answer, explaining why they had chosen that particular answer from the range of choices. Five categories of justification models emerged as a result of the coding (misconception, initial, textbook, synthetic, scientific). Category one *initial* models were based only on students' everyday experience with no scientific justification. Category two *synthetic* models were those that used a combination of everyday and scientific descriptions and justifications, while Category three *scientific* models were justifications that were based solely on scientific conceptions. Category four *textbook* models were justifications based on textbook descriptions of the water cycle, and Category five *misconception* conceptual models reflected a lack of comprehension of the water cycle. Movements across these categories by comparing the pre- and post-tests (refer to Lee, 2010 for details) also emerged during the coding process: (a) *Significant leap*, (b) *Diminutive move*, and (c) *Reverse move*. A diminutive move would be a move to one category above the original position (e.g. from the "textbook" to the "synthetic" conceptual model). If there was a backward shift such as from the "synthetic" to the "textbook" conceptual model, this would be considered a reverse move. On the other hand, a positive shift of greater than a diminutive move would be considered as a significant leap. For instance, when a student's response on a particular concept is first coded as a "misconception" but it has improved to a "synthetic" model then it would be considered as a significant leap.

A rubric was crafted based on the principles espoused by Thagard (2000) and Novak and Gowin (1984) to assess the students' problem representations, and inter-rater reliability was established. Two trained raters independently scored the problem representations and an inter-rater reliability coefficient of $r = .889$, $p < .01$, $n = 20$ was computed to establish the validity of the analysis process. The criteria for assessment of students' Model-It problem representations included semantic associations, total number of nodes, total number of nodes associated with the central concepts (evaporation and condensation), and propositions and causal attributions, including two rules. Rule 1 states that a hypothesis coheres with what it explains, which can either be evidence or another hypothesis, while Rule 2 states that all hypotheses that explain some other propositions cohere with each other and a total score of each problem representation was calculated.

In this study, it was found that the students used a variety of strategies such as asking questions (from teachers and peers), constructing mind maps, writing detailed notes and self-questioning to study science in class. It was also evident that intervening conditions such as *epistemological beliefs, structural knowledge,* and *domain knowledge* exerted an effect on the strategies employed by the students. Two main and diverse types of epistemological beliefs were observed amongst the participating students. While some students maintained that knowledge was ever changing and acquired through constant revisions of one's understanding, others held the belief that knowledge was determined and validated by the textbook or an authority (teacher), which they considered to be a reliable source. Students who believed that knowledge was constant tended not to question the authority and would faithfully take down notes in class and memorize the information recorded. For instance, Jane (pseudonyms are used for all participants) said that she believed that her teacher was always correct when she said: "I always go to my teacher when I have a question ... she always give accurate information," and she was observed to be "over confident" about her work. On the other hand, there were some students who believed that knowledge is ever changing and acquired through constant revision of their understanding. These students were observed to use the strategy of self-questioning. For instance, David was observed to constantly challenge his teacher's and his peers' conceptions both during classroom learning and in the problem-solving sessions. For instance, when his classmate mentioned that evaporation does not exist in a dark corner based on his observation, David challenged him to conduct an experiment in different corners of his house. David also continuously engaged in self-questioning by whispering to himself.

In addition, *domain knowledge* emerged as another intervening condition that affected the students' employment of strategies in the representation of the water cycle problem. When students chose the self-questioning strategy, they did so according to their level of domain knowledge. For instance, during her problem-solving process, Mary stated that she had tried to recall her knowledge on the water cycle and thought about the concepts of evaporation and condensation. She then questioned her understanding of these concepts, especially when she got confused by the output of her problem representation. She emphasised that it was the problem-solving activity that helped her realize her mistake: "I started to question myself. When I went home, I read my textbook and other reference books and then I returned to refine my problem representation (model)."

Students who possessed limited domain knowledge were observed to be rather limited in their choice of strategies and were not observed to use a self-questioning strategy. This was evident in the case of Jane who preferred to use a lot of factual, text-book-type information to elaborate her points. It was also clear that she held some misconceptions in relation to the water cycle.

Structural knowledge was another possible intervening condition. It was more likely for students to engage in self-questioning when they were able to understand the relationships among the variables in the system. For example, Alice, who told the interviewer that she had questioned her own representation of the problem during the problem-solving activity, had obtained a score of 63 (M = 23.7) on the semantic associations for the first version of her problem representation, and a 65 (M = 34) on the same section for the second version of her problem representation. These results may imply that she had sufficient structural knowledge to enable her to construct a more coherent problem representation.

A theoretical model (see Figure 12.3) that explains the interplay of intervening conditions influencing students' problem-solving activity and their learning outcomes was generated as a result of the research program (Lee, 2010).

Restructuring Conceptual Framework

In the problem-solving environment, it was evident that students' epistemological beliefs, domain knowledge and structural knowledge influenced their choice of strategies for building a coherent understanding and representation of science concepts. The interplay of these intervening conditions promoted students' self questioning and this, at times, challenged their existing conceptions. In order to reconcile such perturbations, students had to build a more logical problem representation and restructure their conceptual framework. On the other hand, those students who were adopting strategies other than metacognitive self-questioning experienced less intense interaction between problem solving and conceptual change in their process of learning. These students were observed building simple problem representations and they demonstrated less or no significant leaps, or more

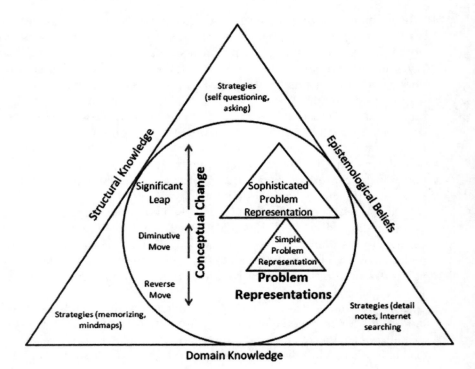

Figure 12.3 The roles of epistemological beliefs, structural knowledge and domain knowledge.

reverse moves in their conceptual models. To illustrate the dynamism between conceptual change and problem solving, two cases are elaborated and presented in the following section.

Simon's Story

Simon's KTI scores revealed that he made 13 moves – four significant leaps, three reverse moves and six diminutive moves. Also, he made three significant leaps for his justifications on the concept of condensation. The following examples show how he improved. In both the pre- and post-test for the following question: Jane's mother parked her car alongside the pavement outside their house. Early in the morning, Jane noticed tiny droplets on the windscreen. These droplets were formed because of water vapour …? Simon chose option B which was: "from the air changing to a liquid state which fell on the windscreen". In the pre-test, he justified his option by saying that: "the night is very cold and thus met the temperature of condensing." This justification was classified as the category 1 (misconception) conceptual model. However, on the same question in the post-test, his justification was categorized as the category 4 (synthetic) conceptual model when he stated:

"At night, it is very cold, so water which evaporated from the ground did not get enough heat for it to rise. As a result, it will turn into water droplets and form mist or low clouds." The researchers found that Simon commonly used strategies such as asking or searching for information as well as self-questioning. He had explicitly told the researchers that he questioned his thoughts very often by saying that: "You know, sometimes I ask what happened? Why is this behaving in that way?" This indicates that Simon perceived knowledge as dynamic and able to be constructed through inquiry methods. During the second interview, Simon told the interviewer that when he encountered problems while building his problem representations, he would question himself (Simon said: "I want to know why by adding a new variable, the output of the model is so different.") in order to refine his model. It was not surprising to the researchers that when his problem representations were examined, it was found that he made a tremendous improvement on his initial representation, judging by his score of 61 for the second problem representation compared to an initial score of 29.

Simon's second problem representation (see Figure 12.4) was more elaborated and complex compared to the first (see Figure 12.5), which was linear and simple. The structure of the representation suggested that he had developed an understanding of the intertwined nature of relationships between variables in a real world system, which resulted in an improved semantic associations score (25 to 44). It was evident in classroom observations and interviews that Simon believed knowledge was not static and that he had employed both the self-questioning and information seeking strategies.

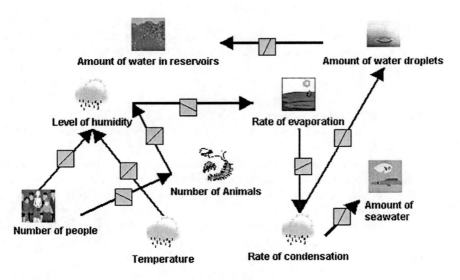

Figure 12.4 Simon's second problem representation.

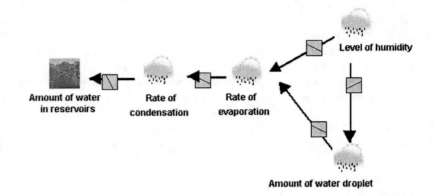

Figure 12.5 Simon's first problem representation.

Jane's Story

Our analysis showed that Jane perceived knowledge as static and that the information provided by the teachers and textbook is, in her opinion, was always accurate. This was apparent in her choice of learning strategies which included both rote memorization of facts, and asking her private tutor for information when in doubt. It became apparent through the study that Jane had misconceptions both before and after the problem-solving activity. For example, when asked whether there would be any evaporation without the sun she replied: "Then the water cannot evaporate." A close examination after the problem-solving activity revealed that she had made five reverse moves, one diminutive move and no significant leaps in her problem representation. In addition, her category 2 (Initial) and category 3 (Textbook) conceptual models were stable. In other words, three of her category 2 and four of her category 3 conceptual models were found to be unchanged in the post-test for the KTI. Jane also experienced a fall in her mean score in her problem representation. Interestingly, her first and second problem representations (see Figure 12.6) were exactly the same, but she deleted some information on the relationships of variables in the second version. Her problem representation retained a simple and linear structured model. This could mean that her knowledge structure was fairly stable throughout the study.

During the post-problem-solving activity interview, when asked whether she had encountered any difficulties in building her problem representation, she confidently said: "Not really, I know what to add." Although she said at a later stage that she might have encountered some difficulties when determining the relationships between the variables, she could not recall what they were and she preferred to work alone. An examination of her KTI showed that she had made five reverse moves and one diminutive move. There was no evidence to show that she had used a self-questioning strategy during the problem-solving activity. However, what was evident was that

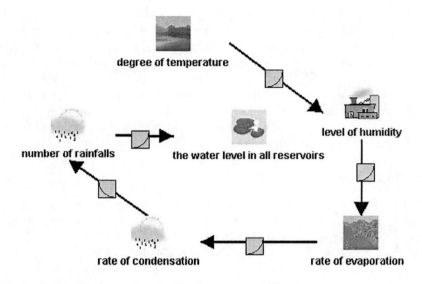

Figure 12.6 Jane's first and second problem representation.

intervening conditions such as epistemological beliefs, and domain knowledge as well as structural knowledge could have had an effect on her choice of strategy. During both interviews, the researchers noted that she was quite firm in her belief that knowledge is determined by the authority and the textbook, and throughout the problem-solving activity it was evident that she had little domain knowledge as she was observed to be asking her friends what variable she could add and what humidity is about. In addition, she did not score well on the semantic associations for either version of her problem representations, indicating that her structural knowledge was relatively weak compared to that of her peers. In the first version of the problem representation, she had obtained a score of 27 (M = 23.7) scoring 26 (M = 34) for the second version.

The two illustrative case studies selected from the extensive data collected delineated the dynamic interactions between conceptual change and problem solving. In the first case, Simon was operating in a *reflective* period (King & Kitchener, 2002) and held sophisticated epistemological beliefs. When learners, like Simon, believe knowledge changes over time and results from reasoned, constructive efforts (Elder, 2002), they are more likely to adopt the *self-questioning* strategy. Such a strategy enables students to not only construct logical and coherent problem representations but also to recognize the inconsistencies in their initial knowledge structure during problem solving; thus engaging them in an interactive process of conceptual change. Alternatively, Jane's case showed that students who are influenced by the three intervening conditions while adopting strategies other than self-questioning tended to experience less intense interaction between problem solving and conceptual change in their process of learning. This leads to the construction of simple and often linear problem representations and fewer significant moves in the development of their conceptual models. In these two cases, it was evident that when the interaction between conceptual change and problem solving was intense, the students produced more sophisticated problem representations and improved their achievement of conceptual outcomes. The students used a variety of learning strategies to develop scientific understandings. Their choice of strategies was affected by three intervening conditions that were domain knowledge, structural knowledge, and epistemological beliefs.

Summary

In this chapter we have discussed the key issues emerging from our review of recent literature in the area of problem solving for conceptual change. It was found that many studies in the field viewed problem solving as a vehicle or process to bring about conceptual change. However, findings from contemporary research suggest that the interaction between the two constructs is far more complex and that there is an interdependent relationship between conceptual change and problem solving. Learning in problem-solving environments is framed by students' epistemological beliefs, and their structural and domain specific knowledge. It has been proposed in this chapter that conceptual change occurs both as part of the problem-solving process and as an outcome. This dynamic processes generates synergy in knowledge acquisition.

References

Bell, R., & Trundle, K. (2008). The use of a computer simulation to promote scientific conceptions of moon phases. *Journal of Research in Science Teaching, 45,* 346–372.

Biemans, H. J. A., & Simons, P. R. J. (1999). Computer-assisted instructional strategies for promoting conceptual change. In W. Schnotz, S. Vosniadou, & M. Carretero (Eds.), *New perspectives on conceptual change* (pp. 247–262). Amsterdam: Pergamon.

Bravo, C., Joolingen, W. R. V., & de Jong, T. (2009). Using Co-Lab to build system dynamic models: Students' actions and on-line tutorial advice. *Computers & Education, 52,* 243–251.

Carey, S. (1985). *Conceptual change in childhood.* Cambridge, MA: MIT Press.

Chang, K., Wu, L., Weng, S., & Sung, Y. (2012). Embedding game-based problem-solving phase into problem-posing system for mathematics learning. *Computers & Education, 58(2),* 775–786.

Clement, J., Brown, D. E., & Zietsman, A. (1989). Not all preconceptions are misconceptions: Finding 'anchoring conceptions' for grounding instruction on students' intuitions. *International Journal of Science Education, 11(5),* 554–565.

Chi, M. T. H. (1992). Conceptual change within and across ontological categories: Examples from learning and discovery in Science. In R. Giere (Ed.), *Cognitive models of science: Minnesota Studies in the Philosophy of Science* (pp. 129–186). Minneapolis: University of Minnesota Press.

De Grave, W. S., Boshuizen, H. P. A., & Schmidt, H. G. (1996). Problem-based learning: Cognitive and metacognitive processes during problem analysis. *Instructional Science, 24,* 321–341.

Diekhoff, G. M. (1983). Testing through relationship judgments. *Journal of Educational Psychology, 75,* 227–233.

Duit, R. (1999). Conceptual change approaches in science education. In W. Schnotz, S. Vosniadou, & M. Carretero (Eds.), *New perspectives on conceptual change* (pp. 263–282). Amsterdam: Pergamon.

Duit, R. T., Treagust, D. F., & Widodo, A. (2008). Teaching science for conceptual change: Theory and practice. In S. Vosniadou (Ed.), *International handbook of research on conceptual change* (pp. 629–646). New York, NY: Routledge.

Duschl, R. A., & Gitomer, D. H. (1997). Strategies and challenges to changing the focus of assessment and instruction in science classrooms. *Educational Assessment, 4,* 37–73.

Elder, A. D. (2002). Characterizing fifth grade students' epistemological beliefs in science. In B. K. Hofer, & P. R. Pintrich (Eds.), *Personal Epistemology: The psychology of beliefs about knowledge and knowing* (pp. 347–364). Mahwah, NJ: Lawrence Erlbaum.

Furio, C., Calatayud, M. L., Barcenas, S. L., & Padilla, O. M. (2000). Functional Fixedness and Functional Reduction as common sense reasoning in Chemical Equilibrium and in Geometry and polarity of molecules. *Science Education, 84,* 545–565.

Hofer, B. K. (2002). Personal epistemology as a psychological and educational construct: An introduction. In B. K. Hofer, & P. R. Pintrich (Eds.), *Personal Epistemology: The psychology of beliefs about knowledge and knowing* (pp. 3–15). Mahwah, NJ: Lawrence Erlbaum.

Jonassen, D. H. (1997). Instructional design models for well-structured & ill-structured problem-solving learning outcomes. *Educational Technology Research and Development, 45,* 656–694.

Jonassen, D. H. (2004). Problem solving: The enterprise. In J. M. Spector, C. Ohrazda, D. Wiley & A. van Schaak (Eds.), *Innovations in instructional technology: Essays in honor of M. David Merrill* (pp. 91–110). Mahwah, NJ: Lawrence Erlbaum Associates.

Jonassen, D. H. (2008). Model building for conceptual change. In S. Vosniadou (Ed.), *International handbook of research on conceptual change* (pp. 676–693). New York, NY: Routledge.

Jonassen, D. H., Beissner, K., & Yacci, M. A. (1993). *Structural knowledge: Techniques for representing, assessing, and acquiring structural knowledge.* Hillsdale, NJ: Lawrence Erlbaum Associates.

Karmiloff-Smith, A. (1992). *Beyond modularity: A developmental perspective on cognitive science.* Cambridge, MA: MIT Press.

Kitchner, K. S. (1983). Cognition, metacognition, and epistemic cognition: A three-level model of cognitive processing. *Human Development, 26,* 222–232.

King, P. M., & Kitchener, K. S. (2002). The reflective judgment model: Twenty years of research on epistemic cognition. In B. K. Hofer, & P. R. Pintrich (Eds.), *Personal epistemology: The psychology of beliefs about knowledge and knowing* (pp. 37–62). Mahwah, NJ: Lawrence Erlbaum.

Leach, J. T., & Scott, P. H. (2008). Teaching for conceptual understanding: An approach drawing on individual and sociocultural perspectives. In S. Vosniadou (Ed.), *International handbook of research on conceptual change* (pp. 647–675). New York, NY: Routledge.

Lee, C. B. (2010). Generating synergy between knowledge building and conceptual change. *Human Development, 53*(3), 134–152.

Lee, C. B., Jonassen, D. H., & Teo, T. (2011). The role of model building in problem solving and conceptual change. *Journal of Interactive Learning Environments, 19,* 247–265.

Limon, M. (2003). The role of domain-specific knowledge in intentional conceptual change. In G. M. Sinatra, & P. R. Pintrich, (Eds.), *Intentional conceptual change* (pp. 133–170). Mahwah, NJ: Lawrence Erlbaum.

Linn, M. C. (2008). Teaching for conceptual change: Distinguish or extinguish ideas. In S. Vosniadou (Ed.), *International handbook of research on conceptual change* (pp. 694–722). New York, NY: Routledge.

Lesh, R., & Harel, G. (2003). Problem solving, modeling, and local conceptual development. *Mathematical Thinking and Learning, 5,* 157–189.

Liu, X. (2004). Using concept mapping for assessing and promoting relational conceptual change in science. *Science Education, 88,* 373–396.

Marbach-Ad, G., Rotbain, Y., & Stavy, R. (2008). Using computer animation and illustration activities to improve high school students' achievement in molecular genetics. *Journal of Research in Science Teaching, 45,* 273–292.

Mason, L. (2002). Developing epistemological thinking to foster conceptual change in different domains. In M. Limon & L. Mason (Eds.), *Reconsidering conceptual change: Issues in theory and practice* (pp. 301–336). Dordrecht/Boston/London: Kluwer Academic Publishers.

Mason, L. (2007). Introduction: Bridging the cognitive and sociocultural approaches in research on conceptual change: Is it feasible? *Educational Psychologist, 42*(1), 1–7.

Mayer, R. E. (1992). *Thinking, problem solving, cognition* (2nd ed.). New York: Freeman.

Muis, K. (2008). Epistemic profiles and self-regulated learning: Examining relations in the context of mathematics problem solving. *Contemporary Educational Psychology, 33,* 177–208.

Muis, K. R., & Franco, G. (2010). Epistemic profiles and metacognition: support for the consistency hypothesis. *Metacognition and Learning, 5*(1), 27–45.

Murphy, P. K. (2007). The eye of the beholder: The interplay of social and cognitive components in change. *Educational Psychologist, 42*(1), 41–53.

Murphy, P. K., & Alexander, P. A. (2008). The role of knowledge, beliefs, and interest in the conceptual change process: A synthesis and meta-analysis of the research. In S. Vosniadou (Ed.), *International handbook of research on conceptual change* (pp. 583–618). New York, NY: Routledge.

Nersessian, N. J. (2008). Mental modeling in conceptual change. In S. Vosniadou (Ed.), *International handbook of research on conceptual change.* (pp. 391–416). NY: Routledge.

Novak, J. D., & Gowin, B. (1984). *Learning how to learn.* Cambridge, UK: Cambridge University Press.

Qian, G., & Alvermann, D. (1995). Role of epistemological beliefs and learned helplessness in secondary school students' learning science concepts from text. *Journal of Educational Psychology, 87,* 282–292.

Robertson, W. C. (1990). Detection of cognitive structure with protocol data: Predicting performance on physics transfer problems. *Cognitive Science, 14,* 253–280.

Scott, P., Asoko, H., & Leach, J. (2007). Student conceptions and conceptual learning in science. In Abell, S. & Lederman, N. (Eds.), *Handbook of research on science education* (pp. 31–56). Mahwah, NJ: Lawrence Erlbaum.

Schoenfeld, A. H. (1985). *Mathematical problem solving*. Orlando, FL: Academic Press.

Sherin, B. (2006). Common sense clarified: The role of intuitive knowledge in physics problem solving. *Journal of Research in Science Teaching, 43,* 535–555.

Sinatra, G. M. (2005). The warming trend in conceptual change research: The legacy of Paul R. Pintrich. *Educational psychologist*, 40(2), 107–115.

Sinatra, G., Southerland, S., McConaughy, F., & Demastes, J. (2003). Intentions and beliefs in students' understanding and acceptance of biological evolution. *Journal of Research in Science Teaching, 40,* 510–528.

Sinatra, G. M, Brem, S. K., Evans, E. M. (2008). Changing minds? Implications of conceptual change for teaching and learning about biological evolution. *Evolution: Education and Outreach, 1,* 189–195.

Smith, M. U. (1992). Expertise and the organization of knowledge: Unexpected differences among genetic counselors, faculty, and students on problem categorization tasks. *Journal of Research in Science Teaching, 29,* 179–205.

Stratford, S. J., Krajcik, J., & Soloway, E. (1998). Secondary students' dynamic modeling processes: Analyzing, reasoning about, synthesizing, and testing models of science ecosystems. *Journal of Science Education and Teaching, 7,* 215–234.

Taasoobshirazi, G., & Glynn, S. (2009). College students solving chemistry problems: A theoretical model of expertise. *Journal of Research in Science Teaching, 46,* 1070–1089.

Tarhan, L., Ayar-Kayali, H., Urek, R., & Acar, B. (2008). Problem-based learning in 9th grade chemistry class: "Intermolecular Forces". *Research in Science Education, 38,* 285–300.

Thagard, P. (1990). Concepts and conceptual change. *Synthese, 82,* 255–274.

Thagard, P. (2000). *Coherence in thought and action*, Cambridge: MIT Press.

Tyson, L. M., Venville, G. J., Harrison, A. G., & Treagust, D. F. (1997). A multidimensional framework for interpreting conceptual change events in the classroom. *Science Education, 81,* 387–404.

Vosniadou, S. (1994). Capturing and modeling the process of conceptual change. *Learning and Instruction, 4,* 45–69.

Vosniadou, S. (1999). Conceptual change research: State of the art and future directions. In W. Schnotz, S. Vosniadou, & M. Carretero, (Eds.), *New perspectives on conceptual change* (pp. 1–14). Amsterdam: Pergamon.

Vosniadou, S. (2007a). The cognitive-situative divide and the problem of conceptual change. *Educational Psychologist*, 42(1), 55–66.

Vosniadou, S. (2007b). The conceptual change approach and its re-framing. In S. Vosniadou, A. Baltas, & X. Vamvakoussi (Eds.), Reframing the conceptual change approach in learning and instruction (pp. 1–16). Amsterdam, Netherlands: Elsevier.

Vosniadou, S. (2008). *International handbook of research on conceptual change.* New York, NY: Routledge.

Vosniadou, S., & Brewer, W. F. (1994). Mental models of the day/night cycle. *Cognitive Science, 18,* 123–183.

Windschitl, M., & Andre, T. (1998). Using computer simulations to enhance conceptual change: The roles of constructivist instruction and student epistemological beliefs. *Journal of Research in Science Teaching, 35,* 145–160.

White, R. T., & Gunstone, R. F. (2008). The conceptual change approach: Theory and practice. In S. Vosniadou (Ed.), *International handbook of research on conceptual change* (pp. 619–628). New York, NY: Routledge.

13 Mobile Technologies as Mindtools for Augmenting Observations and Reflections in Everyday Informal Environments

Susan M. Land, Brian K. Smith, and Heather Toomey Zimmerman

Introduction

For several decades, Jonassen (1996; 2000; 2003; 2006; 2011) has been instrumental in forwarding a vision of technology use that affords new ways of thinking, representing, and visualizing one's experiences for deeper reflection and knowledge construction. His corpus of work around cognitive tools, also referred to as mindtools, frames educational technologies as knowledge construction tools that extend the thinking processes of users, enabling new forms of knowledge representation and task manipulation (Jonassen & Carr, 2000; Jonassen and Reeves, 1996). Mindtools are computer tools that have been adapted or created to extend thinking. His rationale for the concept of mindtools is that even simple, readily-available technology tools, such as databases or spreadsheets, can be powerful intellectual partners for engaging learners in new forms of thinking. Jonassen's mindtools concept is inclusive of general purpose software (such as spreadsheets) as well as designed environments that have been created to facilitate problem solving. Mindtools can include software tools that support knowledge construction and learning-by-design (e.g. programming tools, expert systems, multimedia or web authoring). They can also support semantic organization, dynamic modeling, visualization, multimedia construction, and social networking (Jonassen, 2000). Across the range of approaches and tools, Jonassen (1996) puts forward a unifying concept that "mindtools are cognitive reflection and amplification tools that help learners construct their own representations of a new content domain or visit an old one" (p. 11).

Technology tools can be used to help learners reflect upon and organize ideas and make aspects of the domain under study more explicit and visible (Jonassen, 2000; Linn, 2000). Learner thinking can be made more visible via technology tools that enable the externalization of ongoing understanding (Jonassen 2003; Kafai, 2006), representation of a problem space or conceptual model (Jonassen, 2003), or making connections and comparisons between knowledge and experiences (Collins, 2006). Strategies for supporting reflection using technology tools take many forms and functions, but our synthesis of the literature codifies three primary activities:

(a) *amplify* observations or experiences in ways that encourage deliberate noticing, capturing, or processing of them;
(b) *organize* the products and processes of explorations to support revisiting and revising them; and
(c) *compare, extend, and explain* what students know, considering alternative criteria, audiences, perspectives, representations, or new data

(Collins, 2006; Land & Zembal-Saul, 2003; Lin, Hmelo, Kinzer, & Secules., 1999; Quintana, Reiser, Davis, Krajcik, Fretz, Duncan, Kyza, Edelson, & Soloway, 2002; Schwarz, Lin, Brophy, & Bransford, 1999).

Reflection can be enacted via strategies and technologies, such as mindtools, that can support learners to articulate, visualize, and think about activities and processes (Jonassen & Reeves, 1996).

Since Jonassen's original theoretical conception of mindtools emerged in the mid-1990s, the technology landscape has changed substantially and perhaps in ways that more readily support his vision of seamless tool use for thinking and reflection. For instance, the size and portability of mobile technology tools, including those that are inexpensive and readily available such as iPods and tablets (and their applications, called apps), enable designers to extend learning opportunities into everyday life worlds of people, untethered from classroom desktops or wired indoor facilities. This opportunity expands the potential range of intentions and experiences that can be amplified for learning. Jonassen has often described the work of Donald Norman (1993) as a foundation for mindtools, specifically his distinction between experiential thinking (automatic thinking about ones experiences with the world) from reflective, or more deliberate, thinking. Jonassen's vision was that technology, specifically mindtools, could be a connector between experiential and reflective thinking. Portable, wireless technology tools more readily and immediately support this pairing of experience and reflection, as they can be brought to bear directly in the user's experiential world.

Our discussion here applies the mindtools concept to three cases of everyday learning with informal mobile technologies (i.e. digital cameras, iPods, iPads, smartphones). This shift in context from formal to informal is a departure from the prior research and theory on mindtools for classroom use. The everyday world offers a rich context for learning and extending what is learned in school, yet learners are rarely supported to make such connections, at least in any systematic way. By everyday, we are referring to experiences that routinely occur in daily life that are familiar, informal, and often tacit. Numerous sociocultural studies have tried to characterize differences between the types of learning that occur in formal educational contexts and the world outside schools. For instance, studies of activities such as carpet laying, farming, candy selling (Carraher, Carraher, & Schliemann, 1985;

Saxe, 1991), shopping (Lave, 1988), and game playing (Nasir, 2002, 2005) have examined the connections between mathematics learning and cultural practices associated with activity. These studies recognize that knowledge use and learning occur outside of designed, pedagogical settings. More so, the expression and use of knowledge in these settings rely on tools and artifacts situated in the environment, leading to norms, values, and conventions that generally look very different than those found in designed education contexts.

Anchoring learning in real-world experiences or authentic problems (Jonassen, 2004) potentially enhances the likelihood for discovering the relevance of how and why knowledge is useful (Bransford Brown, & Cocking, 2000). For instance, being able to reflect on the environmental science underlying bee pollination in one's backyard requires intentional observations and interpretations of the surroundings through a scientific lens. Recent mobile computing devices allow for these sorts of investigations and support learners to explore their everyday experiences and use them as objects for knowledge construction (Pea & Maldonado, 2006). In the BioKIDS curriculum, for instance, students used handheld computers to explore their schoolyards, collecting and observing various animals, in order to develop basic understandings of organisms, environments, and interactions between the two (Huber, 2003). Similar biodiversity concepts could be studied with simulations, video clips, and other media (Reiser, Tabak, Sandoval, Smith, Steinmuller, & Leone, 2001), but the use of local, familiar environments and animals may help students better grasp the relevance of the biological theories. Similarly, handheld computer devices, in conjunction with palm-enabled probeware, have been used to enable learners to collect and analyze data from the field (Soloway, Grant, Tinker, Roschelle, Mills, Resnick, Berg, & Eisenberg, 1999), which could include backyards, streams, or parks. The mobility of these devices enables new ways of exploring familiar, everyday experiences, where people learn with, not from, mobile devices, resulting in "an intellectual partnership with the computer is that the whole of learning becomes greater than the sum of its parts" (Jonassen, Carr, & Yeun, 1998, p. 14).

Supporting learners to look at their surroundings with diverse perspectives, including those used by professional practitioners, is a goal of informal educational environments such as outdoor nature centers, where portable technology tools are being explored (see e.g. Liu, Peng, Wu, & Lin, 2009; Rogers, Price, Fitzpatrick, Fleck, Harris, Smith, Randell, Muller, O'Malley, Stanton, Thompson, & Weal, 2004). Our work, which will be the focus of this chapter, seeks to extend the concept of mindtools to include mobile technologies that are integrated into everyday places or experiences for more deliberate reflection and learning. The remainder of this chapter presents three cases of designs for learning outside school, that fall into two broad categories of mobile tools (digital cameras and augmented reality for iPads/iPods) that have been used as technology tools to enable reflection on everyday events, experiences, and places. The first category exemplifies digital cameras as mindtools to capture images of places or experiences, and to organize these images as artifacts to compare, extend, and explain their thinking. The second category is focused on augmented reality as mindtools to amplify observations within a place to encourage deliberate noticing or engagement of disciplinary-relevant practices.

Digital Cameras as Tools to Capture Images as Artifacts for Reflection

In this section, we present two examples that illustrate how Jonassen's framework of mindtools can be extended into everyday places and contexts in support of knowledge construction. Attendant to Jonassen's assumptions of using technology as a tool for thinking, reflection on one's experiences can be better enabled if they are captured in some form – audio, video, written diaries or logs – and used as concrete examples that facilitate shared argumentation, discussion, and reflection. Images collected from videos or cameras provide ways to capture a range of experiences that can be analyzed, compared, or explained (Collins & Brown, 1988). Captured behaviors and experiences allow for reflection (Schön, 1983) as well as being a conversational prop (Brinck & Gomez, 1992; Roschelle, 1992). Asking people to deliberately capture aspects of their experiences often leads them to reflect on observed events as they unfold. Using an expressive medium may somewhat interrupt normal, everyday activities, prompting a photographic eye towards otherwise ordinary events or objects that can be organized and expressed in new ways.

Using digital cameras as tools to document learners' experiences allows them to explore concepts in terms of their experiences. Furthermore, mobile devices such as still and video cameras, potentially become mindtools to capture and represent *images as data* (Smith & Blankinship, 2000). For instance, Rubin's use of video as a form of laboratory instrument (Rubin, 1993) enabled students to film events in the world and analyze them scientifically. Students could capture video of classmates running a race and use the footage to understand the properties of motion (Rubin, Bresnahan, & Ducas 1996; Rubin & Win, 1994). Similar uses of video to capture and reflect on performance have been applied to dance (Cherry, Fournier, & Stevens, 2003), kinesiology (Gross, 1998), visits to science and art museums (Stevens & Hall, 1997; Stevens & Toro-Martell, 2003), classroom learning (Goldman-Segall, 1997), and surgical theaters (Nardi, 1996). All of these examples share the mindtool purpose of extending and amplifying thinking, with the goal of helping learners qualitatively represent the problem space (Jonassen, 2003) and reflect on their observed experiences. In this way, images captured from digital cameras (a) promote reflection on activities that might normally be tacit, (b) build connections between disciplinary practices and the experiential world, and (c) highlight aspects of a developing theory that warrant further investigation (Jonassen & Reeves, 1996; Land, Smith, Park, Beabout, & Kim, 2009).

Case 1: Digital Cameras as Tools for Reflecting on Nutrition Concepts

We have previously explored a series of projects with young children (Kindergartners through fifth graders) in multiple contexts (e.g. health class-rooms, after-school programs) that utilized digital cameras to visualize, ana-lyze, and reflect on everyday food choices (Land et al., 2009; Park, 2007). Typical health and nutrition standards at the primary school level involve identifying the different food groups of the food pyramid, serving sizes, and nutrients. Our projects sought to emphasize learning about nutrition con-cepts using the everyday eating experiences of kids – those that are consis-tent with adult and professional practices around monitoring and improving health and nutrition.

We provided each participating child with digital or disposable cameras to take home and create records of their food choices for a period of time (e.g. three days to one week). The children used these photographs as data to answer a driving question, "How healthy is the food that I am eating?" Using the actual photographs that they took of their food choices, children learned about the different food groups, identified whether they were eating a balanced diet according to USDA-suggested dietary standards, analyzed fats, sugars, and whole grains, and provided justification for whether the photographs of their meals represented a healthy diet. From these analyses, they identified changes they could make to their typical diet.

In order to support learners to represent knowledge as a "mindful task" (Jonassen & Reeves, 1996, p. 696), we designed a multimedia construction activity (Jonassen, 1996) using photo-journals for them to analyze their photos, articulate their beliefs about the healthiness of their food, and to justify these beliefs using basic nutritional concepts. One aspect of the photo-journaling prompted the children to make nutritional analyses of each photographed meal, considering whether the meals were healthy and why they believed this to be the case (Park, 2007). Using digital photo-graphs as media artifacts supported student discussions with each other around their photographs. Furthermore, the children shared their photo-graphs with their parents, and together they could identify specific strategies to improve the healthiness of their food choices, thus crossing the boundar-ies between home and school activities. Using the photographs to develop multimedia artifacts, the children constructed organized knowledge repre-sentations of their data (food choices) that could be revised and revisited using new information and perspectives.

Our research found that using digital cameras as cognitive tools sup-ported learners to reflect on differences between what they were eating and what they believed they were eating (Land et al., 2009; Park, 2007), lending support to Jonassen's premise that mindtools serve an important role as a connector of experiential and reflecting thinking (Jonassen, 1996; Jonassen & Reeves, 1996). The portability of the digital cameras readily enabled this pairing of experience and reflection. Comparing their own choices with

USDA criteria and categories of healthy food choices prompted surprise and reflection as a result of discrepancies they noticed between their photographs and their personal beliefs about their dietary choices. This suggested that capturing and analyzing experiences through self-taken photographs helped learners ground new knowledge of nutrition in their experiences, potentially leading to greater awareness and reflection.

Case 2: Digital Cameras as Tools for Reflecting on the Past and Present of a Place

We also explored the use of digital cameras as tools to reason about history. In particular, we felt it would be useful to have learners study their local communities and consider ways in which they had changed over time. Most communities have gone through large changes in the past hundred years. For instance, city planning has changed with advances in transportation, from horse-drawn carriages to cable cars, to automobiles and subways, and these changes alter the ways that people have moved and lived. Trying to understand a city's design can lead to an increased awareness of the intricacies of the urban environment, what is designed and what is natural (Stilgoe, 1998). More so, everyday travels through a city could lead learners to generate and evaluate hypotheses about its development.

History textbooks typically focus on facts, events, and the names of people rather than the questions, decisions, and heuristics that expert historians use in their work (Paxton, 1999; Voss and Wiley, 2006). Being a skilled historian involves collecting, integrating, and questioning evidence conveyed through multiple sources (Rouet, 1997; Wineburg, 1991), but these skills are not always emphasized in history curricula. As a result, students often associate history with knowing facts and conclusions rather than their underlying justifications and arguments (Voss & Wiley, 2006,).

The mindtools emphasis on meaningful learning through problem solving (Jonassen, 2006) influenced the development of a learning environment called *Image Maps* that connected personal photographs with archival images as a way to understand a community's history. We designed multimedia construction tools that allowed students to trace the development of buildings or locations over time and generate hypotheses about how and why architectural changes were made (Smith & Blankinship, 2000). Approximately 1,000 historical images of Cambridge, Massachusetts along a two-mile route were identified and digitized. Along the route are two major universities (Harvard and MIT) and two major commercial zones (Central and Harvard Square); these targets were chosen for their historical significance and the availability of numerous photographs from the 1890s to the present. Once these images were scanned, students created multimedia evidence to support and refute claims about the evolution of the urban landscape (Jonassen, 2000).

The intention was for students to walk up to a building and have it reveal photographs of its history, much like the Augmented Reality app *Street*

Museum allows users to do on a pedestrian route through downtown London. As students explored and photographed the community, the camera's latitude, longitude, and orientation were captured and inserted into the digital image file. When student photos were uploaded into our application, their position data was matched with historical images stored in a database. If a student took a picture of the newsstand in Harvard Square, the system would retrieve and display historical images of that location taken from the same location and angle. In a sense, the camera and retrieval software acted as a "time machine" (technical details can be found in Smith, 1999); students photographed the present, and the computer returned images of the same location from the past (see Figure 13.1).

The learning environment acted as a mindtool by helping students to make sense of the pictures using multiple representations and perspectives (i.e. historical, architectural, urban planning) (Jonassen & Reeves, 1996). Students began by annotating their pictures with features that changed over time. For instance, some students might have focused on transportation, marking some images with *horse-drawn carriage* tags, others with *automobile* tags. Another group of students might be interested in land use, describing buildings using tags like *commercial* or *industrial* or focus on changes in Cambridge fire stations. Students used labels to compare images, reflect on similarities and differences, and create temporal chains to describe their observations.

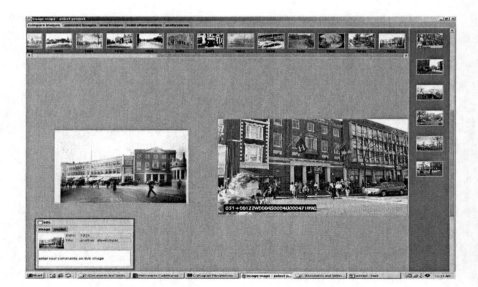

Figure 13.1 An early version of *Image Maps*. Thumbnails along the right side are pictures taken by students. Selecting one of these brings up the thumbnail at the top of the screen, historical images linked to same location. The large image at right center is the student's photograph; the image at left center is an expanded view of a related historical image.

These chains connected historical and student-taken photographs to explain particular aspects of community change. Figure 13.2 shows a set of chains generated by a group of students to illustrate a relationship between traffic and parking over time.

One important characteristic of the image repository is its use of student-collected photographs to drive student inquiry. The goal was to lead students through various tasks, scaffolding the process of observing historical photographs and generating hypotheses about community change.

Augmented Reality as a Tool for Scientific Observation

Another mobile application of technology we have used to support problem solving related to scientific observation in everyday contexts is Augmented Reality (AR). AR combines elements of a real-world physical space with virtual material (e.g. text information, videos, audio, gaming scenarios) in real time (Feiner, Macintyre, & Seligmann, 1993; Rogers et al., 2004). Popular augmented reality environments are available as commercial apps on most mobile devices. For instance, one popular commercial app is *StarWalk*, which enables users to point their mobile devices to a particular location in the night sky and see real-time images of constellations, planets, and stars overlaid onto their device screen. AR also uses Quick Response (QR) bar codes and/or global positioning system (GPS) coordinates to trigger the relaying of such information.

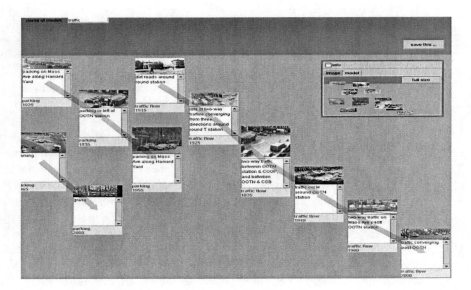

Figure 13.2 An early version of the *Image Maps* timeline tool. Students used this to link historical photographs and explain how and why they were depicted events that were changing over time.

The 2011 Horizon Report (Johnson, Smith, Willis, Levine, & Haywood, 2011) suggests that augmented reality offers "strong potential to provide both powerful contextual, *in situ* learning experiences and serendipitous exploration and discovery of the connected nature of information in the real world" (p. 17). For instance, students can carry mobile, wireless devices through a real-world context and "engage with virtual information superimposed on physical landscapes (such as a tree describing its botanical characteristics or a historic photograph offering a contrast with the present scene)" (Dunleavy, Dede, & Mitchell, 2009, p. 8). In this way, augmented reality apps on mobile devices can serve as tools for reflecting on real-world experiences on demand and within a contextually-rich context outside of school.

Case 3: Using AR to Support Scientific Observations in an Outdoor Nature Center

Land and Zimmerman used AR in a project entitled *Tree Investigators* – where learners explored deciduous and evergreen trees – comparing local trees to each other, as well as to non-native species to make decisions about the scientifically relevant aspects of the garden to make an identification (Land, Zimmerman, Murray, Hooper, Yeh, & Sharma, 2011). Research has found that when learning to make scientific observations, novice learners have to see in new ways (Eberbach & Crowley, 2009); or in problem-solving terms, novices face seasonally dynamic and scientifically situated problems of understanding what is relevant to the situation (Jonassen, 2000). In this sense, learners faced two kinds of authentic science problems, which mapped onto Jonassen's problem-solving processes from a typology (2000):

- strategic performance – applying tactics from science that are relevant to a situation; and
- decision making – identifying and comparing evidence to best fit a problem with appropriate justification.

With the aid of the *Tree Investigators*, learners applied these two problem-solving processes to support their knowledge building and reflection. Learners needed to (a) *apply* tactics from science to identify a tree, (b) *diagnose* which aspect of the tree to focus on to show the biological diversity of trees, and (c) *decide* about the differences between evergreen and deciduous trees to aid in identification. The goal behind *Tree Investigators* was to support youth's knowledge building in the life sciences, in the sense that the AR materials encouraged youth to have a deliberate focus on the scientifically-relevant aspects of the trees. In this way, the AR provided learners with additional resources to engage within the physical space as scientists. The blend of the technology augmentations and key elements from the outdoor learning space changed the activity by combining aspects from two settings (technological and physical) into one.

In this example, the youth's interactions using the technology are mediated in two main ways. First, students' physical observations of eight different trees with text and images were supported through QR (Quick Response) codes (see Figure 13.3) that were indexed to specific trees to highlight variations in physical characteristics. The AR materials focused students' observations on these variations and encouraged them to make additional comparisons in order to highlight species' similarities and differences. In addition, *Tree Investigators* used Microsoft™ Tag Reader to bring specific web-based content to an iPod or iPad that was uniquely relevant to the garden site being explored and to the community. Comparisons, for example, were made between the heights of trees and nearby buildings. Learners were prompted to compare the bark of the tree in front of them to the bark of the tree to their right.

The science content we layered into the garden space via AR tools included three main characteristics of the tree being investigated: (1) leaves/needles, (2) fruit elements, and (3) bark features (see Figure 13.4). Where possible, we augmented images and information that were not directly perceptible to the students at that time (e.g. fall leaf colorings, spring flowering). Organizing the content in this structure served as an intentional scaffold to reveal to students a method of observation of tree species that could help them identify similarities and differences. The link and interface structure suggested a common set of connected ideas that could be applied across instances (Jonassen & Carr, 2000; Quintana et al., 2002).

We also augmented the garden space by creating a "tree mystery" narrative as a context for applying their newly-refined observational practices about trees. Students were told that they were going to help determine the species of a new tree that was donated to the arboretum. Students received clues to figuring out the mystery tree via large AR markers that displayed an

Figure 13.3 QR code for accessing context-specific information in the garden.

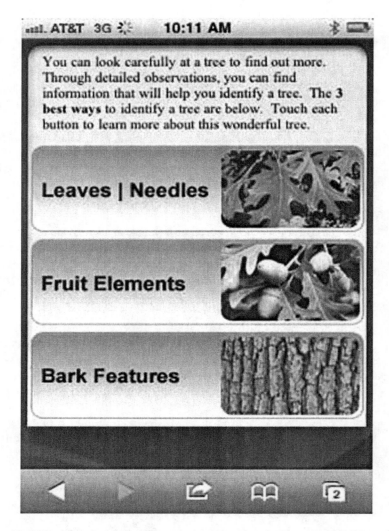

Figure 13.4 Tree characteristics that were augmented and accessed with Microsoft™
        Tag Reader.

image of one of the characteristics of the mystery tree. When the AR markers were held in front of a webcam, the content associated with that marker (i.e. a unique biological feature of the mystery tree) was displayed on the computer screen. Students used a commercial US Trees app to help narrow their search by answering dichotomous key questions. Taken together, our goal was to use AR as a tool for revealing observational methods used by scientists to look at tree species and to facilitate the development of children's own observation skills of the relevant aspects of the local outdoor context.

Conclusion

Mindtools was a concept that grounded learner-centered designs across these three case studies of designs for mobile technologies outside of school (Jonassen & Reeves, 1996). The examples in this chapter all support youth and families in articulating their ongoing understandings, comparing performances or phenomena, and explaining understanding in cohesive ways. Through these cases that focused on learning about disciplinary content connected to everyday places, mobile devices served as mindtools by helping learners connect their experiences with authentic practices, problems, and contextualized knowledge. The success of these three cases suggests that the use of mobile technologies as tools to extend thinking has potential to help learners make deeper connections between their everyday lives and knowledge construction.

Our efforts are intended to provide a starting point to suggest new directions for the application of Jonassen's foundational work on cognitive tools. We see the need for educational researchers and designers to explore tools and frameworks that can transform a *physical* place into a *learning* space by either (a) capturing elements of a place or experience that can be used for further processing, extension, or knowledge construction; or (b) layering data, perspectives, or scaffolds into a physical place in real time to augment how learners can engage the space in ways otherwise conceptually inaccessible to them.

Although Jonassen's mindtools approach was originally intended for, and applied, in school contexts, researchers and designers working with informal environments can adapt the construct to support learners' reflection and articulation. This adaption to learning outside of schools becomes a design imperative to address the needs of the full educational system. For example, Bransford, Brown, and Cocking (2000) noted that students spend only 14 percent of their time in school, but spend roughly 53 percent of their time in the home and community. The informal learning contexts of home, recreation, and community life are largely untapped by designers, researchers, and educators. By applying Jonassen's work into new technologies and new spaces, educational researchers can address questions of how to mobilize people's rich, informal experiences and everyday contexts in their understanding. The theory and application of Jonassen's frameworks for meaningful learning provides a basis for conceptualizing and designing technology tools to support knowledge representation and construction in real places and contexts. The concept of a mindtool is a valuable method for aiding designers to connect individuals' authentic, everyday experiences with systematic reflection and articulation of them.

References

Bell, P., Lewenstein, B., Shouse, A. W., & Feder, M. A. (2009). *Learning science in informal environments: People, places, and pursuits.* Committee on Learning Science in Informal Environments. Washington, DC: National Academic Press.

Bransford, J. D., Brown, A. L., & Cocking, R. R. (Eds.), (2000). *How people learn: Brain, mind, experience, and school.* Washington, DC: National Academy Press.

Brinck, T., & Gomez, L. M. (1992). A collaborative medium for the support of conversational props. In J. Turner & R. Kraut (Eds.), *Conference Proceedings on Computer-Supported Collaborative Work* (pp. 171–178). New York: ACM Press.

Carraher, T. N., Carraher, D. W., & Schliemann, A. D. (1985). Mathematics in the streets and in schools. *British Journal of Developmental Psychology, 3*, 21–29.

Cherry, G., Fournier, J., & Stevens, R. (2003). Using a digital video annotation tool to teach dance composition. *Interactive Multimedia Electronic Journal of Computer-Enhanced Learning, 5*(1). Retrieved from http://imej.wfu.edu

Collins, A. (2006). Cognitive apprenticeship. In R. K. Sawyer (Ed.), *The Cambridge Handbook of the Learning Sciences* (pp. 47–60). Cambridge, MA: Cambridge University Press.

Collins, A., & Brown, J. S. (1988). The computer as a tool for learning through reflection. In H. Mandl & A. Lesgold (Eds.), *Learning Issues for Intelligent Tutoring Systems* (pp. 1–18). New York: Springer-Verlag.

Dunleavy, M., Dede, C., & Mitchell, R. (2009). Affordances and limitations of immersive participatory augmented reality simulations for teaching and learning. *Journal of Science Education & Technology, 18*(1), 7–22.

Eberbach, C., & Crowley, K. (2009). From Everyday to Scientific Observation: How Children Learn to Observe the Biologist's World. *Review of Educational Research, 79*(1), 39–68.

Feiner, S., Macintyre, B., & Seligmann, D. (1993). Knowledge-based augmented reality. *Communications of the ACM, 36*(7), 53–62.

Goldman-Segall, R. (1997). *Points of viewing children's thinking: A digital ethnographer's journey.* Mahwah, NJ: Lawrence Erlbaum Associates.

Gross, M. M. (1998). Analysis of human movement using digital video. *Journal of Educational Multimedia and Hypermedia, 7*(4), 375–395.

Huber, A., Songer, N., & Lee, S.-Y. (2003, April). *BioKIDS: A curricular approach to teaching biodiversity through inquiry in technology-rich environments.* Paper presented at the annual meeting of the National Association of Research on Science Teaching (NARST). Philadelphia, PA.

Johnson, L., Smith, R., Willis, H., Levine, A., & Haywood, K., (2011). *The 2011 Horizon Report.* Austin, Texas: The New Media Consortium.

Jonassen, D. H. (1996). *Mindtools: Computers in the classroom.* Columbus, OH: Merrill.

Jonassen, D. H. (2000). *Computers as mindtools for schools: Engaging critical thinking* (2nd edn) Columbus, OH: Merrill.

Jonassen, D. H. (2003). Using cognitive tools to represent problems. *Journal of Research on Technology in Education, 35*(3), 362–381.

Jonassen, D. H. (2004). *Learning to solve problems: An instructional design guide.* San Francisco, CA: Pfeiffer.

Jonassen, D. H. (2006). *Modeling with technology: Mindtools for conceptual change.* Columbus, OH: Merrill/Prentice Hall.

Jonassen, D. H. (2011). *Learning to solve problems: A handbook for designing problem-solving learning environments.* New York, NY: Routledge.

Jonassen, D. H. & Carr, C. (2000). Mindtools: Affording multiple knowledge representations for learning. In S. Lajoie (Ed.), *Computers as cognitive tools (Vol II): No more walls.* Mahwah, NJ: Erlbaum.

Jonassen, D. H. & Reeves, T. C. (1996). Learning with technology: Using computers as cognitive tools. In D. H. Jonassen (Ed.), *Handbook of research for educational communications and technology* (pp. 693–719). New York: Macmillan.

Kafai, Y. (2006). Constructionism. In K. Sawyer (Ed.), *The Cambridge handbook of the learning sciences* (pp. 35–46). Cambridge, MA: Cambridge University Press.

Klopfer, E. (2008). *Augmented learning: Research and design of mobile educational games.* Cambridge, MA: MIT Press.

Land, S. M., Smith, B., Park, S., Beabout, B., & Kim, K. (2009). Supporting school-home connections through photojournaling: Capturing everyday experiences of nutrition concepts. *Tech Trends, 53*(6), 61–65.

Land, S. M. & Zembal-Saul, C. (2003). Scaffolding reflection and articulation of scientific explanations in a data-rich, project-based learning environment: An investigation of Progress Portfolio. *Educational Technology Research & Development, 51*(4), 65–84.

Land, S. M., Zimmerman, H. T., Murray, O. T., Hooper, S., Yeh, K. C., & Sharma, P. (2011, November). *Mobile computing: Perspectives on design, learning, and development.* 2011 AECT International Convention, Jacksonville, FL.

Lave, J. (1988). *Cognition in practice: Mind, mathematics, and culture in everyday life.* Cambridge: Cambridge University Press.

Lin, X., Hmelo, C., Kinzer, C., & Secules, T. (1999). Designing technology to support reflection. *Educational Technology Research & Development, 47*(3), 43–62.

Linn, M. (2000). Designing the knowledge integration environment. *International Journal of Science Education, 22*(8), 781–796.

Liu, T-C., Peng, H., Wu, W-H., & Lin, M-S. (2009). The effects of mobile natural-science learning based on the 5E learning cycle: A case study. *Educational Technology & Society, 12*(4), 344–358.

Nardi, B. A., Kuchinsky, A., Whittaker, S., Leichner, R., & Schwarz, H. (1996). Video-as-data: Technical and social aspects of a collaborative multimedia application. *Computer Supported Collaborative Work, 4,* 73–100.

Nasir, N. S. (2000). "Points ain't everything": Emergent goals and average and percent understandings in the play of basketball among African American students. *Anthropology and Education Quarterly, 31*(3), 283–305.

Nasir, N. S. (2002). Identity, goals, and learning: Mathematics in cultural practice. *Mathematical Thinking and Learning, 4*(2&3), 213–247.

Norman, D. A. (1993). *Things that make us smart.* Reading, MA: Addison-Wesley.

Pea, R. D., & Maldonado, H. (2006). WILD for learning: Interacting through new computing devices, anytime, anywhere. In K. Sawyer (Ed.), *Cambridge University handbook of the learning sciences,* (pp. 427–442). New York, NY: Cambridge University Press.

Park, S. (2007). *Changing nutrition knowledge and behavior in young children: The role of reflection on personally relevant, technology-rich representations.* Unpublished doctoral dissertation: Penn State University.

Quintana, C., Reiser, B., Davis, E., Krajcik, J., Fretz, E., Duncan, R., Kyza, E., Edelson, D., & Soloway, E. (2004). A scaffolding design framework for software to support science inquiry. *Journal of the Learning Sciences, 13*(3), 337–386.

Reiser, B. J., Tabak, I., Sandoval, W. A., Smith, B. K., Steinmuller, F., & Leone, A. J. (2001). BGuILE: Strategic and conceptual scaffolds for scientific inquiry in biology classrooms. In S. M. Carver & D. Klahr (Eds.), *Cognition and instruction: Twenty-five years of progress* (pp. 263–305). Mahwah, NJ: Lawrence Erlbaum Associates.

Rogers, Y., Price, S., Fitzpatrick, G., Fleck, R., Harris, E., Smith, H., Randell, C., Muller, H., O'Malley, C., Stanton, D., Thompson, M., & Weal, M. (2004). Ambient wood: designing new forms of digital augmentation for learning outdoors (pp. 3–10). *Proceedings of the 2004 Conference on Interaction Design and Children: Building a Community.*

Roschelle, J. (1992). Learning by collaboration: Convergent conceptual change. *The Journal of the Learning Sciences, 2,* 235–276.

Roschelle, J., Rafanan, K., Bhanot, R., Estrella, G., Penuel, B., Nussbaum, M., & Claro, S. (2009). Scaffolding group explanation and feedback with handheld technology: impact on students' mathematics learning. *Educational Technology Research & Development, 58*(4), 399–419. Springer. doi:10.1007/s11423-009-9142-9.

Rubin, A. (1993). Video laboratories: Tools for scientific investigation. *Communications of the ACM, 36*(5), 64–65.

Rubin, A., & Win, D. (1994). Studying motion with KidVid: A data collection and analysis tool for digitized video (pp. 13–14). In *Conference companion to CHI '94* New York: ACM Press.

Rubin, A., Bresnahan, S., & Ducas, T. (1996). Cartwheeling through CamMotion. *Communications of the ACM, 39*(8), 84–85.

Saxe, G. B. (1991). *Culture and cognitive development: Studies in mathematical understanding.* Hillsdale, NJ: Lawrence Erlbaum Associates.

Schön, D. A. (1983). *The reflective practitioner: How professionals think in action.* New York: Basic Books.

Schwartz, D., Lin, X., Brophy, S., & Bransford, J. (1999). Toward the development of flexibly adaptive instructional designs (pp. 183–213). In C. Reigeluth (Ed.), *Instructional-design theories and models: A new paradigm of instructional theory, Volume II.* Mahwah, NJ: Lawrence Erlbaum Associates.

Smith, B. K., & Blankinship, E. (2000). Justifying imagery: Multimedia support for learning through explanation. *IBM Systems Journal, 39*(3&4), 749–767.

Soloway, E., Grant, W., Tinker, R., Roschelle, J., Mills, M., Resnick, M., Berg, R., & Eisenberg, M. (1999). Science in the palms of their hands. *Communications of the ACM, 42*(8), 21–26.

Stevens, R., & Hall, R. (1997). Seeing Tornado: How Video Traces mediate visitor understandings of (natural?) phenomena in a science museum. *Science Education, 81*(6), 735–748.

Stevens, R., & Toro-Martell, S. (2003). Leaving a trace: Supporting museum visitor interaction and interpretation with digital media annotation systems. *Journal of Museum Education, 28*(2), 25–31.

Stilgoe, J. R. (1998). *Outside Lies Magic: Regaining History and Awareness in Everyday Places.* New York: Walker and Company.

Voss, J.F. & Wiley, J. (2006). Expertise in history. In K.A. Ericsson, N. Charness, P. Feltovich, & R. Hoffman (Eds.), *The Cambridge Handbook of Expertise and Expert Performance* (pp. 569–584). Cambridge: Cambridge University Press.

Voss, J. F., & Wiley, J. (2006) Expertise in history. In K. A. Ericsson, N. Charness, P. Feltovich & R. R. Hoffman (Eds.), *The Cambridge Handbook of Expertise and Expert Performance* (pp. 1746–2424). Cambridge University Press.

Wineburg, S. S. (1991). Historical problem solving: A study of the cognitive processes used in the evaluation of documentary and pictorial evidence. *Journal of Educational Psychology, 83,* 73–87.

Wineburg, S. (1991). On the reading of historical texts: Notes on the breach between school and academy. *American Educational Research Journal, 28,* 495–519.

14 Mindtools for Argumentation, and their Role in Promoting Ill-Structured Problem Solving

Brian R. Belland

Introduction

Helping students gain skills in problem solving is a key goal in twenty-first century education (Kuhn, 2007; Warschauer & Matuchniak, 2010). No longer is it enough to simply have a body of accumulated knowledge; rather, one needs to be able to apply knowledge to solve problems (Carnevale & Desrochers, 2003; Casner-Lotto & Barrington, 2006). But the type of problem solving students need to learn is not represented by the classic story problems that many remember from mathematics class. Determining when two trains travelling in opposite directions will meet is not an authentic problem in that it does not represent the kind of problems people face in the real world. As Jonassen (2000) noted, the kind of problems encountered in the real world are ill-structured problems, which cannot be solved by applying a simple procedure or with only the presented information. As such, students need to address ill-structured problems in school (Jonassen, 2000). Simply providing students with an ill-structured problem and expecting them to solve it is not productive.

In this chapter, I explore methods of supporting a critical process involved in ill-structured problem solving – argumentation. First, I explore ill-structured problems, and their role in education and the twenty-first century workforce. Then, I explore the connection between ill-structured problem solving and argumentation. Next, I explore methods for helping students gain skill in argumentation, including scaffolding (as mindtools). Then I discuss controversies in the literature on scaffolding argumentation. Finally, I look forward and discuss argumentation and problem solving and their role in the future of educational technology.

The Need for Ill-Structured Problem-Solving Ability

David Jonassen is a key figure in the emergence of ill-structured problem-solving ability as a focus of education. As he wrote about the importance of ill-structured problem solving, researchers listened, and cited Jonassen's work extensively. According to Google Scholar, as of March 21, 2012, Jonassen has 64 works that have each been cited at least 64 times, including

51 works that have each been cited at least 100 times. This is an extraordinary record of impact, and while not all of Jonassen's works pertain to ill-structured problem solving, much of his highest impact work does.

The Definition of Ill-Structured Problem Solving

Ill-structured (authentic) problems are those for which there is more than one valid solution and more than one possible solution path (Jonassen, 2000). Authentic problems cannot be solved simply by applying a set procedure or by reading a set of problem facts (Jonassen, 2000). Furthermore, there is no one set of criteria for determining the sufficiency of a solution to an authentic problem. Different stakeholders will hold differing sets of criteria by which they judge the sufficiency of problem solutions.

An example of an authentic problem is what should be done to optimize the water quality of a river. There are many different components that combine to indicate water quality, such as (a) oxygen concentration, (b) phosphate levels, (c) nitrate levels, (d) water temperature, (e) turbidity, (f) presence of mayflies, stoneflies, and caddisflies, (g) pH, and so on. Furthermore, no single component has a level that can always be considered ideal. Take temperature for example. Water temperature is important to life in rivers. Water temperature in rivers is not constant; as the day progresses and the sun shines on the surface of the water, the temperature can rise. Water temperature in a river is important because it influences oxygen concentrations. Oxygen concentrations in turn influence the type of fish and other organisms that can live in the river. Colder water will have a greater oxygen concentration, which is conducive to healthy trout populations. Warmer water tends to have a lower oxygen concentration, which is not good for trout but can support fish species such as carp. Having a healthy trout population in a river in mountain regions can be very important to fishermen and environmentalists. If the water is too warm for trout to survive, and yet trout are desired in the river, then it may be desirable to lower the water temperature. However, there is no one procedure for lowering the temperature of water in a river. There are techniques that can help, like planting more trees along the riverbanks, which can provide shade. But this in turn can change other water quality indicators when leaves fall into the river. Not all stakeholders will agree that planting trees along the river is a good solution, or even that the water temperature needs to be lower. Planting trees along the riverbanks may not be enough to lower the temperature, or to sustain a healthy trout population. Furthermore, maintaining a healthy trout population may not be equally valued as a goal by all relevant stakeholders.

Why is Ill-Structured Problem-Solving Ability Needed?

A key argument made by Jonassen to support teaching students to solve ill-structured problems is that in just about any career they pursue, they will be retained and rewarded for solving ill-structured problems, not for reciting memorized information (e.g., Jonassen, 2000; Jonassen, Strobel, & Lee, 2006). This argument stems from the fact that the workplace has changed considerably in the last few decades. It used to be enough to have a certain body of content knowledge and some rudimentary skills (Carnevale & Desrochers, 2003). But that does not suffice any more (Carnevale & Desrochers, 2003; Casner-Lotto & Barrington, 2006; Jonassen, 2000). The monotonous work on assembly lines that used to require legions of workers can now be performed by a few robots (Reich, 2009). But this does not mean that factories are devoid of humans. Rather, workers who are employed in factories need to be able to solve more complex problems (Carnevale & Desrochers, 2003; Feller, 2003; Nordgren, 2002). In fact, in a survey of major employers, problem-solving ability was one of four most highly desired, yet least-developed skill among high school graduates (Casner-Lotto & Barrington, 2006). High school graduates are clearly not being sufficiently prepared to solve complex, ill-structured problems; this can adversely affect their future employment and career advancement prospects.

Process

As Jonassen (2000) noted, the exact process by which ill-structured problems are solved can vary between problem types (e.g., decision-making problems, design problems). But many authors posit that certain general stages exist in all ill-structured problem solving (e.g., Belland, Glazewski, & Richardson, 2008; Jonassen, 2003; Jonassen, 2011). To solve authentic problems, individuals first need to represent the problem (Belland et al., 2008; Jonassen, 2003, 2011). Modeling the presented problem is important not only so the present problem can be solved appropriately, but also so that skills gained can be applied to new problems (Jonassen, 2011). The problem representation that is required when solving authentic problems goes considerably beyond the givens in the problem situation (Jonassen, 2003). It involves creating a rich mental representation of the problem stakeholders, what is happening, and how these entities interact (Jonassen, 2003). It involves causal reasoning in that a problem representation needs to specify how and to what extent certain variables impact other variables (Jonassen, 2011). So in the Intermountain river example, problem solvers need to first determine the ideal state of the river from their stakeholder perspective, and determine how the current state departs from the ideal state. In short, they need to create a mental model of both the current situation and the ideal situation (Jonassen, 2000). But given that it is an authentic problem, there is no single, clear-cut ideal state of the river. To establish an ideal state, problem solvers must engage in argumentation with fellow problem solvers (Garcia-Mila & Andersen, 2008). They must establish a rationale as to why certain characteristics are ideal and are preferable to other characteristics. They need to determine the causal relationships between the problem elements – how changing one element would impact the others. Also, it is important to note that the difference between the ideal state and the current state cannot be represented with a simple quantitative equation.

Next, problem solvers need to determine what else they need to know to solve the problem, and find that information (Belland et al., 2008; Belland, French, & Ertmer, 2009; Hmelo-Silver, 2004). So in the river example, some things they may need to know include the extent to which there are trees on the riverbanks, the flow rate, and the extent to which oxygen-sensitive bugs such as mayflies are present. Because there are no hard and fast rules about the exact types of information that needs to be found, or how to find it again, this stage in the process relies on argumentation.

Then problem solvers need to develop a solution and test its support (Belland et al., 2008; Hmelo-Silver, 2004). Because there are multiple valid solutions to authentic problems, again, this requires argumentation in that the appropriateness of solutions can only be determined by weighing the evidence for and against the solution. One way that evidence can be weighed is to consider the problem from multiple perspectives (Jonassen, 2000; Nussbaum & Schraw, 2007). For example, when examining how to optimize water quality in a river from the perspective of a farmer, it makes sense to think of the problem from other perspectives, such as that of a common citizen. Then, one could think if the same evidence appears to support the same solution from what perspective. One can also consider the same evidence when used to support a counterargument (Nussbaum & Schraw, 2007). Does the evidence appear to support the counterargument to an equal or greater extent than the original argument? The ways in which problem solvers evaluate solutions depends to a large degree on their epistemic beliefs (Jonassen, 2000). As Jonassen (2000) noted, the specific criteria by which solutions are judged depends on the type of ill-structured problem (e.g., troubleshooting problems, dilemmas). For example, in the case of a troubleshooting problem related to a car rattle, a solution may be deemed acceptable when the car stops rattling. In the case of a dilemma, like how to optimize water quality, the measure of a successful solution may simply be that there is an articulated solution with some justification (Jonassen, 2000).

Can One Learn Generalizable Ill-Structured Problem-Solving Skills?

A key goal that can be sensed in Jonassen's work is that of trying to engender students' application of high-quality approaches to ill-structured problem solving in a variety of situations. But it must be made clear that Jonassen's intent is not the same as of many researchers in the era in which information processing theories held sway, who attempted to distill universal approaches to problem-solving that could be learned and then applied to a multitude of problem-solving situations. So for example, methods like means-ends analysis (Simon, 1979) and analogical problem solving (Gentner, Lowenstein,

&Thompson, 2003) were proposed as problem-solving methods that could be applied to a variety of problem-solving situations. Many researchers began to see problems in this conceptualization of problem solving. One issue was that in much of the research that supported the development of these models, participants engaged in relatively constrained problem-solving games like Missionaries and Cannibals and Tower of Hanoi (Gick & Holyoak, 1980). These were not deemed to be representative of real world problems. Another issue is that transfer tasks were often either unrealistic, or transfer was not found in research (Barnett & Ceci, 2002).

Argumentation the Key to Solving Ill-Structured Problems

Much of Jonassen's most recent work has focused on the role of argumentation in helping students learn to solve ill-structured problems. According to Kuhn and Pearsall (2000), science is, at its core, "the coordination of theory and evidence in a consciously controlled manner" (p. 114). By examining the terms in this quote, one would do well to note that theories and evidence are very much involved in both problem solving and argumentation.

Science is problem solving in that it is a way of examining evidence in light of theories to determine how well theories can explain evidence. Scientists create theories to explain and predict reality. But creating theories without reference to evidence would be an exercise in futility, and, indeed, entirely unscientific. When they do not explain a phenomenon, theories need to be adjusted and or new theories need to be added. This process of theory testing and adjustment is scientific problem solving, and is the method by which science advances.

Scientists can justify their decisions in terms of evidence and principles through argumentation. Scientific argumentation can be defined as the process by which individual scientists generate theory and communicate and defend it among the greater community of scientists (Osborne, 2010). Just like problem solving, argumentation involves a type of theory (i.e., a claim) and evidence, and a good argument connects evidence to a claim. In the next section, I explore argumentation more extensively.

Argumentation Definition

In its simplest definition, argumentation can be defined as the process of backing claims with evidence (Perelman & Olbrechts-Tyteca, 1955). However, there are many more nuanced definitions of just what it means to engage in argumentation. There are three main schools of thought: rhetorical, persuasive, and dialectical.

Rhetorical

Classical rhetoric is at once one of the oldest strands in philosophy and the oldest tradition in argumentation. One distinguishing feature of rhetoric is the subject matter about which rhetorical arguments can be made. According to many scholars of rhetoric over the ages, rhetorical arguments cannot be made about specific actions, but rather choices about actions (Kock, 2009). For example, one cannot make a rhetorical argument that actuarial science is the best career. But one could make a rhetorical argument that choosing actuarial science as a career option is good.

Systems of rhetoric were not concerned with rules by which the audience of the argument could accept claims, but rather with the strategy by which orators could produce arguments (Braet, 1987). Rhetorical arguments relied on a system of formal logic that provided chains of evidence from premise to evidence to claim such that the argument could not be falsified (Bricker & Bell, 2008). For any argument, there was an arbiter who could apply "universally accepted yardsticks inherent to the matter under discussion" (Braet, 1987, p. 91). That is, according to rhetorical argumentation, there is a set of universal criteria that can be used to assess the validity of all arguments. Because of this, it does not align well with authentic problem solving. Just as there can be multiple valid solutions to authentic problems, there also can be multiple potentially valid arguments (Jonassen, 2011).

As an example of a rhetorical argument, consider the following scenario. Jimmy wants to prove to his deaf friend Mark that his cat, named Tommy, meows. Mark has never heard Tommy meow for obvious reasons. Jimmy tells Mark: "All cats meow. Tommy is a cat. Thus Tommy meows." As can be seen, if the premise and the evidence are both true, then it will automatically follow that the claim is true.

Persuasive

One of the most prominent models of persuasive argumentation was developed by Perelman and Olbrechts-Tyteca (1955), according to which an evidence-based argument consists of a claim connected to evidence by way of premises. The purpose of argumentation is to lead the audience to agree that the claim is valid (Perelman & Olbrechts-Tyteca, 1955). One can do that by using premises that are jointly held by the arguer and the audience to establish the connection between claims and their associated evidence. The premises need not always be explicitly stated. In this model, there is no such thing as universally accepted yardsticks by which to judge arguments, and there is no such thing as a universally valid argument. Arguments can be considered valid or not by a specific audience. Because persuasive arguments are not judged with respect to universal criteria, they are compatible with authentic problems.

As an example of a persuasive argument, consider the following scenario. Bobby wants to prove to Jonny that trees need to be planted along the Smithfield River. Bobby says: "Trees need to be planted along the Smithfield River because the water temperature in the river is too high. When the water temperature is too high, trout cannot live." In this case, there are two unstated premises. The first is that the Smithfield River should contain trout.

The second is that trees on the banks of a river would provide shade, and thus lead to a lower water temperature in a river. Through his statement of the claim that trees should be planted along the riverside, and the associated evidence, which are connected to the claim by way of unstated premises, Bobby may lead Jonny to accept his claim as valid. But this depends on Jonny's acceptance of the pertinence and validity of the evidence put forward, and the appropriateness of the premises that are used to make the connection between the claim and associated evidence.

Dialectical

According to the dialectical model of argumentation, the goal of an argument is not to win the argument, or prove that your claim is valid. But rather, an arguer aims to arrive at a claim closer to the ultimate truth through discussion with someone with an opposing claim (Jonassen & Kim, 2010). The underlying idea is that each claim related to a topic can hold an element of the truth, but that no human claim can hold the entire truth. But through discussion with someone with an opposing claim, one can get closer to the ultimate truth. This can happen as inconsistencies in each opposing claim are detected and rectified (Walton, 2007). Engaging with arguers with opposing claims in a cooperative rather than an adversarial manner can be likened to the idea of conceptual crisscrossing in cognitive flexibility research (Braten, Britt, Stromso, & Rouet, 2011; Jacobson, 2008). By engaging with multiple perspectives on the same topic, one can build stronger conceptual models related to the underlying data, which can in turn be used to explain the data more effectively (Braten et al., 2011; Jacobson, 2008).

As an example of a dialectical argument, consider Carrie and Sarah's discussion about how to optimize the Smithfield River's water quality. Carrie represents the farmer stakeholder position and Sarah represents that of fishermen. Sarah says that trees should be planted along the river to lower the water temperature, a fence should be installed to keep livestock out of the river, and dams should be removed to allow the river to flow normally. Carrie says that trees should not be planted along the river because that infringes on her rights as a landowner, a fence should not be installed because her animals have as much of a right to use the water as anyone or anything else, and the dams should stay because irrigation water from the associated reservoirs help farmers grow crops. Through discussion of their claims and evidence, Carrie and Sarah may eventually arrive at a claim that is more representative of the ultimate truth, and one that all stakeholders could support.

Connection Between Argumentation and Ill-structured Problem Solving

Argumentation is central to ill-structured problem solving (Belland et al., 2008; Jiménez-Aleixandre, Rodríguez, and Duschl, 2000; Jonassen, 2011;

Jonassen & Kim, 2010; Spector & Park, in press). If problem solving is the coordination of theory and evidence (Kuhn & Pearsall, 2000), then argumentation is the articulation of how theory and evidence interrelate. Authentic problem solving involves an unclear current state, multiple possible goals, and multiple possible solutions. As such, there are many open-ended questions to be answered when solving an authentic problem. For example, what evidence is applicable to the problem at hand? What are good strategies to gather evidence? What is the difference between the current state and the goal state? What is the goal state? What are the necessary elements of an acceptable problem solution? Since there are no single right answers to the questions, problem solvers must engage in a process of argumentation to answer them and justify those answers (Jonassen, 2011). Furthermore, the type of argumentation will be either persuasive or dialectical, because it is not possible to construct a universally valid argument (i.e., rhetorical) about authentic problem solving. This process may be carried out either with fellow problem solvers, in the case of group problem solving, or as an internal dialog, in the case of individual problem solving. In individual problem solving, internal dialog takes place as inner speech, and precedes the production of written problem solutions and/or arguments (Vygotsky, 1962). Inner speech is inherently dialogic in that it responds to other utterances, whether something someone articulated in writing or orally or cultural rules (e.g., what an ideal state would be; Eun, Knotek, & Heining-Boynton, 2008).

People of all Ages and Skills Struggle with Argumentation

Many studies have found that not only K-12 students (Driver, Newton & Osborne, 2000; Keefer, Zeitz, & Resnick, 2000; Ruiz-Primo, Li, Tsai, & Schneider, 2008) but also highly educated adults (Felton & Kuhn, 2001) have difficulty creating effective evidence-based arguments. For example, Kuhn and Udell (2007) compared the performance of middle school students, high school students, and graduate students when selecting an argument to further a personal goal. There were no differences between (a) graduate students and high school students, or (b) high school students and middle school students. The only significant difference was between middle school students and graduate students, and this was only on the order of 0.51 standard deviations. 0.51 standard deviations is a medium-effect size according to Cohen's (1969) effect size guidelines, but one would expect the separation between graduate students and middle school students to be much larger. There is clearly a lack of argumentation skills among the American public.

Methods to Help Students Gain Skill in Argumentation

A central concern in the consideration of methods to promote argumentation ability is whether the overt focus of an instructional unit should be on developing argumentation ability or on the development of problem-solving ability. In short, should students think they are learning to solve problems or learning to create evidence-based arguments?

Focus on Argumentation

One school of thought says that the overt focus should be on developing argumentation ability; that is, that educators should overtly teach students the norms of argumentation and how to create evidence-based arguments (Monte-Sano, 2008; Swartz, 2008). Then, later, once students know the skill of argumentation, they can apply the skill in context.

One difficulty with employing an overt focus on argumentation is that to effectively engage in argumentation, one needs to have something about which to argue (Jonassen & Kim, 2010). So practice activities, which are considered crucial in most instructional theories, would be difficult to facilitate. Much research indicates that one cannot learn process skills effectively without engaging in the process while learning (Schank, 2004). Learning the process of argumentation overtly, and then actually engaging in argumentation can be problematic in that argumentation skills may not be learned effectively in the first place, so students may not be able to apply the skills. In short, the risk with overly teaching argumentation is that students will learn inert knowledge that cannot be generalized.

Focus on Problem Solving

Another school of thought holds that students should learn argumentation while engaged in authentic problem solving (Belland et al., 2008; Jonassen & Kim, 2010). For example, middle school students can develop a project to use $3 million dollars to further the Human Genome Project from stakeholder positions, and then develop evidence-based arguments in support of their solutions (Belland, 2010; Belland, Glazewski, & Richardson, 2011).

By focusing on problem solving, educators can give students a topic about which to argue (Jonassen & Kim, 2010). Furthermore, by arguing about authentic problems, students have the potential to learn argumentation skills that can be applied to new contexts (Schank, 2004).

The Role of Mindtools

Mindtools can help students engage in this process. Jonassen, Carr, and Yueh (1998) proposed that computer applications be used not just as deliverers of information, but as mindtools with which students could do things like represent problems, organize what they are learning, and think critically about information. This connects to research on the use of scaffolding to support argumentation during problem solving (Belland, 2010; Belland et al., 2011; Sandoval & Reiser, 2004). Scaffolding is designed to help students engage in and gain skill at higher-order thinking processes they cannot complete unaided (Belland et al., 2008; Wood, Bruner, & Ross, 1976). It is original conceptualization, scaffolding was provided on a just-in time basis by a teacher or parent (Wood et al., 1976). More recently, the potential of computer-based tools to serve the scaffolding function has been proposed (Hannafin, Land, & Oliver, 1999).

Several reviews of the research on mindtools have indicated the potential of these resources. Belland, Glazewski, and Richardson (2008) reviewed computer-based scaffolds (mindtools) used to support middle school students' creation of evidence-based arguments. Another review was conducted by Clark, Stegman, Weinberger, Menekse, and Erkens (2008). Methods used for supporting argumentation during problem solving include concept mapping, questioning, modeling, and other scaffolding strategies to support problem reformulation, evidence collection, and the connection of claims to evidence (Belland et al., 2008).

Application of Argumentation in Future Situations

Ideally, if students gain argumentation skills, they will be able to apply those skills in future situations. But debate remains as to whether this is likely. The debates relate to whether argumentation skills are context-bound and how to promote the transfer of responsibility from the scaffold to the student.

Controversy 1: Context-Bound Hypothesis

As noted previously, for many years, researchers attempted to distill problem-solving heuristics that could be applied to problems in a variety of domains (for an overview, see Simon, 1979). Much of the research that was done to develop such heuristics used games like the Tower of Hanoi, which involved well-structured problems and the need for little content knowledge (Simon, 1979). However, more recent research suggests that the quest for universal heuristics may not be a productive one. According to Jonassen (2000), ill-structured problem-solving skill tends to be very context-specific in that problem solvers in different disciplines need to deploy domain-specific strategies to effectively solve presented problems. Given that argumentation skills and ill-structured problem-solving skills are so inter-connected, are argumentation skills likewise context-bound?

There are two issues at debate here. The first is if argumentation strategies are subject-specific. So, for example, will a specific argumentation process work only with various problems in the domain of bioengineering, or can it work in problems in other subjects like organic chemistry? Within argumen-tation, there are context-free strategies that can be used. For example, in persuasive argumentation, it is important to back a claim with evidence by way of premises. This generic strategy can in theory work in any domain. But the specifics in how the strategy is deployed can vary by subject. For example, someone who is not an expert in bioengineering may have difficulty identifying subject-specific premises. Or in seeing how collected evidence might relate to a given claim. Sadler and Donnelly (2006) found that there was no relationship between content knowledge and argumentation quality among high school science students.

The second is if argumentation strategies are topic specific. For example, would a specific argumentation process only work with a specific problem in bioengineering, or could it be used with multiple problems in bioengineering?

Kuhn (2010) found evidence that students can learn argumentation skills in one content area and then apply the skills in a different context.

Controversy 2: Transfer of Responsibility Debate

One of the most enduring controversies in scaffolding research is if tools can be called scaffolds if they are not faded. In the original conceptualization of scaffolding, a teacher provided just the right amount of support to allow a student to perform a task that he/she would not be able to complete unaided, and then reduced support as the student gained skill (Wood et al., 1976). This was said to help facilitate the transfer of responsibility from the scaffold to the student such that the student would be able to perform the task independently. In teacher-provided scaffolding, fading is still an option because teachers can engage in ongoing diagnosis of student ability. But current computing technology cannot engage in ongoing diagnosis of ill-structured problem solving (Belland, 2011). Thus, it is impractical to implement fading of computer-based scaffolds based on ongoing diagnosis of student ability (Belland, 2011). When one considers the scaffolding types specified by Hill and Hannafin (2001), it may be possible to implement fading in procedural scaffolds, but not among strategic, metacognitive, and conceptual scaffolds.

So how can the lack of fading be overcome? Belland (2011) considered scaffolds that are not faded as part of a distributed cognition system. If this is done, one can promote transfer of responsibility through front-end work in the design of scaffolds. Specifically, if scaffolds are designed such that students need to (a) maintain executive control throughout the functioning of the distributed cognitive system, and (b) engage mindfully, then the scaffolds can be removed and the remainder of the system can adjust (Belland, 2011).

Argumentation, Problem Solving, and the Future of Educational Technology

Recently, Jonassen (2011) pulled together all he has learned over the years about ill-structured problem solving, and how to support it. Argumentation figures prominently in the book, reflecting the importance Jonassen places on the process. But of course Dave Jonassen would never say argumentation is central to problem solving simply because he says that it is. Rather, he would want readers to look at the evidence.

As noted earlier, the twenty-first century workplace will require the ability to solve authentic problems as a core competency (Casner-Lotto & Barrington, 2006). Being able to build evidence-based arguments is central to authentic problem solving because argumentation is involved in all phases thereof (Belland et al., 2008; Jonassen, 2011; Osborne, 2010). But having students solve word problems is not going to help develop these skills. Rather, having them solve authentic problems with the help of mindtools can help them learn how to (a) represent problems, (b) determine and find needed information, and (c) link evidence to claims (Belland et al., 2008; Clark et al., 2008).

Current Trends

Online Learning in K-12 Schools

As schools progress in the twenty-first century, another initiative is being introduced that will change how authentic problem solving is facilitated. Online education is becoming increasingly prevalent at the K-12 level. A recent report from the National Center for Educational Statistics (2011) indicated that 55 percent of public K-12 districts offered online courses in the 2009–2010 school year; the majority of these courses were asynchronous courses. Furthermore, a major reason that districts offered online courses was to be able to offer courses that enrollment numbers would not otherwise justify offering in a face-to-face format (NCES, 2011). Students in 22 percent of the school districts offering online courses can take a full course load entirely online (NCES, 2011). By many estimates, the proportion of K-12 students taking online courses will increase as time progresses (e.g., Christensen, Horn, & Johnson, 2008; Picciano, Seaman, & Allen, 2010). In fact, Utah recently passed a law guaranteeing K-12 students who meet the prerequisites the right to enroll in publicly funded online courses (Statewide Online Education Program Created, 2011). The emergence of online education will fundamentally change how authentic problem solving and argumentation can be facilitated in K-12 schools. For example, existing mindtools to facilitate such processes largely assume that students are in the same place at the same time. This allows students to engage in the difficult process of consensus building that is central to face-to-face argumentation. It is important to note that consensus building should not mean that the opinion of whoever has the strongest voice is adopted wholesale. Rather, along the lines of dialectical argumentation, the consensus-building process can help individuals point out and rectify inconsistencies in other's claims and associated arguments. Much more needs to be known about how to encourage this crucial process in asynchronous discussions. Many of the online courses that students will be taking will likely involve advanced science. For example, a school in rural Appalachia may not have enough students to justify hiring a highly qualified teacher to teach advanced physics, but throughout the state there would surely be enough students who are interested in taking the class. So if students are taking the course asynchronously and are separated by hundreds of miles, how can the kinds of teamwork, consensus building, and argumentation that are central to authentic problem solving be facilitated? One way might be to mandate synchronous consensus building sessions in which students use chat rooms to discuss ideas and build consensus. Another idea may be to build off of the CSILE/Knowledge Forum Research, in which students articulate ideas in a database, and then peers could go in and comment on the ideas later (Scardamalia & Bereiter, 2006). Another perspective that may inform the consensus-building process in asynchronous work is that of peer scaffolding. Peer scaffolding is the third major type of scaffolding, with the first two being teacher scaffolding and computer-based scaffolding (Belland, in press). In peer scaffolding, students apply a provided framework to their peers' work. The framework could be represented by a rubric or a process modeled by a teacher. The key attribute of peer scaffolding that differentiates it from peer feedback is that it involves both critique and prompting. For example, in Learning by Design, middle school students can critique classmates' designs, and prompt classmates to articulate rationales for both their designs and the associated rules of thumb (Kolodner, Camp, Crismond, Fasse, Gray, Holbrook, Putambeckar, & Ryan, 2003). Teacher modeling of peer scaffolding approaches could work in online education, but such modeling would be of a fundamentally different nature. That is, teacher modeling in an online context would perhaps consist of a screencast. A written rubric may be another good option. Since both the critiquing and the prompting would be done asynchronously, it may be reasonable to examine the consensus-building process in asynchronous education as a three-stage process. In the first stage, students can apply the provided framework to their groupmates' contributions. In the second stage, students should consider side-by-side (a) their critique of their groupmates' contributions, (b) their groupmates' critique of their own contribution, and (c) their groupmates' prompting. In the third stage, students can revise their contribution on the basis of a careful, comprehensive consideration of the feedback and the prompting. This process may need to be repeated until the opposing claims are close enough together.

Information Literacy

Also of critical importance to authentic problem solving and argumentation is information problem solving, defined as the process by which information that can answer specific questions is found, and information literacy, defined as the ability to critically evaluate the appropriateness of information (Partnership for 21st Century Skills, 2008). Students need to be able to assess "the credibility, validity, and reliability of information, including its source and the methods through which the information and related data are derived, in order to critically interpret scientific arguments and the application of science concepts" (Partnership for 21st Century Skills, 2008, p. 7).

Even many university students lack sufficient information literacy (van de Ward, 2010). If the subset of university-bound students do not have sufficient information literacy by the time they get there, then one can imagine that

K-12 students as a whole do not have sufficient information literacy. Argumentation is fundamentally about solving ill-structured problems (Jonassen, 2011). In the process of solving such problems, students will encounter a variety of different sources and information, and they need to be able to sort the information that can help from the information that does not help. Information literacy is key to this process, as students need to critically assess the appropriateness of the information. How can one have enough confidence in evidence to use it to support a claim, or evaluate another's argument if one cannot critically evaluate the credibility and reliability of information? Clearly there is a need for instruction on information literacy to enable students to engage in the kind of authentic problem solving and argumentation that they need to prepare for twenty-first century careers.

Just as solving authentic problems can be iterative, so too can information problem solving (Moore, 1995). That is, when engaging in information problem solving, often the first strategies will not work, and other strategies need to be explored (Moore, 1995). The Big 6 approach can help students engage in information problem solving more effectively (Eisenberg & Berkowitz, 1991). According to the Big 6 approach, students need to (a) define the problem and the information needed, (b) select the best sources, (c) find information, (d) extract information, (e) organize and present information, and (f) judge the product and process (Eisenberg & Berkowitz, 1991). The Big 6 has been integrated into computer-based scaffolds to support authentic problem solving. For example, Wolf, Brush, and Saye (2003) integrated the Big 6 into scaffolds to support students solving of historical problems using primary source documents. Experimental students created better history articles and stayed on task better than control students (Wolf et al., 2003).

Conclusion

As Dave Jonassen has stated many times, people are not paid to recite information or reply to multiple-choice questions. People are paid to solve problems. And the types of problems they are paid to solve are not the familiar story problems that most readers likely recall. People are paid to solve authentic problems, and to do so, they need to be able to articulate what they are doing and why, and provide evidence in support of those decisions. Argumentation is inseparable from problem solving, and through the use of mindtools (scaffolds) students can learn to argue effectively such that they can then build effective evidence-based arguments in the future (Belland et al., 2011; Belland, 2010; Sandoval & Reiser, 2004).

Acknowledgments

The writing of this chapter was partially supported by National Science Foundation Early CAREER Grant # 0953046. However, the opinions and findings expressed herein are those of the author, and do not represent official positions of the National Science Foundation.

References

Barnett, S. M., & Ceci, S. J. (2002). When and where do we apply what we learn? A taxonomy for far transfer. *Psychological Bulletin, 128*(4), 612–637.

Belland, B. R. (2011). Distributed cognition as a lens to understand the effects of scaffolds: The role of transfer of responsibility. *Educational Psychology Review, 23*(4), 577–600.

Belland, B. R. (2010). Portraits of middle school students constructing evidence-based arguments during problem-based learning: the impact of computer-based scaffolds. *Educational Technology Research and Development, 58*(3), 285–309.

Belland, B. R., French, B. F., & Ertmer, P. A. (2009). Validity and problem-based learning research: A review of instruments used to assess intended learning outcomes. *Interdisciplinary Journal of Problem-based Learning, 3*(1), 59–89.

Belland, B. R., Glazewski, K. D., & Richardson, J. C. (2011). Problem-based learning and argumentation: Testing a scaffolding framework to support middle school students' creation of evidence-based arguments. *Instructional Science, 39,* 667–694.

Belland, B. R., Glazewski, K. D., & Richardson, J. C. (2008). A scaffolding framework to support the creation of evidence-based arguments. *Educational Technology Research & Development, 56,* 401–422.

Braet, A. (1987). The classical doctrine of "status" and the rhetorical theory of argumentation. *Philosophy & Rhetoric, 20*(2), 79–93.

Braten, I., Britt, M. A., Stromso, H. I., & Braet Rouet, J. (2011). The role of epistemic beliefs in the comprehension of multiple expository texts: Toward an integrated model. *Educational Psychologist, 46*(1), 48–70.

Bricker, L. A., & Bell, P. (2008). Conceptualizations of argumentation from science studies and the learning sciences and their implications for the practices of science education. *Science Education, 92*(3), 473–498.

Carnevale, A. P., & Desrocher, D. M. (2003). Preparing students for the knowledge economy: What school counselors need to know. *Professional School Counseling, 6*(4), 228–236.

Casner-Lotto, J., & Barrington, L. (2006). *Are they really ready to work? Employers' perspectives on the basic knowledge and applied skills of new entrants to the 21st century US workforce.* Washington, D.C.: Partnership for 21st Century Skills.

Christensen, C., Horn, M. B., & Johnson, C. W. (2008). *Disrupting class: How disruptive innovation will change the way the world learns.* New York: McGraw-Hill.

Clark, D. B., Stegman, K., Weinberger, A., Menekse, M., & Erkens, G. (2008). In Erduran, S., & Jiménez-Aleixandre, M. (Eds.), *Argumentation in science education: Perspectives from classroom-based research* (pp. 217–243). New York: Springer.

Cohen, J. (1969). *Statistical power analysis for the behavioral sciences.* New York: Academic Press.

Driver, R., Newton, P., & Osborne, J. (1998). Establishing the norms of scientific argumentation in classrooms. *Science Education, 84*(3), 287–312.

Eisenberg, M. B., & Berkowitz, R. E. (1991). *Information problem solving: The Big Six skills approach to library and information skills instruction.* Norwood, NJ: Ablex Publishing.

Eun, B., Knotek, S. E., & Heining-Boynton, A. L. (2008). Reconceptualizing the zone of proximal development: The importance of the third voice. *Educational Psychology Review, 20,* 133–147.

Garcia-Mila, M., & Andersen, C. (2008). Cognitive foundations of learning argumentation. In Erduran, S., & Jiménez-Aleixandre, M. (Eds.), *Argumentation in science education: Perspectives from classroom-based research* (pp. 29–45). New York: Springer.

Gentner, D., Lowenstein, J. & Thompson, L. (2003). Learning and transfer: A general role for analogical encoding. *Journal of Educational Psychology, 95*(2), 393–408.

Gick, M. L., & Holyoak, K. J. (1980). Analogical problem solving. *Cognitive Psychology, 12,* 306–335.

Hannafin, M., Land, S., & Oliver, K. (1999). Open-ended learning environments: Foundations, methods, and models. In C. M. Reigeluth (Ed.), *Instructional design theories and models: Volume II: A new paradigm of instructional theory* (pp. 115–140). Mahwah, NJ: Lawrence Erlbaum.

Hill, J. R., & Hannafin, M. J. (2001). Teaching and learning in digital environments: The resurgence of resource-based learning. *Educational Technology Research and Development, 49*(3), 37–52.

Hmelo-Silver, C. E. (2004). Problem-based learning: What and how do students learn? *Educational Psychology Review, 16,* 235–266.

Jacobson, M. J. (2008). A design framework for educational hypermedia systems: Theory, research, and learning emerging scientific conceptual perspectives. *Educational Technology Research and Development, 56,* 5–28.

Jiménez-Aleixandre, M. P., Rodríguez, A. B., & Duschl, R. A. (2000). "Doing the lesson" or doing science: Argument in high school genetics. *Science Education, 84*(6), 757–792.

Jonassen, D. H. (2011). *Learning to solve problems: A handbook for designing problem-solving learning environments.* New York: Routledge.

Jonassen, D. H. (2007). *Learning to solve complex scientific problems.* New York: Lawrence Erlbaum.

Jonassen, D. H. (2003). Using cognitive tools to represent problems. *Journal of Research on Technology in Education, 35*(3), 362–381.

Jonassen, D. H. (2000). Toward a design theory of problem solving. *Educational Technology Research & Development, 48*(4), 63–85.

Jonassen, D. H., & Kim, B. (2010). Arguing to learn and learning to argue: Design justifications and guidelines. *Educational Technology Research & Development, 58*(4), 439–457.

Jonassen, D. H., Carr, C., & Yueh, H. (1998). Computers as mindtools for engaging learners in critical thinking. *TechTrends, 43*(2), 24–32.

Jonassen, D. H., Strobel, J., & Lee, C. B. (2006). Everyday problem solving in engineering: Lessons for engineering educators. *Journal of Engineering Education, 95*(2), 139–151.

Keefer, M. W., Zeitz, C. M., & Resnick, L. B. (2000). Judging the quality of peer-led student dialogues. *Cognition and Instruction, 18*(1), 53–81.

Kock, C. (2009). Choice is not true or false: The domain of rhetorical argumentation. *Argumentation, 23,* 61–80.

Kolodner, J. L., Camp, P. J., Crismond, D., Fasse, B., Gray, J., Holbrook, J., Putambeckar, S., & Ryan, M. (2003). Problem-based learning meets case-based learning in a middle school science classroom: Putting Learning by Design into practice. *The Journal of the Learning Sciences, 12*(4), 495–547.

Kuhn, D. (2007). Is direct instruction an answer to the right question? *Educational Psychologist, 42*(2), 109–113.

Kuhn, D. (2010). Teaching and learning science as argument. *Science Education, 94*, 810–824.

Kuhn, D., & Pearsall, S. (2000). The developmental origins of scientific thinking. *Journal of Cognition and Development, 1*, 113–129.

Monte-Sano, C. (2008). Qualities of historical writing instruction: A comparative case study of two teachers' practice. *American Educational Research Journal, 45*, 1045–1079.

Moore, P. (1995). Information problem solving: A wider view of library skills. *Contemporary Educational Psychology, 20*, 1–31.

National Center for Educational Statistics. (2011). Distance education courses for public elementary and secondary school students: 2009–2010. NCES 2012-08. Accessed 1/14/2012 at http://nces.ed.gov/pubs2012/2012008.pdf

Nordgren, R. D. (2002). Globalization and education: What students will need to know and be able to do in the global village. *Phi Delta Kappan, 84*(4), 318–321.

Nussbaum, E. M., & Schraw, G. (2007). Promoting argument-counterargument integration in students' writing. *Journal of Experimental Education, 76*(1), 59–92.

Osborne, J. (2010). Arguing to learn in science: The role of collaborative, critical discourse. *Science, 328*(3), 463–466.

Partnership for 21st Century Skills. (2008). 21st century skills map: Science. Tucson, AZ: Author.

Perelman, C., & Olbrechts-Tyteca, L. (1958). *La nouvelle rhétorique: Traité de l'argumentation* [The new rhetoric: Treatise on argumentation] (Vols. 1–2). Paris: Presses Universitaires de France.

Picciano, A. G., Seaman, J., & Allen, I. E. (2010). Educational transformation through online learning: To be or not to be. *Journal of Asynchronous Learning Networks, 14*(4), 17–35.

Reich, R. (2009, May 29). The future of manufacturing: Here come the robots. Retrieved 3/19/2012 from http://www.salon.com/2009/05/29/auto_industry_2/.

Ruiz-Primo, M. A, Li, M., Tsai, S., & Schneider, J. (2008). *Testing one premise of scientific inquiry in science classrooms: A study that examines students' scientific explanations.* CRESST Report 733. Los Angeles: UCLA. Accessed 1/15/11 at http://www.cse.ucla.edu/products/reports/R733.pdf.

Sadler, T. D., & Donnelly, L. A. (2006). Socioscientific argumentation: The effects of content knowledge and morality. *International Journal of Science Education, 28*(12), 1463–1488.

Sandoval, W. A., & Reiser, B. J. (2004). Explanation-driven inquiry: Integrating conceptual and epistemic scaffolds for scientific inquiry. *Science Education, 88*, 345–372.

Scardamalia, M., & Bereiter, C. (2006). Knowledge building: Theory, pedagogy, and technology. In K. Sawyer (Ed.), *Cambridge handbook of the learning sciences* (pp. 97–118). New York City: Cambridge University Press

Schank, R. C. (2004). *Making minds less well educated than our own.* Mahwah, NJ: Lawrence Erlbaum Associates.

Simon, H. A. (1979). Information processing models of cognition. *Annual Review of Psychology, 30*, 363–396.

Spector, J. M., & Park, S. W. (In press). Argumentation, critical reasoning and problem solving. In S. Fee & B. R. Belland (Eds.), *The role of criticism in understanding problem solving.* New York: Springer.

Statewide Online Education Program Created, Utah Code Ann. 53A.15 § 1203–1205 (2011).

Swartz, R. J. (2008). Teaching students how to analyze and evaluate arguments in history. *Social Studies, 99*(5), 208–216.

Van de Ward, R. (2010). Distance students and online research: Promoting information literacy through media literacy. *The Internet and Higher Education, 13,* 170–175.

van Eemeren, F. H., Grootendorst, R., & Henkemans, F. S. (1996). *Fundamentals of argumentation theory: A handbook of historical backgrounds and contemporary developments.* Mahwah, NJ: Lawrence Erlbaum.

Vygotsky, L. S. (1962). *Thought and language.* Tr. E. Hanfmann & G. Vakar. Cambridge, MA: MIT Press.

Vygotsky, L. S. (1978). *Mind in society: The development of higher psychological processes.* Cambridge, MA: Harvard University Press.

Walton, D. N. (2007). *Dialogue theory for critical argumentation.* Amsterdam: John Benjamins.

Warschauer, M., & Matuchniak, T. (2010). New technology and digital worlds: Analyzing evidence of equity in access, use, and outcomes. *Review of Research in Education, 34,* 179–225.

Weimer, W. B. (1977). Science as a rhetorical transaction: Toward a nonjustificational conception of rhetoric. *Philosophy and Rhetoric, 10*(1), 1–29.

Wolf, S. E., Brush, T., & Saye, J. (2003). Using an information problem-solving model as a metacognitive scaffold for multimedia-supported information-based problems. *Journal of Research on Technology in Education, 35*(3), 321–341.

Wood, D., Bruner, J., & Ross, G. (1976). The role of tutoring in problem-solving. *Journal of Child Psychology and Psychiatry, 17,* 89–100.

15 A Compendium of Taxonomies

Agustin Tristan

Introduction

The success of the teaching–learning process in education depends on a combination of several factors, including planning, designing learning experiences, curriculum adaptation, assessment and defining educational objectives. One of the main aspects of all educational models or curricula is the specification of set of "descriptors" used to define competencies, select activities and produce and implement resources and assessment tools. These descriptors are known by several names, such as educational objectives, competencies, educational skills, learning products and learning goals. Despite the variety of names, they share the need for a common educational foundation based on a framework or taxonomy.

Frameworks and taxonomies provide a convenient and accepted means of classifying and identifying the levels of complexity of a thinking process, typically associated with the type of knowledge and a set of evidences. Taxonomical categories help to verify that learning of the type and quality established by the curriculum or educational program has occurred. The importance of a taxonomy is beyond dispute, regardless of the educational model. However teachers, evaluators and planners often have doubts about the appropriate framework or taxonomy and its interpretation according to specific educational needs.

A comprehensive and international compendium of taxonomies since 1935 was offered by Tristán and Molgado (2006) who considered fields such as pedagogy, the psychology of learning, instructional technology and specific educational areas related to professional activities, scientific or technological fields. The first part of this chapter introduces the properties of taxonomies and a basic classification of their types.

The present work focuses on taxonomies of "types of knowledge," mainly from references in English. It should be noted that when talking about types of knowledge, three types are generally considered: factual, conceptual and procedural, but this is an incomplete classification. To solve this deficiency, this chapter seeks to present a more comprehensive set of types of knowledge described in several sources. It can be found that the different categories may be organized in four types of knowledge (declarative, procedural, attitudinal and metacognitive) that are presented in tables specially provided for this work. The four tables may be a useful tool for researchers and practitioners in several educational applications, from planning to assessment.

Characteristics and Definitions of a Taxonomy

A taxonomy is a classification model of a set of elements that organizes the categorization of their complex elements or attributes. More recently the term framework seems to be preferred in educational literature to define an organized set of ideas, principles, agreements, or rules that provides the basis of a specific phenomenon or process. The author of this work suggests the following design principles of a taxonomy for the purpose of this chapter and other rules may be found in Bailey (1994) and Jonassen and Tessmer (1996): (a) The classification must follow a single criterion or principle for all of the elements; (b) The classification must be exhaustive or complete; it must contain all of the elements of the species or generic term; (c) The resulting species must be mutually exclusive to prevent an element from being included in two species; and (d) The species or groups of members must follow a systematic order.

Various taxonomic orders can be distinguished within the classification criteria or principles (Bailey, 1994):

- *Generality*. Objects are classified according to their similarity and the degree of generality, from smallest to largest. For instance, this type of criterion is used in zoology and botany and may also be identified as natural classification.
- *Composition or community*. The objects are classified according to the relation of the part to the whole. For example, numbering systems follow this criterion.
- *Hierarchy (synchronic classification)*. This criterion implies a relationship of subordination. The planetary system, from galaxies to satellites, is an example of a hierarchy
- *Genealogy or evolution (diachronic classification)*. This classification includes ancestors and descendants. An example of this type is a linguistic taxonomy.

In addition to these criteria, other options may be considered: from simple to complex, from concrete to abstract or from origin to destination.

The first author to organize educational categories and influence the implementation of other taxonomies in the field of education was Benjamin Bloom (1956). Bloom and his colleagues organized the first taxonomy of the mental processes involved in learning and identified the processes that occur in three key domains: cognitive, affective and psychomotor. Each domain includes a classification of the forms of learning with a criterion of complexity, from simple to complex learning or from lower to higher-order thinking. In recent years, this classification has been expanded to include new knowledge dimensions (Bunderson, Martinez, & McBride, 1999; Huitt & Cain, 2005):

(a) social (establishing interactions and sharing knowledge with other persons);
(b) technological (communication with other persons using information and communication technologies, also known as ICT);
(c) cultural (related to traditions and socio-cultural backgrounds and influencing human well-being, experience and collaboration);
(d) physiological (related to the internal capabilities of the body, such as bladder control and respiration, which are not part of the psychomotor skills); and
(e) a conative dimension (different from the affective domain; making explicit use of volition and motivation and orientations toward goal achievement, self-direction and self-regulation).

There are two basic approaches for the taxonomies of the cognitive domain:

• *Thinking processes*. Taxonomies focus on the classification of the cognitive processes and their complexity levels (from simple to complex), as suggested by Bloom (1956).
• *Types of knowledge*. Associated with specific content, these taxonomies classify the types of knowledge and their manifestation, as proposed by Williams (1977).

Other ways of defining taxonomies depend on the criterion for construction. For instance, according to their aggregation, the author of this work considers that taxonomies can be identified as: (a) combined (a mixture of two approaches to the same cognitive domain); (b) extended (a united approach to two or three domains); or (c) integrated (a holistic approach that do not distinguish between the three classical domains). The work contained in this chapter is focused on the *types of knowledge* while other chapters in this book, or the work by Jonassen and Tessmer (1996) present different approaches to learning and knowledge.

Taxonomy of the Types of Knowledge

Based on theories of human information processing and taking into account various learning schemes, Williams (1977) and other authors have suggested a classical approach distinguishing four types of knowledge:

(1) *Factual*: Knowing what. Its content includes dates, names and data.
(2) *Conceptual*: Knowing why. It concerns classes of objects and events.
(3) *Principle*: Knowing how. It refers to relations among objects and events.
(4) *Procedural*: Doing. It requires the application of methods and algorithms (some psychomotor skills may be included).

This classical taxonomy shows some limitations and deficiencies because it does not satisfy all the classification criteria exposed previously. It has evolved into a more comprehensive taxonomy of the following four types:

(1) *Declarative knowledge*. It refers to knowing, providing evidence of the understanding of facts, concepts, laws and principles.
(2) *Procedural knowledge*. It refers to knowing how as an implementation of internalized actions along with intellectual and motor skills. This type of knowledge includes skills, strategies and processes involving a sequence of actions or operations that run in an orderly manner toward an end. Procedural knowledge permits the use of declarative knowledge in a given situation.
(3) *Attitudinal knowledge*. It refers to knowledge as how to be. This type of knowledge is demonstrated through stable performances and behaviors based on a harmonic relationship with an object or area of reality. It consists of values, norms, beliefs and attitudes intended to balance personal life and social life.
(4) *Metacognitive knowledge*. It refers to all the knowledge about personal cognitive resources and their compatibility with a learning situation. It includes self-regulatory mechanisms that are actively used to solve problems, verify results, identify different solutions and control the qualities and the effectiveness of the resulting actions. Metacognitive knowledge allows learning strategies to be tested, reviewed, evaluated and modified.

Tables 1 to 4 contain an original compendium of taxonomies prepared for this work. It presents definitions and descriptions of the various categories of the four types of knowledge alphabetically organized. Only one reference in English (generally the most important or the most recent) is included in each category, but several papers from other researchers presenting their own definition and interpretation may be found through the Internet. Some particular categories that do not have English references are located at the end of each type of knowledge.

Higher-Order Thinking, Technological and Metacognitive Strategies

The large number of taxonomies of cognitive strategies and metacognitive strategies complicates the selection of the best model for a specific educational purpose and, at the same time, indicates the need for a comprehensive and updated framework for higher-order thinking, mainly interested on analysis, problem solving, creative production and original performances. Yuruk, Ozdemir and Beeth (2003) provided details on six taxonomies developed from 1978 to 2000. Stone and Schneider (1971) proposed a classification of the purposes of John Dewey's democratic education, leading to a taxonomy based on the development of a person under the model of freedom, dignity and human rights.

Table 15.1 Types of declarative knowledge

Categories	Description	References
Conceptual	Knowledge that answers questions such as What is it? How is it? What are its essential characteristics? What are the differences or similarities between concepts X and Y? This category focuses on the mental representation of objects with common qualities in a certain class.	Anderson and Krathwohl (2001)
Episodic	Knowledge and memory about details of experiences, events that allow the reconstruction of previous situations in time, place and context. This knowledge also helps to explain current events compared to past situations and their spatial and temporal relationships.	Najjar and Mayers (2004)
Experiential	The type of knowledge that combines tacit, figurative and formal knowledge. Experience refers to knowledge of the culture, customs and habits that are learned and shared within a cultural group. This knowledge is contrasted with explicit knowledge, but it may require prior declarative knowledge, even if it is not explicitly expressed, articulated or operationalized.	Nishinosono (2003)
Factual	Rote knowledge of unitary elements of information: facts, figures, dates, terminology, events, people, places, objects.	Anderson and Krathwohl (2001)
Figurative or Figural	Allows a person to name, recognize and isolate one or various elements of a complex image. Also known as image knowledge.	Martinez (1998)
Haptic	Knowledge gained by the senses. Primarily refers to the perception of touch.	Forbus and Gentner (1997)
Iconic	Knowledge of objects representing concepts (geometric shapes, textures, models, etc.). Differs from spatial awareness because the icons are closer to ideas than to words. The similarity between the image and its representation requires prior interpretation of the meaning and its content. Knowledge that comes from watching or imagining.	Artess (2003)

(*Continued*)

Table 15.1 (Cont'd)

Categories	Description	References
Parametric	Provides information about a class of objects unrelated to specific data. May include sensory signals, state variables, system components and parameterized language. This type of knowledge is required when establishing positions and control variables and making decisions about the degrees of freedom of a system.	Park and Hunting (2003)
Relational or Associative	Relates to the content of propositions between objects, their functions or associations with statements, relationships, connections, commands, hierarchical nesting and other complex functions.	Merrill (1983)
Semantic	Grounded in verbal knowledge, it organizes networks of propositions or statements concerning facts, concepts and events as well as meanings, rules and procedures.	Najjar and Mayers (2004)
Spatial	Knowledge of the dimensions and component parts of an object, types of projections and representations. Considers the physical dimension of an object or set of objects in a plane or in three dimensions. May include geometric knowledge, iconic and patterns. Spatial knowledge may be considered alone or in combination with temporal knowledge. It is used in maps, images, paths and kinematic models.	Kyllonen (1984)
Structural	Refers to the ability to organize knowledge and the set of processes that lead to cognition and other products, which, in turn, help to improve learning. To represent this knowledge, a person may use letters, maps, conceptual networks and diagrams. Also called a "cognitive strategy," which relates to the structural metacognitive category. However, in this case, the person learns a pre-existing structure, in contrast to the creation of a new structure.	Tombari and Borich (1999)

Table 15.1 (Cont'd)

Categories	Description	References
Symbolic	Used in mathematical language, mathematical or scientific problem solving, musical composition and performance to establish a code for interaction with others. Also includes non-verbal elements used to communicate information and to represent objects by symbols (charts, diagrams, sketches or schemes of any kind).	Park and Hunting (2003)

Other categories from non-English references:

Categories	Description	References
Factorial	Basic criteria used to judge factors that integrate facts and opinions.	Morisette (1992)
Principles	Generalizations or laws that govern a class of objects as a basis for higher-order reasoning. Includes rules, models and laws. The construction of new principles may correspond to the Procedural category.	Morisette (1992)

Table 15.2 Types of procedural knowledge

Categories	Description	References
Algorithmic	Knowledge of strategies, techniques and procedures with a predetermined base of successive actions necessary for the correct or safe resolution of a problem. Includes some psychomotor skills and the knowledge of methods of solution.	Merrill (1983)
Communicative	Ability or competence to produce personal interpretations, purposes and meanings of a message.	Habermas (1983)
Contextual	Knowledge consisting of an ordered set of actions to achieve specific goals, considering the environmental conditions or situations to perform the task and personal capabilities. Can be defined as knowing why, where and in what environment or circumstances.	Tennyson and Nielsen (1998)
Enactive	Knowledge that arises at the time of doing or participating in any activity or action.	Artess (2003)

(Continued)

Table 15.2 (Cont'd)

Categories	Description	References
Executive	The knowledge used in problem-solving methods and procedures that can be performed or used in an automated manner.	Rumelhart and Norman (1985)
Figurative (or Figural)	Ability to solve problems associated with images and shapes and their attributes and qualities. It includes the following:	Martinez (1998)
	1. Showing an element of a picture (contained in the declarative dimension). 2. Evaluation of the image (associating its name, symbol, figure or attribute value and detecting errors and defects). 3. Showing the direction or path of motion (determining direction or path). 4. Showing dimensions extents and boundaries (determining how much, where and position). 5. Assembling items and creating new elements (determining their structure, location, guiding). 6. Producing functional relationships; categorical or ordinal (determining relationships). 7. Identifying continuous, linear and nonlinear relationships among the objects.	
Heuristic	Knowledge of procedures, rules and strategies for problem solving based on previous experience with similar problems.	Verschaffel and De Corte (1997)
Instrumental	The spontaneous "know-how" (either oral or written) of a complex system based on grammatical rules and word webs to convey and interpret messages, meanings and intentions. Also includes skills for managing devices, equipment or instruments, knowledge of computer programming rules, graphic expression and so on. Used to control and manage the environment, focusing on the effects of knowledge on scientific methodologies.	Cranton and Cohen (2000)
Operational	Refers to the ability to use descriptive knowledge in problem solving. Once acquired, this knowledge transforms into habits.	Rumelhart and Norman (1985)

Table 15.2 (Cont'd)

Categories	Description	References
Principle	Integrated through procedures allowing one to carry out principles, rules and other processes. Although the knowledge of the principle, rule or process is declarative, in this case, the focus is on implementing the actions.	Clark (2008)
Procedural executive	Performing actions that allow one to reach an outcome or achieve a goal. Distinguished into the following: 1. Primitive: atomistic or isolated actions. 2. Sequential: sets or sequences of primitive methods.	Najjar and Mayers (2004)
Spatial	Allows the use of parts of an object in the solution of a problem. Spatial knowledge has two sub-categories: 1. Constructive approach. The construction of mental representations of what can be observed and the changes needed to solve the problem. 2. Analytical strategy. Defines a sequence or method to compare, process or analyze a characteristic (feature-by-feature).	Lajoie (2003)
Strategic	Set of operations allowing a person to reach a stated goal or solve a given problem by deciding on the steps or stages to follow in the solution process. Relates to procedures, plans and logistics.	Chi (1987)
Symbolic	Nonverbal language elements used to implement information in technical or special knowledge areas using symbols and codes.	Hauenstein (1998)
Tacit	Knowledge that cannot be written or formally expressed but that allows the performance of certain actions. It can also be defined as knowledge that is used routinely without thinking about it and that cannot be articulated or explained logically, although its method of acquisition can be proven.	Sternberg (1988)
Technological	Includes content that indicates what and how to do things grounded in technological resources, ICT, computer-assisted systems and technological equipment.	Hauenstein (1998)

(Continued)

Table 15.2 (Cont'd)

Categories	Description	References
Other categories from non-English references:		
Conditional	Knowledge that solves when to use a specific content or know-how. Ability to identify the conditions under which declarative and procedural knowledge is appropriate. It relates to the resolution of complex problems in everyday life situations and the combination of different types of knowledge acquired in advance.	Scallon (1999)
Systemic	Knowledge structure that combines a holistic and integrated set of elements that are interdependent and connected. Requires organization, structure, theory and operating rules.	Morisette (1982)

Table 15.3 Types of attitudinal knowledge

Categories	Description	References
Academic instrumental	A combination of knowledge and practices as well as attitudes, values and beliefs. This knowledge improves school performance because it relates to culture and is linked to family and the traditions of the country of origin, specifically for immigrants.	Rueda, Monzo, and Arzubiaga (2003)
Behavioral	Includes behaving, talking or relating to people, institutions and other factors. Integrates initiative, cooperation, respect and values during learning activities.	Hauenstein (1998)
Cognitive	Refers to the attitudes induced by a previous set of ideas and thoughts about a subject during the learning process.	Anderson and Krathwohl (2001)
Communicative	The social knowledge linked to mutual understanding between individuals within a family, community or group as well as knowledge of the customs, social norms, values and traditions of a particular group.	Cranton and Cohen (2000)
Contextual	Knowledge of why, when and where to use concepts, rules and concepts appropriately. This knowledge has a direct association with cognitive skills, which, in turn, are related to cognitive strategies.	Gagné, Briggs, and Wager (1992)

Table 15.3 (Cont'd)

Categories	Description	References
Emancipatory	Knowledge acquired through self-reflection, providing the ability to be aware of the self-condition and potential transformations in life. Emancipatory abilities provide the freedom to make choices and control social forces.	Mezirow (1990)
Emotive	The set of positive or negative emotional charges that affect knowledge, such as feelings of pleasure or displeasure, interests and motivations. Also induced by the first approach or proximity to certain content in a field of knowledge.	Anderson and Krathwohl (2001)
Episodic	Knowledge and memory of emotional details of experiences and events and their spatial and temporal relationships.	Najjar and Mayers (2004)
Prescriptive	Indicates the content related to duty or "what has to be."	Hauenstein (1998)
Symbolic	Set of attitudes towards non-verbal elements or language used to communicate information.	Hauenstein (1998)
Transformative	Reassess the basics of beliefs and act on insights derived from the new meaning perspective. It may participate on communicative and instrumental learning.	Mezirow (1990)

Table 15.4 Types of metacognitive knowledge

Categories	Description	References
Contextual	Knowledge obtained through the regulation and management of cognitive processes, particularized in relation to influential situations, data or information. Usually serves to achieve a relatively concrete goal or objective.	Flavell (1976)
Experiential	Knowledge related to the cognitive and affective experiences that accompany any cognitive process.	Flavell (1976)
Meta-declarative	Includes the cognition process itself as well as the factors that contribute to the cognitive process. This knowledge is acquired through experience and	Chi (1987)

(*Continued*)

Table 15.4 (Cont'd)

Categories	Description	References
	is stored in long-term memory. It can be transformed and used in a domain completely different from the domain in which it was acquired.	
Meta-procedural	Knowledge of procedural rules and evaluation of the procedures in different domains.	Chi (1987)
Meta-strategic	Knowledge of the conditions for using a strategy and mastering the rules that allow such knowledge to be implemented.	Chi (1987)
Regulatory	Defined by the information process in which a system acts to control and regulate knowledge. Demonstrated through activities such as planning, monitoring, controlling, evaluating and other self-regulating cognitive processes.	Barnard, Paton, and Lan (2008)
Self-awareness	Refers to the ability to recognize one's mental processes to achieve learning. The implementation of a series of operations, activities and cognitive functions through mechanisms that allow the intellectual collection and evaluation of information and mechanisms.	Flavell (1976)

Other categories from non-English references:

Conditional	Knowledge that indicates the conditions relevant for using declarative or procedural knowledge. Helps to answer the question: When is it convenient to use a certain procedure or a specific strategy?	Scallon (1999)
Strategic	Strategies or procedures to reach a goal or solve a given problem. Includes reading strategies, problem solving, memory (mnemonics), teamwork, task force groups, use and development of study skills.	Scallon (1999)
Structural	The ability to organize thoughts, communicate and determine a plan. Related to declarative strategic knowledge, but structural knowledge requires the structure to be created or developed by the person, whereas in declarative strategic knowledge, a person learns a predefined structure.	Scallon (1999)

Classifications of problem-solving strategies have been proposed by Polya (1945), whose taxonomy has been used in various educational approaches and also by Harlen (2000), who provided a classification of process skills in science learning from observation to hypothesis, including research and the communication of results.

Flavell (1976) suggested that metacognition is linked to effective regulation and control and grounded in knowledge, metacognitive experiences, goals, actions and strategies. Brown (1987) identified metacognitive skills as a component of information processing. Demetriou and Efklides (1985) proposed a cylindrical, three-dimensional higher-order thinking framework based on exploratory and confirmatory factor analyses and a model of triangulation. The longitudinal axis of the cylinder is associated with levels of development, whereas the drum section is associated with the concept of concentric circles of the information process.

Dick (1991) suggested a taxonomy of 15 cognitive strategies with five types of critical thinking from examples in numerous published references on scientific information. Skills such as deduction, induction and abstraction were part of this taxonomy.

Morisette (1992) proposed a combined taxonomical application (thinking processes and content types) in four domains (observation, treatment, regulation and creation) as well as eight "facets" that corresponded to the types of knowledge (data, factors, concepts, relations, principles, methods, strategies and systems). Fink (2001) proposed two learning components (active and scientific strategies) that may induce changes in thinking abilities.

Dixon (1966) classified engineering design skills and Heywood (1997) provided several classifications related to the tasks of engineers, from application to evaluation and diagnosis. Tomei (2005) defined a taxonomy of six levels of the technological dimension of ICT and computer science, from understanding to the study of technology.

Conclusion

Taxonomies of cognitive processes provide us the opportunity to choose from a structure of types of knowledge that may be conducive to the development of qualitative changes in competencies and abilities of the student. Given that no single all-inclusive framework is available, the compendium provided in this work fills an educational gap documenting the four main types of cognitive processes (declarative, procedural, attitudinal and metacognitive) in tables describing more than fifty categories.

Tables 15.1 to 15.4 show that it is erroneous to use a classification such as factual, conceptual, procedural and attitudinal, because it is a mixture of two types of knowledge (procedural and attitudinal) and two subtypes (factual and conceptual from declarative knowledge) not including metacognition. The tables prepared especially for this chapter contain a comprehensive set of categories in four different types of knowledge with a definition of each category. Since Bloom's taxonomy, some types had been distinguished (facts, principles, relations, codes and concepts), but the tables widen and complete the perspective of types and subtypes along with the contribution of researchers of diverse fields of knowledge.

It is important to observe that declarative knowledge contains more than data, facts and concepts. For example, the types of knowledge defined as iconic, spatial and symbolic, involve abstraction capacities that are different from those of the episodic, factorial and structural types, which can be related to contents of specific subjects in an educational environment or various competencies in everyday life and work.

The mention of procedural and attitudinal knowledge cannot be used as if they covered only one category. The variety of subtypes needs special attention and detail, explaining why authors distinguish among algorithmic, enactive or strategic knowledge. Regarding the attitudinal knowledge, instrumental, contextual or emancipatory manifestations are pointed out, providing the students with important competencies for life.

The abilities related to the metacognitive type of knowledge benefit individuals to develop learning skills, as well as understanding and promoting the best way to learn according to their qualities and personal preferences.

Educational Applications

The definitions of the categories in the four types of knowledge have an impact on education and the academic environment. I suggest some educational applications concerning didactical practices, educational planning and curriculum development.

Diagnosis of the academic orientation of the students is the first application of the tables from this chapter. Teachers must analyze the description and references on these tables, because they imply interesting ideas to increase the learning motivation of students in different academic areas according to age, gender or cultural background. For instance, some students may feel more comfortable with spatial learning while others may prefer episodic or emotive activities, but certainly all of them must learn the same curriculum and content. Following this idea, teachers may design diagnostic tests to identify the academic orientations or preferences of every student and use this information to choose better teaching and learning activities targeting each person.

The second application of the learning types may help teachers and authorities to specify appropriate curriculum contents and planning, to organize the educational goals, to define the best strategies for teaching and learning adapted to the particular competencies and interests of the students and to identify the type of instrument for formative assessment, among other applications. A syllabus should take into account the types of knowledge to offer efficient tools for the teacher and the student according to their academic needs and motivations. With the increasing development of standards as well as national and international tests, there will be an emphasis on the need to explore diverse types of knowledge, so as to being able to judge the competencies of students in multiple manifestations and ways of representing knowledge.

Several additional applications can be foreseeable. For example, in the integration of a portfolio it is convenient to adapt the evidence to the type of knowledge: essays or constructed response items for episodic knowledge, construction of architectural, geometrical and other scale models for iconic and spatial knowledge, live presentation showing the verbal fluency or interaction with a group for communicative knowledge, closed-ended response items for factual or principle types of knowledge, design of a spreadsheet for algorithmic knowledge, videos that show the way to approach a given situation for emancipator knowledge, electronic presentations that allow to show metacognitive capacities. Some evidence requires being adapted for handicapped students whereas others may not be appropriate for certain students or educational levels.

It can be concluded that not all the types of knowledge will be assessed with the same type of evidence. Therefore, the descriptions gathered in the tables must work as a solid base for the educator to decide if the evidence requested in a portfolio is adequate for the type of knowledge. In addition, if the program requires a performance mostly appropriate for a certain type of knowledge, it is important to verify if its learning and development was promoted among students. Has the selection of learning activities been adapted to support students that lack the attitude or preference for a certain type of knowledge? Has the development of metacognitive competencies been promoted for these particular students? It is conceivable that many more applications and educational questions can be proposed by teachers and authorities using Tables 15.1 to 15.4.

This work is focused mainly on English references, however a fully comprehensive compendium would include taxonomies from non-English authors and that is the reason why this work includes a few international examples. Dozens of additional frameworks and references in other languages can also be found in the technical literature, for instance see Tristán and Molgado (2006).

References

Anderson, L. W., & Krathwohl, D. R. (2001). *A taxonomy for learning, teaching, and assessing: A revision of Bloom's taxonomy of educational objectives.* New York, NY: Addison Wesley Longman.

Artess, J. (2003). How adults really learn – or what we think we know about how they learn! *Learning and teaching in action*, 2(2). Retrieved from http://www.celt.mmu.ac.uk/ltia/issue5/artess.shtml

Bailey, K. D. (1994). *Typologies and taxonomies: An introduction to classification techniques.* Sage University Paper series on Quantitative Applications in the Social Sciences, series no. 07-102. Thousand Oaks, CA: Sage.

Barnard, L., Paton, V., & Lan, W. (2008, March 9). Online self-regulatory learning behaviors as a mediator in the relationship between online course perceptions with achievement. *The International Review of Research in Open and*

Distance Learning. Retrieved from www.irrodl.org/index.php/irrodl/article/view/516/1035

Bloom, B. S. (Ed.), (1956). *Taxonomy of educational objectives: Handbook I: Cognitive domain.* New York, NY: David McKay.

Brown, A. (1987). Metacognition, executive control, self-regulation and other more mysterious mechanism. In F. E. Weinert, & R. H. Kluwe (Eds.), *Metacognition, motivation, and understanding* (pp. 65–116). Hillsdale, NJ: Lawrence Erlbaum Associates.

Bunderson, C. V., Martinez, M. E., & McBride, R. (1999 April). *The measurement of ettle in college students and initial readers.* AERA Conference. Montreal, Canada

Chi, M. T. H. (1987). Representing knowledge and metaknowledge: Implications for interpreting metamemory research. In F. E. Weinert, & R. H. Kluwe (Eds.), *Metacognition, motivation and understanding* (pp. 211–232). Hillsdale, NJ: Lawrence Erlbaum Associates.

Clark, R. C. (2008). *Developing technical training: A structured approach for developing classroom and computer-based instructional materials* (3rd ed.). San Francisco, CA: Pfeiffer–John Wiley & Sons. Inc.

Cranton, P., & Cohen, L. R. (2000). Spirals of learning. *The National Teaching and Learning Forum, 9*(5), 1–5.

Demetriou, A., & Efklides, A. (1985). Structure and sequence of formal and post-formal thought: general patterns and individual differences. *Child Development, 56,* 1062–1091.

Dick, R. D. (1991). An empirical taxonomy of critical thinking. *Journal of Instructional Psychology, 18,* 79–92.

Dixon, J. R. (1966). *Design engineering: Inventiveness, analysis and decision making,* New York, NY: McGraw-Hill.

Fink, L. D. (2001). Higher-level learning: The first step toward more significant learning. In D. Lieberman (Ed.), *To improve the academy: Resources for faculty, instructional and organizational development* (pp. 113–130). Bolton, MA: Anker Publishing.

Flavell, J. H. (1976). Metacognitive aspects of problem solving. In L. B. Resnick (Ed.), *The nature of intelligence* (pp. 231–236). Hillsdale, NJ: Lawrence Erlbaum Associates.

Forbus, K., & Gentner, D. (1997). *Qualitative mental models: Simulations or memories?* Proceedings of the Eleventh International Workshop on Qualitative Reasoning, Cortona, Italy. Retrieved from http://groups.psych.northwestern.edu/gentner/papers/ForbusGentner97.pdf

Gagné, R. M., Briggs, L. J., & Wager, W. W. (1992). *Principles of instructional design* (4th ed.). Fort Worth, TX: Harcourt Brace Jovanovich College Publishers.

Habermas, J. (1983). *The theory of communicative action (Vol. 1): Reason and the rationalization of society.* (Thomas McCarthy, Trans.). Boston, MA: Beacon Press.

Harlen, W. (2000). *The teaching of science in primary schools.* London, UK: David Fulton.

Hauenstein, A. D. (1998). *A conceptual framework for educational objectives: A holistic approach to traditional taxonomies.* Lanham, MD: University Press of America.

Heywood, J. (1997). *Outcomes of science based engineering education I: Theory and practice in the derivation of "outcomes". A European historical perspective.*

Proceedings of the 27th American Society of Engineering Education and Institute of Electrical and Electronics Engineers: 'Frontiers in Education Conference. "Teaching and Learning in an Era of Change" (pp. 121–128).

Huitt, W. G., & Cain, S. (2005). *An overview of the conative domain. Educational psychology interactive*, Valdosta GA: Valdosta University. Retrieved from www. edpsycinteractive.org/papers/conative.pdf

Jonassen, D. H., & Tessmer, M. (1996/97). An outcomes-based taxonomy for the design, evaluation, and research of instructional systems. *Training Research Journal, 2*, 11–14.

Kyllonen, P. C. (1984). Information processing analysis of spatial ability. (Doctoral dissertation, Stanford University). *Dissertation Abstracts International, 45*, 819A.

Lajoie, S. P. (2003). Individual differences in spatial ability: developing technologies to increase strategy awareness and skills. *Educational psychologist, 38*(2), 115–125.

Martinez, M. E. (1998). *A taxonomy of methods for demonstration of proficiency in a figural medium*. College Park, MD: Clearinghouse on Assessment and Evaluation. (ERIC Document Reproduction Service No. ED 423 241).

Merrill, M. D. (1983). Component display theory. In C. M. Reigeluth (Ed.), *Instructional-design theories and models: An overview of their current status*. Hillsdale, NJ: Lawrence Erlbaum Associates.

Mezirow, J. (1990). *Fostering critical reflection in adulthood. A guide to transformative and emancipatory learning*. San Francisco, CA: Jossey-Bass.

Morisette, M. (1992). *Élaboration d'activités dont l'objectif d'habileté vise le champ des processus mentaux supérieurs*. Rapport de recherche. l'Université du Québec à Montréal dans le cadre du D.I.R.P.É. Retrieved from www3.sympatico.ca/ michel.morissette/Taxonomi.htm

Najjar, M., & Mayers, A. (2004). *Using human memory structures to model knowledge within algebra virtual laboratory*. Proceedings of the Second IEEE International Conference on Information Technology in Research and Education (ITRE). London, UK.

Nishinosono, H. (2003). *Empirical approach for designing universal learning with ubiquitous ICTs: u-Learning for enhancing the right to learn*. Bukkyo University. Retrieved from www.u-manabi.org/nc/include/netcommons_file.php?path=/ announcement/1/2003-E01-nishinosono.pdf.

Park, J., & Hunting, S. (2003). *XML Topic maps: creating and using topic maps for the Web*. Pearson Education. Boston, MA.

Polya, G. (1945). *How to solve it*. Princeton, NJ: Princeton University Press

Rueda, R., Monzo, L. D., & Arzubiaga, A. (2003). Academic instrumental knowledge: deconstructing cultural capital theory for strategic intervention approaches. *Current Issues in Education, 6*(14). Retrieved from http://cie.asu.edu/volume6/ number14/

Rumelhart, D. E., & Norman, D. A. (1985). Representation of knowledge. In A. M. Aitkenhead, & J. M. Slack (Eds.), *Issues in cognitive modeling*. Hillsdale, NJ: Lawrence Erlbaum Associates.

Scallon, G. (1999). *Planifier l'évaluation certificative à la recherche d'une nomenclature d'objectifs*. Retrieved from www.fse.ulaval.ca/Gerard.Scallon/fascicules/ nomenclature.pdf

Sternberg, R. J. (1988). *The triarchic mind: A new theory of human intelligence*. New York, NY: Penguin.

Stone, J. C., & Schneider, F. W. (1971). *Foundations of education. Commitment to teaching.* Vol. 1 (2nd ed.). New York, NY: Thomas Y. Crowell Company.

Tennyson, R. D., & Nielsen, M. (1998). Complexity theory: Inclusion of the affective domain in an interactive learning model for instructional design. *Educational Technology, 38*(6), 7–12.

Tombari, M., & Borich, G. (1999). *Authentic assessment in the classroom, applications and practice.* Upper Saddle River, NJ: Prentice Hall Inc.

Tomei, L. A. (2005). *Taxonomy for the technology domain.* Hershey, PA.: Idea Group Inc.

Tristán, L. A., & Molgado, R. D. (2006). *Compendio de taxonomías.* San Luis Potosí, Mexico: Instituto de Evaluación e Ingeniería Avanzada, S.C.

Verschaffel, L., & De Corte, E. (1997). Teaching realistic mathematical modeling in the elementary school: A teaching experiment with fifth graders. *Journal for Research in Mathematics Education, 28*, 577–601.

Williams, R. G. (1977). A behavioral typology of educational objectives for the cognitive domain. *Educational Technology, 17*(6), 39–46.

Yuruk, N., Ozdemir, O., & Beeth, M. E. (2003). *The role of metacognition in facilitating conceptual change.* Annual Meeting of the National Association for Research in Science Teaching. Philadelphia, PA. ERIC Document Reproduction Service No. ED 477 315. Retrieved from www.eric.ed.gov/PDFS/ED477315.pdf

16 Mindtools in Online Education
Enabling Meaningful Learning

Rose Marra

Introduction

David Jonassen's contributions to the fields of cognition, educational psychology, instructional technology and the study of problem solving have been, and are, vast. His work has influenced many individuals and organizations, including myself – his wife and professional collaborator for nearly 20 years.

Although Dave will readily tell an audience of one or 1,000 that the last 15 years of his professional life has been dedicated to the study of problem solving (and many chapters in this volume address the impact of this powerful body of work), Dave's influence on my professional endeavors is rooted in his earlier work on mindtools (Jonassen, 2005; Jonassen, 2000a, b; Jonassen, Carr, & Yeuh, 1998). My dissertation many years ago examined the impact of using expert system shells as a knowledge organization exercise on the development of concept maps. Since then I have continued to apply mindtools in my teaching and research.

Mindtools have been shown in many settings to live up to their promise (see e.g. Liu, Horton, Corliss, Svinicki, Bogard, Kim, & Chang, 2009; Liu & Bera, 2005; Rieber, 1996). Mindtools, however, is a rather vintage concept dating back to 1996 or before – which is nearly a generation in technology terms. One may ask do mindtools still hold their promise and potential in today's mobile applications and smartphone-centered world? I propose to make a case for their use in a sector of learning that is rapidly growing – online learning settings.

Increasingly, learning is taking place in online settings – in completely asynchronous courses where one never meets face to face, web-assisted, where face-to-face is supplemented with online components, or perhaps simply using an online learning management system (LMS) to provide an ongoing communication and document portal for an otherwise face-to-face class. No matter the form, online learning has grown by leaps and bounds. A recent study indicates that 77 percent of college presidents say their institution offers online classes (Parker, Lenhart, & Moore, 2011). Additionally, the growth in the K-12 sector is astounding. In 2000, about 45,000 K-12 students were participating in online learning; these numbers had increased to over 4 million in 2010 (Staker, 2011).

There are many challenges to creating meaningful instruction in online settings. By "meaningful" I refer to higher order learning outcomes, for instance at the *apply, analyze, evaluate,* or *create* levels of the revised Bloom's taxonomy (Anderson & Krathwohl, 2001), or, in the language of problem-solving outcomes involving *modeling, designing,* and *decision making* (Jonassen, 2000). In this chapter I will make a case for the use of mindtools in online learning as a way to overcome the challenges of supporting meaningful learning in online settings. Specifically I will:

- provide a brief overview of mindtools: what they are, how they work, their uses and their strengths, and how they can support and enable meaningful learning;
- discuss and provide examples of how mindtools can address some of the challenges of supporting meaningful learning in online settings; and
- address the practicalities of using mindtools in online settings.

The Miracle of Mindtools

In his first mindtools book, *Computers in the Classroom: Mindtools for Critical Thinking* (1995), Jonassen defines a mindtool as:

> ... a concept, not a real entity. You cannot find advertisements for Mindtools. Rather, a Mindtool is a way of using a computer application program to engage learners in constructive, higher order, critical thinking ... .
>
> (Jonassen, 1995, p. iv)

He goes on to distinguish mindtools from traditional computer learning applications. Using mindtools means that learners work *with* the technology to represent what they know versus learning *from* the technology as in traditional tutorial or drill and practice applications. Jonassen says that mindtools are:

> ... computer-based tools and learning environments that have been adapted or developed to function as intellectual partners with the learner in order to engage and facilitate critical thinking and higher-order learning. These tools include (but are not necessarily limited to databases, spreadsheets, semantic networks, expert systems, computer conferencing, multimedia and hypermedia construction, computer programming, and microworld learning environments.
>
> (Jonassen, 1995, p. 9)

Since that first mindtools book was published, the concept has been widely propagated and adopted in both K-12 and higher education settings. Jonassen's mindtools book is now in its third edition (2005), but if the publisher had its way, I'm quite sure it would be in its fourth by now. The book has also been translated into both Mandarin Chinese and Korean.

There are several reasons that mindtools have had quite a bit of staying power – even in the fast-changing world of learning technologies.

Mindtools are ubiquitous. They are – well – not quite everywhere – but they are readily available and easy to find. The sample mindtools listed above – spreadsheets, concept maps or semantic networks – are available from many different sources (freeware, for purchase software) and in many different forms (e.g. resident on your own computer, installed on a school district network, or in the Internet cloud). You don't have to look far to find them. Notably with the advent of the Internet and suites of online tools such as those offered by Google, this is even truer today than it was when Jonassen first introduced the mindtools concept. An important point however, is that even if they are ubiquitous, one still has to know how to use them in a mindtools way. So while you may find many concept mapping applications these days – for them to be a mindtool, one must use them in a student-focused way where students are completing their own concept maps, rather than, say, studying one completed by the teacher.

Mindtools are discipline free. This may be my favorite characteristic. By their very nature mindtools can be applied in pretty much any academic discipline. At the root of the mindtools concept is that students are essentially teaching the technology what they know. This can be done with any academic subject. Students studying English literature or students studying earth science can both effectively construct linked concept maps that represent their growing knowledge of a field of study.

Mindtools are cheap. Just as you don't have to look far to find many mindtool applications, you won't have to look far to find them for a good price – even free or shareware. While this may not be the most esoteric point about these tools, from a practical point of view it is an important one – especially for K-12 teachers that often end up paying for teaching supplies out of their own pockets! Having a technology tool that is both potentially effective and free or inexpensive is a powerful combination.

Lastly – *mindtools are cognitively accessible.* This concept applies at two levels – both for the individual tools as well as for the overall concept of a mindtool. I have heard Jonassen say many times: "I can teach a class to get started using any of the mindtools in about 10 minutes." He does and so can you (I will address how this is done in online settings below). Concept maps, spreadsheets – these are not difficult tools to use – some students may come into your classrooms already knowing the mechanics of such tools.

Although the *how to*s of these tools may be quite simple, one may have to focus training efforts on getting students to understand how to use these tools as mindtools – that is using the tool to externally represent what they know or understand for a particular knowledge domain. I would posit that the general concept of a mindtool is also cognitively accessible. Once you wrap your head around the idea that we want the students to teach the technology rather than thinking of the technology teaching the students, it is a fairly easy concept to apply to multiple tools in multiple settings.

Mindtools' staying power also comes from their effectiveness. The ability of mindtools to support and enable critical thinking and higher order learning outcomes is well documented (see Jonassen & Reeves, 1996). However this chapter is not focused on this body of research but on the application of mindtools in online learning – thus extending their application to a learning setting that is both increasingly prevalent as well as one that faces challenges for supporting meaningful learning.

The Challenges of Supporting Meaningful Learning Online

One of the primary arguments for asserting that educators apply mindtools in online settings is that mindtools can help to overcome some of the challenges of enabling meaningful learning online – particularly within the confines of using a course management systems (CMSs) or learning management systems (LMSs) such as Blackboard. A few years back, the author and David Jonassen described the limitations of online learning environments for supporting constructivist learning activities – a specific instantiation of meaningful learning. In our examination of online learning courses in higher education we found very few that engage learners in solving meaningful problems or other meaningful learning outcomes. Rather, most online learning that we examined replicated in structure and function traditional classroom instruction. We posited that the primary reason that constructive learning is not commonly adopted in online learning contexts is that the affordances of CMSs/LMSs do not support meaningful learning outcomes. In particular – we argued – and this author still asserts that CMSs lack the following abilities:

- The ability to efficiently and effectively accommodate multiple, alternative forms of student knowledge representation. Meaningful, constructive learning must be assessed in multiple ways (Jonassen & Carr, 2000), however online course systems support only quizzes, online discussions (with no evaluative support), and the submission of word-processing documents.
- The ability to provide and support authentic assessment (either with tools for the instructor or tools to help communicate these assessment data to students). The most commonly used assessment in online environments is the quiz. The over-reliance on single forms of assessment (especially quizzes) precludes the assessment of meaningful learning.
- The ability to support distributed tools for meaning making. Constructivist learning environments should provide cognitive tools to scaffold the cognitive requirements of functioning in the environment (Jonassen, 1999, 2000). While face-to-face courses easily provide access to cognitive tools via laboratory instruction, online course developers who require this functionality to support learning find it difficult to provide access to tools and to support the learning of the tools.

Likewise, Naidu (2006) describes similar limitations in online learning. Specifically, Naidu asserts that online learning often puts learners in a passive (rather than active) role, that LMSs lack the tools and capability to engage learners and teachers in the development of complex cognitive and social skills (e.g. collaboration, professional judgment and decision making), and that online courses are often developed as page turning learning sequences (Naidu, 2006).

Bonk and Zhang's (2008) discussion of online learning limitations focuses on the inability of CMSs to work well with diverse learning styles, stating that:

- CMSs best support course materials that are available in text (e.g. syllabi and scanned readings); and
- most communication that is supported in CMSs is in written formats such as emails, discussion boards and chats.

They go on to posit that these characteristics are less appealing to both visual and reflective learners.

While one can get around many of these limitations by programming a complete learning environment outside of a CMS, most online designers and instructors do not have the financial means, the technological know-how, or the time necessarily to develop such an environment. Thus addressing the limitations within CMSs is relevant.

Mindtools in Online Learning Settings

Using mindtools in online courses can help overcome some of the challenges and limitations of CMSs. In this section I will describe a number of different mindtool technologies that can be used in online settings. For each I will describe the tool, suggest potential specific technologies that implement this tool (e.g. a particular spreadsheet package), and provide an example(s) of how this tool can be pedagogically integrated and implemented within a CMS. Following the specific mindtool examples I will address how the use of these tools can ameliorate some of the limitations of attaining meaningful learning outcomes in online settings.

Concept Maps/Semantic Networks

I previously asserted that mindtools are ubiquitous. Semantic networks – also known as concept maps – are perhaps the most ubiquitous of them all; we see them everywhere in educational settings and there are dozens of different software packages out there that support the creating of concept maps. Jonassen (2000) defines a semantic network or concept map as a "spatial representation of concepts and their interrelationships that are intended to represent the knowledge structures that humans store in their minds" (p. 58). Practically, a concept map consists of a graph of nodes that represent concepts and labeled lines that represent the relationships between the connected node/concepts. Figure 16.1 shows an excerpt from a concept map on online facilitation skills generated using CMap (see CMap.ihmc.us).

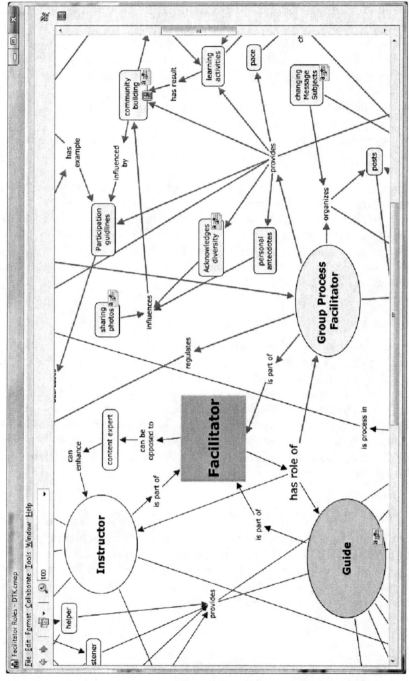

Figure 16.1 Concept map excerpt created with CMap.

Jonassen (2000) describes concept mapping as representing structural knowledge – a type of knowledge that connects declarative knowledge (to put it simply, knowledge about things) and procedural knowledge (knowledge of how). Structural knowledge is "the knowledge of how the ideas within a domain are integrated and interrelated" (Jonassen, 2000, p. 61).

For concept mapping to act as a mindtool, students must *create* their own concept maps rather than simply studying an already created one. Additionally, students must label the links that connect one node to another, as it is in that labeling activity that one must make explicit one's understanding of the relationship between the two concepts. Creating concept maps can engage learners in several learning activities that comprise meaningful learning: organization and reorganization of knowledge, explicit definition of relationships between concepts, relating existing concepts to new concepts and ideas and spatial learning via the spatial representation of concepts in their created maps.

There are many concept-mapping software packages to choose from; both resident to your computer and cloud-based versions are available. These programs provide visual and verbal screen tools for developing concept maps; enable learners to identify the important ideas or concepts in a knowledge domain and then interrelate those ideas in multidimensional networks of concepts by labeling the relationships between those ideas. Table 16.1 summarizes a few of these tools.

Pedagogically, to use concept maps in an online setting is quite simple. You simply have to build a concept map creation activity into course

Table 16.1 Sample concept mapping software Tools

CMap	http://CMap.ihmc.us Free mapping tool available for all hardware platforms (e.g. Mac or PC); appropriate for users of all ages; available in 17 languages. Because it is free and easy to use, it has a growing user base; look forward to more K-12 applications and examples.
Inspiration / Kidspiration	http://www.inspiration.com Popular tool that runs on both Macs and PCs. Kidspiration is the version for younger learners. Both tools are visually appealing but do not offer some features that can better support knowledge organization and idea development. For instance all maps must be created on a single page and learners may focus excessively on choosing pictorial icons instead of on organizing and creating meaningful links between nodes.
MindMeister	http://www.mindmeister.com Online tool available in a free and for-fee version. An "academic" subscription version offers support for unlimited number of maps and the ability to collaborate on maps. Does not support labeled links between nodes.
Visual Thesaurus	http://www.visualthesaurus.com/ A specialized online mapping tool for providing a visual thesaurus look-up of the words related to one that you enter.

activities, and – very importantly – provide some sort of support for learning the concept mapping software. I will address how to support students' learning of a given mindtool later in this chapter.

Figure 16.2 illustrates how I have used concept mapping in a graduate course on "developing online courses." Although the task is focused on creating a map to represent domain knowledge acquired in a reading activity, the activity provides a distinct alternative to the standard "read-the-chapter-and-discuss" activity that normally accompanies students' chapter reading.

Although this is a single activity that students use to organize their domain knowledge (additionally the task was designed to model for students a meaningful task they could insert into their own online courses), an even more worthwhile activity for structuring domain knowledge would be the ongoing use of concept mapping throughout the entire course to provide a changing and evolving view of student's structural knowledge as the semester progresses.

Other possibilities for concept mapping activities in online settings include the following:

- students could post their completed maps to Wiki pages (now provided in CMS Blackboard and also readily available for free from sites such as PBwiki.com) for peer-to-peer commenting. The instructor could structure

---

- Select and read one of the following readings to be the basis of your map. Both are available in the same folder on BB as this assignment description.
  - o Su, B., Bonk, C. J., Magjuka, R. J., Liu, X. & Lee, S. (2005). The importance of interaction in Web-based education: A program-level case study of online MBA courses; *Journal of Interactive Online Learning,4*,1. Retrieved from http://www.ncolr.org/jiol/issues/pdf/4.1.1.pdf
  - o Chapter 3 –"Key Facilitator Roles" from Collison, G., Elbaum, B., Haavind, S., & Tinker, R. (2000). Facilitating Online Learning. Madison, WI: Atwood Publishing.
- Think about a focus question for your map. See Novak reading and ConceptMap_Guide_Aug18 powerpoint.
- Follow the guidelines in the ConceptMap_Guide_Aug18 PowerPoint for creating and revising your map.
- Use "notes", in CMap to add notes, links or other explanatory information for about 20% of your concepts.
- Generate labeled links between all concept nodes.
  - o This is perhaps the hardest part of the assignment. Refer to the "Jonassen links" file for link examples of linking words
  - o Refer to the link characteristics in the PPT file referenced above.
- Your map should be nested at least one level – but see the rubric below for how your map will be assessed.
- Write a short description (a couple of paragraphs) on how you would use this task into an online learning setting
  - o You'll need to submit this in a separate MS Word document.

Figure 16.2 Except from assignment description using CMap.

this activity by suggesting that students' consider the nature of the links and differences or similarities in each other's representations; or

- students can work collaboratively on concept map creation using a "cloud"-based concept mapping software package (e.g. MindMeister).

Spreadsheets

Jonassen has included student construction of spreadsheets as a mindtool since the first edition of his book on the topic (1995). Spreadsheets are computerized record-keeping systems. They have three primary functions: storing, calculating and presenting information. Although we often think of spreadsheets as accounting tools, they can be used as a mindtool to model the inter-relationships between the cells in the sheet. This may sound similar to concept mapping, but because of spreadsheets' abilities to calculate, sort and reorganize the rows it is comprised of, they engage a more precise set of thinking skills as compared to concept maps. Jonassen writes:

> The emphasis in a spreadsheet is on identifying relationships and describing those relationships in terms of higher-order rules (generally numerical), so it is probable that if users learn to develop spreadsheets to describe content domains, they will be thinking more deeply. Thus, spreadsheets are rule-using tools that require that users become rule makers
> (Jonassen, Howland, Marra, & Crismond, 2008, p. 89)

Jonassen describes how spreadsheets can thus be used to model – or build an external representation of – a knowledge domain. When students build a spreadsheet model of a domain, students must use their knowledge of existing rules in a domain, generate new rules, describe relationships and organize (and re-organize) information. As spreadsheet tools become more sophisticated, one can also use them to engage students in creatively and effectively presenting the results of the model using charts, graphs that can be dynamically updated as the values in the spreadsheet cells change.

Figure 16.3 is an example of a student-created spreadsheet (using Microsoft Excel) that represents several nutrition-and-the-human-body relationships: body mass index (BMI), counting calories, and the impact of exercise. To create this spreadsheet the student necessarily had to engage in deep thinking about the relationships she was learning about in the domain of human nutrition; in fact she had to go beyond learning *about* and apply her knowledge of the rules that govern this domain in order to model them in this spreadsheet.

As they are both tools to represent domain knowledge, spreadsheets can be incorporated into online settings in similar ways, pedagogically, to concept maps. Students can create them collaboratively; they can work on a semester-long spreadsheet that grows and is modified as their domain knowledge changes; they can share them with other students and use them as the basis for conversations, online discussions, or Wiki exchanges.

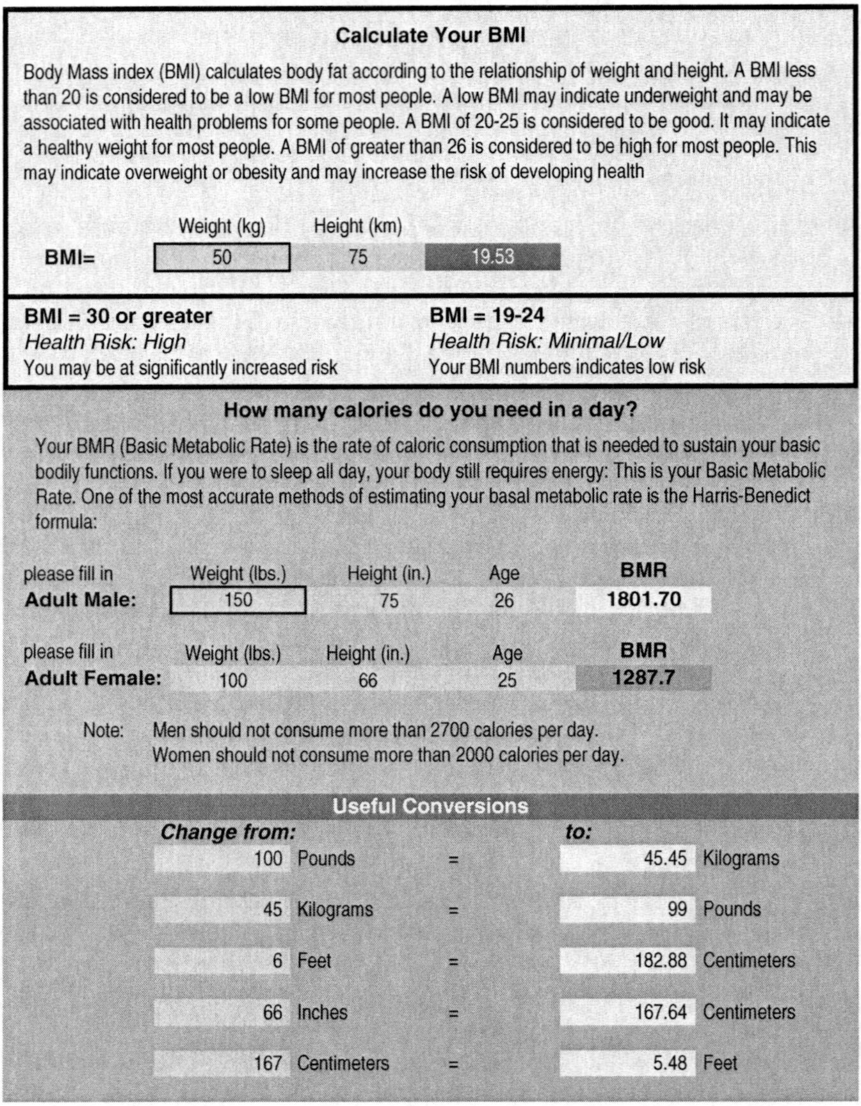

Calculate Your BMI

Body Mass index (BMI) calculates body fat according to the relationship of weight and height. A BMI less than 20 is considered to be a low BMI for most people. A low BMI may indicate underweight and may be associated with health problems for some people. A BMI of 20-25 is considered to be good. It may indicate a healthy weight for most people. A BMI of greater than 26 is considered to be high for most people. This may indicate overweight or obesity and may increase the risk of developing health

	Weight (kg)	Height (km)	
BMI=	50	75	19.53

BMI = 30 or greater
Health Risk: High
You may be at significantly increased risk

BMI = 19-24
Health Risk: Minimal/Low
Your BMI numbers indicates low risk

How many calories do you need in a day?

Your BMR (Basic Metabolic Rate) is the rate of caloric consumption that is needed to sustain your basic bodily functions. If you were to sleep all day, your body still requires energy: This is your Basic Metabolic Rate. One of the most accurate methods of estimating your basal metabolic rate is the Harris-Benedict formula:

please fill in	Weight (lbs.)	Height (in.)	Age	BMR
Adult Male:	150	75	26	1801.70

please fill in	Weight (lbs.)	Height (in.)	Age	BMR
Adult Female:	100	66	25	1287.7

Note: Men should not consume more than 2700 calories per day.
Women should not consume more than 2000 calories per day.

Useful Conversions

Change from:			to:	
100	Pounds	=	45.45	Kilograms
45	Kilograms	=	99	Pounds
6	Feet	=	182.88	Centimeters
66	Inches	=	167.64	Centimeters
167	Centimeters	=	5.48	Feet

Figure 16.3 Spreadsheet used as a mindtool to represent relationships in the domain of human nutrition.

By far the most commonly available spreadsheet tool is Microsoft Excel. It is available on both Apple and PC operating systems and it is a rare computer that does not have the Microsoft Office software suite that includes Microsoft Excel. Many students will already be familiar with the basics of this software package, but further training may be required to use it as a mindtool.

Excel is generally resident software – residing on a particular computer. But recently cloud-based versions of spreadsheet packages have become available. Perhaps most notable because of the Google name, are the Google spreadsheets available in the Google suite of online tools. This cloud package (with data stored on an Internet server and available from anyplace one has Internet access) is available for free by simply registering at the Google tools site (see docs.google.com/spreadsheets). Microsoft is also introducing its own fee-based set of cloud applications: Microsoft Office 365. Internet-based versions of these tools are particularly well matched to online learning settings as they allow simultaneous editing by multiple users – thus allowing learners to collaborate at a distance on their spreadsheet development.

Similar to the assignment concept-mapping activity depicted in Figure 16.2, online instructors can construct a learning activity for students to build spreadsheets as a way to externally represent domain knowledge. It should be noted that spreadsheets' quantitative affordances (e.g. their ability to do fairly sophisticated calculations) makes them particularly amenable for domain representations in science, technology, engineering or mathematics (STEM), and perhaps less suited for applications in the humanities.

Conversation Tools

A pedagogical underpinning of the examples I have provided on how one can use mindtools in online settings is that students can learn not only from the process of constructing the spreadsheet or concept map, but they can also learn from *conversing* about that process, and engaging in dialog with other students on the content and organization of their mindtools. For instance, students would benefit from posting completed or in-progress spreadsheets or concept maps to the online forum for comparisons and discussion with their peers and the instructor. This is a simple instantiation of the social nature of learning and conversations are central to such learning interchanges.

Jonassen first included "conversation" tools in his second edition of the Mindtools book (2000). Conversation tools provide a means to support the social negotiation of meaning – between two or more individuals – that is critical to the concept of mindtools. When he introduced these tools into the mindtools second edition, Jonassen described the transition that was then going on amongst learning theorists as they moved (or at least acknowledged) from understanding learning of learning as an individual activity to one where social interaction is critical to learning (Bruffee, 1993; Lave, 1988). Jonassen emphasized this point saying that "meaningful learning is less focused on transmission and more committed to negotiation and discourse" (p. 238).

Online learning lacks the opportunities for both nonverbal and synchronous communication that can take place in face-to-face settings. Thus the tools that support conversations – both synchronous and asynchronous – are critical to participant interactions and ultimately student learning in line courses. Those conversations can take many forms, but are often mediated through the online discussion forum tools offered in CMSs. Online conversation tools – including asynchronous threaded discussion forums, as well as synchronous chat tools – can enable exchanges between students that allow them to learn from one another. Figure 16.4 illustrates the centrality of the online forum indicating that the online forum can be a way to support a variety of instructional activities (e.g. reflection, community building).

You may say, "Well these tools are built into most course management systems, what makes them a mindtool?" They can be mindtools in part because they are domain-free tools that can be used regardless of what you are teaching. But more importantly, they are mindtools when they are used in particular ways that:

- allow learners to represent what they know, modify their representations and get feedback on them.
- support learners in engaging in higher order learning outcomes and critical thinking activities.

I will mention some of the tools available for implementing these online conversations below, but first I want to provide some examples of instructional activities that can be created to use these conversation tools as mindtools. Table 16.2 provides a number of examples of uses of online conversation tools that go beyond simply tossing a topic out for open discussion, or asking questions about an assigned reading and in fact comprise meaningful learning activities.

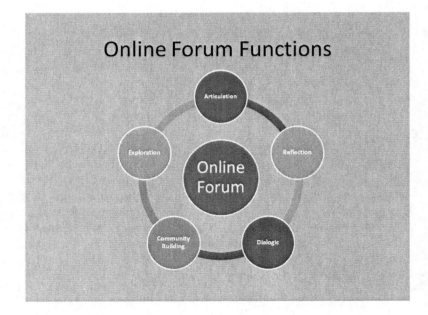

Figure 16.4 Strategies supported by the online forum.

Table 16.2 Conversation activities that engage meaningful learning

Activity	Description
Case analysis	Pose a real-world ethics case to engineering students. Assign different roles/characters from the case to different students and ask them to represent/play that role in a forum discussion to resolve the case. Debrief and reflect on the process and what is learned.
Hypothesis generation	Use the online forum in conjunction with a physics simulation tool like myphysicslab.com. Students would use the forum to present and debate hypotheses that apply to the experiments they are running with the tool. Use it before and after the actual experiment!
Reflection after another activity	Combine the above hypothesis generation activity (that occurs before and perhaps during the use of the simulation or other "lab" work) with a post activity reflection. Ask students to post their original hypotheses along with their actual results. Then ask them to engage in discussions as to why their original hypothesis did or did not prove to be true, and an explanation for their actual results.
Problem solving	Pose an instructional design problem via the discussion forum. Use web-based data to illustrate the problem. Use the forum for brain storming, design, consensus reaching and other group problem-solving tasks.
Peer evaluations	Have students post a final or interim version of an assignment – for instance they might post a rubric they are developing for classwork. Assign students (or have them sign up) a peer to work with AND provide students with a framework or set of criteria by which to provide constructive criticism to their peers. You may also wish to provide students with some canned opening phrases to help them with providing honest and helpful feedback (some students find it difficult to provide what they perceive as negative feedback).An example on writing forced response items: Directions: Post 3 of your forced response type "remember" level items for peer review. Student 1 posts the following item: *Here's one of my items from my unit on geology. "How old is the earth? _____"* Student 2 responds: *It might be clearer to the students if you would indicate that you are looking for a response in years.*
Argumentation	Require students to use formal argumentation skills in analyzing a case and proposing a solution to that case. See Figure 16.5 below for a detailed example.

To accomplish these tasks, the instructor must continually coach and monitor the activities occurring in the conversations. For instance, the instructor may need to prompt students to:

- provide specific examples in their feedback to peers in a peer evaluation;
- redirect students during problem-solving activities to stay on task and reach a consensus;
- provide justifications for their posting BEYOND simply their personal experience (e.g. prompt them to cite research, refer to readings, etc.); and
- direct students' attention to particular posts that represent either an important idea for the content of the discussion (e.g. an important point in the domain of engineering ethics) or to a post that represents a well structured posting (e.g. does a good job of providing peer feedback or is an good exemplar of justifying ones position with external evidence).

These types of coaching and facilitation activities represent instructor-provided scaffolds – or supports – for helping students to attain the most meaningful learning outcomes in their discussion activities. If one uses these activities frequently in an online setting, you would wish to gradually remove the scaffolds or supports as students learn to function effectively in these forums on their own.

A particular type of online conversation tool, however, can provide some of these scaffolds directly within the tool. These are called constrained or scaffolded discussion boards. To explain how these work, let me compare them to a simple threaded asynchronous discussion forum tool like you may find in Blackboard.

In a simple threaded forum, an instructor or a facilitator generally defines what the forum is designed or intended to be focused upon, but participants may post any sequence of postings containing any type of content. There are no actual *enforceable* rules for posting in these forums.

In contrast, a constrained forum is governed by rules on the *types* (e.g. the content) of postings allowed and also rules for the *sequencing* of posting types. The software for the constrained forum allows instructors to define these posting *types* and the *rules* for posting. The software then enforces the rules for participants. In this way, the software provides a built in scaffold to help support the type of thinking or analysis that is structured by the rules defined by the forum designer.

Let's look at an example that illustrates what the constraints and rules would look like for a particular problem, the software that supports these rules, and how it looks to the students as they participate. In this example, I wanted to model and support students' ability to argue for a position as well as engage them in diagnosing and solving issues that arise in facilitating online discussions. I presented them with a small case that presented difficulties that may arise during facilitation of an online discussion forum. My students then used a scaffolded discussion forum tool that was developed at the University of Missouri – called C-Board – to discuss and analyze the case.

Table 16.3 shows the message types they used and the rules that are enforced by the software as to what message types may be used as a reply to a previous message type. For instance, a "hypothesize cause" posting type can only follow "problem identification" or "elaboration" type messages. Figure 16.5 depicts two C-Board screens: on the left is the administrator screen used to define the C-Board "constraints" or rules between message types and on the right is the screen a discussion participant sees as he or she posts a reply message. Note that in this case the reply is to a "problem identification" post and C-Board limits the reply to either a "hypothesize cause" or "elaboration" posting.

There is preliminary research to show that these types of forums can have positive effects on student learning. Specifically, Oh, & Jonassen (2007) found that, as compared to a control group of students who used a standard threaded forum, students who participated in a constrained problem-solving

Table 16.3 Message types defined to use in a constrained forum

Message types	Description	Guiding questions
Problem identification	*Root message in a thread – meaning someone must post one of these to start the discussion; but there can be more than one root type posting*: Describe a problem that is occurring in the forum.	What is the problem you think needs to be addressed?
Hypothesize cause	Why is this problem occurring? You'll have to speculate based on the situation above and your own experiences. This post would follow a *problem identification or elaboration* post.	
Verification	A statement of agreement with a prior post or position. Include evidence for your verification.	I agree because…
Rebuttal	A statement of disagreement with a prior post. Include evidence for your rebuttal.	I disagree because…
Evidence	Statements that provide evidence from a scholar, personal experience, beliefs and/ or research to support or rebut a stated argument.	I can support this view with this evidence…
Elaboration	A request for clarification on a prior post.	Could you clarify? I don't understand…
Solution generation	Describe how you would address the problem via facilitation strategies (e.g. questioning, prompting).	How would you address the problem? What solutions follow from the causes and evidence that have been posted?

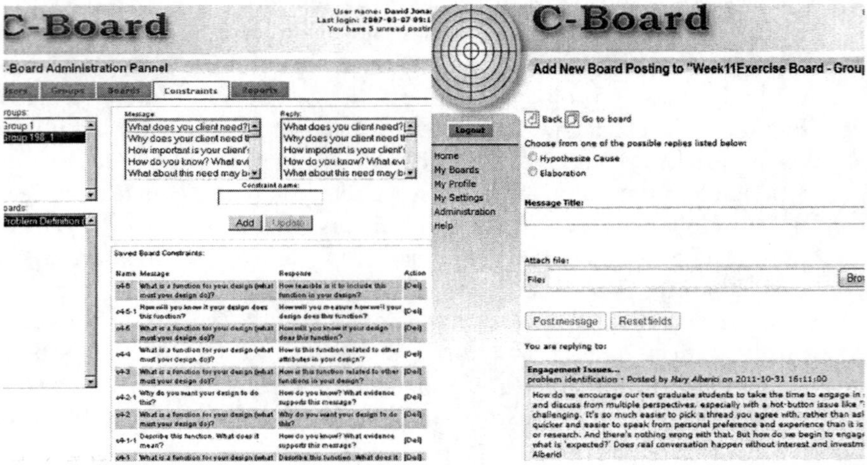

Figure 16.5 Administrator and participant screens from C-board.

activity produced more evidence for their postings, performed better on problem space construction, hypothesis generation, hypothesis testing and solution verification during problem solving, and performed better on follow-up problem-solving activities.

This example illustrates constraints and message types designed to help students learn to structure an argument. But software packages like C-Board or FLE 3 (see fle3.uiah.fi) allow the forum designer to define *any* type of message types and rules they like – depending on what one wishes the students to learn to do. Table 16.4 illustrates message types that scaffold ethical problem solving, and engineering design.

To the author's knowledge, no CMS or LMS supports a constrained forum such as I have described. But there are plenty of both asynchronous and synchronous conversation tools available to today's online instructors – and many of them are actually included in CMSs like Blackboard. In addition to

Table 16.4 Possible conversation constraint formats

Ethical problem solving or case analysis message types	Engineering design message types
Identify dimensions in the case	Identify problem or Need
Recognize instances of ethical problems	Results of research on problem (what do we know already?)
Apply different themes/theoretical approaches to analyze the case	Possible solutions
Decision making	Justifications/rebuttals for solutions
Re-engineer to prevent future occurrences.	Consensus posting

the standard threaded discussion forum, the latest versions of Blackboard, for instance, include Wikis, blogs, a synchronous chat tool, email amongst course members, and Blackboard collaborate which allows for synchronous audio and video communication.

How Mindtools Address Limitations of Online Learning

Incorporating the use of mindtools can address several of the CMS limitations for supporting student attainment of meaningful learning outcomes as well as some of the limitations associated with appealing to diverse learning styles. Table 16.5 summarizes how mindtools can address these limitations.

In essence, CMSs were designed for traditional pedagogies and traditional (mostly text-based) ways of representing content and knowledge. By incorporating mindtools into online courses that otherwise rely on a CMS, instructors can provide *alternatives* ways for representing knowledge, *structure* students' thinking via the affordances of the mindtools (e.g. spreadsheets can support the definition and application of rules in a domain),

Table 16.5 How mindtools address online learning limitations

Limitation	Mindtool solutions
Engage visual, spatial and auditory learners	• Concept map creation is clearly a visual activity providing an alternative to textual presentation of domain knowledge. • Voice thread is a conversation tool includes a visual component. Participants engage in a conversation structured around a visual presentation; student comments can be made both in text and in audio recordings.
Alternative forms of knowledge Representation	• Both spreadsheets and concept maps provide an alternative way to represent knowledge from the predominantly text based modes of knowledge representation available in CMS (e.g. discussion forums).
Alternative forms of assessment	• All of the tools discussed can be used as an alternative form of assessment. When coupled with a rubric, each one of the examples provides a "product" that can be assessed either in a formative or summative way.
Supporting Distributed Cognitive Tools	• Clearly all of these tools are "cognitive" tools and can be used in a distributed fashion – either as resident on individual computers – or in cloud versions that seamlessly support collaboration. Although these tools – with the exception of an appropriate use of a CMS threaded discussion forum – are not part of the CMS packages that most of us use to teach online courses, I argue that they can be used effectively in conjunction with a CMS supported course and thus overcome this limitation in online settings.

incorporate meaningful student-centered activities into online learning, and use the products students produce as alternative assessment products. Although these pedagogical characteristics may be persuasive, the use of mindtools in online courses is not without its implementation challenges. I address these next.

Practical Implications of Using Mindtools Online

The final necessary piece of understanding how to use mindtools in online settings is to address the practical aspects of doing so. Recall that one of the characteristics of mindtools that makes them so imminently usable is that they are accessible – both financially and cognitively. With the possible exception of systems modeling tools, these are software packages that are quite easy to learn to use. I have previously recounted how I have heard Dave Jonassen say many times that he can teach most learners to use these tools in 10–15 minutes. The catch – that was in a face-to-face lab setting where he can wander around and do coaching and troubleshooting as participants learn to use a particular tool.

So how do we facilitate student tool-learning in an online setting where that type of synchronous coaching is not possible? While it may be more challenging to teach these tools in online settings, supporting and creating the online instruction necessary to use mindtools has become much more feasible in the last few years with the advent of easy-to-use technology tools that enable easy screen captures and video production. I briefly explore how these tools can help with the two aspects of helping the students learn to use the mindtool: (1) learning the *how-to*s of the technology (e.g. How do I create a node in CMap? How do I link nodes and label my links?); and (2) learning how to use these *tools as mindtools* (How do I represent domain knowledge in a concept map or a spreadsheet?).

For learning *how to* use the tool, one may not even have to create one's own specialized resources. Many software products and tools such as concept mapping packages now include their own online tutorials that help a learner get started with the basics of tool use. One may also find numerous YouTube videos that illustrate the *how-to*s of a software package. Of course one needs to screen these for quality and accuracy. So an instructor may need to identify these ready-made resources, make them known to the students, and possibly supplement them with a one or two page quick start guide on the tool. Figure 16.6 shows an excerpt for such a guide for using the CMap concept mapping software.

If you cannot find ready-made tutorials that meet your needs, then tools like *screencast* (www.screencast.com) make it relatively easy to produce your own video-based tutorials of how to master the basics of the package you are teaching. Screencast is a tool that makes digital recordings of one's computer screen – basically capturing your screens; additionally you can add audio narration. The tool is free and the service provides a modest amount of online storage as well.

CMapTools 5.0 Job Aid

How to...	Operation
Add a concept	Double click on the white space / Or right click on the white space and select "New Concept"
	→ Type in a concept label to replace the question marks in the shape ⟨????⟩
	→ Click on the white space when you are done with typing.
Add a link	Left click on the concept, drag the arrow on the top of the concept ⬛
	→ If you release the mouse when another concept is selected, a link will be added between them / If you release the mouse on the white space, a new concept will also be added
	→ Next, type in a link label to replace the question mark in the rectangle on the link ⟨????⟩. Click on the white space when you are done
Edit a concept /link	• Double clicking a shape enables you to edit the content of the concept
	• Double clicking the rectangle on a link enables you to edit the link label
Create a CMap	In the window of "Views-CMapTools", select "New CMap" from the File Menu
Save a CMap	Select "Save CMap" from the File menu.
	For the location, select "My CMaps" ⬛ , and name the file.

Figure 16.6 CMap quick guide excerpt.

CMSs are now also providing tools for creating video and doing screen capture. For instance Blackboard now includes Tegrity video capture in its suite of tools. Tegrity is described as a tool for recording lectures. You can use Tegrity at your own computer to capture both your audio as well as video of your choice. The video could be any combination of you (while you talk), and the contents of your computer screen. The latter might include PowerPoint presentations which could be used to show viewers how to use a particular mindtool software package.

A last tactic I have used for both modeling the use of mindtools and teaching software basics is a synchronous session within Blackboard using their version of Adobe Connect (they are now calling it Blackboard Collaborate). To use this feature, you create a session and invite your students to join it at a particular time. Within the session you can simultaneously talk to one another (using headsets), display and share files (such as PowerPoint presentations) and do screen sharing. This last feature is particularly useful for both teaching a software package and modeling how to use it as a mindtool. I can, for instance, run CMap and demonstrate visually how to use the package, answer questions students have about its use, and also show examples that illustrate characteristics of a well-structured CMap being used as a mindtool.

These latter tools – screencasts, Tegrity, and Adobe Connect – are all ways that one can effectively model the use of these technologies as mindtools. As in most good instruction, having examples and non-examples of uses of these tools, and talking through (and visually highlighting) the characteristics that makes them good or bad examples can help students begin to understand how to use these tools effectively. Another tactic I often use, is asking students to post partially completed work to a threaded discussion forum for instructor comments. By providing feedback to one or more students in this public area, all students may benefit and be able to apply the explained principles to their own work.

Conclusions

Mindtools as defined by Jonassen have been around since the mid-90s. In this chapter I argue for and illustrate their application in online learning for supporting meaningful learning. In particular they can easily be used within the context of the CMSs that many online instructors must work with in order to better facilitate and support meaningful learning.

I have provided illustrations of the use of concept mapping, building spreadsheets and using online conversation tools as mindtools in online courses. But these are certainly not the only mindtools that could be incorporated into online courses. The key in all cases of effectively integrating mindtools into an online course (particularly one that uses a CMS) is to build supportive and meaningful instructional activities around the use of that mindtool (e.g. asking students to collaboratively build a concept map to represent domain knowledge). These activities can in turn take advantage of the myriad of online resources available to us as online course instructors. For instance, one might pair knowledge representation tools (e.g. concept maps, spreadsheets or databases) with online simulations and lab environments like the Virtual Autopsy (http://www.le.ac.uk/pa/teach/va/welcome. html). Using these technologies in conjunction with one another takes advantage of the simulation provided in the virtual environment and powerfully couples it with a knowledge representation tool that allows students to reflect upon, analyze and synthesize what they have learned.

To me, the most compelling argument for using mindtools in online settings is that they offer a simple, yet effective means for overcoming some of the limitations instructors encounter in the affordances of CMSs in supporting meaningful learning in online settings (see Table 16.5). I am not arguing that one abandon the readymade tools for displaying and delivering content available within a CMS, however the addition of mindtools to ones instructional bag of tricks greatly expands students' abilities to represent what they know and your ability to assess that knowledge.

So to go back to a question I posed at the start of this chapter – do mindtools still have a place in our mobile-app, Smartphone driven world? Yes! Their ability to enhance online learning activities to support meaningful learning outcomes makes them as relevant today as they were in the mid-nineties. Mindtools may not be my husband's most recent – or some may argue – even innovative work. Using Dave's current language of "problem solving" I offer that integrating mindtools into online learning offers a solution to the very ill-structured problem of supporting higher order learning outcomes in online settings.

References

Anderson, L. W., & Krathwohl, D. R. (Eds.), (2001). *A taxonomy for learning, teaching and assessing: A revision of Bloom's Taxonomy of educational objectives: Complete edition*, New York: Longman.

Bonk, C. J., & Zhang, K. (2008). *Empowering online learning: 100+ activities for reading, reflecting, displaying, and doing.* San Francisco: Jossey-Bass.

Bruffee, K. (1993). *Collaborative learning: Higher education, interdependence, and the authority of knowledge.* Baltimore, MD: Johns Hopkins University Press.

Jonassen, D. H. (1995). *Mindtools for engaging critical thinking in the classroom.* Columbus, OH: Prentice-Hall.

Jonassen, D. H. (1999). Designing constructivist learning environments. In C. M. Reigeluth (Ed.), *Instructional design theories and models: Their current state of the art* (2nd ed.). (pp. 215–236). Mahwah, NJ: Lawrence Erlbaum Associates.

Jonassen, D. H. (2000a). Toward a design theory of problem solving. *Educational Technology: Research & Development, 48*(4), 63–85.

Jonassen, D. H. (2000b). *Mindtools for engaging critical thinking in the classroom* (2nd ed.). Columbus, OH: Prentice-Hall.

Jonassen, D. H. (2005). *Modeling with Technology: Mindtools for conceptual change* (3rd ed.). Columbus, OH: Prentice-Hall.

Jonassen, D. H., & Carr, C. S. (2000). Mindtools: Affording Multiple Knowledge Representations for Learning. In S. P. Lajoie (Ed.), *Computers as cognitive tools, volume two: No more walls: theory change, paradigm shifts, and their influence on the use of computers for instructional purposes* (pp. 165–196). Mahwah, NJ: Lawrence Erlbaum.

Jonassen, D. H., & Reeves, T. C. (1996). Learning with technology: Using computers as cognitive tools. In D. H. Jonassen (Ed.), *Handbook of research for educational communications and technology* (pp. 693–719). New York: Macmillan.

Jonassen, D. H., Carr, C., & Yueh, H-P. (1998). Computers as mindtools for engaging learners in critical thinking. *TechTrends, 43*(2), 24–32.

Jonassen, D. H., Howland, J., Marra, R. M., & Crismond, D. (2008). *Meaningful learning with technology* (3rd ed.). Upper Saddle River: Pearson Education, Inc.

Lave, J. (1988). *Cognition in practice: Mind, mathematics and culture in every day life.* New York: Cambridge University Press.

Liu, M., & Bera, S. (2005). An analysis of cognitive tool use patterns in a hypermedia learning environment. *Educational Technology Research and Development, 53*(1), 5–21.

Liu, M., Horton, L., Corliss, S., Svinicki, M., Bogard, T., Kim, J., & Chang, M. (2009). Students' problem solving as mediated by their cognitive tool use: A study of tool use patterns. *Journal of Educational Computing Research, 40*(1), 111–139.

Marra, R. M., & Jonassen, D. H. (2001). Limitations of online courses for supporting constructive learning. *Quarterly Review of Distance Education, 2*(4), 303–317.

Naidu, S. (2006). *E-Learning: A guidebook of principles, procedures and practices.* Commonwealth Educational Media Center for Asia (CEMCA). Retrieved December 1, 2011 from http://www.cemca.org/e-learning_guidebook.pdf

Oh, S., & Jonassen, D. H. (2007). Scaffolding online argumentation during problem solving. *Journal of Computer Assisted Learning, 23*(2), 95–110.

Parker, K., Lenhart, A., & Moore, K. (2011) *The digital revolution and higher education.* Retrieved December 1, 2011 from http://www.pewsocialtrends.org/2011/08/28/the-digital-revolution-and-higher-education/.

Rieber, L. P. (1996). Seriously considering play: Designing interactive learning environments based on the blending of microworlds, simulations, and games. *Educational Technology Research and Development, 44*(2), 43–58.

Staker, H. (2011). *The rise of K–12 blended learning* [Innosite Institute white paper]. Retrieved December 1, 2011 from http://www.innosightinstitute.org/innosight/wpcontent/uploads/2011/05/ The-Rise-of-K-12-Blended-Learning.pdf.

17 First Principles of Learning

David H. Jonassen

Introduction

Just as Dave Merrill synthesized his prodigious body of research and design into his First Principles of Instruction (Merrill, 2002), in this chapter I too hope to synthesize what I have learned about learning in my First Principles of Learning. Merrill (2002) synthesized five principles of instruction: activation, demonstration, application, and integration wrapped around a problem. In Figure 17.1, I suggest five principles of learning: problem-based, analogizing, modeling, reasoning causally, and arguing. Both Merrill's First Principles of Instruction and my First Principles of Learning may be regarded as the epitome of our work (see Reigeluth & Stein, 1983, for the notion of an epitome).

In the early part of my career, much of my learning was guided by Merrill's work, which continues to present perhaps the most coherent model of instructional design. Although impressed by the coherence of Merrill's work for the Navy in the 1980s, it became obvious that I could not deny my constructivist orientation, so I came out of the closet (Jonassen, 1990, 1991). The assumption of instruction is that it results in learning. As a constructivist, how much of the variance in learning that is actually accounted for by instruction is questionable epistemologically, ontologically, and teleologically. That is why I have always been more interested in learning than I am in instruction – *ergo*, the First Principles of Learning. Please note that I am not arguing against instruction. I have provided a lot of it. My interest in learning is more pre-eminent.

The purpose for my research focus on problem-solving and related activities is captured best perhaps by the distinction that Gilbert Ryle (1949) made between knowing that vs. knowing how. My work has nearly always focused on knowing (learning) how vs. knowing (learning) that. This is more than a semantic distinction. The overwhelming majority of formal education is designed to help students to learn *about* the world. In universities everywhere, students learn about sociology, psychology, biology, and a host of other theoretical *ologies*, although too seldom are students required to learn *how* to do much of anything, such as solving sociological, psychological, biological or other kinds of problems.

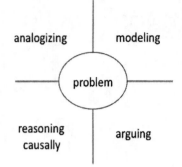

Figure 17.1 First principles of learning.

I argue that problem solving, analogizing, modeling, reasoning causally, and arguing are the most powerful modes of thinking that lead to the most meaningful learning. These are the most cognitively engaging and epistemically productive learning activities that students may complete. All are replete with cognitive load and other cognitive challenges.

Problems

Problem solving is most often the implicit goal of informal learning, as we learn to solve the myriad problems that we encounter in work and our everyday lives. I have long argued that problem solving should be the primary intellectual focus of nearly all formal education. Why should problem solving be considered the pre-eminent goal of education?

- *Authenticity* – In everyday, and especially professional life, people constantly solve problems. Problems are everywhere. Employees in corporations, the military, and other agencies are hired, retained, and rewarded for solving problems. Karl Popper (1999) made the bold assertion that living is essentially problem solving.
- *Intentionality* – Problems provide a purpose for learning. Students learning to solve problems must think in order to succeed. They construct conceptual understanding while solving problems because they must articulate or at least embrace an intention to solve the problem.
- *Conceptual anchoring* – Knowledge constructed while solving problems, as opposed to simply learning about a problem domain, is more meaningful, more integrated, better retained, and more transferable when encountering other problems.
- *Ontology* – The knowledge that is constructed while solving problems is phenomenologically (experiential knowledge) and epistemologically meaningful and at a higher or deeper level than knowledge resulting from simply reading or hearing about a problem domain (Jonassen,

2009). Problem-based learning, compared with traditional didactic instruction, generally results in higher levels of understanding, problem-solving transfer, higher order thinking, and self-directed learning with slight decrements in basic domain knowledge acquisition (Hung, Jonassen, & Liu, 2008).

My theory of problem solving diverges from traditional models of problem-solving that articulate process models for solving all kinds of problems (e.g. Bransford & Stein, 1994). Problems and problem solving vary in several ways. Foremost among these differences is the continuum between well-structured and ill-structured problems (Jonassen, 1997; Simon, 1969). Most problems encountered in formal education are well-structured problems. Well-structured problems typically (a) present all elements of the problem, (b) engage a limited number of rules and principles that are organized in a predictive and prescriptive arrangement, (c) possess correct, convergent answers, and (d) have a preferred, prescribed solution process.

Ill-structured problems, on the other hand, are the kinds of problems that are encountered in everyday practice. Ill-structured problems have (a) many alternative solutions to problems, (b) vaguely defined or unclear goals and constraints, (c) multiple solution paths, and (d) multiple criteria for evaluating solutions.

Problems also vary in complexity. The complexity of a problem is a function of (a) the breadth of knowledge required to solve the problem, (b) the level of prior knowledge, (c) the intricacy for the problem-solutions procedures, and (d) the relational complexity of the problem (number of relations that need to be processed in parallel during a problem-solving process) (Jonassen & Hung, 2008). Ill-structured problems tend to be more complex than well-structured problems. Another dimension of problem complexity is *dynamicity*. In dynamic problems, the relationships among variables or factors change over time and are often non-linear. Changes in one factor may cause variable changes in other factors that often substantively changes the underlying nature of the problem. The more intricate these interactions, the more complex the problem becomes. There may also be delayed effects in a complex problem, which is yet another aspect of dynamicity. Ill-structured problems tend to be more dynamic than well-structured problems, which tend to be static because all of the information needed to solve the problems is contained in the problem statement.

A final dimension of problems and problem solving is domain specificity. In contemporary psychology, there is a common belief that problems within a domain rely on cognitive strategies that are specific to that domain (Mayer, 1992; Smith, 1991; Sternberg & Frensch, 1991). These are often referred to as strong methods, as opposed to domain-general strategies (weak methods). Problems vary according to the domain (physics problems are different from social psychology) and especially by the context in which they occur.

If problems vary along so many dimensions, then it is possible to describe and categorize different kinds of problems. I (Jonassen, 2000) have previously described a typology of problems that vary primarily along a continuum from well-structured to ill-structured, including puzzles, algorithms, story problems, rule-using problems, decision making, troubleshooting, diagnosis-solution problems, strategic performance, systems analysis, design problems, and dilemmas. This typology assumes that there are similarities in the cognitive processes for solving problems within a particular problem category. Within each category, problems may vary with regard to abstractness, complexity, and dynamicity, each of which poses somewhat different cognitive challenges (e.g. more abstract problems may require more analogical reasoning; dynamic problems involving delayed effects and non-linear relationships may require reasoning about changes over time; etc.).

An underlying assumption in instructional design is that conditions of learning should be altered to most effectively address different learning outcomes (Gagné, 1977). Therefore, learning how to solve different kinds of problems requires different learning activities. Instructional models for different kinds of problems are presented in Jonassen (2011). In the remainder of this chapter, I argue that the key epistemic components for learning to solve problems or otherwise engage meaningful learning are analogizing, modeling, reasoning causally, and arguing. The development of these skills will assist learners in completing myriad cognitive tasks. For me, they represent key critical thinking skills.

Analogizing to Learn

The use of analogies to facilitate concept development has a rich research history (Glynn, 1989; Paris & Glynn, 2004). Analogizing is the process of transferring (mapping) information from a particular subject (source) to another particular subject (target). Inferring analogies helps learners to understand a new idea by comparing its attributes to the attributes of an existing, better-understood idea.

Analogies are also useful for learning to solve problems. A primary purpose for learning to solve problems is transfer – that is, developing the ability to solve related problems. Although conceptions of transfer vary dramatically, problem-solving transfer means that learners can solve similar problems when encountered. In order to transfer problem-solving skills, it is essential to develop robust schemas for different kinds of problems (Jonassen, 2011). In order to develop those robust problem schemas, two different kinds of analogizing have proven useful. For more well-structured problems, analogical encoding supports problem schema induction. That is, provide analogical examples for comparison in order to help learners induce better problem schemas. For more ill-structured problems, case-based reasoning supports the recall of analogous problems (experiences) when trying to solve a current problem.

Analogical encoding is a process that provides multiple analogical problems to compare to the problem being solved. Well-structured problem-solving transfer is based on schema induction and reuse, which is a form of analogical reasoning. In order to induce more robust problem schemas, students should analogically compare the problem being solved to one or more structurally similar problems. Rather than attempting to induce and transfer a schema based on a single example, Gentner and her colleagues have shown that comprehension, schema induction, and long-term transfer across contexts can be greatly facilitated by comparing two analogous problems for structural alignment (Gentner & Markman, 1997, 2005; Loewenstein, Thompson, & Gentner, 1999, 2003). Analogical encoding fosters learning because analogies promote attention to structural commonalities, including common principles and schemas (Gick & Holyoak, 1983).

The second kind of analogizing is from experience. When we encounter a problem without a solution, we first search our memories for similar problems that we have solved. An encountered problem (a new case) prompts the reasoner to retrieve similar cases from memory, to reuse the old case if it works (i.e. interpret the new in terms of the old), which suggests a solution. If the suggested solution will not work, then the old and or new cases are revised. When the effectiveness is confirmed, then the learned case is retained for later use. This is a process known as case-based reasoning (Kolodner, 1993).

In order to enhance problem solving with case-based reasoning, we construct databases of previous experiences in the form of stories, known as case libraries. The simplest method for eliciting stories is to present a problem to an experienced practitioner and ask him/her if they have encountered a similar problem before. More often than not, they are reminded of many similar stories. After recording those stories, they must be indexed in order to explain the lessons learned from the experience. Indexes may include, among other issues, the problem goals and expectations, the context in which the problem occurred, the solution that was chosen, or the outcome of the solution, or the points that each story makes (i.e. the lessons to be learned from the experience). In addition to providing advice on how to solve a problem, those stories may also yield an abundance of conceptual and strategic knowledge that can be included in your instruction. Why? Because when eliciting stories, practitioners naturally embellish their stories with contextual information, heuristics, practical wisdom, and personal identities (Henning, 1996; Schön, 1983). Both analogical encoding and case-based reasoning use similar problems as analogies. Analogical encoding provides new problems in order to help learners construct robust problem schemas, while case-based reasoning provides reminded experiences of previously solved problems in order to help learners solve problems. The analogical processes are similar and both emphasize the importance of analogizing to problem solving.

Modeling to Learn

Model building is a powerful strategy for engaging, supporting, and assessing conceptual change in learners because these models scaffold and externalize internal, mental models by providing multiple formalisms for representing conceptual understanding and change (Milrad, Spector, & Davidsen, 2003; Jonassen, Strobel, & Gottdenker, 2005). Not only does model building engage students in meaningful learning, but it results in conceptual change. Although models are commonly provided to students to study and also used to design interactive learning environments, it is the construction and testing of models by students that offers the greatest potential for learning. The models that students construct also provide evidence of the growth and reorganization of learners' conceptual models. Conceptual change may result from studying models, we learn so much more from building and manipulating models (Morrison & Morgan, 1999).

Why is model building so much more productive for learning and conceptual change than model using? When solving a problem or answering a complex conceptual question, learners must construct a mental model of the phenomena and use that model as the basis for prediction, inference, speculation, or experimentation. Constructing a physical, analogical, or computational model of the world reifies the learner's mental model. So, when students construct, manipulate, and test their own technology-mediated models, they learn more and change conceptually more than they do from trying to induce the underlying model in a black box simulation. Among the most effective ways of engaging, supporting, and assessing conceptual change is by building and comparing models that represent different kinds of knowledge (Jonassen, 2008).

Models are conceptual systems consisting of elements, relations, operations, and rules governing interactions that are expressed using external notation systems (Lesh & Doerr, 2003). Although the most commonly used system for modeling scientific phenomena is the equation, many other kinds of modeling tools may be used to represent phenomena being studies, including images, structural diagrams, metaphors, and demonstrations (Jonassen & Henning, 1999) and computer-based tools such as databases, concept maps, spreadsheets, expert systems, hypermedia, systems dynamics tools, visualization tools, and teachable agents (Jonassen, 2006a). Each different kind of modeling tool includes its own constraints on the knowledge construction process as well as its affordances for constructing different kinds of knowledge.

What should students model? Most commonly, students focus on subject matter content, so any models they build typically focus on content topics. In addition to domain content, Jonassen (2006a) claimed that students should learn to model the problems they solve, the systems that organize ideas, and the thinking processes they use to learn (a form of metacognitive reflection).

Model building is a powerful learning strategy because:

- Model building is a natural cognitive phenomenon. When encountering unknown phenomena, humans naturally begin to construct theories about those phenomena as an essential part of the understanding process.

- Modeling supports hypothesis testing, conjecturing, inferring, and a host of other important cognitive skills.
- Modeling results in the construction of cognitive artifacts (mental models) by constructing physical or computational artifacts.
- When students construct models, they own the knowledge. Student ownership is important to meaning making and knowledge construction. When ideas are owned, students are willing to exert more effort, defend their positions, and reason more effectively (Duffy & Jonassen, 1993).
- Modeling provides shared workspaces and a basis for meaningful collaboration.

Reasoning Causally to Learn

Concepts are the basis of semantic processing. Most forms of understanding require humans to learn and apply dynamic combinations of concepts (Jonassen, 2006). Those combinations of concepts define various propositions. Propositions are sets of concepts that are connected by associative and dynamic relationships. The most common type of proposition that underlies all thinking is a causal proposition (one that implies cause and effect) (Carey, 2002). David Hume (1739/2000) claimed that causal reasoning is the *cement of the universe*. As intellectual cement, causality binds together reasoning processes that are common to all disciplines.

Causal reasoning enables us to make predictions, draw implications, make inferences, and articulate explanations. Given a set of conditions or states of an event, predictions state the possible effect(s) that may result. The two primary purposes of prediction are forecasting an event (e.g. economic or meteorological forecasting) and testing of hypotheses to confirm or refute scientific assumptions. A less deterministic form of prediction is drawing implications from a set of conditions based upon plausible cause–effect relationships. To imply is to entail or entangle events or to involve an effect as a necessary consequence of some cause without necessarily knowing what the effect will be. When an outcome or state exists for which the causal agent is unknown, then an inference is required. The primary purpose of inferences is diagnosis. Finally, causality is essential for understanding all forms of scientific reasoning (Klahr, 2000).

While causal reasoning is central to most kinds of learning, it is absolutely essential to problem solving. For example, Jonassen and Hung (2006) showed how troubleshooting relies on a functional model of the system being diagnosed. That functional knowledge is described by the causal relationships among the elements of the problem. So, problem solvers must develop an understanding of the causal relationships that comprise the problem space for virtually any kind of problem to solve it. Problems may be defined by the causal relationships among the entities that comprise the problem. In order to solve problems, the solver must understand the causal relationships in the problem.

Understanding the causal relationships in a problem is a complex cognitive phenomenon requiring comprehension of the covariational attributes of the causes as well as the underlying mechanisms behind those causes (Jonassen & Ionas, 2008). Causes are usually inferred from observational data. Covaration summarizes these empirical data in the form of quantitative descriptions. Covariational properties of causal relationships include the direction, strength, probability, and the immediacy of the effect (Jonassen & Ionas, 2008). Mechanisms are conceptual descriptions of causal relationship. They describe why and how the cause changes the effect. Covariational and mechanistic explanations are reciprocal. Both are necessary for understanding; neither is sufficient. Although learners can induce a correlation (covariation) between two variables using statistical methods, failure to provide an explanatory mechanism that shows how and why the covariation occurs results in lack of comprehensions of the relationship.

Jonassen and Ionas (2008) described a number of methods for enhancing causal reasoning in learners. Causality may be described using influence diagrams (Spector & Koszalka, 2004) or prompted using questions to focus student attention on important attributes of the relationships. Learners may also induce causal relationships from interacting with simulations. Students may construct causal models (see modeling discussion above) using expert systems, systems modeling tools, or a variety of available causal modeling tools. Including one or more of these methods while learning to solve problems will enhance student understanding of the problems they are learning to solve.

Arguing to Learn

Meaningful learning requires deep engagement with ideas. Deep engagement is supported by the critical thinking skill of argumentation. Learning to argue represents an important way of thinking that facilitates conceptual change and is essential for problem solving. "Argumentative thinking lies at the heart of what we should be concerned about in examining how, and how well, people think" (Kuhn, 1992, p. 157). Argumentation is the means by which we rationally resolve questions, issues, and disputes and solve problems. Embedding and fostering argumentative activities in learning environments promotes productive ways of thinking, conceptual change, and problem solving.

Although many definitions and theories of argumentation exist, Kuhn (1991) claims that complete arguments contain five essential components: (a) causal theories to support claims (see also the section in this chapter on Reasoning Causally to Learn), (b) evidence to support theories, (c) alternative theories, (d) conditions that would undermine the theories they hold (counterarguments), and (e) rebuttals to alternative theories.

Argumentation has been shown to support learning to solve both well-structured and ill-structured problems. When students answered well-structured physics problems incorrectly and later constructed an argument for the scientifically correct answer, Nussbaum and Sinatra (2003) found that those students showed improved reasoning on the problems and long–term retention. On the other hand, Cho and Jonassen (2003) showed that the production of coherent arguments to justify solutions and actions is a more important skill for solving ill-structured problems than for well-structured problems. Ill-structured problems are the kinds of problems that are encountered in everyday practice and are characterized as having (a) alternative solutions to problems, (b) vaguely defined or unclear goals and constraints, (c) multiple solution paths, and (d) multiple criteria for evaluating solutions; so they are more difficult to solve (Jonassen 2000). Groups that solved ill-structured economics problems produced more extensive arguments (Cho & Jonassen 2003). Because ill-structured problems do not have convergent answers, learners must be able to construct arguments that justify their own solutions. We have begun to establish a clear relationship between argumentation (justification) and ill-structured problem solving, and this deserves further investigation by educational researchers and practitioners.

Summary

This chapter has synthesized what I believe to be the most important cognitive processes that lead to the most meaningful learning. Learning that is problem-focused necessarily engages deeper processing of information and results in more meaningful kinds of knowledge. In order to enhance learning to solve problems, learning environments should scaffold analogical reasoning, modeling, causal reasoning and argumentation. In addition to supporting problem solving, these activities provide valuable assessment information on problem-solving abilities. There exist a virtually unlimited list of research questions about these learning strategies and how they relate to problem solving and different learning outcomes. Which strategies are most important to supporting which kinds of problem solving? To what extent do these strategies supplant or supplement each other? How do these strategies relate to different instructional components? The important lesson is that learning outcomes are more likely to be scaffolded by learning strategies such as analogical reasoning, modeling, causal reasoning and argumentation than they are by instructional presentations. Learning environments should support productive thinking by students.

References

Bransford, J. D., & Stein, B. S. (1984). *The IDEAL problem solver*. New York: W. H. Freeman.

Carey, S. (2002). The origin of concepts: Continuing the conversation. In N. L. Stein, P. J. Bauer, & M. Rabinowitz (Eds.), *Representation, memory, and development: Essays in honor of Jean Mandler* (pp. 43–52). Mahwah, NJ: Lawrence Erlbaum Associates Publishers.

Cho, K. L., & Jonassen, D. H. (2003). The effects of argumentation scaffolds on argumentation and problem solving. *Educational Technology Research and Development, 50*(3), 5–22.

Duffy, T., & Jonassen, D. H. (Eds.), (1992). *Constructivism and the technology of instruction: A conversation.* Hillsdale, NJ: Lawrence Erlbaum Associates.

Gagné, R. M. (1977). *The conditions of learning.* New York: Holt, Rinehart & Winston.

Gentner, D., Lowenstein, J., & Thompson, L. (2003). Learning and transfer: A general role for analogical encoding. *Journal of Educational Psychology, 95*(2), 393–405.

Gentner, D., & Markman, A. B. (1997). Structure mapping in analogy and similarity. *American Psychologist, 52*(1), 45–56.

Gentner, D., & Markman, A. B. (2005). Defining structural similarity. *Journal of Cognitive Science, 6*, 1–20.

Glynn, S. M. (1989). The Teaching-with-Analogies (TWA) model: Explaining concepts in expository text. In K. D. Muth (Ed.), *Children's comprehension of text: Research into practice.* (pp. 185–204). Newark, DE: International Reading Association.

Henning, P. H. (1996). *A qualitative study of situated learning by refrigeration service technicians working for a supermarket chain in Northeastern Pennsylvania.* Unpublished Ph.D. Dissertation. The Pennsylvania State University.

Hume, D. (1739/2000). *A treatise of human nature* (Eds. D. F. Norton & M. J. Norton). Oxford, UK: Oxford University Press.

Hung, W., Jonassen, D. H., & Liu, R. (2008). Problem-based learning. In J. M. Spector, J. G. van Merrienboer, M. D., Merrill, & M. P. Driscoll (Eds.), *Handbook of research on educational communications and technology*, 3rd ed. (pp. 485–506). New York: Lawrence Erlbaum Associates.

Milrad, M., Spector, J. M., & Davidsen, P. I. (2003). Model Facilitated Learning. In S. Naidu (Ed.), *Learning and teaching with technology: Principles and practices* (pp. 13–27). London: Kogan Page

Jonassen, D. H. (1990). Toward a constructivistic conception of instructional design. *Educational Technology, 30*(9), 32–34.

Jonassen, D. H. (1991). Objectivism vs. constructivism: Do we need a new paradigm? *Educational Technology: Research and Development, 39*(3), 5–14.

Jonassen, D. H. (1997). Instructional design model for well-structured and ill-structured problem-solving learning outcomes. *Educational Technology: Research and Development 45*(1), 65–95.

Jonassen, D. H. (2000). Toward a design theory of problem solving. *Educational Technology: Research & Development, 48*(4), 63–85.

Jonassen, D. H. (2006a). *Modeling with Technology: Mindtools for Conceptual Change.* Columbus, OH: Merrill/Prentice-Hall.

Jonassen, D. H. (2006b). On the role of concepts in learning and instructional design. *Educational Technology: Research & Development, 54*(2), 177–196.

Jonassen, D. H. (2008). Model building for conceptual change. In S. Vosniadou (Ed.), *International Handbook of Research on Conceptual Change* (pp. 676–693) New York: Routledge.

Jonassen, D. H. (2009). Reconciling a human cognitive architecture. In S. Tobias & T.M. Duffy (Eds.), *Constructivist Theory Applied to Instruction: Success or Failure?* New York: Routledge.

Jonassen, D. H., & Henning, P. (1999). Mental models: Knowledge in the head and knowledge in the world. *Educational Technology, 39*(3), 37–42.

Jonassen, D. H., & Hung, W. (2006). Learning to troubleshoot: A new theory-based design architecture. *Educational Psychology Review, 18,* 77–114.

Jonassen, D. H., & Hung, W. (2008). All problems are not equal: Implications for PBL. *Interdisciplinary Journal of Problem-Based Learning, 2*(2), 6–28.

Jonassen, D. H., Strobel, J., & Gottdenker, J. (2005). Model building for conceptual change. *Interactive Learning Environments, 13*(1–2), 15–37.

Klahr, D. (2000). *Exploring science: The cognition and development of discovery processes.* Cambridge, MA: MIT Press.

Kolodner, J. (1993). *Case-based reasoning.* New York: Morgan Kaufman.

Loewenstein, J., Thompson, L., & Gentner, D. (1999). Analogical encoding facilitates knowledge transfer in negotiation. *Psychonomic Bulletin & Review, 6*(4), 58–597.

Loewenstein, J., Thompson, L., & Gentner, D. (2003). Analogical learning in negotiation teams: Comparing cases promotes learning and transfer. *Academy of Management Learning and Education, 2*(2), 119–127.

Mayer, R. E. (1992). *Thinking, problem solving, cognition* (2nd ed.). New York: Freeman.

Merrill, M. D. (2002). First principles of instruction. *Educational Technology: Research and Development, 50*(3), 43–59.

Morrison, M., & Morgan, M. S. (1999). Models as mediating instruments. In M. S. Morgan, & M. Morrison (Eds.), *Models as mediators: Perspectives on natural and social science* (pp. 10–37). Cambridge, UK: Cambridge University Press.

Nussbaum, E. M., & Sinatra, G. M. (2003). Argument and conceptual engagement. *Contemporary Educational Psychology, 28*(3), 384–395.

Paris, N. A., & Glynn, S. M. (2004). Elaborate analogies in science text: Tools for enhancing preservice teachers' knowledge and attitudes. *Contemporary Educational Psychology, 29,* 230–247.

Popper, K. (1999). *All life is problem solving.* London: Routledge.

Ryle, G. (1949). *The concept of mind.* New York: Barnes and Noble.

Reigeluth, C. M., & Stein, R. (1983). The elaboration theory of instruction. In C. M. Reigeluth (Ed.), *Instructional design theories and models* (pp. 338–381). Hillsdale, NJ: Lawrence Erlbaum Associates.

Schön, D. A. (1983). *The reflective practitioner – how professionals think in action.* New York: Basic Books.

Simon, H. A. (1969). *The sciences of the artificial.* Cambridge, MA: MIT Press.

Spector, J. M., & Koszalka, T. A. (2004). *The DEEP methodology for assessing learning in complex domains* (Final report to the National Science Foundation Evaluative Research and Evaluation Capacity Building). Syracuse, NY: Syracuse University

Sternberg, R. J., & Frensch, P. A. (1991). *Complex problem solving: Principles and mechanisms.* Hillsdale, NJ: Lawrence Erlbaum Associates.

Glossary

3D virtual environments   Computer generated, three-dimensional, graphical spaces that can be based on real or fantasy environments and in which users are typically represented as avatars.

Agency   The human capacity to act in the world; agency suggests that people act freely and not simply according to pre-established structures and expectations.

Analogizing   The process of transferring (mapping) information from a particular subject (source) to another particular subject (target).

Aplomb   Self-confidence – a desirable characteristic to nurture as learners progress.

Argumentation   The means by which we rationally solve problems; arguments generally consist of (a) theories to support claims, (b) evidence to support theories, (c) alternative theories, (d) counterarguments, and (e) rebuttals.

Argumentation   The process of supporting and defending claims with evidence.

Augmented reality   Technology tools or applications that augment a real physical space with virtual materials (text, video, images) in real time.

Case-based reasoning   A process invoked when encountering a new problem that involves retrieving a previously encountered problem believed to be similar and using analogical reasoning to address the new one.

Causal reasoning   A process cutting across many disciplines that enables us to make predictions, draw implications, make inferences, and articulate explanations.

Cognitive tool   Any technology such as mathematical notation or a computer program that enhances or extends the mental powers of human beings during thinking, problem solving, and learning; tools aimed at scaffolding cognitive processing; see *mindtool*.

Complexity   A situation or task that involves many interrelated factors or components, often with nonlinear relationships, delays, and incompletely defined factors; perceived complexity is associated with an individual's lack of familiarity with the problem type, lack of relevant background knowledge, lack of confidence to solve such problems, and so on.

Concept maps External representations depicting relationships among concepts (nodes).

Conceptual change Occurs when an existing concept is modified by some form of learning; the dynamic process of revising or changing a set of beliefs as a result of experience and education.

Constatively A give and take of arguments between the parties engaged in the communicative action; provides the learner with a facilitated feedback without giving the correct answer but clues to continue processing the solution individually.

Content area reading comprehension The ability to construct a meaningful interpretation of texts in a particular domain area.

Continuing healthcare education A form of continuing education for healthcare professionals that is designed to maintain, modify, and/or extend the competencies of healthcare professionals.

Craftsmanship Sustained dedication to excellence in the making of something, requiring a honing of skill and cultivation of wisdom based on professional experience.

Design theory A theory of design aimed at engaging learners in high level thinking in the context of solving real-world problems.

Direct instruction Learning that involves a teacher or tutor or instructional system in making decisions for learners, indicating which resources to use and what activities to pursue.

Dynamic interaction In the context of this volume, the dynamic interaction between problem solving and conceptual change; the notion is that there is or can be a relationship of mutual influence rather than the one-way influence often assumed.

Educational design research Educational design research is distinguished from other forms of scientific inquiry conducted by educators by its commitment to developing theoretical insights and practical solutions simultaneously in real-world (as opposed to laboratory) contexts.

Embodied learning In a 3D virtual environment, the way our understanding of phenomena is affected by (1) being represented virtually as an avatar; (2) interacting with virtual objects; and (3) being able to experience and interact with objects and environments in ways that would be impossible in the real world (i.e. flying or seeing at a nano-scale).

Epistemology The study of the nature and limits of knowledge and how knowledge is acquired and developed.

Experience Direct engagement with the world that results in knowledge through interaction with the world.

Experiential learning Experiential learning in its simplest form refers to learning from experience in contrast to learning from some type of formal instruction.

Formative feedback and assessment Support for learning that involves providing a learner meaningful and timely information pertaining to a specific learning task.

Framework   An organized set of ideas, principles, agreements, or rules that provides the basis of a specific phenomenon or process.

Gaming   The act of playing a video game and the use of game thinking and mechanics to design an activity.

Higher-order thinking   Upper levels of a thinking process involving analysis, creativity, problem solving among other mental performances.

Ill-structured problem solving   Solving problems that are incompletely defined and which lend themselves to multiple solution approaches and solutions.

Influence diagrams   External representations that depict causal connections among concepts and problem factors.

Instructional design   The process of devising engaging activities and supportive cognitive tools to promote learners' abilities to solve complex and challenging problems.

Intelligent tutoring systems   A computer system intended to replace a human tutor and provide instructional support and learning activities with appropriate feedback to learners.

Learning environment model   A model that guides and constitutes the design, implementation and use of a learning environment.

Learning   Involves a recognized and persistent change in a person's attitudes, beliefs, capabilities, knowledge, or skills.

Machinima   Video capture of a game or a simulation on the computer screen.

Meaningful learning   Involves practical learning outcomes that can be applied to solve problems likely to be encountered.

Mental model   Internal representations containing subjective plausible and meaningful declarative and procedural knowledge that people use to understand specific phenomena.

Millennials   Those who were born into an environment where computers and the Internet were present; roughly, those born after 1982 in developed countries; also known as digital natives.

Mindtool   A computer application that allows students to represent information, engage in solving problems, and develop higher order thinking skills; a computer system that supports the representation of knowledge and construction of meaning by learners; computer-based applications that engage learners in constructivist learning.

Mobile technologies   Devices that are portable and used in everyday life, such as cell phones, tablet devices, or portable media players.

Model-based learning   The formation and subsequent development of mental models by a learner.

Modeling   A process involving the construction of cognitive artifacts that support hypothesis testing, conjecturing, inferring, and a host of other important cognitive skills.

Online learning   Learning that is significantly supported using Internet-based resources and which typically takes place outside traditional classrooms.

Play   Engagement in an activity that is enjoyable and includes challenge, fantasy and/or curiosity.

Practice theory   A theory that takes practice or human activity as a unit of study, such as activity theory, actor-network theory, ethnomethodology, and Bourdieu's theory of practices and dispositions.

Practice-centered instructional design   Framing instructional-design work in terms of activity mediated by tools and circumstance, where opportunities for innovation emerge from new technologies, ideas, and systemic tensions, as well as the craftsmanship, character, and agency of participants.

Problem conceptualization   An important but neglected early phase of problem solving in which a learner develops a personal theory to explain the situation.

Problem solving   An activity aimed at resolving a situation which involves one or more undesirable, undefined or unknown (as yet) aspects; an engaging and dynamic process that may influence conceptual change and/or be influenced by conceptual change.

Scaffold   A kind of mindtool that helps students develop desired skills such as argumentation and problem-solving.

Schema   Represents the *generic* and *abstract* knowledge a person has acquired in the course of numerous individual experiences with objects, people, situations, and events.

Self-regulated learning   Learning that focuses on individual sense-making and monitoring one's own learning processes.

Simulation   A type of learning environment wherein critical aspects of professional performance are replicated with some degree of fidelity so that learning and assessment are enabled.

Social learning   In a 3D virtual environment, learning that is promoted within a social context which leverages conversations, identity and co-presence as key elements.

Systems models   External representations that can include mathematical models to depict behavior over time so as to promote hypothesis testing.

Taxonomy   A classification model of a set of elements that organizes the categorization of their complex elements or attributes.

Teaching with technology   Integrating one or more technologies to support learning.

Transmedia   A single experience that spans across multiple forms of media.

Visualization   The ability to represent to oneself and/or others a set of facts, events or circumstances in a graphical manner that meaningfully encapsulates a visual message.

Web 2.0   Second-generation web pages and tools that typically involve interactive pages and support the participation and sharing of information and resources.

Index